The Good Cartesian

The Good Cartesian

Louis de La Forge and the Rise of a Philosophical Paradigm

STEVEN NADLER

OXFORD
UNIVERSITY PRESS

Oxford University Press is a department of the University of Oxford. It furthers the University's objective of excellence in research, scholarship, and education by publishing worldwide. Oxford is a registered trade mark of Oxford University Press in the UK and certain other countries.

Published in the United States of America by Oxford University Press
198 Madison Avenue, New York, NY 10016, United States of America.

© Oxford University Press 2024

All rights reserved. No part of this publication may be reproduced, stored in a retrieval system, or transmitted, in any form or by any means, without the prior permission in writing of Oxford University Press, or as expressly permitted by law, by license, or under terms agreed with the appropriate reproduction rights organization. Inquiries concerning reproduction outside the scope of the above should be sent to the Rights Department, Oxford University Press, at the address above.

You must not circulate this work in any other form
and you must impose this same condition on any acquirer.

Library of Congress Control Number: 2023048145

ISBN 978-0-19-767171-9

DOI: 10.1093/oso/9780197671719.001.0001

Printed by Integrated Books International, United States of America

Contents

List of Figures	vii
Acknowledgments	ix
Introduction: Cartesian Beginnings	1
1. Louis de La Forge	7
2. Cartesianism, 1650–1663	18
3. Illustrating the World	44
4. A Disciple's Commentary	70
5. The Cartesian Mind	91
6. The Union of Mind and Body	118
7. Occasionalisms	162
8. The World of Bodies	194
9. Mind and Motion	214
10. Ideas and Volitions	236
Conclusion: How Important Was La Forge?	252
Gallery of Figures	263
Notes	279
Bibliography	315
Index	327

Figures

1. Gerard van Gutschoven's illustration of the muscles around the eye; from Clerselier's edition, *L'Homme de Rene Descartes* (Descartes 1664). — 263

2. Louis de La Forge's illustration of the muscles around the eye; *L'Homme* (1664). — 264

3. Descartes's illustration (re-drawn by Clerselier) of the muscles around the eye; *L'Homme* (1664). — 265

4. An original drawing by Descartes of the eye muscles; from Florent Schuyl's edition, *Renatus Des Cartes De homine* (1662). From the Daniel and Eleanor Albert Collection. By courtesy of the Department of Special Collections, Memorial Library, University of Wisconsin-Madison. — 266

5. Figure by Schuyl, *De homine* (1662). — 267

6. Figure by Schuyl, *De homine* (1662). — 268

7. Figure by Schuyl, *De homine* (1662). — 268

8. Figure by Schuyl, *De homine* (1662). — 269

9. Figure by Schuyl, *De homine* (1662). — 269

10. Figure by La Forge, from *L'Homme* (1664). — 270

11. Figure by Gutschoven, from *L'Homme* (1664). — 271

12. Figure by Gutschoven, from *L'Homme* (1664). — 271

13. Figure by La Forge, from *L'Homme* (1664). — 272

14. Figure by La Forge, from *L'Homme* (1664). — 272

15. Figure by La Forge, from *L'Homme* (1664). — 273

16. Figure by Gutschoven, from *L'Homme* (1664). — 273

17. Figure by Schuyl, *De homine* (1664). — 274

18. Figure by Gutschoven, from *L'Homme* (1664). — 274

19. Figure by Frans van Schooten the Younger, from Descartes, *La Dioptrique* (Leiden: Maire, 1637). — 275

20. Figure by Gutschoven, from *L'Homme* (1664). — 276

21. Figure by Van Schooten, from Descartes, *La Dioptrique* (1637). — 276

22. From Caspar Bauhin, *Theatrum anatomicum* (Frankfurt: Moenem, 1605). Courtesy of Ebling Library, Rare Books & Special Collections, University of Wisconsin-Madison. — 277

23. From Bauhin, *Theatrum anatomicum*. — 278

Acknowledgments

It takes a (small) village to produce a book on Louis de La Forge. Several colleagues—friends, really—were gracious and generous enough to take time from their own work to help me during the research and writing of this book. I am extremely grateful to Delphine Antoine-Mahut (ENS-Lyon) and Tad Schmaltz (University of Michigan), who read and provided remarkably insightful feedback on an early draft manuscript; their comments, corrections, and suggestions were invaluable. A conversation and follow-up exchange with Jeremy Hyman when I presented some material on occasionalism at a seminar at Princeton University in the fall of 2022 made me rethink some of my assumptions about varieties of causation in the early modern period. And my thanks to Sandrine Roux (Université de Montreal à Québec) for sharing her thoughts on La Forge and related topics; and to Elise Whatley, PhD student in philosophy at the University of Wisconsin-Madison, for their proofreading skills.

I also want to take this opportunity to acknowledge, with enormous gratitude, the encouragement and support that Dan Garber and Tom Lennon have provided me, not only on this project—they both served as readers of the penultimate draft for Oxford University Press—but from the very start of my career. I first met Dan when I was still a graduate student (in 1985, during his visit to Columbia University to give a colloquium talk), and Tom shortly after receiving my PhD (in 1989, at a conference, Ideas in Early Modern Philosophy, at the University of Iowa). Over nearly four decades, their books and articles, and our conversations—at meetings; over meals; during plane, train, and taxi rides; and (with Tom) during runs in the Jardin de Luxembourg in Paris—inspired me to pursue my own projects and to try as best I could to emulate not only their groundbreaking scholarship, but their warm collegiality as well.

Finally, my thanks to Peter Ohlin and his team at Oxford University Press—not only for taking on this project and producing a terrific-looking book, but for their general support of research in early modern philosophy and the OUP's superb (and still growing) list of studies on seventeenth-century Cartesianism.

X   ACKNOWLEDGMENTS

An earlier version of the material presented in Chapter 3 was previously published as "The Art of Cartesianism: The Illustrations for Clerselier's Edition of Descartes's *Traité de l'homme* (1664)," in *Descartes's Treatise on Man and Its Reception*, edited by Stephen Gaukroger and Delphine Antoine-Mahut (Springer, 2017). My thanks to Springer Nature for permission to include that material in the book.

Introduction

Cartesian Beginnings

On 4 August 1671, François de Harlay de Champvallon, the archbishop of Paris, acting at the behest of King Louis XIV, ordered the University of Paris to be on guard against the teaching of certain new philosophical ideas that had been determined to be a danger to Christian piety.

> The king, having learned that certain opinions that the Faculty of Theology had at one time censured and that the *parlement* had prohibited from being taught or published, continues to spread, not only in the university but also in the rest of this city and in some other cities of the kingdom, whether by foreigners or by people within, and wanting to prevent the progress of this opinion which could cause some confusion in the explication of our mysteries, pushed by his zeal and his ordinary piety, has commanded me to tell you his intentions. The king exhorts you, sirs, to make it so that no doctrine is taught in the universities or put into theses other than that which is prescribed by the regulations and statutes of the university, and relies on your prudence and your wise conduct to take the necessary steps for this.[1]

The earlier censure to which the archbishop refers is a 1624 condemnation by the Sorbonne (the Faculty of Theology at the University of Paris) of a number of anti-Aristotelian theses that had been proposed for public defense. The university's theologians found the theses "false," "temerarious," "scandalous," and, most disturbing of all, "heretical" and "erroneous in faith," and took all due measures to punish their authors. What primarily concerned the learned doctors was that the theses in question, which rejected the prime matter and substantial and accidental forms so essential to Aristotelian physics and metaphysics, "in some way undermine the sacrosanct sacrament of the Eucharist."[2] Medieval Scholastic explanations of the Eucharistic mystery in terms of forms and matter had practically become as much a part of Catholic Church dogma as the "real presence" itself of Christ's body in the consecrated

The Good Cartesian. Steven Nadler, Oxford University Press. © Oxford University Press 2024.
DOI: 10.1093/oso/9780197671719.003.0001

2 THE GOOD CARTESIAN

host. Without that traditional explanatory apparatus—whereby it still *looks* like there is bread and wine because the accidental forms or "real qualities" (that is, the sensory appearances) of bread and wine remain, miraculously suspended, without their respective underlying substances—it was thought that there was no way to account properly for what happens during the transubstantiation of the bread and wine into the body and blood of Christ.

The sanctity of the Eucharist was clearly of concern again in 1671, as the archbishop's reference to "our mysteries" attests. While neither Descartes himself nor his philosophy is mentioned in this new censure and prohibition, there can be little question that Cartesianism is the target of the *arrêt*. This becomes clear later that year, when the *Sacra Facultas Parisiensis*— the Sorbonne—rendered its concurrence with what it called the order "against the doctrine of Descartes [*contra Doctrinam Carthesi*]," and in general against "teaching and propagating novelties in philosophy."[3] Why was the 1624 censure renewed in 1671? Almost certainly because of the publication that year, in Amsterdam, of a book titled *Considérations sur l'état présent de la controverse touchant le Très Saint-Sacrament de l'autel* (Considerations on the Present State of the Controversy concerning the Very Holy Sacrament of the Altar). The author was Dom Robert Desgabets, a member of the Benedictine order. In his treatise, Desgabets offers an explanation of Eucharistic transubstantiation on Cartesian principles, without any appeal to elements from the Aristotelian-Scholastic metaphysical toolbox.[4]

The archbishop's order against philosophical novelties and the University of Paris's affirmation were soon followed by condemnations and prohibitions against les opinions et les sentiments de Descartes at the University of Angers (1674–75) and the University of Caen (1677) as well as within the Jesuit and Benedictine orders and the society of the Oratory.[5] Additional censures followed over the next few decades.

All of this anti-Cartesian activity was but a vain, rearguard action against a philosophical movement that was not only continuing to make great inroads into the teaching at universities and *collèges*, but had already taken over the "secular" French intellectual world of private academies and salons. Descartes's philosophy was well on its way to becoming *the* dominant philosophical paradigm of the second half of the seventeenth century. It set the agenda for reflection and research, both for its partisans and for its numerous critics, in metaphysics, epistemology, and natural philosophy for many decades after Descartes's death in 1650. Not just in France, but in the Netherlands, the German lands, and elsewhere, Cartesianism was *the new philosophy*, until it was finally supplanted by Newtonianism in the next century.

The story of how this happened has been told many times, from studies by Victor Cousin and Francisque Bouillier in the nineteenth century—especially Bouillier's magisterial *Histoire de la philosophie cartésienne* (1868)—to, in the mid-twentieth century, Paul Mouy's *Le Développement de la physique cartésienne, 1646–1712* (1934), Henri Gouhier's *Cartésianisme et Augustinisme au XVIIe siècle* (1978), and C. Louise Thijssen-Schoute's *Nederlands Cartesianisme* (1954), to recent books by Thomas M. Lennon (*The Battle of the Gods and Giants: The Legacies of Descartes and Gassendi, 1655–1715* [1993]), Tad Schmaltz (*Radical Cartesianism: The French Reception of Descartes* [2002] and *Early Modern Cartesianisms: Dutch and French Constructions* [2017]), and the collection edited by Delphine Kolesnik-Antoine (*Qu'est-ce qu'être cartésien?* [2013]).

A considerable but underappreciated part in the successful promotion of Cartesian philosophy in the mid-seventeenth century was played by a young, provincial medical doctor: Louis de La Forge. It would not be accurate to say that La Forge has been entirely ignored by scholarship. His place in the history of occasionalism, in particular, is well acknowledged. Occasionalism is the causal doctrine according to which natural substances (minds and bodies) have no true and efficacious causal power. God alone, occasionalists argue, is the sole causal agent of everything that happens in nature, of all bodily and mental events and processes. When one body collides with another, the contact between the bodies is only an "occasion" for God to modify the motion and rest of the bodies involved, as determined by the laws of motion. When a human being's body is pricked by a needle, the breaking of the skin's fibers is the occasion for God to cause in that individual's mind a feeling of pain. And when a person wills to raise an arm, the volition in the mind is the occasion for God to cause the arm to rise. Thoroughgoing occasionalists also deny that the mind has any power to cause its own thoughts or volitions. While the doctrine has its ancestral roots in medieval Arabic and Latin theories of natural causation, it really flourished, albeit rather briefly, in the seventeenth century among Descartes's more and less orthodox followers—primarily in France, the Netherlands (both the southern Low Countries and the Dutch Republic), and the German lands. Though occasionalism might seem to be either an excessive expression of religious enthusiasm or, as it was long portrayed in scholarship, an ad hoc retreat to a *deus ex machina* to resolve the mind–body

4 THE GOOD CARTESIAN

problem, its various dimensions were grounded in serious metaphysical, physical, epistemological, and theological argumentation.

As many scholars have shown—from Heinrich Seyfarth's 1887 study *Louis de la Forge und seine Stellung im Occasionalismus* and Joseph Prost's 1907 *Essai sur l'atomisme et l'occasionalisme dans la philosophie cartésienne* to recent books and articles on causation in early modern philosophy, including a fair number of essays on La Forge himself—La Forge did indeed have an important role to play in the genesis of Cartesian occasionalism. But there is also a good deal of disagreement and confusion on just what that role was, and especially how thoroughgoing La Forge's occasionalism may or may not have been and what his arguments were supposed to show. This is especially true, as we shall see, if we distinguish what La Forge *meant* to say from what he was *justified* in saying or *should* have said.

But La Forge's contribution to the fortunes of Descartes's philosophy goes well beyond his role in the Cartesian occasionalist tradition. Despite his short life and very brief philosophical career far from the lively intellectual world of Paris, he was one of the most important members of the second generation of Cartesians—that cohort of philosophers who, in the first two decades after Descartes's death, worked to complete, correct, update, and expand his metaphysics, epistemology, and especially his physics or natural philosophy, sometimes into domains where Descartes had been reluctant to go, and even in directions he would most definitely not have sanctioned. La Forge, along with several others—including, as well as Desgabets, his fellow Frenchmen Claude Clerselier, Géraud de Cordemoy, Jacques du Roure, and Jacques Rohault; the Flemish-Dutch philosopher Arnold Geulincx; and the German Johannes Clauberg, all active before Nicolas Malebranche published the first volume of his *De la recherche de la vérité* (On the Search after Truth) in 1674—was instrumental in so promoting Cartesianism and bringing it to what he saw as greater internal coherence and better correspondence with the progress of experimental natural philosophy that it came to rule the European Republic of Letters.

La Forge was also the most loyal of all Cartesians—*the good Cartesian* who strove to remain faithful not just to what Descartes actually did do but also (he claims) to what Descartes would have done had he lived longer and managed to complete all the different parts of his system that he envisioned. La Forge was not above correcting Descartes when necessary, for the sake of consistency and truth, but he always did so in ways he believed Descartes would have approved had he examined things a little more closely, performed a few more anatomical investigations, and had the chance to consult the work of others in the years since his death. To be sure, La Forge also went beyond Descartes in drawing out what he saw as the implications of his principles and doctrines, and he did this in ways that he must have known Descartes was not planning to take and probably could not even envision. This is true, it seems, of his occasionalist account of the motion of bodies. But even here, as La Forge lays out "what Descartes would have said," I am convinced he sincerely believed that he was doing something with which Descartes, once sufficiently alerted to its necessity, might eventually be brought to agree.

By contrast, other important Cartesians of La Forge's generation and the next purposively departed from orthodoxy, usually with the aim of rendering the system more conceptually coherent, empirically accurate and/or theologically acceptable, but sometimes because they simply thought that Descartes got it wrong. Cordemoy, rejecting Descartes's claim that body, *qua* extension, is indefinitely divisible, opted for atomism; and Malebranche, an Oratorian priest, modified Descartes's account of the human mind and its ideas in radical ways he believed necessary to reconcile it both with the thought of Saint Augustine and with his own religious vision. Then there is Desgabets, whose "radical Cartesianism" caused a good deal of trouble for the movement.[6] Desgabets was not interested in merely expositing and elaborating on what Descartes had said, and he had no patience for those Cartesians unwilling to be critical of their mentor when appropriate or to take his philosophy into new domains. "I will content myself here," he says in the preface to his *Supplément à la philosophie de Monsieur Descartes*, "with working as well as I can on the reasonings and on the things that he [Descartes] has brought forward in order to make known their strengths and weaknesses with all the good faith that one can expect from a person exempt from passion in this regard." Desgabets will not be sparing in his assessments. He promises

> to show in what follows that after he [Descartes] has saved us from an infinity of errors, he let himself be ambushed by imperceptible prejudices in fundamental matters, which deprived the world of the greatest fruit of his work. I will take the opportunity of his own discoveries to indicate the points where he failed to push things as far as he ought to have. I will reveal contradictions that exist between the things that he has proposed and how he himself ceased sometimes to be a good Cartesian, abandoning his most beautiful discoveries in order to embrace popular opinions.[7]

6 THE GOOD CARTESIAN

La Forge was not an uncritical disciple, and he did take some things further than Descartes had or would have. But unlike Desgabets, he did not intentionally go into matters that Descartes himself would not have addressed or offer solutions that Descartes would not ultimately have endorsed . . . or so he wants us to believe.

La Forge's importance for the cause was recognized by no less a figure than Clerselier—and he should know, since he was Descartes's good friend and literary executor. Writing shortly after La Forge's death in 1666, Clerselier notes that

> We have, in his person, experienced a loss that cannot be overly regretted. For beyond the fact that from what he has done we can judge what he could have done, he communicated to me some of his plans, which would have gone nowhere but to achieve those which M. Descartes himself had proposed; and I saw in him a genius [*un genie*] capable of executing them all. But instead of uselessly expressing our regrets, let us try rather to imitate his virtue and approach as near as we can the knowledge [*science*] and wisdom that he had acquired. It began in him with the high esteem that he had for Monsieur Descartes, it increased by the reading of his works, and it was perfected by the reflections that he made over these.[8]

Despite La Forge's significance, and notwithstanding the increasing attention given to him by Cartesian scholars in recent years, there has never been, in any language, a full and thorough study of La Forge's philosophical contributions: his role in illustrating and critically commenting on Descartes's *Traité de l'homme* (Treatise on Man) in its first original-language edition (1664),[9] and his own *Traité de l'esprit de l'homme* (Treatise on the Human Mind) in which he completes Descartes's study of the human being, in particular the mind and its relation to the body. With this book I hope to fill in that lacuna in the literature on early modern Cartesianism.

1
Louis de La Forge

Louis de La Forge was destined by geography to be the century's champion of Cartesian philosophy. He was born and spent all of his brief life within a relatively small circle of towns in the Loire Valley that was, after Paris, the epicenter of Cartesianism in seventeenth-century France. Lying southeast of Angers are Châtellerault, in the province of Poitou, where Descartes's parents resided; and, in the adjacent province of Touraine, La Haye—later named La Haye-Descartes, in 1802, and changed to simply Descartes in 1967—where the great philosopher was born in his maternal grandmother's house (because his father was away from Châtellerault, in Rennes on business). Then, in the province of Anjou and closer to Angers, there is Saumur, which was home to several religious academies and houses of study, Catholic and Protestant, where the new philosophy found devoted partisans. Finally, northeast of Angers, also in the province of Anjou, is La Flèche, site of the Collège Henri IV, a Jesuit institution founded in 1603 and where Descartes was sent as a boarding student from 1607 to 1615 for his early education.

La Forge—his name appears in his baptism record as Louis-François de La Forge—was born in La Flèche on 24 or 26 November 1632.[1] His father, Thomas-Louis de La Forge (1601–1652), from nearby Lude, was a medical doctor, like *his* father Guillaume de La Forge. His mother, Urbaine Virdoux, was from Saumur. After their wedding the couple settled in La Flèche, where they had five children, with Louis the first child to survive infancy.[2]

We can be fairly certain that Thomas-Louis sent his eldest son to Descartes's alma mater, the local *collège*, for his schooling. This was thirty years or so after the young Descartes's time at Henri IV–La Flèche, but some of the same men were still engaged in preparing the courses in philosophy and mathematics. Most prominent among these was Father Etienne Noël (1581–1659), who between 1612 and 1615 taught logic, physics, and metaphysics, and then, after some years away, returned to become rector in 1636. He would remain at La Flèche until 1644 (with a break of two years in Rouen), when he went off to Paris. However, Father Noël returned again to La Flèche in 1649 and stayed there until his death ten years later.[3] For

The Good Cartesian. Steven Nadler, Oxford University Press. © Oxford University Press 2024.
DOI: 10.1093/oso/9780197671719.003.0002

8   THE GOOD CARTESIAN

the most part an Aristotelian, Noël was not dogmatic about his philosoph-
ical commitments. He never became a true Cartesian, but over the years he
did grow sympathetic to aspects of Descartes's metaphysics and physics. In
June 1637, Descartes sent his former professor a copy of the just published
Discours de la méthode and its accompanying scientific essays;[4] and in 1646
Father Noël returned the favor and wrote to Descartes with copies of two
of his own works in physics.[5] A few years later Noël responded critically to
Blaise Pascal's barometric experiments, appealing to Cartesian principles to
argue against the possibility of a void or vacuum. Since this relatively open-
minded but still rather orthodox Jesuit was, as *préfet des études*, overseeing
the curriculum during what would have been La Forge's time at the school,
there can be little doubt that La Forge, if he did indeed attend La Flèche, at
least heard something about the "new philosophy" there.

La Forge would have received at La Flèche a standard Jesuit education informed by the order's *Ratio Studiorum* of 1599. The focus was on classical
languages and the liberal arts, broadly construed to include "humanities"
disciplines as well as fields now classified as "sciences." The classes in a nine-
year course of study were all conducted in Latin. They were intended to properly cultivate students intellectually, socially, and religiously, so as to prepare
them for professional careers and, if such was their vocation, higher studies
in theology, law, or medicine.

The program began with a six-year sequence of Latin and Greek grammar,
rhetoric, and literature, so that "the youths entrusted to the Society's care may
acquire not only learning but also habits of conduct worthy of a Christian."[6]
The texts were drawn from both classical antiquity (Homer, Hesiod, Pindar,
Demosthenes, Thucydides, Plato, Aristotle—including the *Poetics*—Cicero,
Caesar, Horace, Ovid, Livy, Virgil, Quintilian) and early Church writings
(the *Ratio* lists Saints Gregory of Nazianzus, Basil, and John Chrysostom).
After completing this elementary stage, students moved on to the three-
year "philosophy" curriculum, which involved logic, physics (supplemented
by mathematics, mainly Euclid), metaphysics, and moral philosophy, all
based almost exclusively on texts from Aristotle: selections from the *Prior
Analytics, On Interpretation, Topics, Physics, On the Soul, On Generation and
Corruption, Metaphysics*—"passing over the questions on God . . . which depend on truths derived from revelation"—and, the syllabus notes, "all ten
books of Aristotle's *Ethics*." They also read commentaries on these works by
medieval and early modern Aristotelians, such as Thomas Aquinas and the
sixteenth-century Jesuits Francisco de Toledo and Pedro da Fonseca.

LOUIS DE LA FORGE 9

Classes at La Flèche were primarily lectures by professors, whose job was to "interpret well the text of Aristotle and be painstaking in this," although after the lecture the students were expected to gather in small groups of about ten and spend half an hour reviewing on their own the material just covered.[7] This lecture/discussion format was supplemented once a month by a disputation, in which students would "pose objections" on a given topic, to which other students were to respond, followed by an hour-long argument or debate overseen by a philosophy professor or theologian. In both structure and content, it was a classic and conservative Scholastic education, subject to minor modifications here and there, and consistent with the Counter-Reformation principles of the Council of Trent in the sixteenth century. According to the *Ratio*'s "rules for the professor of philosophy," the teachers should have "a heart set on advancing the honor and glory of God . . . and above all lead [students] to a knowledge of their Creator."[8]

Typically, a student who wanted to advance from this liberal arts education to higher studies in theology, law, or medicine had to move on to a university faculty in one of these disciplines. However, the Collège Henri IV at La Flèche was sufficiently well endowed that in addition to its arts lecturers it had several professors of jurisprudence and theology; a student seeking to become an ordained Jesuit priest could thus remain at La Flèche for an additional three to four years. Most important for the La Forge family, there were also four professors of medicine and two of anatomy and surgery. What a *collège* could not do, however, was confer a doctorate. Thus, in order for La Forge to become a *docteur en médecine*—and we know that he did obtain this status—he would have to have received a university degree, very likely from the nearby Université d'Angers.[9]

*

It is possible that La Forge began his medical practice while still living in La Flèche. In his wedding banns of 1653, in which he is said to be a resident of Saumur, he is noted as already being a *docteur*. However, he was not yet twenty-one years old, and so there would have been very little time between finishing his degree and moving to Saumur to actually set up a practice in La Flèche.[10] A more likely scenario is that La Forge, whose father had died in 1648, decided at some point to accompany his widowed mother back to her hometown after his medical studies. Once in Saumur, by 1653, he began practicing medicine. In May of that year, he married Renée Bizard, a Saumur

10 THE GOOD CARTESIAN

native, in the parish church of Notre-Dame de Nantilly.[11] La Forge and his wife had four children: the first, a boy named Louis, was born just nine months after the marriage and baptized in Saumur. A daughter Renée came a year and a half later, followed by two more daughters, Urbane (b. 1657) and Perrine (b. 1661).

Though far from the academic and cultural riches of Paris—philosophy of various species flourished in the capital city's university, *collèges*, academies, and salons—Saumur was no intellectual backwater. It was home to several religious establishments that hosted eclectic and relatively open-minded theological and philosophical colloquia, some even going so far as to entertain discussions of "the new philosophy" that was under assault elsewhere. As Prost explains, "Saumur . . . happened to be a cultivated milieu, one that was very hospitable to new doctrines."[12]

The Protestant Academy in Saumur, informally organized in the late sixteenth century, was officially established 1607. It received at least a wink if not direct support from the king, Henri IV (who, always suspect because of his early years as a Protestant, certainly would have had to answer to his Catholic subjects were he to give his imprimatur to a Huguenot educational enterprise). The academy's mission was the study of "three languages [Hebrew, Latin, Greek] and arts and sciences," including philosophy.[13] In 1611, the year after Henri's assassination by a Catholic zealot, it became a "royal academy" when Louis XIII issued a writ stipulating that "the same privileges are to be granted to Protestant colleges as are enjoyed by other colleges."[14] (The toleration would end and the Academy would be forced to close in 1685, when Louis XIV revoked the Edict of Nantes.) Most of the academy's professors, as might be expected, came from Protestant nations, especially England but also the Dutch Republic. The Leiden scholar Franco Burgersdijk (1590–1635)—an ecumenical early modern Aristotelian who, through teaching or his writings, would later influence Adriaen Heereboord (1614–1661), Johannes Clauberg (1622–1665), Arnold Geulincx (1624–1669), and Bento de Spinoza (1632–1677)—was there as professor of philosophy from 1614 to 1619. Clauberg himself—not yet the Cartesian he would later become—paid a visit to the academy in 1646, after finishing his studies at the University of Groningen, while the Danish anatomist Nicolas Steno dropped by for a brief period in 1665.

The Protestant Academy maintained a devotion to Aristotle in its teaching, at least officially. Most of the curriculum was based on Scholastic texts providing standard Peripatetic lessons in metaphysics, physics, logic, and rhetoric. However, this seems to have been more a matter of maintaining appearances and decorum and forestalling intramural disputes than a dogmatic intellectual orientation. In fact, a pair of pastors associated with the academy but unhappy with the philosophy curriculum, and possibly interested in more progressive ideas, made a formal request in 1656 that they "not at all be required to follow or teach the philosophy of Aristotle, but that each be free to teach philosophy according to that which they judge to be most proper."[15] The academy's governing council rejected the request, ruling that such academic freedom was "neither reasonable nor tolerable, as it would generate great confusion and trouble in the school between the professors and the students, as well as contention and divisions among those who teach who, having no certain rule for their tradition, one would teach in one manner, and another in another manner."[16] Aristotle remained the standard, but clearly there were other philosophical ideas circulating among the academy's faculty and the local clergy.

Saumur was also the site of two Catholic establishments. In 1619, the Congregation of the Oratory established in the town a learning and conference residence for theologians associated with the society. Many of the intellectuals who spent time at Ardilliers—so-called because the seminary was near the chapel of Notre Dame des Ardilliers—had received their training at the Sorbonne. Then there was the Collège Royal des Catholiques, also run by the Oratorians. Both of these institutions trained or hosted a number of prominent intellectuals over the course of the century, some of them already or soon-to-be devoted Cartesians. Saumur was a relatively open academic environment, and its Catholics seem to have been no less interested than its Protestants in giving a hearing to new, even controversial philosophical ideas.

Far from the intolerant ecclesiastic milieu of Paris, and despite the religious tensions that roiled so much of France in this period, the faculty at Saumur's Catholic and Protestant academies enjoyed a respectful, even amicable relationship. If they could not agreeably share each other's religious doctrines, they could at least engage in fruitful intellectual intercourse, and so they did. There were frequent meetings bringing the Catholic and Protestant professors together for "courteous discussions," they attended each other's lessons and seminars, and the local Catholics reportedly participated in thesis defenses by their Protestant colleagues.[17]

*

12 THE GOOD CARTESIAN

If Cartesianism was going to insinuate itself in France in the mid-seventeenth century, Saumur was as likely a place as any. And by the early 1650s insinuate itself it did, as it found in this provincial town a reception unexpectedly warm for any philosophy that represented a departure from Aristotelian orthodoxy. Saumur's Catholics and Protestants began introducing Descartes's ideas into their curricula and discussions shortly after the philosopher's death in 1650, with those ideas usually made more palatable by demonstrating their Augustinian roots. Around 1652, just before La Forge's arrival in Saumur, the Oratorian André Martin (1621–1695), writing under the pseudonym "Ambrosius Victor" and teaching at Ardilliers before moving on to the *collège* in nearby Angers, was putting the final touches on his *Sanctus Augustinus de existentia et de veritate dei* (Saint Augustine on the Existence and Truth of God). This work blending Augustinian and Cartesian principles would later be compiled with his other, similarly oriented writings into his *Philosophia Christiana*. Martin saw no conflict between an orthodox Christian faith and Descartes's philosophy, although his more conservative superiors when he had been teaching in Marseille just a year earlier saw fit to suspend him from his teaching duties for introducing Cartesian themes into his lectures. Martin was also close with the Bishop of Angers, Henri Arnauld, who happened to be the older brother of a young Sorbonne theologian named Antoine Arnauld (1612–1694). The Arnauld family was at the center of the embattled Jansenist movement, a rigorous Augustinian faction within the French church that was persecuted by ecclesiastic and civil authorities. The good bishop no doubt gave some protection to Martin and other Cartesians in his domain, while his younger brother Antoine would go on to become one of Descartes's most outspoken defenders in the second half of the century. Bernard Lamy (1640–1715) was another Oratorian resident at Ardilliers, present there from 1659 to 1660. Still a young man during his time in Saumur—he would not be ordained until 1667—he developed a taste for Cartesianism early in his career, perhaps under the tutelage of Martin, and would go on to teach the new philosophy as professor at the University of Angers and author a variety of works in physics, mathematics, and theology.

Meanwhile, in the local Protestant Academy, there was Jean-Robert Chouet (1642–1731). Chouet taught philosophy in Saumur from 1664 until 1669, when he left to become a professor in Geneva, and may have been the most devoted Cartesian in town during La Forge's lifetime. Chouet attracted to Saumur a large number of students from across France and even from abroad. In his teaching and his later writings, he insisted that all questions of natural philosophy are to be determined by reason alone, not by appeals to the Bible or ancient authorities. Chouet was, in fact, fiercely critical of Scholastic thinkers, whom he accused of "investigating not the nature of things but only the philosophy of Aristotle."[18] To Chouet, Descartes had discovered *la véritable philosophie*.[19] He was apparently allowed freely to pursue his interest in Cartesian science and metaphysics, with no interference by his superiors in the academy.

Chouet may have been the most openly welcoming of Cartesianism at the Academy, but he was, it seems, not the first. His predecessor as professor of philosophy, from 1661 to 1664, was a man named Etienne Gausson. When Gausson moved into the theology faculty, Chouet took over his position in the arts faculty. According to Chouet, who had been Gausson's student—and so he would know—Gausson had been "giving his students a smattering of the new philosophy . . . even though it was against the regulations of the academy."[20]

*

Gausson was cautious, and apparently dispersed the smattering in and among his more orthodox lessons based on "our Aristotle."[21] Chouet, on the other hand, was a major player on the Cartesian scene in Saumur. Nonetheless, we can rule him out as the person who first introduced La Forge to Descartes's philosophy; Chouet's arrival in Saumur came too late, since by 1661 La Forge had already completed his commentary on Descartes's *Traité de l'homme* and had made great progress on his own *Traité de l'esprit de l'homme*. Indeed, as we shall see, La Forge was already invested in Cartesian ideas by the late 1650s. Still, Chouet's and La Forge's shared passion for the new philosophy did bring the two men together. Very soon after landing in Saumur, Chouet got to know La Forge and spent a good deal of time with him in conversation on various matters. In a letter from November 1664, Chouet relates that

> I again made an acquaintance that I hold in infinite esteem, a skilled Catholic doctor named Monsieur De La Forge, who is a great philosopher and who knows admirably well the Philosophy of Monsieur Descartes, so much so that he has had diverse treatises of this philosophy printed.[22]

Another remarkable instance of cross-confessional intellectual relations in this provincial town.

14 THE GOOD CARTESIAN

If not from Chouet, then where *did* La Forge, a young medical doctor, pick up his predilection for Descartes? Was it in Paris, at one of the private academies or salons that devoted at least some of their meetings to Cartesian topics? La Forge never lived in Paris for any extended period of time, as far as we know, but did he at least visit the city? In his preface to his *Traité de l'esprit de l'homme*, he describes himself as "a man who has spent almost all his life [*presque tout le temps de sa vie*] far from the Court and the Academy."[23] The 'almost' here has given rise to speculation that there was a Parisian period.[24] One reason for giving some credence to this hypothesis is the fact that the *Traité* is dedicated to *Monsieur de Montmor, Conseiller du Roy en tous ses conseils et Maistre des Requestes Ordinaire de son Hostel*—that is, Henri Louis Habert de Montmor (c. 1600–1679), a wealthy scholar and literary patron who, starting in 1654, hosted a regular philosophical salon in his Parisian home that was the site of a good deal of Cartesian activity. The dedication might be taken to indicate that La Forge was, at one point, an attendee at Montmor's gatherings. La Forge says in the 1665 dedicatory letter that he has resolved "for a long time" to present the treatise to Montmor. He is grateful to Montmor for the fact that "you have often made your home the theater of his [Descartes's] glory," and his words of praise for Montmor's intellect and character—"I know no one else whose intellect is more lively and brilliant and whose judgment is more reliable and sound," "I also thought of you as a model from which I could draw a picture of a mature mind. . . . The admirable virtues which shine in you made me notice its various perfections"—seem to go beyond the niceties of literary flattery to suggest a personal acquaintance.

Unfortunately, no confirmation of this is extant. In fact, that La Forge did *not* know Montmor personally is intimated by a letter that Jean Chapelain sent to La Forge in July 1665, several months before the publication of the *Traité*. La Forge had apparently asked Chapelain to recommend *un Mécène*, that is, a patron to help subvent the publication of the work. Chapelain replied that

> I cannot point you to anyone who is better suited to your request than M. de Monmor [sic], sub-dean of the *maîtres des requêtes*, man of letters, endowed with goods and credit, and the greatest protector of the sect that you profess [i.e., Cartesianism] in all of France, and I do not think that you can set eyes on anyone else who would be more grateful for your offer [of the book's dedication].[25]

LOUIS DE LA FORGE 15

That Chapelain needs to explain to La Forge who Montmor is suggests that La Forge was not yet acquainted with the *maître des requêtes*.[26] It also belies La Forge's claim that the idea to dedicate the work to Montmor was something that he had been contemplating "for a long time."

Be that as it may, we do not need to travel so far from Saumur to find sources of inspiration for La Forge's Cartesianism. It seems very likely that he had already been exposed to the new philosophy at La Flèche. During what would have been La Forge's time at the school, a Jesuit priest named Denis Mesland (1615–1672) was on its faculty. A former student of the *collège* himself, Mesland stayed on at La Flèche and taught there between 1636 and 1645. Mesland was a true fan of Descartes, and sometime before May 1644 he composed a *précis* of the *Meditationes de prima philosophia*, very likely to be used in his classroom. According to Descartes's early biographer, Adriaen Baillet, "Father Mesland read the *Meditations* with great penetration. Not content to have digested them for his own use, he wanted to render them even more useful for others. To put them in a format accommodated for more people, he thought to reduce them into a method more scholastic and more intelligible to common minds."[27] Mesland sent a copy of this manual to Descartes, who was very impressed with the cleric's effort.

> I know that it is very difficult to enter into another person's thoughts, and experience has taught me how difficult many people find mine. So I am all the more grateful to you for the trouble which you have taken to examine them; and I cannot but think highly of you when I see that you have taken such full possession of them that they are now more yours than mine.[28]

Mesland's gift to Descartes initiated a brief correspondence (before Mesland shipped off for missionary work in the New World) in which he was able to draw out Descartes's thoughts on important theological matters, including Eucharistic transubstantiation.

Mesland thus seems a very likely candidate to have first introduced La Forge to Descartes's philosophical writings. Deeper study of Cartesian physics, philosophy of mind, and human physiology, as these are presented in the *Discours de la méthode* and its scientific essays *La Dioptrique*, *Les Météores*, and *La Géométrie* (1637), the *Principia philosophiae* (1644) and *Les Passions de l'âme* (1649), could have come during La Forge's medical training in Angers, or at the latest soon after his settling in Saumur, where, as we have

16   THE GOOD CARTESIAN

seen, Descartes's natural philosophy was an object of some interest among the local Oratorians and Huguenot academicians.

Even in a relatively small place like Saumur—or, perhaps, especially in Saumur, with the well-stocked libraries at Ardilliers, the Collège Royal and the Protestant Academy—La Forge, if he did not have his own copies, would have had easy access to those published works. Moreover, in 1657 and 1659, Claude Clerselier (1614–1684) brought out the first two of three volumes of Descartes's correspondence (he would publish the third volume in 1667), and we know that La Forge was in possession of both of these soon after their appearance.[29] Thanks to Clerselier, La Forge, by the spring of 1660 at the latest, also had the rare privilege of possessing one of the few circulating manuscript copies of Descartes's unpublished *Traité de l'homme*, which Clerselier was preparing for publication.

(It is tempting to think that La Forge might have been influenced by another young Oratorian from Paris who also came to Saumur. Nicolas Malebranche (1638–1715) was at Ardilliers from April to October 1661. However, though Malebranche would become the most important Cartesian in the latter part of the century, he was, in that spring and summer in Saumur, just a new member of the society, not yet an ordained priest, and certainly not quite the philosopher of his later years. If there was any influence here, it will be not Malebranche to La Forge but, as we shall see, the other way around.)

La Forge was thus no doubt into his Cartesian ways by his mid-twenties. Jacques Gousset (1635–1704), a native of Blois and student of theology and philosophy at the Protestant Academy in Saumur in the late 1650s, recalls many years later that in 1658 he became friendly with La Forge and began meeting with him regularly to discuss various philosophical matters. He describes especially La Forge's attempts to make sense of the relationship between mind and body on Cartesian terms.[30] "Rare in those times and places," Gousset says, "were those who read Descartes, even rarer those who took him seriously, who followed him diligently."[31] In the *Remarques* or commentary that La Forge prepared for Clerselier's edition of the *Traité de l'homme*, which would be published with that work in 1664 but which he had completed by 1661, La Forge presents himself as already an expert and enthusiastic disciple of Descartes.[32] The appearance of his own book on the human mind based on Descartes's principles, nearly fully drafted by 1661 but not published until late 1665, only confirmed that status in the public eye and brought him a fair amount of recognition well beyond Saumur.

Had La Forge lived longer, he was, he had told Clerselier, planning "to do no less than complete those [projects] that Monsieur Descartes had set himself" but did not get around to doing.[33] Presumably, this meant investigating further the nature of the human mind, its immortality, and moral matters, beyond what he had already accomplished with the *Traité de l'esprit de l'homme*. Unfortunately, La Forge never had the opportunity to follow through. He died soon after the publication of his *Traité*, sometime between July and September 1666, not yet thirty-four years old. Clerselier mourned the passing of such a genial colleague who did so much for the cause, and who no doubt would have done a lot more. "We have suffered such a loss that cannot be too much regretted."[34]

Clerselier was not the only person who missed the young doctor. La Forge was, by all accounts, a kind and generous person. Gousset calls La Forge "a truly good natured man [*vir profecto comis*]."[35] Despite their differences in religion and *métier*, Gousset reports, the two men bonded over their shared enthusiasm for Descartes and for experimentation. Gousset says he helped La Forge with the illustrations for the *Traité de l'homme*, and the two men would spend hours breaking chicken eggs to determine the circulation of the blood. Writing many years later, he praises La Forge both for his intellect and for his amicability. "He was such an animated man, and he used to take great pleasure in my uninterrupted visits to his house."[36]

2

Cartesianism, 1650–1663

An intellectually curious visitor to Paris in the late 1650s and early 1660s in search of lively and informed discussion of Descartes's philosophy would have had a nice variety of options from which to choose. Cartesianism was all the rage in the city's salons, academies, and conferences, and he—or she—could have spent each day of the week (except Sunday) at a different venue where men and women were engaged in an examination of these new ideas.

On Monday, there was the Académie Bourdelot, held at the home of Pierre Michon, Abbé de Bourdelot, in Faubourg St. Michel. The gatherings began informally sometime in the 1640s, but were interrupted in 1651 when their host went off to Stockholm to serve as physician for Queen Christina. They were back in session again by 1662, a few years after Michon's return to Paris, and officially established in 1664.[1] Several Cartesians, including the natural philosopher Jacques Rohault (1618–1672) and his friend Géraud de Cordemoy (1626–1684), were known to have been attendees.[2]

Tuesdays were devoted to the Académie Montmor, at Montmor's home on the rue Sainte-Avoye. The host was a lawyer and, as a *maître de requêtes*, civil servant. A man reportedly of "great delicacy and wit," he had been a good friend of Descartes himself, even offering him at one point the use of his country house as a retreat to carry out his researches (though the offer was politely declined). Montmor began welcoming intellectual company by 1653, with the meetings formalized in 1657 but ending by 1664.

On Wednesdays it was Rohault's turn. The *conférences* at his home on the rue de Quincampoix began around 1655 and ended with Rohault's death in 1672.[3] Known around town as *les mercredis*, they were famous for Rohault's lectures on the finer points of the new physics and many other topics. Clerselier notes that there was "a great number of people of status to be found at this assembly, where even women often held first rank."[4] Among the regular attendees were Madame de Bonnevaux (Marie-Madeleine de Vignerot de Pontcourlay) and Madame de Geudreville (Marie Thiersault).

Thursdays were for the conferences hosted by the "famous Cartesian" Gilles de Launay, while Friday's meetings were presided over by Claude de

The Good Cartesian. Steven Nadler, Oxford University Press. © Oxford University Press 2024.
DOI: 10.1093/oso/9780197671719.003.0003

CARTESIANISM, 1650–1663   19

Fontenay and devoted to "all the parts of philosophy and mathematics"; the latter, one writer noted at the time, "had great merit."[5]

Saturday offered an assortment of opportunities for Cartesian conversations. One could join the gatherings held by Jean-Baptiste Denis, a disciple of Pierre Gassendi (1592–1655)—Descartes's nemesis and the author of the hostile Fifth Set of Objections to the *Meditationes*—who nonetheless opened his home to members of the opposing camp. Or, if one were in the Marais district, there was the salon of Madame de Scudéry on the rue de Beauce. These were a kind of sequel to the salon at the Hôtel de Rambouillet on the rue Saint-Thomas-du-Louvre that Catherine de Vivonne, the Marquise de Rambouillet, held in the 1640s. Descartes's niece, Catherine Descartes, reportedly attended the Scudéry affairs, also known as *les Samedis de Sapho*.[6] Or one could show up at the home of Madame de Bonnevaux. Her salon attracted such notables as the Dutch scientist Christiaan Huygens, who spent a good deal of time in Paris, and Cordemoy, who on at least one occasion there discussed the vortices composing the Cartesian universe. In her well-appointed rooms, Bonnevaux also gave her own lectures on Descartes, as did her friend Mme. de Geudreville.[7] One contemporary, Marguerite Buffet, describes Bonnevaux as

> very learned in [the philosophy] of Monsieur Descartes; no one ever understood him with more facility than this illustrious woman. When she held conferences at her home for the most learned men in France, this learned philosopher seemed to be a beacon to provide light . . . for dealing with philosophical questions.[8]

There were several other venues for the discussion of Cartesian matters, some organized by Descartes's partisans (*cartésiens* and *cartésiennes*) and some by his critics. The Académie Thévenot, also known as the Compagnie des Sciences et des Arts, met at the home of Melchisédich Thévenot; it was formally inaugurated in 1664 after the demise of the Montmor academy, but there had been informal meetings as early as 1662. The Thévenot group did not last long, however, and was over by 1666. One could also attend the salon at the Hôtel Carnavalet, where, we are told, "discussions were held, with great vivacity, both for and against Descartes."[9] (The Carnavalet home, it should be noted, was also known for less elevated activities. Pierre Bayle reports that friends of the Duc du Maine would meet there in order to *faisoient débauche avec des femmes de joie*.[10])

20 THE GOOD CARTESIAN

All of these academies and salons flourished well before the creation by royal decree of the Académie des Sciences in 1666, and provided Cartesians, anti-Cartesians, and neutral observers occasions for lectures, demonstrations, and conversations. As Bouillier notes, albeit with some exaggeration,

> After the publication of the *Méditations métaphysiques*, Descartes . . . was the subject of all learned conversations in Paris and in the provinces. For more than half a century, there was not a single book of philosophy or a single philosophical discussion which did not have Descartes as its object, which was not for or against his system. Among the clergy, in the religious congregations, in the academies, at the bar [*le barreau*], in the magistrature, in high society [*dans le monde*], in the chateaus, in the salons, and even at court, everywhere, we will find fervent disciples of the new philosophy, who took it to new heights, who worked fervently to disseminate it.[11]

There were Cartesians everywhere. "No one could claim rank among fine minds [*les beaux esprits*] without mixing more or less with Cartesian philosophy."[12]

In terms of the promotion of Cartesianism, the most important of these intellectual and social assemblies were the Montmor Academy and *les mercredis* of Rohault. Attendees at Montmor's included Clerselier, Cordemoy, Rohault, and Desgabets. But Montmor enjoyed mixed company, and despite his preference for Descartes his academy also welcomed partisans of Gassendi. The formal program of Montmor's meetings, drawn up in 1658 by Samuel Sorbière, who was secretary, indicated only that they were a private affair, by invitation only, and established for "receiving into his [Montmor's] house a certain number of men chosen to discuss natural questions, or experiments and inventions," and that "the purpose of the conferences shall not be the vain exercise of the mind on useless subtleties, but the company shall set before itself always the clearer knowledge of the works of God, and the improvement of the conveniences of life, in the arts and sciences which seek to establish them."[13] Whether that knowledge and improvement comes by way of Cartesian or Gassendist or the representative of some other party was, at least in theory, immaterial. Indeed, Descartes's critics were often among the presenters at the academy. Pierre Daniel Huet, for one, no fan of Cartesianism—he says he preferred Gassendi's system—reports that "I

CARTESIANISM, 1650–1663   21

frequently attended [Montmor's meetings]; and I occasionally presented dissertations of my own for their judgment."[14]

The company *chez Montmor* did, nonetheless, spend most of its time reading, discussing, and defending Cartesian principles, focusing on both Descartes's original texts and new works in progress by his followers. Desgabets gave a lecture on blood transfusion in 1658, while in 1663 Cordemoy and Rohault presented their soon-to-be-published treatises: a *Discours du mouvement local* and a *Discours des fièvres*, respectively.[15] Huet's impression was that Montmor "secretly favored Descartes" and that "the sole object of Montmor in instituting this philosophical meeting was to accustom men's minds to the Cartesian principles and gradually bring them over to his sect."[16]

While the ambiance in most of the Parisian salons and academies was genteel and respectful, as befitting the social rank of their participants, one contemporary, Ismail Boulliau, writing in 1658, says that "the Montmorians [*Mommoriani*] are sharper [*acriores*], and dispute with vehemence, since they quarrel about the pursuit of truth; sometimes they are eager to rail at each other, and jealously deny a truth, since each one, although professing to inquire and investigate, would like to be the sole author of the truth when discovered."[17] Writing to Christiaan Huygens in December 1658, Boulliau recalls a rather unpleasant incident at Montmor's involving Gilles de Roberval, one of the century's leading mathematicians and an implacable (and irascible) foe of Descartes.

> As for Monsieur Roberval, he did something stupid at the home of Monsieur de Montmor, who is as you know a man of honor and quality. When he [Roberval] was annoyed by one of the opinions of Monsieur Descartes of which Monsieur de Montmor approved, he was so uncivil as to say to him [Montmor] in his own house that he [Roberval] had more wit [*esprit*] than he, and that he was a lesser man only with respect to goods and the responsibility of *maître des requêtes*, and that if he were *maître des requêtes*, he would be worth a hundred times more than him.

Their host took it all in stride. "Monsieur de Montmor, who is very discreet, said to him that he could and should act more civilly than to quarrel and treat him with contempt in his own house. The whole company found the boorishness and pedantry of Monsieur Roberval very strange."[18] A month later,

22 THE GOOD CARTESIAN

Boulliau tells Huygens that the mathematician has yet to be seen again at one of Montmor's Tuesdays.[19]

Rohault's regular Wednesday conferences (occasionally held on a Saturday) were a more public affair, but less amenable to the presentation of non-Cartesian opinions. In fact, they consisted mostly of Rohault himself, whose *Traité de physique* would be published in 1671, lecturing on topics in Cartesian natural philosophy. Many of the Cartesian attendees at Montmor's academy showed up at the Wednesday meetings as well. Clerselier and Desgabets were regulars, and the ever curious Huygens was an occasional visitor. We also know that among those whom Rohault initiated into the "sect" was a young man named Pierre-Sylvain Régis (1632–1707), who would soon be off to Toulouse to bring the new philosophy to the provinces; he will become a major Cartesian player on the philosophical scene in the final three decades of the century. Clerselier says that Rohault's affairs were very popular and attracted "people of all sorts of qualities and conditions, prelates, abbés, courtesans, doctors, physicians, philosophers, geometers, regents, scholars, provincials, foreigners, artisans, in a word people of all ages, of every sex, and of every profession." Each week, the meeting followed the same general plan:

> The method that Monsieur Rohault followed in his conferences was to explain, one after another, all the questions of physics, beginning with the establishment of its principles and then descending to the proof of their most particular and rarest effects. To do this, he would begin with a discourse of about an hour, which was never studied and in which he simply said what his subject provided him on the spot. That is why he allowed anyone to interrupt him when it happened that someone either did not sufficiently understand what he had said or found some objection to make. And so, with a patience and moderation that I have admired a hundred times and of which he alone was capable, he calmly listened to whatever one wanted to object, however extravagant it might be, without ever interrupting the speaker; and after having responded to his objections, he picked up the thread of his discourse right where he left off and continued to explain the rest of the matter that he had set himself. After this, the discussion was opened up to everyone—not a tumultuous dispute consisting of a lot of noise, but a peaceful and honest dispute, where each modestly and succinctly proposed difficulties that he had noticed on the matter that was brought up that day, in order to learn more and to derive the fruit of these conferences.[20]

CARTESIANISM, 1650–1663   23

Over the years, Rohault covered a broad range of topics, from mathematics and logic to physics and more general philosophical questions. There were sessions devoted to the weight of the air; the vacuum; Aristotle's "prime matter"; the distinction between solids and liquids; light and colors (as well as reflection and refraction); sensory phenomena such as odors and tastes; magnetism; the tides—no natural phenomenon seems to have been out of bounds.[21]

With the passing of Descartes's friend, the Minim priest Marin Mersenne (1588–1648)—who, from his base in Paris, ran a wide-ranging corresponding network in the international Republic of Letters—Clerselier had assumed the mantle of Descartes's literary executor and prime functionary at the center of the Cartesian cosmos. And in his eyes, no one was better suited for leading a Cartesian seminar than Rohault (who also happened to be his son-in-law, having married Clerselier's daughter Geneviève). "Among all my acquaintances," Clerselier says, "he is the most knowledgeable in this philosophy."[22] Nor were Rohault's conferences limited to lecturing. Unlike many of the other academies and salons, his *mercredis* saw a fair amount of serious experimental work, devoted to demonstrating the explanatory power of the mechanical philosophy. Clerselier boasts that

nature, by a truly singular advantage, has provided him [Rohault] with a completely mechanical mind, perfectly suited for inventing and imagining all sorts of machines, along with artistic and adroit hands suited for executing whatever his imagination might represent. Also, he took pleasure in going to the studios of all sorts of workers to watch them work, each at his craft, and to examine attentively the diverse tools they used for executing their works.[23]

Rohault enhanced his oral presentations with "many beautiful experiments [*de belles expériences*] that he performed in front of everyone, and most often he alerted everyone to the effects of the experiments (according to the principles he had already established), before even getting to the demonstration itself."[24]

Supplementing all this Cartesian activity among audiences in Paris's private and public spaces were the works coming off various presses. Clerselier was busy preparing for publication manuscripts that Descartes had left behind, both in Stockholm, where the philosopher had died, and in Holland, where he had spent most of his adult life. The first two volumes of selected

24 THE GOOD CARTESIAN

correspondence appeared in 1657 and 1659, and the first edition of the *Traité de l'homme* in its original French in 1664.[25] Cordemoy was putting the finishing touches on his own treatises, including a *Discours touchant le mouvement et le repos* (Discourse on Motion and Rest), to be published in 1664 within an edition of the first part of Descartes's *Le Monde* (the *Traité de la lumière*), and *Le Discernement du corps et de l'âme en six discours* (The Distinction between the Body and the Soul in Six Discourses), which would appear two years later, around the same time as La Forge's *Traité de l'esprit de l'homme*. The prolific Jacques du Roure (b.?, d. 1685), one of Descartes's first French followers, had already published *La Physique expliquée* in 1653, followed one year later by *La Philosophie divisée en toutes ses parties, établies sur des principes évidents*, in which the "evident principles" came right out of Descartes; now, in the early 1660s, he was at work on several new treatises, including the *Abrégé de la vraie philosophie*.[26]

Not everything these early French Cartesians were working on made it into print, at least right away. Desgabets's first writings on the Eucharist, in which he defends Descartes's account of transubstantiation in the sacramental host, drawing from Descartes's letters to Mesland in the 1640s (copies of which Desgabets had received from Clerselier, who did not include them in the published editions because of their controversial content), were composed around 1663. His goal, he says, is "to give in good faith an explication of the manner in which the body of our Savior is present in the Sacrament of the Altar, according to the new principles and discoveries."[27] These texts remained in manuscript, however; his mature thoughts on the topic would not be published until 1671, with the *Considerations sur l'état présent de la controverse touchant le T. S. Sacrement de l'autel*.

*

France was not the only realm where Cartesian philosophy flourished in the decade after Descartes's passing. The Dutch Republic (United Provinces of the Netherlands), which had only recently won its formal independence from Spain with the Treaty of Münster in 1648, also saw the spread of—and many vicious disputes over—the new philosophy. It all began there even earlier than in France, in the 1640s, and it was a very different affair. In France, the dissemination of Cartesian ideas was left mostly to civilians operating outside the formal educational institutions: aristocrats and middle-class professionals like lawyers and physicians, as well as independent scientists.

CARTESIANISM, 1650–1663   25

The university and college faculties, where the Catholic ecclesiastic hierarchy exercised strong oversight, were still populated mostly by conservative Aristotelians; if there were Cartesians there, they kept a very low profile.

In the more politically decentralized and confessionally cluttered Dutch Republic, on the other hand, a lot of the Cartesian activity took place in the arts, medical, and theology faculties of the universities, with varying degrees of openness and toleration according to province and city. Bouillier aptly describes the different situations:

> In Holland, even before the death of its author, we saw the Cartesian philosophy spread in the universities, penetrating the chairs of philosophy, physics, medicine, mathematics and even theology. In France, it made its inroads through society [par le monde] and the academies more than through the universities, which were severely closed to novelties.[28]

If the French had Clerselier, Du Roure, Desgabets, Cordemoy, Rohault, and Régis, the Dutch had, in their first and second generations of Cartesians, professors such as Henri Reneri (1593–1639), Henricus Regius (Hendrik de Roy, 1598–1679), and Johannes de Bruyn (1620–1675) at the University of Utrecht; Abraham Heidanus (1597–1678) and Johannes de Raey (1622–1702), along with Heereboord and, after 1658, Geulincx at Leiden University; and De Raey's student Clauberg at the University of Groningen (before he returned to Germany in 1649). In 1662, Florent Schuyl (1619–1669), working out of Leiden, published, for the first time and in a Latin translation, Descartes's *Traité de l'homme* (*De homine*). The physician Cornelis van Hogeland (1590–1662), also based in Leiden, was a good friend of Descartes and the author of *Cogitationes quibus Dei existentia, item animae spiritualis, et possibilis cum corpore unio, demonstratur* (Thoughts by Which the Existence of God Is Demonstrated, and Similarly of the Spiritual Soul, and [Its] Possible Union with the Body, 1646), which includes a mechanistic account of the human body that hews closely to the principles of the *Traité de l'homme*.

During the 1640s and early 1650s, in fact, it was the Dutch and the Flemish who were far ahead of the French in pushing publicly the new philosophy. (As La Forge slyly notes in 1665, in the dedicatory letter of his *Traité de l'esprit de l'homme*, "the place of his [Descartes's] birth is almost the last to do him justice . . .his own country is so stubbornly opposed to the adoption of his principles."[29]) Between 1647 and 1660, Clauberg published no fewer than five

26 THE GOOD CARTESIAN

treatises, including the *Defensio cartesiana* (1652) and the *Initiatio philosophi sive dubitatio cartesiana* (1655), as well as his two major metaphysical works on "*ontosophia*." At the University of Leuven (in Flanders, one of the provinces of the southern Low Countries that still belonged to Spain), Gerard van Gutschoven (1615–1668), professor of mathematics since 1646, was but one of many members of the faculty who was devoted to Cartesianism; by 1662 he was, along with La Forge, working on illustrations for Clerselier's forthcoming edition of *L'Homme*. His colleague Guillaume Philippi, a professor of medicine, published between 1661 and 1664 several works—on logic, metaphysics, and physics—informed by Cartesian principles.[30] Baillet, writing in 1691, claims that "the University of Leuven has been composed almost exclusively of Cartesians for nearly forty years."[31]

Because of their institutional standing, Dutch Cartesians had to be a bit more creative and subtle than their French colleagues, and they often sought to show that Descartes's philosophy was compatible with Aristotelian principles. Sometimes this was a rhetorical strategy, but often it was a matter of doctrinal substance. Heereboord, for example, in his *Philosophia naturalis cum novis commentariis explicata* (1663), while not uncritical of Peripatetic metaphysics of form and matter, also rejected some basic Cartesian elements—such as the reduction of matter to extension—when they seemed irreconcilable with Aristotelian physics.[32]

Not that it was smooth sailing in any country. The French, Dutch, and Flemish Cartesians faced serious resistance from academic, civil, and church authorities. The troubles in the United Provinces and the Spanish Netherlands started in Descartes's lifetime and continued for decades after. In the 1640s, there was strong opposition to teaching the *nova philosophia* from university administrators in Utrecht and Leiden. Gisbertus Voetius, the rector at Utrecht, and Jacob Revius, a theologian at Leiden, were, along with their minions, especially vicious in their attacks on Descartes himself and his local partisans.[33] They argued that his philosophy, with its "method of doubt," undermined the belief in God and Christian faith, while the appeal to the will as the source of human error was, to these Calvinists, just a latter-day Pelagianism (the heresy, from the fifth century, that a post-Lapsarian human being is not so tainted by original sin as to be without free will to accept or reject God's grace, and thus bears responsibility for his or her own salvation). The city council in Utrecht and university officials in Leiden, hoping to calm things down, ended up banning all discussion of Descartes's philosophy, both for and against. In Leuven, a decade or so later, the anti-Cartesian campaign

CARTESIANISM, 1650–1663   27

was led by Vopiscus Fortunatus Plempius, a member of the medical faculty and erstwhile friend of Descartes—they performed some dissections together in Amsterdam before falling out—who would write that "soon we will hear the condemnation by the primate of the theologians, who will thrust into hell Cartesian philosophy, which is contrary to Scripture, in dissent from the Fathers, far removed from the sentiments of the Church."[34]

In 1663, a young thinker of Portuguese-Jewish background named Spinoza living in Voorburg, in the province of Holland, gained a reputation as a prominent Cartesian with the publication in Amsterdam of his book *Renati Des Cartes Principiorum philosophiae Pars I & II* (René Descartes's Principles of Philosophy, Parts I and II), a summary of the main points of the first two parts of Descartes's 1644 "textbook" of philosophy. The appearance of this work, composed outside the confines of any university faculty but still written in Latin—it derived from lessons on Descartes that Spinoza was giving to a student—was an important moment both in the dissemination of Cartesian ideas among the educated Dutch public and in giving new impetus in the Republic to attacks upon them. (Spinoza, of course, would go on to compose "scandalous" and "atheistic" works—the epithets come from his many critics—that, despite their Cartesian conceptual framework, Descartes would never have sanctioned. Indeed, contemporary Dutch Cartesians strongly attacked Spinoza's ideas in order to distance themselves from someone whom hostile authorities regarded as a representative of their philosophical cause.[35])

The troubles in France began somewhat later than they did in the Dutch Republic, but were no less vigorous. In this Catholic nation, the problem was not so much freedom of will as the effort by Descartes's partisans to advance an explanation of Eucharistic transubstantiation in Cartesian terms, accounting for the "real presence" of Christ in the sacraments without Aristotelian contrivances to preserve the appearances of bread and wine in the absence of the underlying substance of the bread and wine.[36]

The problem was first raised, in a somewhat friendly and constructive way, by Antoine Arnauld, at the time (1640) a young Sorbonne theologian, in the Fourth Set of Objections to the *Meditationes*. Among "points which may cause difficulty to theologians," he notes that

> What I see likely to give the greatest offense to theologians is that according to the author's doctrines it seems that the Church's teaching concerning the sacred mysteries of the Eucharist cannot remain completely intact. We

believe on faith that the substance of the bread is taken away from the bread of the Eucharist and only the accidents remain. These are extension, shape, color, smell, taste and other qualities perceived by the senses. But the author thinks there are no sensible qualities, but merely various motions in bodies that surround us which enable us to perceive the various impressions that we subsequently call "color", "taste" and "smell." Hence, only shape, extension and mobility remain. Yet the author denies that these powers are intelligible apart from some substance for them to inhere in, and hence he holds that they cannot exist without such a substance.[37]

Because Descartes has emptied the material world of sensible qualities such as color, taste, and smell, leaving behind only extension and its modes (shape, size, divisibility, motion, and rest), his philosophy appears to Arnauld to be incompatible with the standard explication of transubstantiation in the sacramental host.

To understand the problem, it is useful to take a brief detour into medieval and early modern Aristotelian metaphysics. For Aristotelians, the proper objects of scientific inquiry were individual substances. They sought especially to understand the properties and behaviors that substances have and the changes they undergo. A substance, which in its primary sense is simply any particular existing individual (a tree, a horse, a human being), is a compound "hylomorphic" entity consisting of matter (*hyle*) and form (*morphé*). The matter provides the materiality and "thisness" of the substance. What gives that underlying substratum its determinate nature is the form—an immaterial, soul-like item that provides the "whatness" of the substance, its identity as a being of such and such a kind. The form, which is the more active constituent of the substance, is causally responsible for all the qualities by which a thing is what it is and for all the characteristic behaviors it exhibits. When a parcel of matter is informed by the form "horse," for example, the result is a particular horse that looks and acts in horse-like ways. Its shape, its tendency to trot or gallop, its whinnying are all generated by the form.

Forms are distinguished as substantial or accidental according to whether the properties and activities they ground are essential or accidental to the substance. The substantial form of human being imposes on the particular matter it informs just those properties essential to being a human: say, animality and rationality.[38] The other features or powers belonging to an individual that distinguish it from other members of the same species—in a human being, these would be hair, eye and skin color, height, and so on—result from any number of accidental forms also informing the same matter.[39]

Under an Aristotelian hylomorphic metaphysics, moreover, any account of how a substance undergoes alteration and even a complete change of nature necessarily involves specifying determinate forms. Because the forms are responsible for the substance being what it is and acting as it does, a change or alteration in a substance occurs when that substance loses or acquires some form(s) or other. In substantial change, whereby a thing is transformed into something of another kind altogether, the material substratum loses one substantial form and gains a different one. In the more common case of alteration, the substance remains what it is essentially but undergoes some change in one or more of its accidental properties—its color or one of its powers—through the loss and gain of accidental forms.

This general model of explanation is also at work in Aristotelian physics and informs the Scholastic account of the dynamic behavior of bodies in motion and rest. Aristotle had identified four species of fundamental elements or primary bodies, out of which all the matter of physical bodies is composed: fire, air, water, and earth. Each of these four elements is in turn generated from a combination of two out of four primary qualities—heat, cold, dryness, and moisture—which determine the nature of that element. Fire, for example, is made up of heat and dryness. As the primary qualities combine in various proportions in the elementary bodies, and then in the macroscopic physical bodies for which those elementary bodies provide the matter, they account in part for the observable behavior of things in the world. The properties and effects of ordinary fire—its power to burn or dry other bodies—are explained by the preponderance in it of the element fire and thus of that element's primary qualities of heat and dryness.

This was the general metaphysical and physical schema of Thomas Aquinas and other medieval Aristotelians. In late Latin Scholasticism of the sixteenth and early seventeenth centuries—in works by Francisco Suarez, the Jesuit authors of the Coimbrian Commentaries on Aristotle (so-called because they were produced at the University of Coimbra, in Portugal), and especially Eustacius a Sancto Paulo (Descartes called his *Summa philosophiae quadripartita* "the best book of its kind ever made"[40])—one still finds an unwavering commitment to the hylomorphic doctrine of substance and the theory of elements and qualities. At the same time, the primary qualities were supplemented with two motive qualities—heaviness (*gravitas*) and lightness (*levitas*)—as well as additional "sensible" qualities to explain

30 THE GOOD CARTESIAN

natural phenomena. These were called "real qualities" and "virtues," and practically every sensible and insensible property or behavior in bodies was to be explained in terms of a body's possession of the relevant form or quality. The forms and qualities, conceived as active powers, were regarded as the efficient causes of their respective visible and invisible effects. Thus, the real quality "heat" (*calor*) begets sensible warmth in a body or that body's power of warming another body, while the quality "dryness" (*siccitas*) begets sensible dryness or the power to dry. A swan is white (*albus*) because of the presence of "whiteness" (*albedo*) in it, while gold is yellow because its matter is informed by the quality "yellowness." Even so-called occult powers such as magnetism and gravity, whose operations are undetectable, are amenable to this kind of explanatory schema. The lodestone affects iron the way it does because it has the "attractive quality" or "magnetic virtue."[41] A heavy body falls toward the earth because it is endowed with the form "heaviness." As the Coimbrian commentators put it, "since heavy and light things . . . tend toward their natural places, there must be some means present in them . . . by the power of which they are moved. This can be nothing other than their substantial form and the heaviness and lightness which derives from it."[42]

To return to the Eucharist: Catholic theologians since the Middle Ages had explained the mystery of transubstantiation—whereby there is a "real" and not merely symbolic presence of Christ in the sacraments—with the use of Aristotelian forms, both substantial and accidental. On the account favored by the followers of Thomas Aquinas, the substance of the bread of the host is, through God's action on the occasion of the priest's utterance of the words '*hoc est corpus meus*,' converted into Christ's body; on the account preferred by the followers of Johannes Dun Scotus, the substance of the bread is annihilated and replaced by Christ's body. In both cases, although the bread substance is no longer present after consecration, the accidental forms or real qualities of bread (its visual appearance, its texture, its odor, its flavor) remain, present with the substance of Christ's body but not inhering in it, and thus existing without any substratum. This is why, despite being substantially Christ's body, the host *looks* and *smells* and *tastes* like bread. This Scholastic account, over time, became so intimately connected with the Eucharistic mystery itself that it was practically treated as a part of Catholic dogma.[43]

On Descartes's metaphysics, however, such a real and autonomous existence of accidents without their original substance—or, indeed, without inhering in *any* substance—is ruled out in principle. If something is capable of independent existence, then it is a substance; the notion of independently existing accidents is, according to Descartes, an oxymoron.[44] The bread is nothing but a particularly shaped parcel of extension of a certain size and texture, minute particles of matter organized in a certain way. There is no appearance or smell or taste to be miraculously suspended without an underlying (bread) substratum.

The exchange between Arnauld and Descartes on this point—and they appear only in the second (1642) edition of the *Meditationes*, which was published in the Protestant Dutch Republic and thus less likely to raise hackles—entered into what Descartes and Mersenne rightly saw as dangerous theological terrain.[45] Dealing with "truths of revelation" (as opposed to truths of reason) was something that Descartes tried to avoid as much as possible. However, he recognized the force of Arnauld's point and needed to address the problem, especially if he was not to alienate the "learned doctors of the Sorbonne" whose approval of the work he sought. Thus, after a half-hearted attempt to clarify that "I have never denied that there are real accidents"— he meant only that one can do quite well without them—Descartes makes a bold effort to reconcile his metaphysics with the real presence of Christ in the host. What affects the senses in perception, he says, is only the superficies of a body: the texture formed by the outermost particles of matter, with all of its microscopic nooks and crannies. "For contact with an object takes place only at the surface, and nothing can have an effect on any of our senses except through contact." Therefore, in transubstantiation, if the substance of Christ's body is confined by God within material "boundaries" or dimensions that exactly match those that had characterized the now-absent bread, "it necessarily follows that the new substance [Christ's body] must affect all our senses in exactly the same way as that in which the bread and wine would be affecting them if no transubstantiation had occurred."[46] Christ's body looks and smells and tastes like bread because it has taken on an extended figure identical to that of the bread and so affects our senses as the bread did.

Arnauld certainly did not intend to get Descartes into trouble, but ultimately that is what happened. Descartes will later, in a 1645 letter to Mesland, offer a somewhat different account of transubstantiation. To the Jesuit he explains that just as the particles of bread that we ingest in ordinary eating become a part of *us* because they congeal with the parts of our body that are united with our souls—a kind of "natural transubstantiation" in digestion, he calls it—so the conversion of the host occurs when the matter of the bread gets "informed by his [Christ's] soul simply by the power of the words of consecration" and thereby becomes Christ's body.[47]

32 THE GOOD CARTESIAN

Descartes feared that this philosophical foray into revealed theology would be "shocking"—he asked Mesland not to publicly attribute the view to him—and he was right. As we have seen, the question of the Eucharist, especially as Descartes's remarks were later interpreted and developed by Desgabets and others, would eventually lead to the 1671 royal edict in France against his philosophy, followed by condemnations in French universities. But this issue of Catholic dogma seems first to have become a matter of especially serious concern already in 1662, in the Spanish (Catholic) Low Countries. It was the Leuven theologians, urged on by Rome to take a closer look at the philosophy that was insinuating itself into the arts and medicine faculties, who first issued a condemnation of the "Cartesian errors." Among other items—that the human soul is the only substantial form, that the corporeal universe has no end to its extension (that is, that it is infinite)—they objected to the fact that since, on Descartes's account, there are no "real accidents," it follows that "the accidents of the bread and the wine do not remain in the Eucharist without a subject."[48]

In the fall of 1663, the Vatican, responding to the affair in Leuven, undertook its own examination of Descartes's texts. Censors commissioned by the Holy See found much that was problematic in the *Discours de la méthode* and its scientific essays (in their Latin edition), the *Meditationes*, the *Principia philosophiae*, and *Les Passions de l'âme*. They highlighted in their reports the Copernican heliocentrism, the limitless universe, the fact that there was no a posteriori demonstration of God's existence (which they deemed contrary to Scripture, insofar as God's attributes should be evident "through those things He has created"), the lack of indifference in the will's freedom—and, notably, the fact that "what [Descartes] says about accidents that inhere in substance is not compatible with the sacred mystery of the Eucharist, in which the outward appearances of the substance of the bread remain, that is, the accidents defined by the Council of Trent."[49]

In October of that same year, the Congregation of the Holy Office in Rome, in response to the reports by the Pope's censors, decreed that Descartes's own published writings "are prohibited until they are corrected."[50] This was followed by the Holy Congregation of the Index placing those writings on the Index of Prohibited Books, also *donec corrigantur*. This decree would have little meaning in the Dutch Republic, where the Reformed Church was in control, and only slightly more consequence in France, where the Catholic hierarchy jealously guarded its religious independence from Rome. Editions of Descartes's published and unpublished texts continued to be produced posthumously in both countries. Even though by 1682 there was still not

CARTESIANISM, 1650–1663   33

a single "out" Cartesian in the Académie des Sciences, this was probably more an effect of both the king's earlier edict and perceived methodological differences over speculation versus experimentation in natural philosophy than obedience to any Vatican prohibition.[51]

Spinoza's first published treatise and Descartes's placement on the *Index Librorum Prohibitorum* mark 1663 as a most consequential year in the history of Cartesianism.

*

What did it mean to be a "Cartesian" in the seventeenth century, particularly before Malebranche—with his highly unorthodox, extremely Augustinized Cartesianism—appears on the scene, and eventually dominates it? Is there some set of doctrines or positions that unites those disparate members of the first and second generations—Regius, De Raey, Clauberg, Geulincx, Du Roure, Clerselier, Desgabets, Rohault, Cordemoy, La Forge, and others— with all their intramural differences, into the "sect" that so concerned academic, ecclesiastic, and civil authorities?

For one thing, being a Cartesian generally involved opposition to the Aristotelian-Scholastic philosophy that ruled the curricula of the educational faculties in France, the Spanish Netherlands, and the Dutch Republic and informed much contemporary theology as well. But there were many anti-Aristotelians in the period who cannot, under any circumstances, be regarded as Cartesians. Being critical of "the philosophy of the Schools" might, at best, serve only as a sine qua non and merely negative desideratum for Cartesian membership. Even this, however, is problematic since, as we have seen, there were some proponents of Cartesianism—such as Leiden's Heereboord, author of the *Parallelismus Aristotelicae et Cartesianae philosophiae naturalis* (Parallelism of the Aristotelian and Cartesian Natural Philosophy, 1643), and, in France, René Le Bossu, author of the similarly titled *Parallèle des principes de la physique d'Aristote et de celle de René Descartes* (1674)—who were willing to adopt a conciliatory approach to at least certain features of Peripatetic Scholasticism.

Descartes's enemies themselves could only vaguely define what made one a Cartesian; at best they could say only that they knew one when they saw one. Recent scholars have shown how difficult it is to come up with a clear set of necessary and sufficient conditions for a thinker to fall neatly into that category. Thomas Lennon and Patricia Easton warn that

34 THE GOOD CARTESIAN

philosophical schools or movements, and even the doctrines they espouse, are usually characterized in terms that construe them as natural kinds or even Platonic Forms. References to Platonism, Aristotelianism, Thomism, rationalism, empiricism, logical positivism, etc., often suggest semantic monoliths that are clearly defined and agreed upon by their exponents. Not much history is required, however, to reveal such characterizations as caricatures.

"Even in the case of Cartesianism," they show in their study of the Cartesian empiricist François Bayle, "which is perhaps the paradigmatic philosophical 'ism', there was hardly a doctrine, view or argument that was advanced by everyone thought, and rightly thought, to be a Cartesian."[52]

Sophie Roux, likewise, has argued that the search for an "essence" of Cartesianism is a vain undertaking. "Abandoning the essentialist response and its weaker naturalist version, it is possible to look at more conventional and social determinations as to what it is to be Cartesian." The "definition" or boundaries of Cartesianism, she insists, are best sought "polemically," whereby the meaning and extension of "Cartesian" emerges only in the context of disputes, both between Cartesians and their opponents and among Cartesians themselves. "Anyone who seeks to respond to this question [What is it to be Cartesian?] would do well to pay attention to the controversies in which Cartesians and anti-Cartesians are opposed to one another and to the internal polemics in the course of which Cartesians are forced to define what constitutes their identity."[53]

Nonetheless, even with these reasonable caveats in mind, it does seem possible to identify some essential theses of Cartesian philosophy.

First, there is the framework of substance/attribute/mode ontology. Whatever is, is either a substance, defined by Descartes as "a thing which exists in such a way as to depend on no other thing for its existence"; the principal attribute of a substance ("which constitutes its nature and essence, and to which all its other properties are referred"); or a mode or quality of a substance, "when we are thinking of a substance as being affected or modified" or existing in such and such a way.[54] Strictly speaking, only God is a substance, since only an infinite, necessary being depends ontologically on absolutely nothing for its existence. However, Descartes concedes that the term 'substance' is equivocal, and that finite beings are substances in a secondary sense, since they depend only on God.[55]

CARTESIANISM, 1650–1663 35

Equally important and non-negotiable (although, as we shall see, subject to some modification, within bounds) is the way that ontology is more specifically divided into what has come to be known as substance dualism. There are two, and only two, kinds (or principal attributes) of substance: thought or thinking substance and extension or extended substance. As Descartes puts it, there is a "real distinction" (and not merely a modal distinction or a "distinction of reason") between mind as substance and body as substance. "We can perceive that two substances are really distinct simply from the fact that we can clearly and distinctly understand one apart from the other."[56] Mind or thinking (immaterial) substance and body or extended (material) substance are radically different, mutually exclusive, and universally exhaustive categories. *Everything*, without exception, is *either* a mind or mental state *or* a body or bodily state. The principal attribute of mind is thought, and the principal attribute of body is extension or three-dimensional spatiality. The modes or properties of minds are thoughts (ideas, volitions, doubts, passions, etc.), and the modes or properties of bodies are shape, size, divisibility, motion and rest, and impenetrability. No mind can have a bodily property (minds do not occupy space), and no body can be the subject of a mental property (bodies do not have thoughts).[57] Immaterial minds can exist without bodies, and throughout nature there are innumerable bodies that are not united with minds.

Mind–body substance dualism excludes from the Cartesian camp such thinkers as Thomas Hobbes (1588–1679), a materialist who explicitly rejects the notion of an immaterial or incorporeal substance as "absurd"; Gassendi, who (especially in his Fifth Set of Objections to the *Meditationes*) adopts a mitigated skeptical stance as to the true, substantial nature of the mind; John Locke (1632–1704), who, like Gassendi, is unwilling to commit himself to the claim that the substance of thought is radically different from the substance of body, and even entertains the possibility that matter might be endowed with thinking; and, if we go into the early eighteenth century, George Berkeley, who rejects the notion of material substance as incoherent.[58] One could argue that it also rules out Spinoza to the extent that he recognizes only one substance, God or Nature, an infinite and eternal substance to which an infinity of attributes (including thought and extension) belong.

In the domain of natural philosophy, a critical aspect of Cartesianism was a commitment to a mechanistic science of nature. There is but one kind of matter, and everything in the physical universe, terrrestrial or celestial—but nothing in the mental realm—can be explained by the motion, rest, collision, conglomeration, and separation of particles of matter having shape and size. There are no "forms," mind- or soul-like entities partly constitutive of bodily substances that cause them to move and behave in their characteristic ways. There are laws of nature, and these are "causes" in the sense that any true understanding of a natural phenomenon must refer to them. But there are not embedded in bodies any kind of dynamic forces operating in non-mechanical ways.[59] Neither is there, nor can there possibly be, action at a distance. Whatever effects there are in nature, whatever natural phenomena one is seeking to explain, are accounted for solely through local contact of micro- and macroscopic parcels of matter. The active, incorporeal "forms" and teleological "entelechies" that Gottfried Wilhelm Leibniz (1646–1716), self-consciously following the Scholastics, introduces into corporeal substances are inadmissible in the Cartesian universe. A similar fate among the Cartesians is in store for Newtonian matter and forces that operate in ways that cannot be captured in strictly mechanistic terms.[60]

With respect to the human mind, the Cartesian distinguishes between two basic faculties: intellect and will. The intellect, broadly construed, is home to ideas and perceptions.[61] These include both clear and distinct concepts and the reasoning performed upon them, and the obscure and confused testimony of the senses, emotions, and imagination. The will is the active faculty in the mind that allows the mind to assent to or reject the content of the ideas presented to it by the intellect. The intellect is responsible for understanding; the will is responsible for volitions, desires, assertions, denials—any activity of an appetitive or assertoric nature.

The mind operates at its best through the testimony of clear and distinct ideas in the intellect. Descartes says that "we never go wrong when we assent only to what we clearly and distinctly perceive . . . the minds of all of us have been so molded by nature that whenever we perceive something clearly, we spontaneously give our assent to it and are quite unable to doubt its truth."[62] Any such giving or withholding of assent by the will, whether in the face of a clear and distinct idea or an obscure and confused one, is free and unconstrained (but not necessarily undetermined, insofar as it is difficult, even "morally" impossible, for the will to withhold its assent before a clear and distinct idea).

Rejecting any one of these doctrines in a wholesale way makes one's Cartesianism unorthodox, even problematic; rejecting all of them removes one from the Cartesian circle altogether. Of course, as Roger Ariew has noted, "to be a Cartesian . . . does not entail agreeing with everything Descartes propounded," no more than being an Aristotelian means adopting every single one of Aristotle's own doctrines.[63] Mind–body dualism, the mechanistic philosophy of nature, and the Cartesian philosophy of mind provide only the most general parameters within which a Cartesian must work. When we descend to more particular matters, there seems to be room for negotiation, correction, innovation, even striking departures from the precise views of Descartes or his most faithful followers. Indeed, we find *most* Cartesians in the second half of the seventeenth century expanding on, modifying, or even rejecting this or that item on which Descartes had explicitly insisted, whether for the sake of greater internal and systematic consistency or in order to catch up with recent developments in natural science (especially physics and human physiology).

For example, Descartes was quite clear that matter, as nothing but pure extension, is indefinitely divisible; any body or determinate parcel of matter, by virtue of having dimensions, is capable at least in principle of being divided. In other words, there are ever-increasingly minute corpuscles but no atoms.[64] Moreover, if matter is extension, then any extended space is necessarily matter; there is no empty space, no vacuum—the cosmos is a plenum.[65] Cordemoy, however, rejected both of these claims in his *Le Discernement du corps et de l'âme en six discours*. He defines 'body' as "extended substance." So far, so good. He also notes that the extension of any particular body must be limited, and so a body will have figure or shape. Again, there is nothing out of the Cartesian ordinary here. But then comes the surprise:

> Since each body is only one and the same substance, it cannot be divided; its shape cannot change; and it is necessarily so continuous that it excludes every other body. This is what is called *impenetrability*.[66]

The term 'body' properly refers to an indivisible, shaped, impenetrable, mobile, extended substance. Because they are indivisible, bodies have no parts. They are also insensible, because any singular body is too small to have an effect on our sense organs. Bodies, in other words, are simple and (to the naked eye) invisible atoms. Matter, on the other hand, is a collection of individual bodies (*un assemblage de corps*). As such, matter has parts. Discrete parcels of matter, in turn, are "portions" that make up more compound matter. Depending upon how the collected atoms (parts) of a portion of matter are situated relative to each other, and how that portion of matter relates to other

38 THE GOOD CARTESIAN

portions of matter constituting a larger parcel of matter, that larger parcel of matter will be a "heap [*tas*]," a fluid, or a solid.

Cordemoy insists that, strictly speaking, extension belongs only to bodies, not to matter. This is because of the unity and simplicity of a body, which means that its figure is truly continuous. Matter, on the other hand, has "quantity" but not extension.

> Any single body is never a quantity, although it may be a part of a quantity, just as unity is not a number, although it constitutes part of number. The upshot is that quantity and extension are two different things: one pertains properly to body and the other pertains properly to matter.[67]

A conglomerate of bodies or portions of matter that make up a visible body (a macro-portion of matter) might seem to a perceiver to have extension. This is because of the extension of the constituent bodies and the appearance of unity and continuity when they come together to form portions. However, the empty spaces between the matter's parts and portions rule out the true continuity necessary for extension. And Cordemoy, unlike Descartes, does believe that there are indeed empty spaces. The void (*vuide*) is not only possible, but actual, since it constitutes the necessary space that separates atoms and which they need in order to move.

> The bodies that compose heaps, fluids, and masses are not everywhere so tightly packed that they do not leave some gaps in various places. When these gaps are perceived, they are called *holes*. And when they are not perceived, they are called *pores*. It is not necessary that these gaps are filled; and it is conceivable that there should be no body between bodies that do not touch each other.[68]

Cordemoy takes Descartes head-on when he insists that "it is not at all true to say that these gaps cannot be conceived without extension, and that consequently there are bodies that fill them." The shape of a space should not be confused with the real extension that constitutes a body. Should the contents filling a vase be removed, it does not follow—"as some [i.e., Descartes] maintain"—that the "empty" vase keeps its shape only because of the (invisible) matter within it, that only a body taking the place of the contents would keep the vase from collapsing in on itself and its sides from coming together.[69]

The identification of matter with extension, with the consequent rejection of atomism and the denial of a void in nature, would seem to be central metaphysical features of Cartesian natural philosophy. And yet, despite Cordemoy's deviations from orthodoxy on these points, it would be wrong to deny that he was a true and devoted Cartesian. He took himself not to be rejecting Descartes's philosophy but to be moving it in the right directions.

There are other topics on which bona fide Cartesians departed from what Descartes himself would have regarded as dogma. Innate ideas, so central to Descartes's epistemology, are rejected by Cartesian empiricists such as Desgabets, Régis, Lamy, and François Bayle (1622–1709). Also in the epistemological domain, Desgabets and Régis—whom Tad Schmaltz identifies as the "radical Cartesians"[70]—denied the need for any propadeutic use of skepticism or "method of doubt," such as that employed by Descartes in the *Meditationes*. Some Cartesians insisted, again contrary to Descartes, that the mind is *not* better or more easily known than the body (Desgabets, Malebranche); others, rebuffing Descartes's claim that some of the mind's ideas are purely intellectual, with no corporeal correlate, insisted that all thoughts in the human mind are grounded in the mind's union with the human body (the radicals Desgabets and Régis again).[71]

No less subject to revision was Descartes's natural philosophy. Cartesians were not obliged to adopt a plenist cosmos structured by vortices or to agree with Descartes on the laws of motion, either their content or their derivation. There are no vortices in Cordemoy's universe; and Malebranche was but one of many who corrected Descartes's rules governing the collision of bodies. All of this could be done while remaining essentially and steadfastly faithful to Descartes's version of the mechanistic philosophy.

It should be clear from this brief survey of the different ways in which Cartesians distinguished themselves from Descartes that there was a good deal of familial squabbling among them as well. Descartes's seventeenth-century acolytes were far from a unified cohort. Writing to Clerselier in 1666, Desgabets proclaimed Cordemoy's atomism to be "contrary to the doctrine of Monsieur Descartes." He composed a refutation of Cordemoy's text, declaring it to be "thoughtlessly creating a schism which is all the more considerable given that he, at one strike, eliminates from the true philosophy one of its strongest columns and remarkably strengthens the party of Monsieur Gassendi, which already seems very likely to support itself and overthrow that of Monsieur Descartes."[72]

40 THE GOOD CARTESIAN

Desgabets, along with Régis, also took issue with Malebranche on a matter that Descartes himself recognized might be seen as problematic by theologians and philosophers. In letters to Mersenne from 1630 and in the Sixth Replies, Descartes had proclaimed that all truths, even those we regard as necessary and eternal, were freely created by God. To the "philosophers and theologians" of the Sixth Objections, he says that

> If anyone attends to the immeasurable greatness of God he will find it man-
> ifestly clear that there can be nothing whatsoever that does not depend on
> him. This applies not just to everything that subsists, but to all order, every
> law, and every reason for anything's being true or good. If this were not so,
> then ... God would not have been completely indifferent with respect to the
> creation of what he did in fact create.[73]

Mathematical propositions such as $1 + 1 = 2$ and that the interior angles of a triangle add up to 180 degrees are true only because God has so decreed them. In an absolutely simple God, will and understanding are one and the same, and thus for God to know those truths is the same as for God to will them. To Mersenne's query as to what kind of causality God established the eternal truths, Descartes replied, "by the same kind of causality as he created all things, that is to say, as their efficient and total cause."[74] However, he also warned his friend not to publicize this as his view. "I beg you to tell people [about the eternal truths] as often as the occasion demands, provided you do not mention my name."[75]

Desgabets and Régis toed the Cartesian line here. But they also criticized Malebranche for his opposing view that the eternal truths are uncreated, that they necessarily and timelessly exist in God's understanding beyond the reach of God's will. According to Malebranche's "Vision in God" doc-trine, which makes its first appearance in 1674–75 with the publication of his *De la recherche de la vérité*, human beings come to know these truths only because God chooses to reveal the eternal ideas on which they are based to finite minds, which naturally enjoy a cognitive union with the divine understanding.

The critique of Malebranche by Desgabets and Régis, however, was nothing like the assault launched against him by yet another Cartesian, Arnauld. The public debate between these two Augustinians—one a Jansenist, the other an Oratorian, but both committed to Descartes's philosophy—was arguably the most vicious and personal in the second half of the century. Arnauld essentially initiated the Cartesian attack on Malebranche's claim that the intellectual ideas we perceive—including the ideas of ordinary bodies—are not modes of the human mind but are in God. But what really troubled him was Malebranche's theory of causation and his occasionalist account of God's modus operandi in the realms of both nature and grace. And yet, Arnauld and Malebranche were on the same side—facing off against Desgabets and Régis—on the question as to whether there were any purely intellectual thoughts independent of the body.[76]

All of these internecine battles, among others, were usually waged not only in pursuit of "the truth" but also for the sake of establishing one's claim to be the better or more authentic or more progressive Cartesian. As heated as the disagreements might have been, and despite the not insignificant differences on matters of metaphysics, epistemology, and natural philosophy, all of these individuals were self-consciously participating in a common project: the success of the Cartesian philosophy. They were all working on behalf of its enshrinement as the dominant philosophical paradigm in educated society, scientific research, and institutions of learning.

To be a Cartesian—truly a Cartesian[77]—then, meant taking one's start from Descartes's fundamental principles and, rather than slavishly reproducing the consequences Descartes had drawn from them, doing what one could to shore up and improve the system: repair its errors, supplement its shortcomings, enhance its agreement with the progress of science, and respond to objections both philosophical and theological, even if this meant pushing that system in directions that Descartes never intended and probably would not have endorsed.

Being a Cartesian meant, above all, *seeing oneself* as a Cartesian, as someone engaged in at least some, and perhaps all, of this range of tasks. Spinoza, for one, might have envisioned his own substance metaphysics as a matter of driving Cartesian principles to their ultimate logical conclusion, but he most certainly did not regard himself as a Cartesian. (Neither did contemporary Cartesians, whom he referred to as "the stupid Cartesians [*stolidi Cartesiani*]" for their efforts to distance themselves from him, regard him as a fellow traveler offering only friendly amendments.[78]) Spinoza was not working on behalf of the success of Descartes's philosophy in the way that Clerselier, Rohault, Desgabets, Cordemoy, Régis, and others were. The latter were not only seen by their opponents as "Cartesians," but regarded themselves as such. What Desgabets says of his approach to Descartes and the

42 THE GOOD CARTESIAN

proofs in the *Meditationes* of the existence of God and the immortality of the soul represents well the Cartesian's self-image:

> I find many considerable defects [in the *Meditationes*] that can be corrected only for the glory of this great philosopher who himself provided the means to bring them to their final perfection and the remedies for whatever he did wrong [*au mal qu'il a fait*]. I have thus set myself the task of working on something so necessary, in this treatise that I call the first supplement of his philosophy, insofar as I try to rectify in it his own thoughts on things in which it seems to me that he strayed from the right path leading to the truth; this is different from what might be called the second supplement, which is the new application that can be made of his incontestable principles to phenomena that he did not know or to truths of which he did not speak.

Desgabets notes that he will limit himself to the first "supplement" or project—fixing things, rather than introducing new applications—as "it is on behalf of the kind of second supplement that Messieurs de Cordemoy, Rohault, de la Forge, Clauberg and others have labored in the beautiful works that they have given to the public."[79]

What Schmaltz says about Desgabets's project seems to capture nicely the more general point: "Cartesianism is not a fixed position that can simply be extracted from Descartes, but rather a work in progress that starts with Descartes's insights but that subjects his views to revision and correction."[80] He suggests that we should speak in the early modern period not of "Cartesianism" but rather of "Cartesianisms." What brings them together is less a doctrinal homogeneity than a family resemblance à la Wittgenstein. Quoting the *Philosophical Investigations*, Schmaltz implies that it is best to see Cartesianism as "a complicated network of similarities overlapping and crisscrossing: sometimes overall similarities, sometimes similarities of detail." What unites Clerselier and company is "a particular historical origin and line of descent." All of these individuals are "engaging in a research program that is continuous with [Descartes's] own work."[81]

*

We do not know how well La Forge was acquainted with the members of this internationally dispersed, religiously disparate, relatively loose but nonetheless distinct and identifiable network—even whether he was personally acquainted with any of them at all. He was at least in touch with Clerselier, via correspondence, by 1660, when they began their collaboration on the edition of Descartes's *Traité de l'homme*. But unless La Forge had attended some of the meetings of the Montmor Academy—and, as we have seen, there is no direct evidence that he did—he is not likely to have met Clerselier in person. Or Du Roure. Or Rohault or Régis.

Clauberg paid a visit to the Protestant Academy in Saumur in 1646. This was way too early for a meeting with the fourteen-year-old La Forge, who was still doing his studies in La Flèche. By the time he had reached his philosophical maturity, however, La Forge was well acquainted with the older Cartesian's works. In his *Traité de l'esprit de l'homme*, La Forge does cite, somewhat critically, Clauberg's *De cognitione Dei et nostri* (1656) and his *Ontosophia nova* (1660; La Forge refers to it as *Metaphysica*). Their views on the union of mind and body are quite similar—both see it as consisting solely in a mutual correspondence of states—and the two men reportedly exchanged letters.[82] None of the correspondence has survived, however, and so there is no extant documentation of a personal relationship.

What about Cordemoy, whose own treatise on "the distinction between the body and the mind" is very similar to La Forge's *Traité*? Cordemoy's work appeared in print just months after La Forge's, and the two men are often linked as the "first" of the Cartesian occasionalists. Was there some connection between them, if not in person in Paris at Montmor's then somewhere else or via correspondence? The circumstantial evidence is compelling, but the most we can do is agree with one scholar who wrote "*la chose est possible.*"[83]

Whether or not La Forge was acquainted with any of Clerselier's colleagues, and however tenuous may have been his connection with the Cartesian networks operating in Paris, Utrecht, Leiden, or Amsterdam, he knew what they were up to and closely followed their progress. There can be no question of La Forge's Cartesian credentials. He was, in fact, a Cartesian par excellence, and arguably the most faithful of all. We know that had La Forge lived longer, he was, he told Clerselier, planning "to do no less than complete those [projects] that Monsieur Descartes had set himself" but did not get around to doing.[84]

3

Illustrating the World

By early 1662, Clerselier's patience was wearing thin. The Parisian lawyer was in possession of an unpublished manuscript of a treatise by his late friend, the century's greatest philosopher, and several years of effort to get it into print still had not paid off. The text itself was ready to go to press, but some essential artwork he had commissioned to illustrate the work was long overdue. To make matters worse, a Latin translation of the treatise would soon appear with a foreign (Dutch) publisher. Clerselier was concerned that this translation was based on a poor, unreliable copy of the original, and so he tried to postpone that book's appearance with a polite letter. But a failure to communicate due to the Dutch translator's insensitivity to the niceties of the French language had led to the impression that Clerselier was, in fact, endorsing the project.[1]

Clerselier was convinced that his edition of the treatise, in the original French, would be better than the Latin version: more authentic, based on what he claims to be the philosopher's autograph manuscript,[2] and more valuable and marketable to a broad European audience. If only he had those illustrations.

*

In late 1653 or early 1654, Clerselier had acquired many of the papers left behind by Descartes when he died in Sweden.[3] In the first two volumes of the philosopher's correspondence, he exercised a little editorial discretion in his selection of letters, and often had to do serious reconstructive work from old and mutilated scraps of paper. Moreover, in his preface to the second volume, Clerselier tells the reader that, unlike the first volume, which contained a mix of letters in Latin and French, the contents of this one are entirely in French. Various booksellers had complained that the first volume did not sell well, just because of the large number of letters it contained in Latin, and "many people who have no familiarity with this language had not bought it."[4]

The Good Cartesian. Steven Nadler, Oxford University Press. © Oxford University Press 2024.
DOI: 10.1093/oso/9780197671719.003.0004

Now, in 1659, while working on the third volume of letters—it would not appear until 1667, in part because of the time required for him to draw the relevant illustrations for it[5]—Clerselier was also readying for the press two closely related parts of Descartes's earliest philosophical project.[6] Taken together, they constitute the first and second sections of *Le Monde* (The World) an ambitious work composed in the late 1620s and early 1630s in which Descartes lays out, for the first time, the fundamental principles of his philosophical system and uses them, with great audacity, to explain (as he said to Mersenne) "all sublunary phenomena."[7]

In Part One of *Le Monde*, eventually to be called *Traité de la lumière* (Treatise on Light), Descartes uses the phenomena of light to lead an investigation of inanimate bodies in the celestial and terrestrial realms solely according to the principles of his physics, including an account of the origin and structure of the cosmos. Part Two, *Traité de l'homme* (Treatise on Man; abbreviated as *L'Homme*), concerned "animals, and in particular men," and it was devoted to showing how the human body, like any living body, operates on purely mechanical (i.e., material) principles.[8] A discussion of "the rational soul," both by itself and in its relation to the human body, initially intended for a Part Three, would appear only in several of his later works: the *Meditationes de prima philosophia*, the *Principia philosophiae*, and especially *Les Passions de l'âme*.[9]

Putting aside for the time being the *Traité de la lumière*,[10] Clerselier began with a separate edition of the *Traité de l'homme*, an essay on human physiology that presents "all the principal functions of the human being" according to strictly mechanistic principles, without assuming that the body is endowed with any kind of soul or mind.[11]

*

For most camps in the Aristotelian philosophy, while only human beings had a rational soul, the organic internal processes and basic motions of the human body were explained through the introduction of lower-level souls (forms) into the body's matter. Generation, growth, the circulation of the blood and other fluids, the digestion of food, and so on depended on a vegetative soul, which was present in all living things, whether animal or plant. Sensory perception and the active and responsive movements of the body were a function of a sensitive soul, which informed the bodies of all animals, human and non-human.[12] Descartes, pursuing his earliest attack on

46 THE GOOD CARTESIAN

the substantial and accidental forms of Scholastic thought, dispenses with all such non-rational souls and non-mechanical powers and operations. The human body he describes in *L'Homme* is a kind of machine, no less so than other animate and inanimate bodies. In its ordinary operations, it is simply a collection of material parts moving and interacting with each other and with other bodies according to the laws of nature.

> We see clocks, artificial fountains, mills and other similar machines which, even though they are only made by men, have the power to move of their own accord in various ways. And, as I am supposing that this machine [the human body] is made by God, I think you will agree that it is capable of a greater variety of movements than I could possibly imagine in it, and that it exhibits a greater ingenuity than I could possibly ascribe to it.[13]

Through empirical investigation involving dissection and other modes of experimentation, supplemented by clear and distinct reasoning, Descartes carefully determined the structure of the human skeleton, musculature, and organs and the actions of its sensory, circulatory, respiratory, nervous, and digestive systems.

Of primary importance in the living human body as described by Descartes is the heat of the heart. In contrast with the Aristotelian and Galenic traditions, the ultimate source of everything that happens in the body is not some immaterial spiritual principle informing its matter, but simply the heart and the heat that it spontaneously generates—a "fire without light," he calls it.[14] In the final article of the work, he says

> I desire that you consider that all the functions that I have attributed to this machine, such as the digestion of food, the beating of the heart and the arteries, the nourishment and growth of the bodily parts, respiration, waking and sleeping; the reception of light, sounds, odors, smells, heat, and other such qualities by the external sense organs; the impression of the ideas of them in the organ of common sense and the imagination, the retention or imprint of these ideas in the memory; the internal movements of all the bodily parts that so aptly follow both the actions of objects presented to the senses, and the passions and impressions that are encountered in memory: and in this they imitate as perfectly as possible the movements of real men. I desire, I say, that you should consider that these functions follow in this machine simply from the disposition of the organs as wholly

naturally as the movements of a clock or other automaton follow from the disposition of its counterweights and wheels.

To explain all these functions, he continues,

> It is not necessary to conceive of any vegetative or sensitive soul, or any other principle of movement or life, other than its blood and its spirits which are agitated by the heat of the fire that burns continuously in its heart, and which is of the same nature as those fires that occur in inanimate bodies.[15]

The heart's heating action, aside from explaining the circulation of the blood as it is caused to expand in and depart from the heart's chambers, also generates the agent that, as it moves throughout the body, plays a role in all of that body's operations—the internal motions that regularly maintain it, its passive and active responses to external stimuli, and even its interactions with the soul. Descartes calls this agent the "animal spirits." The spirits are not actually spiritual at all, but a highly rarified vapor or neural fluid generated from the blood by the separation of its finer parts by the heat of the heart as the blood circulates through it. This distillation produces "a very fine wind, or rather a very lively and very pure flame."

The spirits are transported throughout the body by the channels that contain and protect the nerves, which are simply tiny fibers connecting the extremities of the body to the brain. The body moves when the muscles are inflated by the spirits sent there by the brain or deflated as the spirits depart. In instinctive motions—for example, flinching at the sight of a threat—the spirits are stimulated in a purely mechanical manner, as their minute parts are pushed in this or that direction by other bodily parts in motion, which in turn are responding to the impression caused by an external body. The human body in this case acts just like that of a sheep that flees at the sight of a wolf. The sheep's turning around and running away is a purely mechanical response, a matter of motions in muscles generated by the image of the predator in the sheep's optical apparatus affecting the flow of the spirits.

Descartes compares the role of the animal spirits in the human body to the air that is forced through the pipes of an organ by a bellows, or to the water that, through a hydraulic system, moves animated statues such as those in the French king's estate at Saint-Germain-en-Lay.

48 THE GOOD CARTESIAN

You may have observed in the grottoes and fountains of the royal gardens that the force that drives the water from its source is all that is needed to move various machines, and even to make them play certain instruments or pronounce certain words, depending on the particular arrangements of the pipes through which the water is conducted.[16]

Of course, the human being is more than a machine operating on strictly mechanical principles. The human body is united with a soul.

I hold that when God unites a rational soul to this machine, as I intend to explain later on, He will place its principal seat in the brain and will make its nature such that the soul will have different sensations depending on the different ways in which the nerves open the entrances to the pores in the internal surface of the brain.[17]

The animal spirits are, in fact, always responding to and affecting one particular part of the brain: the pineal gland, which Descartes locates right at the brain's center. It is the position and motion of this gland that directs the spirits that flow through it into the pores of the brain that are the endings of the nerve channels, and through these into the limbs and sense organs.

In sensory awareness—whether through sight, touch, smell, hearing, or taste—other bodies impinge, either directly or through a medium, on the exterior of the human body. The motions caused on the surface of the human body constitute a kind of kinetic isomorphic image of that external body. The image is communicated in a purely mechanical manner by the nerves in their channels to the brain, where they impress the image on the brain's interior surface by causing its pores to open or close in that same pattern. Spirits flowing toward this pattern on the brain's interior surface from the pineal gland form into and maintain the image as they cause the gland to move in this or that way, which in turn stimulates the soul to have this or that sensation or idea. This is how we perceive things and have other kinds of sensations in their presence. Thus, in tasting salt, "the tiny fibres that make up the marrow of the nerves of the tongue and which serve as the organ of taste in this machine" are easily moved in different ways by the particles of salt, whose shape and size affect the tongue differently from particles of brandy.[18] When those motions terminate in the brain and, by means of the animal spirits, determine the particular movement of the pineal gland, we experience the salty sensation.

ILLUSTRATING THE WORLD   49

It is crucial to Descartes's account of human experience that, as much in the case of a salty or sweet taste as in the perception of red or blue or the sound of a musical note, there is no resemblance whatsoever between "our sensations and the things that produce them." He reminds us, right at the beginning of *Le Monde*, that "words . . . bear no resemblance to the things they signify, and yet they make us think of those things." Likewise, then, "why could Nature not also have established some sign which would make us have the sensation of light, even if the sign contained nothing in itself which is similar to this sensation?"[19] The motions in the brain (pineal gland) are a kind of natural sign that, on the occasion of their occurrence, stimulate the mind to "interpret" them and produce the appropriate qualitative sensory experience.

Descartes's *Le Monde* represents a crucial stage in the development of the mechanical philosophy in the seventeenth century, with *L'Homme* serving to reorient the study of the human body away from opaque and "mysterious" Aristotelian-Scholastic explanations and render its vital processes— circulatory, respiratory, digestive, and muscular—just as perspicuous as any physical event in nature, where material bodies are nothing but parcels of pure extension in motion.

There were problems, however. An essential feature of Descartes's "world" was its Copernican heliocentric cosmology. In his account, the sun sits at the center of the vortices that contain, and cause the revolutions of, the earth and other planets that move around it. Nor is the sun the only luminous body that has orbiting planets.

> Even though all [the planets] tend towards the centers of the heavens containing them, this is not thereby to say that they could ever reach those centers. For as I have already said, these are occupied by the sun and the other fixed stars. . . . Thus, you see that there can be different planets, at varying distances from the sun. . . . The matter of the heaven must make the planets turn not only around the sun but also around their own center.[20]

Descartes knew that he was treading on dangerous ground. The heliocentrism is, in part, the reason why he decided to present his overall account of the universe in purely hypothetical terms, "as if my intention were simply to tell you a fable."[21] He says in the treatise that he is not describing this actual world, the one that the Bible tells us God created. Rather, he is talking about "another world—a wholly new one which I shall bring into being before your mind in

50 THE GOOD CARTESIAN

imaginary spaces."[22] He hoped that by presenting his Copernican cosmology as a counterfactual fiction—the way a cosmos *might* be constructed—he would be afforded some protection from theological critics who would otherwise attack him for expounding a doctrine that was regarded by the Catholic Church as "contrary to Holy and Divine Scripture." Besides, did not the Catholic Church allow the discussion of heliocentrism, so long as it was considered merely a "hypothesis" and not presented as the truth?[23]

Descartes's faith in his strategy was shaken in November 1633, just as he was about to send *Le Monde* to Mersenne for publication. Having been unsuccessful in his attempts to get a hold of a copy of Galileo's *Dialogo sopra i due massimi sistemi del mondo* (Dialogue Concerning the Two Chief World Systems), published just a year earlier, he was shocked to hear the rumor that Galileo's book had been burned in Rome and that Galileo had been convicted by the Catholic Church of heresy and punished. Descartes, who thought himself a good Catholic—and, more to the point, who was fearful of any repercussions—now had second thoughts. He told Mersenne, "I was so astounded at this that I almost decided to burn all my papers or at least to let no one see them. For I could not imagine that he [Galileo]—an Italian and, as I understand, in the good graces of the Pope—could have been made a criminal for any other reason than that he tried, as he no doubt did, to establish that the earth moves." Descartes concedes that if that view is false, then "so too are the entire foundations of my philosophy." The heliocentric model, he claims, "is so closely interwoven in every part of my treatise that I could not remove it without rendering the whole work defective."[24] Moreover, Descartes reminded his friend, Galileo himself had used the maneuver of presenting that model as a mere hypothesis; if that did not save a Florentine who enjoyed the pope's favor, it was unlikely to save Descartes. Rather than incur the wrath of the Church, Descartes decided not to publish either part of *Le Monde* after all. "I have decided to suppress the treatise I have written and to forfeit almost all my work of the last four years in order to give my obedience to the Church, since it has proscribed the view that the earth moves." Many years later, he would remind Mersenne that "the only thing that has stopped me publishing my Philosophy up to now is the question of defending the movement of the earth."[25]

In the fall of 1633, Descartes put both parts of *Le Monde* away; they would not be published in his lifetime.

*

Now, several years after Descartes's death, with the author safely beyond the reach of the Holy Office, it was up to Clerselier to bring Descartes's abandoned treatises to the public. He started with the *Traité de l'homme*.

The text was just about ready to go. However, from certain letter-labels in the manuscript that he possessed, Clerselier could tell that this relatively short work was missing illustrations that Descartes had envisioned for it. He knew, then, that before he could publish the treatise he would have to find a way to supply these—which is precisely where, like the final volume of letters, things seem to have gotten held up.

Despite working on the "figures" for the correspondence, Clerselier did not believe himself to have the artistic skills for this more specialized and detailed anatomical work; he claims that he did not feel "strong enough to come up with them myself."[26] Thus, he was quite thrilled—he calls it *une faveur du Ciel*—when, in 1657, he learned from Louis and Daniel Elzevirs, of the Dutch publishing firm which that year had brought out the first volume of Descartes's letters, that a man named Huyberts had already done some illustrations for the treatise, which the Elzevirs were planning to publish.[27] Clerselier feared that Huyberts had worked from an unreliable copy of the manuscript, however, and so he sent a fair copy of what he claimed to be the original to the Elzevirs to forward to Huyberts, in order that he might refine his figures accordingly. Huyberts wrote back to Clerselier promising to deliver the illustrations "when he had given them the best form he could."[28] Unfortunately, this seems to have been the end of the trail. Clerselier never heard back from Huyberts—perhaps, Clerselier suspects, because the latter had become rather ill and maybe even died—and he soon gave up hope on this lead.

In April 1659, Clerselier made a second attempt to secure illustrations. He believed himself to have a natural candidate in Henricus Regius, professor of medicine at the University of Utrecht and a disciple of Descartes—although, as disciples go, he was a rather unorthodox (and somewhat troublesome) one. Given Regius's Cartesian credentials and his medical background, Clerselier could say, "I did not know of anyone whom I believed more capable of executing this project."[29] Regius had had an unpleasant falling out with Descartes some years earlier—Descartes did not feel that Regius was representing his philosophy in a proper and responsible way—and there were bitter recriminations on both sides. Regius was also not on good terms with Clerselier, since he apparently resented Clerselier's including Descartes's letters to him in the first volume of correspondence without permission, while

52 THE GOOD CARTESIAN

Clerselier had taken Regius to task for removing in the second edition of his *Fundamenta physices* the praise of Descartes that he had included in the first edition. But a collaboration on the *Traité de l'homme* seemed to Clerselier like a good opportunity to mend fences and for Regius to publicly reconfirm his *ancienne amitié* with the late Descartes and re-enter the good graces of his followers.

Regius, however, declined the offer. As Clerselier tells it, Regius was afraid that, were he to work on the illustrations for *L'Homme*, people would suspect that he had long been familiar with the essay, and thus that his own work in physics and human physiology was nothing but a plagiarization of Descartes. Regius's relationship with Descartes had been poisoned in part by disagreement over who should get credit for what, and he was again worried about being perceived as the pupil and not as the master. (Among other things, Descartes complained to Princess Elisabeth of Bohemia that Regius, in his *Fundamenta physices* [1646], merely "transcribed the whole section" in *L'Homme* dealing with the eye muscles.[30]) Clerselier, for his part, was skeptical that Regius could, all on his own, really have come up with exactly the same ideas—and in the same words!—as Descartes, and he claimed to have the letters to prove who really learned from whom.[31] Be that as it may, with Regius's rejection of the commission, it was back to square one.

At this point—probably the summer of 1659, just after the disappointment with Regius—Clerselier decided to make a more public plea for help with the illustrations. In the final paragraph of his preface to the second volume of Descartes's letters that was published later that year, he wrote that among the items from Descartes "which were put into my hands by him who was the repository of all of the goods of his [Descartes's] mind"—that is, by Pierre Chanut, Descartes's friend, France's ambassador to Sweden and Clerselier's brother in-law[32]—is a manuscript titled *L'homme*, "an altogether curious work which we can only wish had been put into its final perfection by the hand of the author himself." Clerselier notes that he is now trying to arrange this text into the best form possible. But because, among other things, it lacks the necessary illustrations, "I hereby invite all learned men who want to help me to supply them." He continues this solicitation as follows:

> If some obliging person, envious of the reputation of Mr. Descartes and of his own, wanted to offer himself for this glorious work, I beg him to give me notice of it. If he is a foreigner, provided that he can give me a certain and precise address, I will put into his hands everything that is necessary;

and I will stipulate to him no further condition other than that this Treatise not be printed in our language in foreign lands until it is first printed in France.[33]

At around the same time, Clerselier, persuaded that Descartes himself must have created some illustrations—or even just sketches—for the treatise to match up with the labels in the manuscript, sent a young emissary to the Netherlands to see what he could discover. Pierre Guisony did not find any figures by Descartes during his travels, but in Flanders he did come into contact with Gerard van Gutschoven, at the University of Leuven. As a physician, anatomist, and mathematician—and as someone who, during a visit to Holland in the late 1630s, got to know Descartes personally and admired his philosophy—Van Gutschoven seemed perfectly well qualified to take on this task. Best of all, he was willing to do so.

Unfortunately, Clerselier did not have any information on how to send Van Gutschoven the manuscript. After a year went by with still no word from Leuven, Clerselier was ready to write this off as yet another dead end. However, in mid-1660, he received a visit in Paris from one Monsieur de Nonancourt, a Flemish gentleman who was acquainted with Van Gutschoven and who brought word that the professor was indeed still interested in doing the illustrations, and he would begin just as soon as he received a copy of the manuscript.

By great coincidence, on that very same day (or so he says) Clerselier also received a letter out of the blue from a man, previously unknown to him (*que je ne connoissois point alors*, he says), who happened to be a medical doctor in Saumur, France, and who was a devotee of Cartesian philosophy. This is where La Forge enters the picture. He had learned of the *Traité de l'homme* project from Clerselier's preface to the second volume of Descartes's correspondence, and, in response to Clerselier's plea, was eager and willing to contribute to the edition and do the illustrations, if someone were still needed. He was also, he said, prepared to provide some commentary on the text.

Clerselier now faced an embarrassment of riches. He had two highly qualified people willing and exceptionally able to provide the book with the requisite figures. On the one hand, he did not want to insult Van Gutschoven by now rescinding the invitation; on the other hand, he did not want to pass up the opportunity being offered by La Forge, "a person of our Nation, whose profession corresponds to the knowledge this work requires of someone who offers to undertake it."[34] Clerselier decided to make a kind of competition of

54 THE GOOD CARTESIAN

it and have them both do the work, independently of each other. He says he would let neither man know that someone else was preparing illustrations as well, lest they become "lazy and negligent" and unwilling to put their best effort into a job in which there was a risk that they would not derive all the glory.[35] He gave each of them a copy of the manuscript, and his plan was that at any point in the book where an image was needed he would use whoever's illustration was better.

All of this was neatly arranged by the fall of 1660 at the latest.[36] At around the same time, Clerselier also learned from Descartes's friend Alphonse Pollot about the Latin translation of the treatise being prepared in Leiden by Florent Schuyl, a naturalist and professor of philosophy at the Latin school in Den Bosch (and later professor of medicine at the University of Leiden); as we have seen, Schuyl's *De homine* would appear in 1662. Pollot also told Clerselier about some illustrations (*quelques figures*) for the treatise by Descartes himself that Schuyl had in his possession. Clerselier thus wrote to Schuyl and asked if he would send him Descartes's drawings, a copy of the manuscript he was using for the translation, and any illustrations he may have himself done for the Latin edition. "If I find them suitable," Clerselier added in his letter, he would use them in his own edition.[37]

Schuyl was happy to accommodate Clerselier's request and forwarded everything to Paris: Descartes's drawings—Schuyl refers to them as "two figures crudely drawn by the hand of Monsieur Descartes"[38]—his own drawings for the text (or prints thereof), and a copy of the manuscript he was using. Clerselier was careful not to show any of Schuyl's illustrations to either La Forge or Van Gutschoven, so that they might do their best work on their own. (Even after receiving a copy of Schuyl's book, Clerselier says he did not bring it to the attention of his two anatomist-artists, in order to safeguard their claims of originality.[39])

Less than a year after receiving La Forge's letter—and so probably by mid-1661—Clerselier received from the Saumur physician more than he ever hoped for: not only the promised illustrations, but an extensive, detailed commentary on the treatise, as well as a draft of La Forge's own *Traité de l'esprit de l'homme*, in which La Forge supplements Descartes's study of the human body with an account, on Cartesian principles, of the human mind and its relationship to the body.[40]

However, Clerselier did not yet have Van Gutschoven's figures. A clean copy of the treatise itself was almost certainly ready to go to the printer by this time. It is possible that as late as the spring of 1662, Clerselier still did not

ILLUSTRATING THE WORLD 55

have the other set of illustrations promised by his perpetually tardy Flemish collaborator.[41] From Clerselier's account of this whole process in his preface to *L'Homme*, however, we can infer that Van Gutschoven's figures did arrive sometime *before* the publication of Schuyl's Latin translation in later 1662.[42] Still, it would be two more years before Clerselier could finally bring out his own, original French edition of Descartes's work on human physiology.

In the end, Clerselier had five sets of illustrations to consider for the *Traité de l'homme*. First, there were two "crudely drawn" figures by Descartes that he is supposed to have received from Schuyl. Then there were Schuyl's own figures from the Latin translation, which Clerselier apparently had permission to use in his French version if he so wanted. He also had the images provided by La Forge and those finally rendered by Van Gutschoven. Moreover, Clerselier claims that at some point before publication he came across yet another, previously unknown original figure from Descartes.

What purpose did Clerselier think such illustrations should serve and what criteria did he have in mind when deciding which figures to include in his edition?

As we have seen, the project of *L'Homme* is to describe the human body (or an imaginary facsimile thereof) on its own—that is, a body unrelated to a human soul or any other immaterial animating power, such as an Aristotelian substantial form. In keeping with the strategic rhetorical posture adopted in the first part of *Le Monde* (the *Traité de la lumière*)—in which the origin, elements, and processes of the world that Descartes describes are presented as "a Fable"[43]—the body under consideration in *L'Homme* is only a hypothetical body of a hypothetical being, although the ruse is rather thin and Descartes often calls attention to this body's resemblance to the actual human body.

> I suppose the body to be nothing but a statue or machine made of earth, which God forms with the explicit intention of making it as much as possible like us. Thus God not only gives it externally the colors and shapes of all the parts of our bodies, but also places inside it all the parts required to make it walk, eat, breath, and indeed to imitate all those of our functions which can be imagined to proceed from matter and to depend solely on the disposition of our organs.[44]

56 THE GOOD CARTESIAN

Descartes's ploy alone raised at least one particular artistic challenge: should the illustrations of the hypothetical body render it simply to look like an ordinary human body? But Clerselier was clearly aware of more general difficulties with Descartes's text. He admits that the density, even occasional opacity, of Descartes's discussion might cause trouble for readers trying to grasp the finer details of his account of human physiology, and especially the explanations of muscular changes, sensation, digestion, memory, and other kinetic phenomena that take place in the body. The text, Clerselier says, "is compact, and . . . says lots of things in few words."[45]

The basic structure of Descartes's *homme*—including the circulatory system, the arrangement of nerves and muscles, and the constitution of the brain and its pores—may itself be rather simple; as Descartes says, "Nature always acts by the easiest and most simple of all means."[46] But the text still demands serious effort to be followed and understood. It especially requires some work on the part of the reader's imagination, and not only because Descartes makes frequent reference to labeled elements of illustrations that are assumed to have originally accompanied the treatise. One needs to be able to picture what exactly Descartes is describing when, for example, he says that a muscle has a number of interior valves that move back and forth over some opening in a nerve canal. Like the figures embedded in the demonstrations of Euclid's *Elements of Geometry*, the illustrations of *L'Homme* were not intended by Descartes to prove or confirm anything, but they were at least supposed to facilitate an understanding of the work's scientific content. As one scholar notes, "the text of Descartes, which was written entirely around the pictures, is often incomprehensible without them."[47]

Clerselier was concerned by this. He notes in his preface that what Descartes says in one article (about the muscles responsible for moving the eyes) is "very concise, and quite difficult to understand without any figures, as anyone can see for themselves if they want to take the trouble to read the text without glancing at them [the illustrations]."[48] He is thus quite clear about what he expects from the illustrations. He says that they should be able to "serve to make . . . the text comprehensible" and "make for an easier understanding of it."[49] The figures are to function as aids for the reader in visualizing, literally—in seeing on paper—the bodily elements and processes that Descartes is describing and to help him understand how everything is supposed to work. The point of "the figures in this book" is "to help one understand what is Monsieur Descartes' thought in it"[50] and "simply to explain . . . what Monsieur Descartes is proposing in his book, in which

ILLUSTRATING THE WORLD   57

he very often discusses only things that never fall under the senses, which he had to make sensible in order for them to become more intelligible."[51] The illustrations must allow even the non-specialist reader to "divine his [Descartes's] thought."[52]

By the same measure, Clerselier does not intend the illustrations to provide insight as to what the elements and processes being discussed might actually look like were one to peer inside the body. Some of the things that Descartes talks about are not visible in fact; others are not even visible in principle, and so do not have a "look" that can be captured on paper. Other than the gross organs, musculature, connective tissues, and circulatory channels, many of the items in Descartes's anatomical picture are much too small to be seen by the naked eye, while some are presumably so minute that they would not be accessible even to microscopic view, given the state of the art of microscopy at the time. And a good number of the functional components of Descartes's *homme* are simply invisible—for example, the animal spirits. Still other features of Descartes's explanations cannot possibly be represented in a single image: how, for example, can motion be depicted in one figure? Conversely, many of the bare diagrammatic illustrations that Clerselier ended up using in the text do not look at all like anything that would be found in an actual human body or medical text.

In other words, what guided Clerselier in his selection of figures was their adequacy as illuminating schematic representations, not any kind of naturalistic verisimilitude. Claus Zittel is thus right to insist that "the criterion of 'faithfulness to the object'—a confirmation of the image's truthfulness through personal observations—therefore had to be ruled out" as a criterion for assessing the adequacy of the images.[53] As Clerselier himself says, this is not an anatomy book.

> If the figures do not resemble anything natural, one should not be surprised, since the plan was not that this should be a book on anatomy that allows one to see exactly how the parts of the human body are made and the relation or proportions among them.[54]

He adds that nothing is easier than drawing pictures that naturalistically resemble the way things actually look. It is a much more difficult task to come up with illustrations that facilitate understanding of objects and mechanisms "which do not at all appear to the senses." The book needed to be accessible to lay readers who might not be willing or able to take the trouble to "examine

58 THE GOOD CARTESIAN

things more closely"; thus, Clerselier has, with the figures, attempted to tailor the treatise "for everyone."[55]

With illustrations of this kind, however, what the reader sees on paper provides only the first step in the process of understanding. Because the figures are schematic diagrams and not naturalistic representations, they need to be aided by the reader's own imagination. Together with the text, they stimulate and guide the reader's mind to fill in the missing details. This is especially true when Descartes discusses various kinetic features of the circulatory, nervous, and sensory systems. The images do not—indeed, they cannot—actually show the animal spirits inflating and deflating muscles; and when Descartes talks about how the pineal gland is moved this way or that because the spirits flow out of it toward these or those pores in the brain lining, all one can do is try to visualize what he has in mind. Clerselier seems to be aware of this, insofar as he notes that the illustrations by Van Gutschoven and La Forge still leave some things "to be supplied by the imagination."[56]

Clerselier suggests that at times the illustrations not only help the reader by supplementing the text and allowing one to visualize (with the senses and the imagination) what Descartes is talking about, but even do a better job than Descartes at explaining something, especially when the text is too short on words (*fort concis*).[57] And if one image will not do the trick in clarifying a particular matter and making Descartes's meaning clear, Clerselier will include two or three, by different hands, so that, as he says, what was not seen through one might be seen through another. Thus, in one instance, a specific application of Descartes's general account of the motion of parts of the body, "the most important action that the author undertook to describe and to explain," Clerselier saw fit to publish the relevant figures from Van Gutschoven, La Forge, *and* Descartes himself (re-drawn by Clerselier). Referring to the three figures related to the explanation of the motion of the eye by its surrounding muscles [figs. 1, 2, 3], Clerselier says, "I thought it necessary to include the one that each came up with; because they are all three very different, what cannot be understood through one can perhaps be supplied by the other."[58] As we shall see, on at least one other occasion, Clerselier informs us, the illustrator—La Forge—went beyond the call of duty and actually corrected Descartes.[59]

*

With the criteria of selection at hand, we can now consider the various options that Clerselier had and what he ended up doing with them. This

ILLUSTRATING THE WORLD   59

will allow us to see and assess La Forge's own pictorial contributions to the treatise.

First, there were the two illustrations by Descartes that Clerselier says he received from Schuyl. The fate of these are a bit of a mystery. Schuyl included only *one* figure by Descartes in his Latin translation [fig. 4]; presumably it was one of the drawings that he forwarded to Clerselier. But Clerselier did not include either it or its missing companion in his edition. From Schuyl's claim that these two images were poorly drawn (*duabus figuris a Des Cartes rudi Minerva exaratis*), we can infer that Clerselier found them unsuitable for his own purposes.

However, Clerselier says that independently he did come across another illustration by Descartes, which he assumed was meant for the *Traité de l'homme*. What he found, he says, is a rough draft on a small, torn, disfigured piece of paper, something that was in such bad shape that someone else might easily have overlooked it:

> In a draft [*brouillon*] that, because it was so small, torn and disfigured, anyone other than I would have thrown into a fire, I found an attempt that M. Descartes once scribbled when he was trying means for imagining a figure that could respond to and satisfy what he had in mind.[60]

To judge from the sketch that Schuyl included in his edition, as well as some other figures hand-drawn by Descartes,[61] the philosopher seems not to have had great artistic skills, or at least not to have taken great care in such matters. Thus, the *brouillon* that Clerselier found needed to be redrawn and better rendered not just because of its poor physical condition and its low artistic quality (he calls it *mal desseiné*[62]), but also in order to serve as a proper illustration for the text. Clerselier did this himself as best he could. "The figure ... below which there is a D is a copy of this draft by Monsieur Descartes, of which I have spoken which I did as best as I could."[63] Among the things he had to do to improve Descartes's drawing was clarify one of its details so it better fit the text. Apparently, Descartes's original image seemed to have three folds (*replis*) on each valve in the nerve extending into the muscles around the eye and through which the animal spirits would flow, whereas the text speaks of only two folds. After comparing the drawing with the text, however, Clerselier realized that what he was taking for a third fold was only a small hook that serves to facilitate the transit of the spirits from one muscle to the next by holding down the valve to which it is attached.[64]

60 THE GOOD CARTESIAN

Having improved the image to make all this clear, Clerselier then included it in his edition as one of the three illustrations of the eye muscles [fig. 3]. As we shall see, while Clerselier did correct Descartes's image for consistency with the text, what he did *not* do was correct it for scientific accuracy.

What is striking is the degree to which this finished illustration can be seen to resemble, in a general enough way, the rough figure by Descartes that Schuyl included in his translation [fig. 4], minus the eyeball but including many of the labels. This suggests two possibilities: either Schuyl and Clerselier each had a different sketch by Descartes of the same thing (the eye's muscles), or the sketch that was redrawn by Clerselier and included in his edition was not in fact some *brouillon* that (he claimed) he found on his own but just the drawing that he received from Schuyl or saw in his book. What may seem to count against this second possibility, however, is the fact that the Descartes drawing published by Schuyl does not exhibit the ambiguous valve flaps that Clerselier says had him confused. Moreover, Clerselier says that he still has Descartes's *brouillon* in his possession, and is willing to show it to "those who are curious about it."[65]

Another issue is the remarkable similarities in design between Clerselier's polished "D" (for "Descartes") image and Van Gutschoven's figure for the same text [fig. 1]. These suggest that Clerselier might have referred to Gutschoven's rendering for guidance in his improvement of Descartes's drawing. It is hard to believe that, relying on the complicated text alone, Clerselier and Van Gutschoven would have come up with such similar figures. Perhaps, then, Clerselier took Descartes's rough sketch of the eye muscles that he found on his own (or saw in Schuyl's edition) and drew up a finer and more detailed version based on Van Gutschoven's illustration.[66] Why would he bother with an improved copy of Descartes's drawing if he had Van Gutschoven's meticulous illustration of the text in question? After all, he concedes that, with respect to these eye muscles, "I find that Messieurs de Gutschoven and de la Forge have rendered [them] better than Monsieur Descartes himself, and that the disposition that they have given to the valve and its two folds conforms better to the text and the play of the valve easier to understand."[67] Perhaps Clerselier wanted to be able to say that his edition, like Schuyl's, contains one of Descartes's own original figures.

Before turning to the illustrations by La Forge and Van Gutschoven, it is useful to review, for the sake of comparison, the images that Schuyl created for his Latin translation. This text contains a large number of original illustrations, fifty-seven in all (some repeated throughout the text). Clerselier

ILLUSTRATING THE WORLD   61

had access to all of them, both because Schuyl sent at least some of them to him before publishing his edition and because the book was published in 1662, while Clerselier was still at work on the French edition. Schuyl's illustrations include relatively schematic, bare-bone illustrations—literally, in some cases, as Schuyl depicts the human skeletal structure—of the relevant text [fig. 5]; and more elaborate and naturalistic representations [figs. 6 and 7]. Some of these latter images, which show a relatively high degree of artistic flair, include elements (such as landscapes, architectural ruins, even weapons of war and punishment) that are, strictly speaking, extraneous to their supposed role in elucidating the scientific and philosophical content of the text [fig. 8].[68] Some of the illustrations even combine a realistic rendering with a schematic figure [fig. 9].

Clerselier was impressed by Schuyl's draftsmanship and the care he took in creating such detailed images. Compared to the figures he would end up putting in his own edition, he found Schuyl's illustrations expertly produced and aesthetically superior. He says that Schuyl's figures, which were done as copper-plate engravings, "far outweight those that I have put in this book, if one attends simply to the engraving and printing."[69] However, Clerselier ended up using none of Schuyl's material, at least directly. He finds "some flaws [quelques défauts]" in Schuyl's figures.[70] Some of these, it seems, are a matter of substantive content, insofar as Schuyl has used a faulty manuscript copy of the original work (or so Clerselier claims). But more important from Clerselier's point of view is the character of the illustrations themselves. They simply do not suit his purposes. Schuyl's illustrations are "for the most part . . . less intelligible than the others [by La Forge and Van Gutschoven], and less suitable for understanding the text."[71] As naturalistic renditions, they are nicely done and well drawn, but they are too opaque, too fussy to do the work that Clerselier expects his book's illustrations to do. As we shall see, this becomes particularly clear when Schuyl's diagrams are compared with the figures that La Forge and Van Gutschoven sent to him.

*

Clerselier received a large number of illustrations from his Flemish and French collaborators. We do not know how many figures altogether were submitted, but we know (from Clerselier's preface) that it was more than actually appear in the 1664 edition. He decided against including a figure either when it was unnecessary for clarifying a part of the text which was

62 THE GOOD CARTESIAN

sufficiently clear in itself and easy enough for the reader to visualize on his own, or when it would have led to a needless duplication of illustrations (an exception being the instance mentioned above, where he decided he had good reason to include all three illustrations—by La Forge, Van Gutschoven, and Descartes—for the text discussing the eye muscles). Clerselier ended up publishing forty figures altogether: six by La Forge, his own copy of the drawing by Descartes, and the rest by Van Gutschoven. If he had figures by La Forge and Van Gutschoven on the same text and there was no reason to use both, he generally went with the one by Van Gutschoven. Here is how Clerselier describes his selection process, and especially his decision to give priority to Van Gutschoven's illustrations over those of La Forge, primarily on the basis of their higher artistic quality:

> Because most of the figures that these two Messieurs have drawn, each on his own, were similar, or that the difference between them was not essential and related only to the exterior disposition of the body of the figure, I thought it useless to display the same thing two times, and so contented myself with using, for the most part, the figures of M. de Gutschoven, which were better drawn than the others. As for those in which the difference between the two was noticeable and was useful in particular ways, such as those of the muscles and the brain, I included both of them.[72]

Clerselier then notes that when he did end up reproducing figures by both illustrators, he labeled the one by Van Gutschoven with a 'G' and the one by La Forge with an 'F.' There are in fact only two instances where Clerselier included figures by both Van Gutschoven and La Forge for the same textual item: in the case of the eye muscles [figs. 1 and 2], and in the case of the interior of the brain with the pineal gland [figs. 10 and 11]. It is odd, then, that Clerselier still labels quite a few of the solo figures by Van Gutschoven with a 'G,' when there is no corresponding figure by La Forge.

In contrast with his assessment of Schuyl's figures, Clerselier was quite pleased with the illustrations that he received from La Forge and Van Gutschoven. First, he appreciated the degree to which both illustrators were willing to heed his critical recommendations and make changes to their figures. They sent drafts of their images to Clerselier, who offered "some few comments" on how to make revisions so that some of the illustrations might do a better job of illuminating the text. On at least one occasion, Clerselier himself modified Van Gutschoven's figure, changing its orientation from a frontal view to a side view, in order "to make more visible" what Descartes was talking about when he discusses the arterial pathways taken by the parts of the blood that circulate to and from the brain.[73]

As we have seen, Clerselier considered Van Gutschoven the better artist, and for this reason most of the figures in the 1664 edition are his. However, Clerselier also notes that La Forge was *plus hardy*, bolder or more daring. What he means by this is that La Forge did not uncritically follow Descartes's lead, and that he tailored his illustrations not only to fit the text and do the explicatory work that Clerselier expected, but also, on occasion, to make sure that what was shown in the figure was scientifically correct. "He had no difficulty in distancing himself from the thought of the author and substituting his own in its place."[74] La Forge would then, in his extensive commentary— and, in Clerselier's estimation, "for good reasons"—justify any ways in which his figures departed from Descartes's text.

The clearest example of this concerns the way in which the animal spirits are directed into a muscle. As Clerselier notes, La Forge's illustration of the muscles around the eyeball and responsible for its movement places the valves between the muscle tendons rather than in the nerve channels leading into the muscles, which is how Descartes had it in his drawing (and which Clerselier kept in his rendering of that *brouillon*). Similarly, La Forge's image shows the nerves discharging the animal spirits directly into the eye muscles—more precisely, into the membranes surrounding the muscles' fibers—to inflate them; by contrast, Descartes says in his text (and shows in his illustration) that the nerve channels themselves extend into the muscle tissue and the muscles inflate as an indirect result of those channels being filled by the spirits [figs. 2 and 3].[75] However, because Clerselier wanted the illustrations "to clarify Descartes's thought [*faire comprendre quelle est . . . la pensée de Monsieur Descartes*]" on various matters, in addition to La Forge's relatively simple, artistically inferior but scientifically correct figure, he felt he should also include his enhanced copy of Descartes's useful but, he agrees, incorrect illustration (as well as Van Gutschoven's detailed figure for the same passage).[76]

La Forge is quite aware that, in his illustration of the nerve channels entering the eye muscles and discharging the animal spirits therein, he is departing from Descartes's view. As he will explain in his commentary on the text,

> This is something on which I add to the opinion of Monsieur Descartes, as opposed to what he says about the canals of the nerves entering the muscle

64 THE GOOD CARTESIAN

and dividing into several branches. . . . I take here the liberty of explaining my thought, which I submit to the judgment and the censure of the learned, and without pretending to have understood it better than our Master, to show as well as possible that if I follow him for the most part, it is not his authority but his reason that persuades me.

He adds,

What has led me to stray here from the way that he [Descartes] has followed is that unless I establish these small channels in the muscles as I do, there is no way to explain why, when a muscle is cut longitudinally along its fibers it does not lose the faculty of moving, since there would be nothing to prevent the animal spirits from exiting the muscle.

La Forge's revised account of how the nerves discharge animal spirits into a muscle applies not only to the eye muscles, but generally to all the muscles of the body. This is essential to understanding how the body moves, which La Forge calls "the most difficult function of the body to understand."[77]

In short, La Forge is doing what a good and faithful disciple would do. His goal in interpreting and completing Descartes's project, as much in his illustrations as, we shall see, in his commentary, and then in his own *Traité de l'esprit de l'homme*—and as a philosopher and a physician—is not simply to proceed in exactly the way Descartes did and would have, although this was an important consideration. He is out also to improve the system and its constituent parts by moving everything toward great internal consistency and, no less crucial, toward greater correspondence with the latest scientific and medical discoveries.[78] La Forge's fealty was as much to reason and experience as to Descartes.

*

In many instances, and without looking at Clerselier's labels, it is not too difficult to tell which figures are by La Forge and which are by Van Gutschoven, once we know each illustrator's style. Clerselier was quite right to say that Van Gutschoven is the better artist. His pictures are, for the most part, denser and richer in detail, capturing more information with finer lines, whereas La Forge seems to opt for clarity and ease of reading. Compare, for example, the illustrations of the eye muscles examined above [figs. 1 and 2], or their respective images of the brain and the pineal gland [figs. 10, 11, and 12]. As the latter case shows, La Forge often goes for a two-dimensional cut-away view, whereas Van Gutschoven tends to give his illustrations some depth. There is a certain flatness to La Forge's figures, and they can, in fact, seem quite primitive [figs. 13 and 14]. This may be why Clerselier adopted the policy of going with the images by Van Gutschoven when he had figures from both illustrators on the same passage and no compelling reason to display both. (However, the difference between a Van Gutschoven and a La Forge is not *always* so clear cut [see figs. 15 and 16].)

La Forge himself is conscious of the occasional disparity between their illustrations. He notes in his commentary that his own spare, structural diagram of the skull and the nerves descending from the brain [fig. 13], while adequate for displaying what La Forge wanted it to show relative to the text, is in fact not quite at the level of Van Gutschoven's illustration.

> My [figure] represents the brain such as it would appear if it were cut from the mammillary apophyses up to the brain's own substance. . . . The first part of the figure of Monsieur de Gutschoven is more exact than mine.[79]

Van Gutschoven's picture, with its richer detail, succeeds in displaying a number of things that La Forge's own figure, he concedes, leaves only to the imagination. As for most of the others, however, he insists that they are "similar in all ways, and merely say the same thing."

La Forge also highlights the way in which he has illustrated the muscular function in respiration, which is just a particular instance of what Descartes considers the most important process in the body, namely, the way in which the animal spirits, which flow to and from the muscles, "are able to cause movements in all bodily parts in which the nerves terminate."[80] In Article 24, "How This Machine Breathes," Descartes explains,

> In order to understand specifically how this machine respires, imagine that it is the muscle d that serves to raise its chest or to lower its diaphragm, and that the muscle E is its opposite; also that the animal spirits that are in the brain cavity marked m, running through the pore or little channel marked n, which is by its nature constantly open, proceed first to the tube BF where, lowering the little membrane F, they cause those from muscle E to come and inflate muscle d.[81]

66 THE GOOD CARTESIAN

A salient feature here is the way in which muscles can work together or against each other to help us "understand how the machine that I am describing to you can be moved in all the ways that our body can, just by the force of the animal spirits that flow from the brain into the nerves."[82] In the previous article, Descartes explained that if the animal spirits enter the two muscles around the eye with equal force and inflate those muscles at the same time, the eye is held in position. On the other hand, if the spirits enter the two muscles with differential force, certain membranes and passages are closed and others opened, and the spirits then flow from the one muscle to the other. This causes one muscle to contract and the other to dilate, which in turn causes the eye to move in a particular direction. Both La Forge and Van Gutschoven supplied illustrations for this ocular muscular process, with La Forge's simpler, more abstract picture easier to read. However, the text includes only La Forge's illustration for respiration, in which the same "antagonism" of the muscles is at work. La Forge notes that while his and Van Gutschoven's illustrations of the eye muscles could have served adequately to represent the muscular dynamic in respiration, he chose to provide an illustration of the chest muscles as well.

> I have not used the preceding figure [of the eye muscles] to explain the way in which respiration operates, although I could, like Monsieur Gutschoven, have done this, because it is good to see that it is not just in the case of the eye muscles, which is what appears from the communication that the author speaks of. This is why I preferred to take the two chest muscles, that is, the inferior serratus posticus and the serratus major, whose tendons are clearly antagonistic, and so are better suited to showing the same thing occurs in muscles that we do not see.[83]

La Forge seems to be aware that Van Gutschoven did not supply a separate illustration of the chest muscles. Either Clerselier asked him for this supplementary figure, or he simply took it upon himself to provide the additional diagram. Either way, La Forge's contribution serves to reinforce Descartes's point that the same mechanical process is at work throughout all of the body's main functions.

*

A more telling and interesting comparison among the illustrations is between those by La Forge and Van Gutschoven in the 1664 French edition, on one hand, and, on the other hand, the ones by Schuyl in the 1662 Latin edition.

A natural question arises with respect to the illustrations by La Forge and Van Gutschoven when looked at beside those of Schuyl. Clerselier claims in his preface that his two illustrators worked totally independently of each other and without consulting Schuyl's work. However, one might suspect that Van Gutschoven, at least, did in fact have a look at Schuyl's figures. For example, Gutschoven's schematic depiction of the internal structure of the eye is remarkably similar to the one rendered by Schuyl [figs. 17 and 18]. One wonders whether Clerselier sent copies of Schuyl's images to him, or maybe Clerselier is not to be trusted when he says that he had Van Gutschoven's figures in hand before the publication of Schuyl's book. Fortunately, we need not suspect Clerselier of violating the letter (if not the spirit) of his challenge to Van Gutschoven to come up with illustrations all on his own, and especially without seeing those of Schuyl. For the more obvious explanation of the similarity between Van Gutschoven's eye and Schuyl's eye is that they both took their lead from the same source, namely, Frans van Schooten the Younger, the illustrator of Descartes's *La Dioptrique* (Dioptrics), which was published as one of the essays accompanying the *Discours de la méthode* in 1637. Van Schooten's diagram of the eye is clearly the model for both of the later artists [fig. 19].[84] Moreover, it seems obvious that Van Gutschoven was consulting Van Schooten's figures for some of his other illustrations as well [figs. 20 and 21].[85]

There is little mystery as to why, given his stated goals for the illustrations in his edition, Clerselier rejected the figures by Schuyl. While often intriguing to look at, they do not have the rational clarity of the figures by La Forge and Van Gutschoven. Schuyl's figures do not really succeed as diagrams that are supposed to supplement and illuminate a scientific text. They are busy, with unnecessary detail and extraneous features, and thus hard to read. Even when there is no landscape setting, the renderings offer too naturalistic a representation to be intellectually useful. Clerselier is quite right to say that they are "less intelligible, and less suitable for understanding the text [*moins propres à l'intelligence du texte*]."[86] In this sense, and contrary to Clerselier's express purpose, the illustrations in Schuyl's edition might indeed look like the illustrations of an anatomy textbook. This is especially clear when we consider his figures along with those in a contemporary anatomical study— Caspar Bauhin's *Theatrum anatomicum* (first published in 1605)—that, as Annie Bitbol-Hespériès has shown, Descartes consulted while composing

68 THE GOOD CARTESIAN

L'Homme [see figs. 5, 6, 22, 23].[87] Compare, for example, Schuyl's illustration of the brain with the pineal gland in the center [fig. 7] with Van Gutschoven's rendering of the same thing [fig. 11]. Schuyl's picture looks like a brain; Van Gutschoven's, not at all. But Van Gutschoven's image helps the reader see what Descartes is talking about much better than Schuyl's.

Part of the "problem" for Schuyl may be the respective media in which the illustrators were working. Schuyl's illustrations are copper-plate engravings, and this technique, popular for art prints of the period (especially reproductions of paintings and sculpture), affords the artist richer graphic opportunities. An engraving allows for finer detail than the older and artistically more primitive technique of woodblock printing, which is what was used for the figures by La Forge and Van Gutschoven. Clerselier even alerts the reader to the fact that on at least one occasion, regarding the diverse, criss-crossing paths that can be taken by the animal spirits as they descend from the brain cavity through the nerves, the woodblock technique was not up to the task of providing the requisite fine detail, and so the reader will have to use his imagination to fill in what is missing. "The wood that was used for carving the figures did not allow such delicacy . . . and the imagination will have to do the rest."[88] But it is precisely the fact that he took advantage of engraving's opportunity for greater detail that worked against Schuyl, at least in the eyes of Clerselier.[89]

(The interesting question here is why Clerselier opted for woodblock prints for his illustrations rather than engravings. One possible answer is economic—a book using woodblock prints would be significantly less expensive to produce than one using copper-plate engravings; it could also therefore be priced more affordably for a larger audience. Moreover, bear in mind that Clerselier was, by 1664, anxious to see his edition of *L'homme* finally published; and woodblock prints could be produced much more quickly than the time-consuming method of engraving, which would have delayed publication even longer.)

*

The illustrators for Clerselier's edition of Descartes's treatise faced a difficult task, as Clerselier himself notes. They had to come up with figures that would illuminate for a wide range of readers a dense, often terse and elliptical text of human physiology according to the principles of the new mechanistic science. Some of the images are more successful than others. In the end, however, we have no choice but to admire their handiwork. La Forge and his colleague Van Gutschoven may not have been great artists, but they understood the charge they were given and the challenges they faced. La Forge, for one, seems to have been aware of Clerselier's demand that the illustrations not be modeled on the kinds of pictures one would find in an anatomy book, and that they need not resemble what one would see when looking into the body itself during a dissection. As he says about his illustrations involving the very small pineal gland, he represents it "considerably larger than it naturally is, and as the anatomists are not accustomed to doing in their illustrations." He adds that "the things Descartes describes cannot be perceived by our senses" and so he "represented them not in the same way they really appear but in the same way that we would see them if our senses were subtle enough to discover them."[90]

La Forge and Van Gutschoven more than satisfied the expectations of their client. Clerselier believed that they had succeeded admirably. So did a reviewer in the very first issue of the *Journal des sçavans* (5 January 1665), who had this to say about the book: "Monsieur Des Cartes left behind this treatise in such a greatly confused state that it would not be intelligible if Monsieur Clerselier had not put it in order, and if Messieurs de la Forge et Guscoven [*sic*] had not clarified it with figures."[91]

La Forge's illustrations for the *Traité de l'homme* constitute an important supplement to the book. They were also his first major (and public) contribution to the advancement of the Cartesian philosophy, especially its mechanistic account of the living human body. But they pale in comparison to what La Forge, unsolicited, included with the pictures in the packet that he sent to Clerselier in the summer of 1661.

4
A Disciple's Commentary

When, in the spring of 1661, Clerselier in Paris received the packet from Saumur, there was a pleasant surprise to be found among the papers in it. The medical doctor who had agreed to supply illustrations for Descartes's *Traité de l'homme* sent not only the promised images, but a long and meticulous commentary on the work—one that was twice as long as the treatise itself.

Far from being put out, Clerselier was quite pleased by this unsolicited essay from La Forge. So pleased that he decided that it should be included in the edition of *L'Homme* that he was preparing. In his preface to the book, he notes,

> there is no need for me to extend myself here on his [La Forge's] praises, since the greatest part of this book speaks to his advantage, as both the figures and the learned commentary he has added to this treatise will serve better to make known his mind and his merit than anything I could say. I have never seen so much diligence in one person.[1]

He says that it is in his *sçavantes remarques* that La Forge "reveals the extent and power of his mind."

> There is no difficulty that he has not resolved, no qualms that he did not raise, no obscurities that he did not clarify; so much so that I could almost say that his commentary is a perfect text, which says everything and assumes nothing, which leaves nothing behind, and which contains the solution of all the most difficult questions which the author only proposed and reserved to explain at another time. . . . He has omitted nothing of all that can serve for explaining the machine of the human body.[2]

What seems especially to have struck Clerselier is La Forge's intellectual independence, his willingness, despite being dedicated to Descartes's philosophy, to go beyond what Descartes says and even on occasion to correct him. La Forge was "bold," he says, and "no slave to Monsieur Descartes's opinions."

The Good Cartesian. Steven Nadler, Oxford University Press. © Oxford University Press 2024.
DOI: 10.1093/oso/9780197671719.003.0005

A DISCIPLE'S COMMENTARY   71

> If sometimes he approves of them, it is only out of deference to reason, never to authority; he never has any difficulty in distancing himself from the author's thought and in substituting his own in its place; not in order to propose it as better, but only to have it examined and to learn, through the judgment that might be made of it, the estimation that he himself should give it.

For Clerselier, La Forge's intelligence, his expertise on matters dealing with human anatomy and physiology, and, not the least, his confidence shine through in the labors he devoted to this project. Clerselier might indeed have been interested in having La Forge submit a short interpretative and clarificatory essay to include with the *Traité de l'homme*, had La Forge inquired in advance. In the end, Clerselier took what he got and chose not to exercise his editorial prerogative by cutting out La Forge's more critical remarks in the final text.

> As very ingenious as his [La Forge's] thoughts no doubt are, and that he defends them in his commentary with good and forceful reasons (although in this respect he is not acting simply as an interpreter), I did not want, using the liberty he has given me, to remove them from his commentary, in order that he might enjoy the fruit of his labor and so as not to deprive the reader of the pleasure of judging between the Author and him.[3]

Even making allowance for the courtesies required by literary protocol in the seventeenth century, this is effusive (and apparently sincere) praise. Clerselier—now the standard bearer for the Cartesian camp and protector of the brand—is clearly impressed.

*

La Forge's extensive commentary on *L'Homme* is all the more remarkable given how quickly he composed it—less than a year after receiving the manuscript from Clerselier—and how detailed and erudite it is. Aside from his close study of Descartes's text, La Forge appeals to his own experimental knowledge of the human body and to the work of earlier and recent anatomists. Moreover, whether he is defending and justifying Descartes or correcting him, he supplies careful rational arguments for his claims and responds to potential objections. The physician's *Remarques* are, thus, not

72 THE GOOD CARTESIAN

merely an empirical and descriptive anatomical supplement to this posthumous publication of Descartes's work. Rather, they include a good deal of philosophical physiology, grounded in both abductive reasoning and informed speculation. La Forge does not hesitate to revise Descartes's account when it fails to account for the phenomenon. We have already seen this, for example, with respect to how the nerves discharge the animal spirits into the muscles, when Descartes's description cannot explain why a muscle cut longitudinally along its fibers does not lose the faculty of moving. La Forge explains not just how the body is visibly constructed and operates, but how in all probability it must be operating when its structures and processes are inaccessible to observation. As he notes, referring to the way in which the animal spirits work the muscles, "because our senses do not discover anything of what he [Descartes] says, it is left to reason to justify his thought."[4]

*

The commentary starts, like the treatise itself, rather abruptly, with La Forge simply—and, of course, correctly—noting that this *Traité de l'homme*, whose first article opens with the phrase "these men [*ces hommes*]," appears to be "a piece detached from a much larger work."[5] La Forge has not seen the first part of *Le Monde*, the *Traité de la lumière*, and so he can only surmise its contents from what Descartes had said about it in the *Discours de la méthode*.[6] From here he moves to what is practically an article-by-article review of Descartes's essay.

La Forge begins with all due praise and deference to Descartes's project. On the view of the human body as a "machine," La Forge notes "this assumption is very true," and lays out what this effectively means:

> For by the word 'machine,' one cannot understand anything other than a body composed of many organic parts which, being united, agree [*s'accordent*] in producing some movements of which they would not be capable if they were separate. I call 'organic parts' all sorts of simple or composite bodies which, being united together, and by their conformity, figure, motion rest and situation, can contribute to the production of movements and functions of their machine of which they are parts. This being so, not only clocks and other automata are machines, but also the body of the human being, that of all animals, and even the entire universe itself can be considered a machine.[7]

A DISCIPLE'S COMMENTARY   73

What seem, in La Forge's eyes, to be the most novel and important contributions of Descartes's work are (a) the role played by the heart and its heating power as the source of life in a living body (human or non-human), and (b) the function of the nerves and the animal spirits in both involuntary and voluntary movements of the body. A good deal of La Forge's attention in the commentary is directed at these features of Descartes's analysis. He wastes no time getting down into the details.

La Forge's *Remarques* can, for the most part, be sorted into four basic categories: clarification; justification and defense; expansion, supplementation, and contextualization; and correction or revision.

Clarification

Many of La Forge's comments are devoted to clarifying or explaining what Descartes has in mind, especially when Descartes's text is terse or when it might be possible to mistake what he is saying on this or that matter. In Article 11 of the *Traité de l'homme*, for example, which describes how some parts of the blood descend to the stomach and bowels, "where they act like *aqua fortis*" and help in the digestion of food, Descartes says that these blood particles, "because they are carried here from the heart almost instantaneously through the arteries, are always very hot, which enables their vapors to rise easily through the gullet toward the mouth, where they make up the saliva."[8] La Forge warns the reader, based on what Descartes says later in the work in his description of the brain, that Descartes should not be understood to be claiming that the saliva is composed *only* of the vapors of the acidic liquid that ascends from the ventricule through the throat. Though Descartes is focused here on the vapors, "he is not denying, for all that, that the moisture secreted by the arteries of the pharynx in the glands of this part, and that which distills from the brain by means of the opening called Funnel [*Entonnoir*], contribute."[9]

Likewise, La Forge wants to make it clear that while, "as no one doubts," the nerves that terminate in the muscles play a role in the body's movements, nevertheless, according to Descartes the fibers [*filamens*] of the nerves, which are guided throughout the body by the nerve casings, do not play any role in moving the muscles and limbs. In the matter of voluntary motion, when the body is informed by a soul, it is not the case that, as the "ancient physicians seem to have believed," the soul pulls on this or that nerve cord according to

74 THE GOOD CARTESIAN

how it wants this or that part of the body to move, "much as we do with the bridle of our horses."[10] The nerves—or, more precisely, their casings—that meet the muscles do serve to convey the animal spirits into the muscles, and thus cause the inflation of the muscle and the movement of the limb. What the nerve fibers themselves do is limited to transmitting motions from the body's exterior and interior parts to the brain and thus convey therein sensory images of things impinging on the body.[11]

Sometimes the clarification is needed because of what La Forge sees as a poor choice of words by Descartes. In Article 5, Descartes says that

> The fire in the heart of this machine that I am describing to you has as its sole purpose to expand, warm, and refine the blood that falls continually a drop at a time through the passage from the vena cava into the cavity on its right side, from where it is exhaled into the lung [d'où il s'exhale dans le poulmon], and from the vein of the lung which anatomists have called the 'venous artery' into its other cavity, which where it is distributed throughout the body.[12]

La Forge notes that "this term [s'exhale dans le poulmon], and the term 'vapors' that follows [in the next article], do not express well Monsieur Descartes's thought, and are contrary to anatomical truth." The problem is that what is in the arteries is blood, not vapors. And yet,

> it truly seems from this passage that he had believed that the two drops that fall into the heart, or at least that which falls from the right side, acquires the form of air or vapor in being rarefied by means of the fermentation that takes place there ... and that these vapors reassume the form of blood when they cool in the lung by means of the air that enters there.

However, La Forge insists, "this is not Descartes's real thought; but only that the two drops of blood that enter the heart are rarefied, dilated and heated there, and by this means expand, one into the arterial vein and the other into the aorta."[13]

Justification and Defense

La Forge's defense of Descartes in his commentary takes two forms: providing arguments for claims that, in Descartes's text, are simply asserted; and addressing objections to Descartes's account on this or that topic, whether the objection has actually been lodged by some opponent or is a conceivable difficulty that needs to be resolved.

One of the contentious issues facing seventeenth-century anatomists concerned the beating of the heart. It was the Englishman William Harvey, in his *Exercitatio anatomica de motu cordis et sanguinis in animalibus* (Anatomical Exercise on the Motion of the Heart and Blood in Animals, 1628), who firmly established that the blood actually circulates throughout the human body, rather than being produced in the heart and consumed by the rest of the body. Harvey also claimed that the heart beats (expands and contracts) on its own, not because it is caused to expand and contract by the expansion and departure of some contents within it. Functioning like a pump, the heart's natural and spontaneous expansions and contractions cause the blood to enter its cavities and then flow out through the arteries to the rest of the body, whence it returns by way of the veins.

The thesis of circulation was still regarded with suspicion in France in the early 1660s. The medical faculty of the University of Paris led the way by rejecting Harvey's claims. Descartes, on the other hand, praised Harvey in the *Discours de la méthode* for his discovery, for "having broken the ice on this subject."[14] At the same time, he did not accept Harvey's account of the beating of the heart. According to Descartes, the heart expands because the blood within it is heated by the heart (with its "fire without light"), which causes that blood "to swell and expand," which in turn "makes the whole heart swell."[15] As the blood is then forced by the increasing pressure out of the heart's cavities into the arteries, where it cools, the heart contracts.

La Forge believes that Descartes, not Harvey and his followers, got it right (although, of course, Descartes got it wrong).

> Most physicians do not attribute the beating of the heart to the fermentation that happens to the blood which ceaselessly runs into it with each pulse, but to a Faculty of the Soul that they call "pulsific." As for me, I have so much respect for these masters that I certainly want to retain the word 'Faculty' rather than displease them. Besides, it cannot be doubted that the heart has, in effect, the faculty of beating, since it, in effect, beats. Just as one cannot deny that anything that tends to sink has the faculty, that is, the power to tend to do that.

What is problematic, however, is the assumption that this "faculty" is some real, active attribute of the heart, much like the active substantial or accidental forms of the "Peripatetic Doctors," that is, the Scholastics:

76 THE GOOD CARTESIAN

Just as they will not, I believe, have any difficulty in admitting that, in this and other cases, the word [*faculté*] is useless, and does not at all explain how the thing happens, so I hope that they will permit me to ask what is this faculty? It cannot be said that it is the soul itself, at least in human beings, who know [*sensent*] quite well that their soul is not the master of these sorts of motions, and that they do not directly depend at all on their thoughts. To say, too, that it is a quality of the body, or a property of the soul, serves in no way to explain what it is; no more than if I were to ask what is an elephant I were to be told that it is an African animal.

For La Forge, as for Descartes, there is no other cause of the beating of the heart than "the boiling or fermentation that the remnants of the blood in the chambers of the heart produce in those drops that fall anew into its ventricles." Only this "will satisfy a mind that wants to know things and not merely pay lip service."[16]

La Forge then goes on to consider three potential objections to the Cartesian account.[17] First, it might be claimed that the heat of the heart is not sufficient to cause the blood to rise up. La Forge responds to this on Descartes's behalf with a mundane analogy from baking: in fact the heat need not be that great, "for one sees leavening that is actually cold which yet does not fail to do this." La Forge backs up his point here with experimental evidence.

> To demonstrate that it is the heat which causes the elevation [of the blood]: if you bring close to the fire the heart of an eel that is already cold, and does not beat any longer, you will find that it begins to beat. The same thing will happen if you plunge it into the blood of the same eel although it is cold.

The second objection considered by La Forge is that the expansion or *élevation* of the parts of the blood in the heart does not typically take place so quickly and so can hardly account for the relatively rapid beating of the heart and the pulsing of the arteries. "To which," La Forge says, "Monsieur Descartes responds that there are different types of rarefication," some requiring a good deal of time but others occurring in but a moment, "as we see in milk which has been for some time on the fire."

Third, La Forge addresses the objection that sometimes the heart of an animal does not cease to beat even when it has been removed from the body and no blood can flow into it. This, he grants, is "the principal objection," but,

A DISCIPLE'S COMMENTARY   77

he claims, is easy to resolve. Even in a heart removed from an animal's body, with no new blood entering, there remains some blood in the cavities that continue to be heated and rarefied by the heart. Here La Forge is repeating precisely what Descartes had said in a 1638 letter to Plempius in Leuven.[18] The letter, in which the two men discuss the circulation of the blood— which Plempius initially denied—was available in the first (1657) volume of Clerselier's edition of Descartes's correspondence.

La Forge is current in his reading of anatomical studies, for in the course of his discussion of the beating of the heart he rejects the theory of the Danish anatomist Caspar Bartholin the Elder, author of the *Anatomicae institutiones corporis humani* (1611), citing the *Anatomia reformata*, essentially a revised edition of Bartholin's work published by his son Thomas first in 1641, and more recently in 1660, just when La Forge is composing his commentary. According to Bartholin, as La Forge reads him, the heat of the arterial blood is "an effect of the sensible and exterior motion that we see in the heart." This, La Forge responds, is wrong. "We do not say that, but rather that it is an effect of the fermentation that takes place in [the heart's] ventricles, which causes the particles of the blood to move noticeably faster . . . as we see in all other fermentations, where the matter becomes hotter for the same reason."[19]

La Forge also considers several objections to the role that, on the Cartesian account, the animal spirits play in bodily motion through the inflation of the muscles, and provides both experimental evidence and rational arguments to supplement Descartes's brief remarks. To those who would deny that the belly of a muscle becomes larger as the muscle contracts, and who would rather say that its fibers close up among themselves, La Forge responds as follows:

> Besides the fact that it is in no way plausible that the animal spirits that descend from the brain precisely at the instant that we want to move one of our members are capable of causing such an occlusion in all the fibers of a muscle—they seem, on the contrary, more likely to separate a bit; it also appears that if this were the case, there would remain some vestige of this occlusion in the large muscles that often cause this movement; and yet we do not see this at all when an animal is dissected after its death.[20]

La Forge also defends Descartes's view that, in voluntary motion of a limb, a muscle expands only because "the animal spirits descend from the brain more quickly and abundantly than usual at the instant when we want to move

78 THE GOOD CARTESIAN

our members." He considers the objection that the expansion must be due to leftover spirits already in the muscle being caused to ferment by spirits newly descending and thus taking up more space than before. La Forge recognizes the force of this objection, "which seems to me that strongest of all that can be raised on this matter." He agrees that as the new spirits enter the muscle with great speed, they must cause some increased motion among the spirits already there. But, he insists, this is certainly not sufficient to cause rarefication by fermentation.

First, because the spirits are already the most subtle and lively parts of the blood, with the exception of those of the first and second element; such that there are none more delicate or more lively, according to the nature of each animal. How, then, could other [spirits] similar to them cause them to become rarefied? Second, there are three conditions that render these spirits incapable of being so fermented. First, they have no pores, or if they do they are so small that they admit only the first element, or at best the second. Second, they have no branches, or if they do, they are few . . . because of the violence of their agitation will have broken them. Third, they are moved very promptly. This is why, besides having no or only a few pores in themselves, they cannot join together to have any. How, then, could they be capable of fermentation, which, according to Monsieur Descartes, happens when the particles of the third element, accompanied only by the first, enter the pores of some body.[21]

Given the important role that the animal spirits play in even the most basic motions of the body, it is no surprise that La Forge devotes a good deal of his commentary to protecting Descartes's theory against real and imagined attacks.

La Forge at one point considers the charge that Descartes contradicts himself in Article 100, in which he wants to explain "how one and the same action, without changing, can move now one foot of this machine, now another, as is required to make it walk." Descartes claims that in both strides of the act of walking, especially when it is mindless, unintentional wandering, the animal spirits pass through the same pores of the brain, but the extremities of the casings leading from those pores are so disposed as to direct those spirits into some nerves to move the right foot and into other nerves to move the left foot. Descartes adds that this "ordinarily does not depend on any idea."[22]

A DISCIPLE'S COMMENTARY   79

In his remarks on this article, La Forge, taking into account the equivocation of the term 'idea' to refer both to corporeal images in the brain and mental representations in the soul, proposes the objection that

> Monsieur Descartes contradicts himself here. For, since corporeal ideas are nothing other than the form through which the spirits depart more abundantly from certain pores in the mesh [of the brain], and from certain pores in the gland, than others, it is impossible for them to be able to go in greater abundance into some muscles than opposing ones without them tracing the idea of this movement.[23]

True enough, La Forge notes. However, he continues, one should remember that the movement of the legs depends not so much on the way in which the spirits exit from the gland—and he reminds us that it is the pattern traced on the gland by the departing spirits that *is* the corporeal idea—than on how the nerve channels downstream are flexibly situated. Thus, "[Descartes] was right to say that these movements do not depend on any idea."

Of perhaps equal importance, both for understanding the course of the animal spirits but especially when it comes to speculation on how the body interacts with the mind once a soul is united with it, is La Forge's defense of Descartes's theory of the pineal gland.

As we have seen, according to Descartes the animal spirits that rise to the brain from the heart are always responding to and affecting the pineal gland located at the center of the brain. La Forge fully accepts the role accorded the gland in directing spirits from its pores into the openings of the nerve channels on the interior surface of the brain (to be then transmitted to the muscles). He also acknowledges, conversely, the gland's role in receiving material images or impressions transmitted from the body's extremities to the brain by the nerves that open the brain's pores in certain patterns. These patterns, as they are imprinted on the gland when the spirits exit it toward those select openings, give rise to sensory ideas in the mind and explain imagination and memory. As La Forge elaborates on Articles 65 and 66 of the *Traité de l'homme*—for which La Forge and Van Gutschoven together have supplied four illustrations—and focusing in particular on the discussion of "how ideas of objects are formed in the place assigned to the imagination and for the common sense, and how they are preserved in memory," he notes that what Descartes is referring to here is

80 THE GOOD CARTESIAN

> how the action of objects [on the exterior of the body], opening certain links in the mesh [of the interior surface of the brain], force the spirits to leave [the gland], which is the organ of the imagination and the common sense, otherwise than as they were doing.... And how they are preserved in the memory, that is, how these spirits, in crossing these links, imprint in the fold of the brain a figure similar to that which they took on as they exited the gland and the mesh.[24]

To several objections raised by Thomas Bartholin in his *Anatomia reformata* against "this new and ingenious opinion" promoted by "Descartes and his followers," including a concern that a single, small gland could not do so much work without generating confusion, as multiple images might be imprinted on the gland at one and the same time—Bartholin, in his fifth objection, predicts a "confusion of different ideas [*idearum diversarum confusio*]"—La Forge responds that any single material image rarely lasts longer than a moment on the gland, unless the external object continues to exert its pressure on the body. Moreover, while the gland is indeed quite small, one should not suppose that it is so small that it cannot handle more than one image or imprint at a time in a clear fashion, without those images interfering with each other. "However small it [the gland] may be, it will always have more points and holes than the different impressions we receive at the same time."[25]

Four of La Forge's illustrations for *L'Homme* are clustered around Articles 63 to 65, and focus on the pineal gland and the interior of the brain. The gland will, as we shall see, play an important role in La Forge's own *Traité de l'esprit de l'homme*. La Forge may, in fact, be the last of Descartes's defenders on this crucial aspect of his theory of human anatomy, as later Cartesians either minimize its function or drop it altogether.[26] I will return to this in Chapter 6.

Expansion, Supplementation, and Contextualization

In *L'Homme*, Descartes is rather selective in his choice of what topics to pursue in detail and which to present in only a cursory manner, or even not at all. This gives the more unrestrained La Forge the opportunity to expand on Descartes's text, either by bringing in supplementary material from other sources or by providing additional context for what Descartes does say.

Right at the beginning of the work, Descartes says,

A DISCIPLE'S COMMENTARY   81

I shall not pause to describe to you the bones, nerves, muscles, veins, arteries, stomach, liver, spleen, heart, brain, nor all the other different parts from which this machine [the human body] must be composed, for I am assuming that they are just like those parts of our own bodies having the same names, and that you can get some learned anatomist to show them to you . . . if you are not already sufficiently acquainted with them.[27]

These macro and visible parts of the body—as opposed to its indiscernible and unsuspected elements and operations—are not Descartes's main concern.

La Forge, however, in order to counter the errors of others, deems it worthwhile to go into such matters. He cites approvingly Harvey's *De generatione animalium* (1651), a work of embryology in which Harvey explains, among many other things, that the liver, which has its origin in the blood flow from the vessels in its channels, is generated only after the blood has begun to circulate. La Forge, alluding to his own observation of the generation of a chicken—perhaps during his experiments on eggs with Gousset—finds this to be quite right, and an effective rebuff to "the ancients," who, believing that it is the liver that generates the blood, claimed that it is one of the first parts of the body to be formed.[28]

Something else that Descartes decided to skip is the constitution of the brain (aside from discussing the essential work done by the pores of its interior lining, as the animal spirits enter into the nerve channels there). Where Descartes, in Article 9, simply includes the brain among those solid parts of the body that are composed by *certains petits filets*, La Forge, in his discussion of this article, wants to prove that the brain is a fibrous body, like "all the parts of the animal and the plant . . . if you except the humors, the spirits, the fat and perhaps some gland"—so much so that plant and animal bodies "are nothing other than a mass of small fibers."[29] While "the senses" and experimental investigation show this clearly to be the case with plants and, in the human body, such parts as the muscles, skin, cartilege, and bone, "reason" is required to establish it for the brain. Though the brain is soft and does not reveal any fibers to the naked eye, nonetheless,

to be assured that it, too, is a fibrous body, one need only consider that it was generated, like all the other parts, from the largest particles [of the blood], which pass through the pores of the arteries and which are

82 THE GOOD CARTESIAN

determined to stretch into strands by the small gaps through which they pass, which like small channels serve to give them the form they take and thereafter retain.

Moreover, there would be no way to explain how the nerve fibers could communicate motions from an external body to the inner chamber of the brain if those nerve fibers were not themselves extensions of the brain's own fibers.[30]

Sometimes La Forge cites other works by Descartes to expand on one point or another. In Article 12, Descartes says that the most lively and subtle parts of the blood issuing from the heart will go to the cavities of the brain, insofar as the arteries that lead there take the most direct line from the heart than any others, and all bodies in motion tend, as much as possible, to continue their motion in a straight line. For a proof of this latter point, La Forge directs the reader to Part II, Article 39 of the *Principia philosophiae*, where Descartes demonstrates the second of his three principal laws of nature—that the tendency of the motion of each and every part of matter, considered in itself, is in a straight line—on the basis of the immutability of God, who is the primary cause of motion in the cosmos.[31] Meanwhile, anyone who would doubt that it is the force alone with which the blood pushes against the membranes of the arteries that causes these to pulsate is directed to read that 1638 letter from Descartes to Plempius. This is where Descartes describes a number of experiments—including one involving vivisection on a rabbit—that prove that the arteries "pulse" only because the blood flowing through them strikes their walls.[32]

Interestingly, La Forge uses that same letter by Descartes yet again to show that something that he says in the *Traité de l'homme* is in fact contrary to his own considered position as expressed elsewhere. In Article 5 ("How the blood is heated and dilates in the heart"), Descartes had responded to anyone who doubted that the blood that enters the right chamber of the heart from the veins "is promptly inflated and expanded" that it "can be demonstrated experimentally that the blood or milk of some animal will be dilated if you pour it a drop at a time into a very hot flask."[33] La Forge points out, however, that liquids that are capable of being fermented do not have to be very hot, and that Descartes himself had suggested as much in the letter to Plempius. What La Forge seems to have in mind is the paragraph in that letter in which Descartes, explaining to Plempius why a heart removed from a body continues to beat because there will still be some blood in it to be heated and expanded, says that "even a tiny drop of blood falling from one part

A DISCIPLE'S COMMENTARY   83

of the heart into another, slightly warmer part was sufficient to cause this
pulsation."[34]

More often, La Forge puts Descartes's views in the context of other anatomical texts, marking out points of agreement and of disagreement. This
includes works by *les médecins* such as Harvey and Bartholin, as we have
seen, but also by the Flemish anatomist Andrea Vesalius, author of *De hu-
mana corporia fabrica* (1543), and the Dutch physician Johannes Wallaeus in
Leiden, who defended Harvey's view on circulation.

In Article 7, which deals with the beating of the pulse, Descartes had
explained how there are certain *petits peaux*, small membranes, that,
functioning as "so many small doors" or valves, control the flow of blood into
the two cavities of the heart. When a beat of the heart ceases, the valves that
allow blood to flow into the arteries are closed while the valves that let blood
into the heart from the veins are open. Two drops of blood then flow from
the veins, one into each cavity of the heart. The heat of the heart causes those
two drops to become rarefied and swell. This expansion of the blood and the
heart forces the valves from the veins to shut and pushes open those to the
arteries. The blood rushes through the arterial valves "quickly and forcefully,"
which causes the arteries to swell. This is the systolic part of the heartbeat.
At the diastolic moment, with a smaller volume of blood in the heart and as
the blood now in the arteries cools and condenses and before more blood is
introduced from the veins, the heart and the arteries contract. This leads the
arterial valves to close and the valves from the veins to open, letting in another two drops.

La Forge says that *tous les medecins* agree that the valves are situated where
Descartes has placed them and that they function in the way he describes.
However, while

> all the physicians are also in agreement that there are two movements in the
> heart: one in which the point [of the heart] approaches the base, the other
> in which it pulls away from it, they do not agree with respect to the time at
> which the blood enters or leaves the heart, nor the time in which, for these
> two movements, its chambers enlarge or shrink further, which they all call
> diastole and systole.

Harvey and Bartholin had insisted that at the moment of systole the tip
of the heart approaches the base, while Descartes "with all the rest of the
physicians"—that is, in the Galenic tradition—thinks that at systole the tip

84 THE GOOD CARTESIAN

pulls away from (*s'éloigne de*) the base. Moreover, according to La Forge, Harvey claims that it is when the tip is pulling away from the base that the blood exits the heart, while Bartholin and Descartes believe that this happens when the tip approaches the base—an opinion that La Forge declares to be *tres-veritable*.[35]

Revision and Correction

La Forge is a good Cartesian. But his fealty is not so much to Descartes himself, as great as his admiration for the philosopher may be, but to the Cartesian philosophy. Thus, it is not surprising to see him revising and updating Descartes's claims in the treatise. He seems, in fact, to feel that he owes it to Descartes to render his system as consistent as possible both within itself and with current scientific knowledge. Thus, we often find La Forge departing from certain features of Descartes's anatomical study on the basis of experimental evidence and rational argument. At the same time, he wants to show that recent developments in anatomy and physiology do not undermine Descartes's general principles but—at least in most cases—reinforce them, even if a little adjustment is needed in the details.

In Article 3, which concerns the process of digestion, whereby food is broken down "in the stomach of this machine by the force of certain fluids," Descartes had described how "the finest and most agitated" particles of food flow through small pores in the bowels into a large vein that carries them to the liver. La Forge identifies that mass of particles as the chyle, which he says Descartes apparently regards as being carried out of the intestines by "the mesenteric veins of old [*les anciennes venes Meseraïques*]." This passage, he then notes,

> is sufficient to show that this treatise was made a long time ago. For it is indubitable that if he had written here in accordance with the latest knowledge available, he would have followed the experiments of Asellius and Monsieur de Pecquet, which were not unknown to him . . . and which do not allow for any doubt that all of the chyle, or at least most of it, is carried to the heart.[36]

La Forge is referring here to Gaspar Aselli, an Italian physician active in the first decades of the century, who discovered the "lacteal" capillaries that draw the chyle, a milky white substance composed mostly of lymphatic fluid

A DISCIPLE'S COMMENTARY   85

and fats, from the small intestine. These capillaries, as the French anatomist Jean Pecquet later explained in his *De circulatione sanguinis et chyli motu* (1653), do not go to the liver but to a sac at the start of the thoracic duct called the *cisterna chyli* (chylic reservoir, later renamed the Pecquet reservoir). Descartes's error here was also made by Bartholin, who was overly dedicated to "the old view."

As we have seen when examining La Forge's illustrations for the book, he does not hesitate to revise, as well, a significant detail in the crucial mechanism by which the human body moves, namely, the manner in which the animal spirits are introduced into the muscles.

> I recognize how obliged I am to him [Descartes] for all the truths he has taught me, but principally for having allowed me to conceive distinctly how this movement [of the body], which is in my view the function of the human body that is the most difficult to understand, takes place.[37]

However, he insists, Descartes's conception of the inner constitution of the muscles and the cause of their inflation cannot be correct. It is not the case that the nerve channels, by which the animal spirits are conveyed throughout the body, continue into the muscle and branch off within it, with their expansion and contraction by the spirits within them causing the changes in the muscle. Rather, the spirits leave the nerve channels and enter into the sheaths of fibers in the muscle directly, which they then cause to inflate.

> This is something on which I add to the opinion of Monsieur Descartes, as opposed to what he says about the canals of the nerves entering the muscle and dividing into several branches. . . . I take here the liberty of explaining my thought, which I submit to the judgment and the censure of the learned, and without pretending to have understood it better than our Master, to show as well as possible that if I follow him for the most part, it is not his authority but his reason that persuades me. What has led me to stray here from the way that he has followed is that unless I establish these small channels in the muscles as I do, there is no way to explain why, when a muscle is cut longitudinally along its fibers it does not lose the faculty of moving, since there would be nothing to prevent the animal spirits from exiting the muscle.[38]

As for the *petite glande* from which the animal spirits depart toward the nerve openings in the brain's inner lining on their way to the muscles, La

86 THE GOOD CARTESIAN

Forge does offer a minor correction to Article 74, on Descartes's description of the structure of the gland in the center of the brain. Descartes, trying to account for the easy mobility of the gland, had claimed that it is connected to the brain only by "two small arteries" and suspended thereby "like a balance by the force of the blood that the heat of the heart pushes toward it."[39] La Forge, through his anatomical investigations, discovered that "besides these arteries that sustain [the gland], it is also united to the rest of the substance of the brain by two small nerve fibers . . . which are so relaxed that they do not prevent it from being able to move in a thousand different ways."[40]

*

Seemingly in a class of their own are La Forge's extended remarks on the puzzling Article 83 of the treatise. He here offers a revision—or, perhaps better, an emendation—of the very brief paragraph in which Descartes mentions, but does not explain, a role for memory in allowing the human body-machine to imitate the motions or other observable features of another body. All Descartes says in this article is this:

> The effect of memory that seems to me to be most worthy of consideration here is that, without there being any soul present in this machine, it [the machine] can naturally be disposed to imitate all the movements that real men—or many other similar machines—will make in its presence.[41]

La Forge finds this article inadequate as it stands, since so little is said and what *is* said seems off. He suggests that either there is a lacuna in the manuscript or, if this is indeed all Descartes meant to say, then he has isolated the wrong thing as the principal mechanism at work in the familiar phenomenon of involuntary imitative behavior.

> It seems to me that something is missing from this article. For besides the fact that it is too short to be so beautiful, I think that what can dispose our machine to imitate the actions that true human beings or other similar machines will do in its presence is an effect not so much of memory as of the action of objects on the senses; otherwise [i.e., if Descartes had really meant to focus on memory], he would have had to say 'will have made in its presence.' This is because memory is only of past things, and is nothing other than a remnant of the impression that the senses have made on the

A DISCIPLE'S COMMENTARY   87

[pineal] gland, and subsequently on the brain, which allows for the same ideas to be retraced anew and to reproduce the same movements of the muscles that originally accompanied them.

It is, La Forge argues,

principally and primarily the presence and action of the object to which we should attribute the disposition of our machine that renders it capable of, and even incites it to, imitate the actions made in its presence by other, similar machines, and to repeat them when they have already done them once.

There is no soul, and thus no knowledge, at work here. The mimicry is not intentional, or even consciously done.

This sort of involuntary imitation is seen quite clearly in those who yawn when they see others yawn, or who cough or spit having seen others do the same. I even know of men whom one can make drink until they have lost their reason, provided that, drinking in their company, one makes sure to put next to them glasses full of wine; one need not even warn or ask them to drink.[42]

There are only motions being conveyed by the senses through the nerves to the brain, which in turn sends the animal spirits to this or that organ or muscle. This leads La Forge to an extended discussion of the way in which sight and hearing, especially, can generate the thoughtless imitation of actions seen and sounds heard based solely on the strength of a present sensory impression.

Involuntary imitation in the case of hearing is less complicated and more likely to happen than in the case of sight. Through a strictly mechanical process, without any input from a mind and not unlike musical harmonics, the vibrations of the auditory nerves caused by a sound hitting the ear are transmitted to the brain, opening up the pores there in the same pattern and allowing the animal spirits dispersed by the pineal gland to flow in that pattern into the muscles of the tongue and the throat, thereby causing a similar sound tone to be emitted.

Consider that when these fibers [of the nerves] are struck by sounds, that is, by the wobbles and tremblings that strings or other things imprint on the

88 THE GOOD CARTESIAN

air, they [the fibers] imitate them in the same way in which the string of a lute that is not plucked imitates the sound of another string right next to it that is plucked.[43]

The inclination to repeat a sound in this way is rather weak, La Forge concedes (*cette disposition est forte legere*). The mimicry rarely takes place on the first occasion, and it can easily be opposed by the will. But nonetheless it can, and does, happen, without any contribution from memory, corporeal or otherwise. This is the point that Descartes's article is missing.

The disposition is, however, greatly strengthened if one has heard or uttered the sound once before. This is where La Forge says (corporeal) memory does indeed have a role to play. It is especially clear in the case of sight, where the influence of a present external object in generating an imitation on the very first occasion is even slighter than in the case of sound. We are more likely to mimic the action of another that we see when it is an action we have seen or performed several times in similar circumstances, especially if we have done so in an imitative manner. Memory—and what is at issue here is a purely mechanical, bodily memory, not involving the mind at all—is nothing but a vestige of the particular path taken by the animal spirits flowing from the pineal gland into certain pores of the brain, which makes it easier and more likely for them to take the same path in the same pattern to the same muscles again. "I do not believe that one can otherwise explain the principal effect of memory, which allows the machine that we are describing to be able to imitate the actions that true human beings or other similar machines make in its presence, when it has at other times done similar such things on a like occasion." La Forge adds, "I am not afraid to add these last words to the text, because without them it does not seem intelligible to me."[44]

*

La Forge's commentary on the *Traité de l'homme* is a remarkable (yet relatively neglected) document in Cartesian physiology, and a substantial contribution to the advancement of the mechanistic scientific program. La Forge's text constitutes a much more detailed account of the human body and analysis of its processes than Descartes offers in the treatise itself.

Despite his occasionally critical treatment of the text, La Forge ends his long set of remarks with effusive praise of his mentor,

A DISCIPLE'S COMMENTARY 89

a man whom we can call Divine, with much more right to that title than Plato, and whom we can believe, with more justification than some have provided for Aristotle, to have been sent by God to teach us how to philosophize well. For although there is no sect of philosophy that has principles as simple and as few as his, there is none that has used them to explain so many things nor so clearly as he has.[45]

It is clear, however, that La Forge saw his *Remarques* merely as but the beginning of a larger project. His ultimate goal is to pursue further the study of the human being that Descartes would have had the chance to complete "if death had not taken him from us."

For one, there remains the problem of the generation of the human (and animal) body, that is, "how two seeds from a man and a woman can engender a machine capable of all the corporeal functions that we notice in ourselves, and similar to that which we have just described."[46] La Forge is referring here to a topic taken up in an essay that, in the Stockholm inventory of Descartes's papers, bore the title *La Description du corps humain*.[47] Clerselier included this work in the 1664 volume with the *Traité de l'homme* and La Forge's commentary. However, on the volume's title page and on the running headers of the essay, he gave it the title *Un traitté de la formation du foetus* (only the first page of the published essay within the volume has *La Description du corps humain et de toutes ses fonctions*).[48] Though this later reworking of material from the early *L'Homme*, which Descartes was composing in his final years, appears in Clerselier's volume in five parts, the manuscript that Descartes's literary executor had was incomplete.

La Forge knows that the account of generation and growth in Descartes's extant manuscript is really only a sketch (*ce qu'il n'a quasi qu'ébauché*); he calls it "half done." He proposes that, by conjecturing what Descartes would have said on the basis of what he has said, "someone who has the honor of being among his disciples" should undertake to finish the job and explain the formation of all the parts of the body and their functions.

La Forge could certainly be the one to do it—"if I were satisfied that the clarifications that I have tried to provide for the places that seemed to me obscure in the first part [i.e., *Traité de l'homme*] show that I am not very far either from the dogmas of our author or from correct reason." But it is not something he is going to undertake now.[49] He has a more pressing project in mind.

90 THE GOOD CARTESIAN

The reader of La Forge's commentary on *L'Homme* will notice that the soul or mind is not entirely absent from his account of the body "machine." It seems, in fact, to inform—sometimes explicitly, sometimes subtly—his own discussion more than it does Descartes's text. The soul is present on those occasions when La Forge addresses voluntary motions of the body and the way in which, when we want to move our limbs, the animal spirits descend from the brain more quickly and more abundantly than usual.[50] And where Descartes claims in Article 28 only that "when God unites a rational soul to this machine . . . he will place its principal seat in the brain, and will make its nature such that the soul will have different sensations depending on the different ways in which the nerves open the entrances to the pores in the internal surface of the brain"[51], La Forge adds the clarification that God "will unite its thoughts not immediately with all those motions that take place in this machine, but only with those that can be communicated to the brain by the nerves." La Forge even needs to amend Descartes's account of sensation by reminding us (in his comments on Article 51, regarding the "internal senses") of the distinction between sensation as motions in the body, on one hand, and, on the other hand, sensation as a confused perception in the soul. There is thirst as dryness in the throat, which is a purely bodily state, and there is thirst that, as the mind's perception of that dryness, is the desire for drink in the soul. La Forge insists that there is no discernable relation between these two kinds of events other than their concomitance, "no more than there is between the sensation of the thing that causes pain, and the thought of sadness to which this sensation gives rise."[52]

It was no secret to this generation of Cartesians that Descartes had intended to supplement the doctrine of the body-machine in the *Traité de l'homme* with an account of the human soul, both on its own and in its union with the body. He had claimed as much in his published writings. This is among those things that, as La Forge says, Descartes's untimely demise prevented him from doing. These topics are not entirely absent from the Cartesian corpus; they are addressed in the *Meditationes*, in Part Four of the *Principia philosophiae*, and in *Les Passions de l'âme*, as well as in his correspondence. La Forge felt, though, that they needed a more adequate treatment, a detailed and systematic investigation. Taking this on was the obvious next step for a good Cartesian.

5

The Cartesian Mind

La Forge's generosity on behalf of the Cartesian cause seemed to know no bounds. There was more in the packet that Clerselier received from him in 1661 than illustrations for the *Traité de l'homme* and an extensive commentary on the work. In his preface to *L'homme*, Clerselier tells the reader that, besides *ses figures et ses remarques*, his new-found medical colleague in Saumur had enclosed, as well,

> a quite extensive treatise on the mind, in which he has collected and put in order what Monsieur Descartes has already said in several places, and he has added, on his own, everything he judged that he [Descartes] should have said about it if he had achieved his goal.

This *Traitté de l'esprit de l'homme, de ses facultez & fonctions, & de son union avec le corps, suivant les principes de René Descartes* is, Clerselier adds, "one of the most beautiful pieces I have ever seen." He was initially inclined to include it with La Forge's commentary in the 1664 volume of *L'Homme*. However, he soon thought better of it, since the long treatise was in need of "some touching up [*quelques coups de lime*] in order to bring it to perfection."[1] Thus, he says,

> I thought it would be better to save it for another time, rather than delay further our printing [of *L'Homme*]. Besides, it certainly deserves to appear in a separate volume, or to be the principal part of a body to which it could be joined. So much so that, if the great occupations of Monsieur de Gutschoven had not prevented him from giving all the necessary attention to complete in a short time what he had promised me, we would have had this treatise [*L'Homme*] nearly two years ago.[2]

In the end, La Forge's own *Traité* was printed in Paris—*Chez Theodore Girard*—in November 1665, and, with its *Privilege du Roy* and dedication to

---

The Good Cartesian. Steven Nadler, Oxford University Press. © Oxford University Press 2024.
DOI: 10.1093/oso/9780197671719.003.0006

92 THE GOOD CARTESIAN

Montmor, available for sale in early 1666. It was one of the first full-length treatises of Cartesian philosophy published in France.[3]

La Forge was already working on his *Traité* before he began composing his commentary on *L'Homme*.[4] Several times during the commentary he refers to parts of the work that are either already completed or in progress. In his remarks on the ambiguity of the word 'senses'—it can mean the impression made on the nerves of human body by an external object, the perception in the mind of this impression, or the judgment in the mind that follows the perception (essentially Descartes's three grades of sensation[5])—he notes that this is something "I have explained and proven in the *Traitté de l'esprit*."[6] And when explaining the errors the mind can make on a sensory basis—although one and the same pattern that is imprinted on the pineal gland can be generated by different bodily causes, it will (from divine providence) always give rise to the same sensory idea in the mind—he says that "we have explained this at greater length in the *Traitté de l'esprit*, which will follow this one."[7]

The *Traité* was thus likely begun in 1660, if not earlier; perhaps La Forge had undertaken such a project before seeing Clerselier's call for illustrations for *L'Homme*. Given Clerselier's assessment that the work he received in 1661 was still in need of revisions (or at least some touching up), La Forge seems also to have continued to work on it right up until 1665. In June or July of that year, La Forge asked Jean Chapelain—the same friend who, we have seen, had recommended that he dedicate the treatise to Montmor—to look over the manuscript and suggest any necessary changes. Chapelain demurred: "You underestimate yourself too much when you put yourself in my care for the revision and correction your work. The disciple does not teach the master, and the most he can do is to propose to him some difficulties."[8]

*

In his commentary on *L'Homme*, La Forge, in a remark that, almost word for word, clearly prompted Clerselier's own description of the *Traité*, declares that in his forthcoming work "I have tried to set out everything that Monsieur Descartes has already said, and to add what I believe he would have said if he had continued his project [*son dessein*]."[9]

La Forge is not merely speculating on what Descartes might have done had he not died in Stockholm at the age of fifty-four. There really is no mystery here. Descartes himself tells us, several times, what his plans were. The very

THE CARTESIAN MIND   93

first sentence of the *Traité de l'homme* spells out the envisioned three parts of the work.

> These men [the "hypothetical" subjects of the treatise] will be composed, as we are, of a soul and a body. [A] First I must describe the body on its own; then [B] the soul, again on its own; and finally [C] I must show how these two natures would have to be joined and united in order to constitute men who resemble us.[10]

[A] represents the uncompleted treatise such as we have it. Although the soul makes a cameo appearance here and there in this first part of *L'Homme*, particularly when it is a question of the role of the pineal gland in generating sensations, the subject of these chapters is, as we have seen, "the machine without any vegetative or sensitive soul or other principle of movement and life, apart from its blood and its spirits." Descartes concludes the extant work with a few final remarks "before going on to describe the rational soul," that is, [B].[11]

Likewise, in the *Discours de la méthode*, after reviewing the work he carried out on the human being three years earlier, he reports that after dealing with the body-machine,

> I described the rational soul, and showed that, unlike the other things of which I had spoken, it cannot be derived in any way from the potentiality of matter, but must be specially created. And I showed how it is not sufficient for it to be lodged in the human body like a helmsman in his ship, except perhaps to move its limbs, but that it must be more closely joined and united with the body in order to have, besides this power of movement, feelings and appetites like ours and so constitute a real man.[12]

This obviously corresponds to his plan in *L'Homme* to examine the rational soul "on its own" and, then, its union with the body. While this passage would seem to imply that Descartes did indeed complete these sections of the work, no such manuscripts have survived; if they were completed they must have been lost or destroyed. Still, traces of those investigations into the soul and the soul-body union can be found in later treatises. The nature of the mind as a thinking substance, its radical distinction in essence from the human body, its most essential functions (especially perception or understanding and will), the nature of its union with the body, and those

94   THE GOOD CARTESIAN

powers it acquires through that union (sensation, imagination, memory) are all treated a few years later in the *Meditationes* and especially *Les Passions de l'âme*.

The *Principia philosophiae*, as well, while devoted mostly to topics in metaphysics and physics, concludes with a number of articles on the soul and its relationship to the body. To be sure, this Cartesian textbook, extant in four parts, was originally supposed to include an additional two parts, one of which was to be devoted to animate bodies generally and the other to "man." Apparently, and despite his earlier work on the latter, Descartes was still not satisfied with what he had.

> I would not add anything further to this fourth part of the *Principia philosophiae* if, as I originally planned, I was going to write two further parts—a fifth part on living things, i.e., animals and plants, and sixth part on man. But I am not yet completely clear about all the matters which I would like to deal with there, and I do not know whether I shall ever have enough free time to complete those sections. So, to avoid delaying the publication of the first four parts any longer, and to make sure there are no gaps caused by my keeping material back for the two final parts, I shall here add a few observations concerning the objects of the senses.[13]

It is unclear whether, when Descartes mentions here a "sixth part on man," he is talking only about the human body and its purely physical operations— that is, a reworking of the material from *L'Homme*, which in fact he would go on to do in the late 1640s in *La Description du corps humain*, also left unfinished at his death—or also about the complete human being, a mind–body union. That it is the latter is suggested by the fact that the "few observations" that he includes toward the end of Part Four (articles 189 to 198) deal with the external sensations and the emotions or passions of the human soul, which, "while informing the entire body, nevertheless has its principal seat in the brain"; the soul's essential nature as a thinking and willing substance was already treated in Part One.

It thus cannot be argued that Descartes has not left us a good deal of material on the human soul and its relationship to the human body, even if it is scattered among various writings, including his correspondence. Still, La Forge, seeking to complete Descartes's project and fulfill his mentor's promissory note to give us a systematic treatment of the soul and its union with the body, has his work cut out for him. Essentially, what he is doing with his

Traité de l'esprit de l'homme is of a piece with what he did with his commentary on *L'Homme*: explaining, expanding, and completing what Descartes has done.

La Forge's thorough and highly detailed account of the mind, like the finer points of his examination of the human body in the *L'Homme* commentary, goes well beyond Descartes's own written summaries, but (he claims) never departs from the principles that Descartes laid out and the spirit of his philosophy. This is something that La Forge does not tire of reminding his reader. "Death prevented [Descartes] from providing what he still required to demonstrate in order to inform us fully about human nature. . . . [I] believed I could draw enough material to write this whole work from the books which he himself had published and from the two volumes of correspondence which one of his friends gave us." Descartes, La Forge says, "never revealed his thoughts about [human nature] completely," but he did at least "leave us many clues in his writings by which we can rather easily know how he would have spoken about the mind if he had decided to write about it."[14] Thus, he continues, "I only claim to borrow his ideas here and to provide a supplement to what he would have said about the nature of the mind at the end of his *Traité de l'homme*."[15] Everything La Forge has to say about the mind and its union with the body in his own treatise "follows so clearly from the first truths which Monsieur Descartes demonstrated that, even if I could not locate all of them in the books which he left us, there would still be no room to doubt that they are consequences drawn from his principles."[16]

While La Forge does say, "I do not stray from [Descartes's] views [*je ne m'éloigne par de ses sentimens*]" and that he will "follow the truth and footprints [*traces*] of Monsieur Descartes," without deviating from him "even minimally,"[17] it is clear that, as with the *L'Homme* commentary, this must be taken with a grain of salt. There are, as we shall see, points on which La Forge goes not only where Descartes did not go but might or even would have gone, but in a direction that Descartes would almost certainly not have sanctioned. La Forge does allow himself to "stray" from his mentor; but, he would say, all such deviations are justified—and justified on Cartesian grounds, "according to his [Descartes's] principles."

*

Along with fealty to Descartes, there are two other sub-themes running through La Forge's *Traité*. The first is an anti-Scholasticism. To La Forge, "the

96   THE GOOD CARTESIAN

Scholastic philosophers [*les Philosophes de l'Ecole*]" do nothing but slavishly adopt and employ the principles of Aristotle without ever having closely read his texts after their college studies; they "do not know the teaching of Plato and Aristotle, apart from what was dictated in their notebooks or remembered from the explanations of their professors." These are, he adds, "the most troublesome opponents of Monsieur Descartes's disciples and, although they are not the most formidable, they are nevertheless the most difficult to convince."[18]

'Scholasticism' is often used lazily as a catch-all term for medieval thinkers who employ generally the concepts and explanatory principles of Aristotle. In fact, there is no such single thing as Scholasticism, any more than there is a single Aristotelianism (or, as we have seen, a single Cartesianism). There is significant philosophical and theological variety among medieval and early modern Aristotelians teaching in the university and college faculties ("the schools"), such that it is more accurate to refer to Scholastic Aristotelianism*s*. As La Forge himself notes, "the views which are often attributed to the Schools are not always found in every school, and there are even some among them who glory in finding in Aristotle today all the completely novel things which have been discovered in this century."[19] By the latter La Forge may have in mind certain eclectic thinkers—such as Heereboord, whom he calls a "*savant peripatetique*"—who try to show that Descartes's philosophy is compatible with central elements of Aristotelian thought.

It is nonetheless safe to say that the Scholastic Aristotelianism that La Forge and other Cartesians are most concerned to combat typically involves that reliance on prime or secondary matter informed by substantial and accidental forms and real qualities for the explanation of natural phenomena—and, as we have seen in the case of the controversies around the Eucharist, for the explanation of supernatural phenomena as well. For Descartes and his followers, however, a model of science that operates by infusing bodies with spiritual forms and qualities defined by the phenomena they are supposed to explain easily lent itself to critique and ridicule. Progressive early modern philosophers, including Descartes, found such explanations trivial and useless. It is totally uninformative to be told that the reason why a body fell was because it was "heavy," or that an object was white because it contained "whiteness." Scholastic thinkers, Descartes notes,

> have all put forward as principles things of which they did not possess perfect knowledge. For example, there is not one of them, so far as I know,

THE CARTESIAN MIND 97

who has not supposed there to be weight in terrestrial bodies. Yet although experience shows us very clearly that the bodies we call "heavy" descend toward the center of the earth, we do not for all that have any knowledge of the nature of what is called "gravity," that is to say, the cause or principle which makes bodies descend in this way.[20]

In other words, the explanations offered by latter-day Aristotelians are no explanations at all. They simply take the property to be explained ("heavy") and make it part of the explanation ("heaviness"). A famous parody of this technique was offered by Molière in his 1673 play *Le Malade imaginaire*. When Thomas, a candidate in medicine, is asked at his degree disputation to explain why opium causes sleep, he responds, "Because it has the dormitive virtue, which makes one sleep." The chorus of examiners enthusiastically applaud him and welcome him into "our learned body."[21]

La Forge grants that there are commonalities between Aristotle and Descartes: for example, the method of doubt in the epistemological exercise of the *Meditationes*.

This method is completely consistent with the opinion of Aristotle. . . . Aristotle would not have been among those who criticized the First Meditation of Monsieur Descartes as unnecessary because there is at least as much need to doubt everything once in a lifetime when looking for the foundation of all the sciences, in order subsequently not to doubt them, as to begin incessantly at the start of each science as Aristotle requires.[22]

What does trouble La Forge is the way in which Aristotelians fail to respect the basic categories of the new philosophy, especially the radical metaphysical distinction between mind and body. Like Descartes, he cannot abide the ontologically uncategorizable entities that Scholastic thinkers use to try to explain natural phenomena. Their principles are, he insists, "useless . . . because it is impossible to solve the simplest problem in physics by means of such principles," and "obscure" because "there is no idea in the mind which corresponds to the meaning [of the terms]." The most offensive of all, he notes, are those imaginary beings that are neither themselves minds or bodies nor related to minds or bodies as properties or accidents that can be understood as modifications of the respective underlying nature (thought or extension). These ontological oddities include those beings which are called substantial forms of bodies, and real, impressed, intentional, occult, sympathetic or specific qualities, and the heating, retentive, or expulsive faculties, etc.—it is impossible for any idea in the mind to correspond to them or for what is said about them to have any meaning which can be understood.[23]

Despite their name, substantial forms are not substances, since they cannot exist by themselves but only as they inform or inhere in matter; nor are real accidents truly accidents, since as "real" they are (at least in principle) capable of existing on their own.

Descartes's *Traité de l'homme* and La Forge's commentary on it were intended to demonstrate that no such entities are required to understand the constitution and processes of the human body (or any living body); everything happens by virtue of extended matter and motion. La Forge's *Traité de l'esprit de l'homme* carries that project forward to show that neither the mind itself nor its union and interaction with the body involves anything that cannot be accommodated strictly to the terms of Cartesian dualism.

The other sub-theme of the work, one which takes up a good deal of La Forge's preface, is his demonstration that the Cartesian philosophy, and especially his own contributions to it on "the nature of the soul," are in perfect agreement with Saint Augustine's views. "I will show here in a few words that the thoughts of Monsieur Descartes concerning the nature of the soul are completely consistent with the doctrine of Saint Augustine."[24] This was a common trope in seventeenth-century Cartesianism. Descartes himself seems to have been relatively unmoved when his interlocutors would point out echoes of Augustine in his texts, perhaps because he was protective of his originality. Arnauld, for one, immediately recognized that the *ego sum, ego existo* argument of the Second Meditation had its precedent in Augustine's *De libero arbitrio* (Book 2, Chapter 3). Referring to Descartes's discovery of the indubitability of one's own existence, even if one is in a state of complete doubt and uncertainty about all other things, Arnauld in his Fourth Set of Objections notes that "the first thing that I find remarkable" is that "our distinguished author has laid down as the basis of his entire philosophy exactly the same principle as that laid down by St. Augustine."[25] Descartes gives this remark only the briefest of attention: "I shall not waste time here by thanking my distinguished critic for bringing in the authority of St. Augustine to support me."[26] Around the same time, when one of his correspondents—most likely the Dordrecht minister Andreas Colvius, referring to the French

THE CARTESIAN MIND 99

version of the argument in the *Discours de la méthode* (*je pense, donc je suis*, famously appearing in Latin in the *Principia philosophiae* as *cogito, ergo sum*)—also highlighted for Descartes the similarity between his reasoning and that of the Bishop of Hippo, Descartes replied at somewhat greater length, if not in all honesty: "I am obliged to you for alerting me to the passage of St. Augustine, to which my 'I think, therefore I am' bears some relation. I went to read it today in the library of this city [Leiden], and I found, truly, that it serves well for proving the certainty of our being."[27] (Is it really possible that Descartes had not read Augustine's *De libero arbitrio* by this point?[28])

Descartes may not have cared very much about precedents in Augustine, or any other ancient thinkers for that matter, or so he pretended. But second- and third-generation Cartesians often defended their philosophy against its many opponents by appealing to its Augustinian pedigree. These Cartesians would even fight among themselves over whose views represented a proper amalgam of the old and the new. The long and rancorous debate between Arnauld and Malebranche, for one, was between two Cartesians equally inspired by Augustine but at odds over who was the more faithful disciple.[29]

In his preface, La Forge offers an extended catalogue, including copious citations of Augustinian texts, of items on which Descartes and Augustine are in essential agreement. These include the *cogito* argument, where La Forge also cites *De libero arbitrio* ("there is nothing in this context which is contrary to the thought of Saint Augustine"); the fact that the human soul is an immaterial substance whose essence is thinking, and thus which is always thinking, "in the same sense as Monsieur Descartes proved it"; the proof that the soul is immortal on the basis not just of faith and revelation but on philosophical grounds as well, because of its metaphysical distinction from the body; and the reduction of the soul's faculties, "which are not distinct from it," to two: "one for perceiving and one for willing." This last point is particularly important insofar as it is of a piece with the Cartesian view that it is not the soul that gives life to the body, and thus with the rejection of the Aristotelian hylomorphic account. "Saint Augustine also recognized, just as Monsieur Descartes did, that the human mind is not the principle of vegetative and nutritive functions."[30] As for the union and interaction of soul and body, La Forge notes, Augustine's account foreshadows the dualist interface defended by Descartes and himself. The mind does not confer any sensitive powers on the body; rather, motions impressed on the body by external objects occasion thoughts or perceptions in the mind. "One could not deny

100 THE GOOD CARTESIAN

that the way in which Saint Augustine explains sensation is very far from that of the Schools, and that there is little or no difference between him and Monsieur Descartes on this issue. . . . I do not think one could find a greater degree of agreement than between what Saint Augustine wrote and what I proposed on this subject [of mind–body union]."[31]

*

With the preliminaries over, La Forge lays out his plan in the *Traité de l'esprit de l'homme*.

> I shall say, firstly, what the human mind consists of; secondly, what its functions are when it is considered in itself and, as it were, separated from its body. I shall then show the way in which the mind and body are united together and, fourthly, what are the actions which result from this union. Finally, I shall discuss the principal ways for performing all the actions of the mind properly in order to be as happy as possible in this life.

He goes on to remind the reader that "this is a purely philosophical work in which I had no other aim but to search for what the natural light of reason alone teaches us about the nature of the mind, its faculties and operations"; there will be no appeals to "truths which the faith has revealed to us" nor "any proofs from Scripture."[32]

So, "what the human mind consists of," for La Forge, as for Descartes, is thought. The mind, that is, is unextended thinking substance. Its "modes" or properties are individual thoughts.

> By the human mind we understand this inner principle of all our knowledge, desires and decisions, by means of which we produce all of our actions which include an element of thought and in which they are all received as in their primary subject. . . . This principle must be a substance.[33]

Moreover, he adds, "we know [this substance] better and are more convinced of its existence and of what it is insofar as it thinks than we are of the body or of extended substance."

La Forge's use of the term 'subject [*sujet*]' as that in which thought occurs and his description of the mind as that in us "which has the faculty of thinking," as well as his description at one point of the mind as "the substance

THE CARTESIAN MIND   101

which provides a support for [*qui sert de soutien*] thought,"[34] should not be misinterpreted to imply that the mind itself is some bare, attributeless substratum in which thinking inheres. Rather, a mind or mental substance just is its "principal attribute" or essence or nature—it is thought itself, with one mind distinguished from another by its particular thoughts. Such particular thoughts or mental states—whether they are ideas of the understanding or volitions of the will—are thought's modes, particular determinations or realizations of the principal attribute. There is no real distinction between a substance and its essence, La Forge insists. "Since the nature of the mind consists in its faculty of thinking, it must be identical with it. Otherwise, if there could be a real distinction between a substance and its essence, the same thing would be different from itself."[35]

There is nothing here that is not perfectly orthodox from a Cartesian perspective.

*

La Forge is equally faithful to Descartes when he defines the essence of thought as consciousness.

> I understand thought as that perception, consciousness [*conscience*], or inner knowledge which each one of us experiences directly in ourselves when we are aware of what we do or of what takes place in ourselves. Thus, all knowledge of our own understanding and of all the movements of our will, all our imaginings and all the actions of our senses are nothing but different kinds of thinking.[36]

The distinctive and essential feature of any thought or mode of thinking, of any mental state, is consciousness or the immediate subjective awareness of that thought or state. (This is what has come to be called "phenomenal consciousness," to distinguish it from self-consciousness. It is one thing to account for a mental state being a *conscious* mental state, for my being consciously aware of x, and another thing to account for my knowing that it is *my* conscious state, for my being conscious that *I* am aware of x.)

La Forge is here echoing Descartes's own definition of 'thought' as the "awareness or internal testimony" that essentially and necessarily accompanies every state of mind. That is, thinking, for Descartes, is defined by consciousness: "By the term 'thought,' I understand everything which we are aware of [*nobis consciis*] as happening within us, in so far as we have awareness [*conscientia*] of it."[37] There are no thoughts that are not episodes of conscious awareness, there are no non-conscious mental events. "There can be nothing in the mind, in so far as it is a thinking thing, of which it is not aware [*conscia*] ... we cannot have any thought of which we are not aware at the very moment when it is in us."[38]

The famous "hard problem," of course, is how to explain phenomenal consciousness.[39] What gives rise to it and accounts for the difference between a conscious mental state and a non-conscious one? And why are some beings conscious while others, apparently, are not? While contemporary philosophers and neuroscientists continue to wrestle with these questions, they were, in fact, first isolated and addressed in a sustained and (sometimes) systematic manner in the seventeenth century.

Descartes's achievement early in the *Meditationes*—in the Second Meditation—is to direct our attention to the indubitable presence constituted by the contents of the mind, and thereby to consciousness itself. As thought is the principal attribute or property of the immaterial substance that is the soul, the soul's thinking includes all the sensory phenomena, imaginings, beliefs, volitions, doubts, intellectual conceivings, and other immediately accessible data that fill the theater of the mind. While he admits that it is quite hard to define just what thought is, he insists that it is the easiest thing in the world to experience, basically because it is experience itself and is right there before us. As Descartes has Eudoxus say in the dialogue *Recherche de la vérité*, "to know what doubt is, what thought is ... we [do not] have to rack our brains." There are, he continues, "some things which are made more obscure by our attempts to define them: since they are very simple and clear, they are perceived and known just on their own, and there is no better way of knowing and perceiving them." The only way, in fact, in which we can learn about such things is "by ourselves: what convinces us of them is simply our own experience or awareness—that awareness or internal testimony which everyone experiences within himself when he ponders on such matters."[40]

Descartes unfortunately does not have much more to say about the nature of consciousness. He does note that what consciousness involves is basically thought thinking about itself. In his conversation with his young Dutch disciple Frans Burman, he reportedly claimed that "to be conscious [*conscium esse*] is both to think and to reflect on one's thought." Moreover, this reflection on a thought or mental event is simultaneous with the mental event itself; it

THE CARTESIAN MIND 103

is not a subsequent memory of an earlier thought. He says "it is false that this reflection cannot occur while the previous thought is still there."[41]

Descartes's use of the term 'reflection,' and the way in which he continues his remarks here, may seem to imply that the activity that constitutes the awareness accompanying a conscious thought involves a concomitant but second-order, even voluntary thought directed at a primary thought distinct from it: "This is because . . . the soul is capable of thinking of more than one thing at the same time, and of continuing with a particular thought which it has. It has the power to reflect on its thoughts as often as it likes, and to be aware of its thought in this way."[42] Although the reflection that accounts for consciousness occurs "while the previous thought is still there," it might seem from this passage that it is a discrete mental act, distinct from the act that is its object.

However, other comments by Descartes suggest that phenomenal consciousness should be distinguished from an explicit, higher-order reflection directed at one's thinking, in part because such a second-order thought would indeed have to occur subsequent to the original thought that is its object. Knowing what thought is, he says,

> does not require reflective knowledge or the kind of knowledge that is acquired by means of demonstrations; still less does it require knowledge of reflective knowledge, i.e., knowing that we know, and knowing that we know that we know, and so on ad infinitum. . . . It is quite sufficient that we should know it by that internal awareness [cognitione illa interna] which always precedes reflective knowledge. This inner awareness of one's thought and existence is so innate in all men that . . . we cannot fail to have it.[43]

While much remains obscure here—particularly whether in this passage Descartes, when he refers to knowing "what thought is [quid sit cogitatio]," is talking about the immediate awareness of or acquaintance with one's thinking that characterizes phenomenal consciousness, or about a more cognitive grasp (or implicit, even propositional knowledge) of what thought is[44]—it does seem to be the former that he has in mind. Consciousness for Descartes, then, appears primarily to be a kind of immediate self-relation that is an essential feature of any mental state; it does not require forming a second thought directed at a first thought.[45] My conscious awareness of an external object (an apple, for example) would involve both my perception of that object and the perception's own reflection on itself. The mind is

104 THE GOOD CARTESIAN

thereby, as Descartes puts it, "thinking of more than one thing at the same time" insofar as it is thinking of both the apple and its own thinking of the apple, and doing so by the same act of thinking. Each act of thought directed at an external object would also be directed at itself, and thus have both its external object (the apple) and an internal object (itself, the act of thinking of the apple). As one commentator puts it, "whenever I think of object x . . . there is [for Descartes] only one act, the act of thinking of x, which has x as its primary object and itself as its secondary object."[46]

Similarly, writing about the conscious awareness that accompanies all acts of volition, Descartes says that "we have ideas not only of all that is in our intellect, but also of all that is in the will. For we cannot will anything without knowing that we will it, nor could we know this without an idea; but I do not claim that the idea is different from the action itself."[47] Descartes makes this same point in the *Les Passions de l'âme*: "It is certain that we cannot will anything without perceiving by the same means [*par mesme moyen*] that we are willing it."[48] The coherence of Descartes's position here on the will, however, is uncertain. An act of volition is not itself an act of perceiving—it is an act of willing. So while an ordinary idea or act of perceiving can have itself as one of its (perceived) objects (in addition to its external object), it would seem that the consciousness of an act of volition cannot come through the act of volition itself, but would require a second-order act of mind, a perceiving, directed at the act of volition. It is unclear how an act of volition can *perceive* itself since it is not a perceiving at all. Still, as an act of thought it somehow necessarily involves consciousness of itself.

Be that as it may, this distinction between phenomenal consciousness as first-order awareness involving a mental act reflecting on itself and explicit reflection as a second-order act of thinking directed at a first-order act forms the core of what is the clearest and most important discussion of consciousness among Cartesians in the seventeenth century.

Arnauld took on the problem of consciousness right at the beginning of his long dispute with his fellow Cartesian, Malebranche, over the nature of the mind's ideas.[49] The key to Arnauld's account of consciousness lies in his notion of "virtual reflection [*réflexion virtuelle*]." In *Des vraies et des fausses idées* (1683), his opening salvo in the debate, Arnauld insists that every perceptual act (taken broadly to mean not only acts of perception per se, but any thought activity whatsoever) is a conscious act, is accompanied by awareness. There are no non-conscious mental states. One cannot perceive or think of something without being aware that one is perceiving or thinking of

THE CARTESIAN MIND   105

something. "The thought that our soul has of itself" is a constant feature of mental life, since

> whatever it is that I am knowing, I know that I know it, by means of a certain virtual reflection which accompanies all my thoughts. . . . I thus know myself while knowing other things. And, in effect, it is principally this which, it seems, distinguishes intelligent beings from those which are not intelligent—the former *sunt conscia sui et suae operationis*, the latter are not.[50]

Adding a bit more explanatory detail, he says that

> our thought or perception is essentially reflective on itself, or, as it is said more aptly in Latin, *est sui conscia*. For I never think without knowing that I am thinking. I never know a square without my knowing that I know it; I never see the sun, or, to put the matter beyond all doubt, I never seem to see the sun without my being certain that I seem to see it . . . . at the same time that I conceive [something], I know that I am conceiving it.[51]

More explicitly than Descartes, Arnauld accounts for consciousness by insisting that every mental act is self-reflective and thus accompanied by awareness. Every perception, in addition to being the perception of some external object, is also turned upon itself and has itself (an act of the mind) as its (internal) object. Virtual reflection does not involve a second perceptual act distinct from the first and directed at it; rather, it is the self-awareness possessed by the first-order perception. This is an essential part of any mental act, identical with the act. The immediate awareness of a perception is not an experience distinct from simply having a perception. Whenever one perceives, no special effort is required to be aware that one is perceiving and thus for the perceiving to be a *conscious* experience. Arnauld thus, like Descartes albeit in clearer terms, distinguishes the virtual reflection that involuntarily and necessarily accompanies every perceptual act from what he calls "explicit reflection [*réflexion expresse*]," a deliberate and voluntary second-order act of perception directed at the first and having it as its primary object. "Besides this reflection which can be called virtual, which is found in all perceptions, there is another, more explicit reflection by which we examine our perception by means of another perception."[52] With virtual

106 THE GOOD CARTESIAN

reflection, I am (consciously) perceiving the world; with explicit reflection, I am (consciously) perceiving my perceiving of the world. (The act of explicitly reflecting on another act of perception, because it is itself an act of perception, would have to be characterized by virtual reflection as well.)

In the passages above, Arnauld seems to stress the first-person content of awareness ("I know that I know it") and the presence therein of the self ("I thus know myself"). This might seem to suggest that the process of virtual reflection is meant to explain *self*-consciousness. This is misleading, however. It is not clear that Arnauld believes that the "I" or self is explicitly a part of the content of first-order consciousness. Possibly, virtual reflection only lays the foundation for self-consciousness, which itself occurs at the level of explicit reflection. The proper content of virtual reflection when I am perceiving a table would thus be only: "Here is a table presentation" (or "table-awareness is taking place"), but not "*I* am perceiving a table"; the latter would be the content of an explicit reflection. Nonetheless, even if virtual reflection does account for some low-level kind of self-consciousness, it is intended primarily to explain phenomenal consciousness.

This notion—broached by Descartes (although perhaps also found in Augustine and others) and explicitly elaborated by Arnauld—that consciousness *qua* conscious awareness (as opposed to explicit self-consciousness) is accounted for by the virtual reflection of a first-order act of thought rather than an explicit second-order act of thinking directed at a first-order act— became the standard view among seventeenth-century Cartesians. Which brings us back to La Forge.

La Forge, like all later Cartesians—including Malebranche and Régis— accepted Descartes's definition of thought in terms of consciousness: to be a mental event is to be a conscious event. Thus, as we saw above, he says that "the nature of thought consists in this consciousness [*conscience*], this testimony, this inner sentiment by which the mind attends to all that it undergoes, and generally all that passes immediately in it, at the same time that it acts or it suffers." From this and other passages it seems that, likewise, for him consciousness does not appear to demand a second-order thought directed at a first-order perception. Rather, that first-order perception is self-reflective, undoubtedly much in the same way as Arnauld would describe it some years later. As La Forge says in the passage, this *sentiment* in the soul that is consciousness occurs "at the same time that it [the soul] acts or suffers," and thus presumably by the numerically identical means—that is, through the perception itself. This is reinforced by his claim in that same chapter of the *Traité*

THE CARTESIAN MIND 107

that the phenomenon of consciousness is part of the first-order act of mind. He wants to make sure that

> you know that this testimony and this inner feeling [*sentiment*] is not distinct from the action or the passion, and that the actions and passions themselves make the mind aware of what is taking place in itself. Thus you will not confuse this inner feeling with the reflection that we sometimes make on our actions, which is not found in all of our thought.[53]

He insists that "the substance which thinks is nothing but a being which is aware of everything going on in itself, whether it acts itself or whether something else acts on it, and which is aware of it at exactly the same time as it occurs."[54] For La Forge, we know a thought, we are aware of it, as it occurs, "through itself [*par elle*]," and not because it is the explicit object of another thought. For good measure, he adds that this is also the view of Saint Augustine, who

> must have believed that the soul, insofar as it acts, is immediately aware of its operations. No one can fail to realize how consistent that is with the opinion of Monsieur Descartes who generally applies the term 'thought' to all the things that we perceive immediately in virtue of the fact that we do them.[55]

*

So far we have been considering what might be called La Forge's "functional" definition of the mind. The mind characterized as *thinking* substance is identified primarily by what it does, its actions and its passions. But of course La Forge, no less than Descartes, is concerned with the metaphysical status of the mind—not just as substance, but as *immaterial* substance. "Everything which thinks is immaterial," he notes;[56] thought and matter cannot occur in the same simple substance (although they can be united in a composite substance—the subject of the next chapter). La Forge, in other words, is a vigorous and uncompromising defender of mind–body ontological dualism.[57]

Descartes presents his account of the exclusive and exhaustive divide between mind and body in several contexts. It appears in summary form in the *Discours de la méthode*, where he reviews his "discovery" that "this 'I'—that is, the soul by which I am what I am—is entirely distinct from the body."[58] In

108 THE GOOD CARTESIAN

the *Principia philosophiae*, there is a series of articles in Part One in which Descartes introduces the notion of a "real distinction" (as opposed to either a modal distinction or a distinction of reason), which captures the differences between "two or more substances" whose defining natures or essences—their principal attributes—can be clearly and distinctly conceived as real things "one apart from the other."[59] His most well-known and extended argument for the doctrine, however, is in the *Meditationes*.

There is robust scholarly disagreement as to whether Descartes has sufficiently established the real distinction between mind and body in the Second Meditation, or the case is not closed until the Sixth Meditation, after he has proven the existence of a non-deceiving God and, thus, the epistemic reliability of clear and distinct perception.[60] In metaphysical terms, putting aside any epistemological worries about the validity of clear and distinct perception, it does seem that the considerations brought forward in the Second Meditation do draw the fundamental ontological division between mind and body and the essential and exclusive features of each kind of substance.

After arriving at the certainty of both "I am" and "I am a thing that thinks," Descartes seeks to understand the nature of the thinking thing that he is. He can clearly conceive of himself as a mind whose sole essence is thought. "Thought . . . alone is inseparable from me." He also has a clear conception of body as something extended, as revealed in the wax example. Finally, he recognizes that thought and extension are both radically distinct natures and that each constitutes a principal attribute of a substance. In the Fourth Replies, for example, he tells Arnauld that

> the mind can be perceived distinctly and completely (that is, sufficiently for it to be considered as a complete thing) without any of the forms or attributes by which we recognize that body is a substance, as I think I showed quite adequately in the Second Meditation. And similarly a body can be understood distinctly and as a complete thing, without any attributes which belong to the mind.[61]

In the Sixth Meditation, he reviews just those clear and distinct conceptions that the power of God can instantiate in reality "so as to correspond exactly with my understanding of [them]," and these conceptions seem to be precisely those he had achieved by the end of the exercises of the Second Meditation:

THE CARTESIAN MIND 109

Simply by knowing that I exist and seeing at the same time that absolutely nothing else belongs to my nature or essence except that I am a thinking thing, I can infer correctly that my essence consists solely in the fact that I am a thinking thing. It is true that I may have (or, to anticipate, that I certainly have) a body that is very closely joined to me. But nevertheless, on the one hand I have a clear and distinct idea of myself, in so far as I am simply a thinking, non-extended thing; and on the other hand I have a distinct idea of body, in so far as this is simply an extended, non-thinking thing. And accordingly it is certain that I am really distinct from my body and can exist without it.[62]

As Marleen Rozemond has shown, Descartes's argument for the real distinction between mind and body does not, as many scholars have insisted, rely on a premise about their separability (by God); rather, their separability follows from the fact that these are two radically distinct substances or "complete things." In other words, the argument for dualism does indeed seem complete by the end of the Second Meditation. The demonstration, as Rozemond reconstructs it, is based on Descartes's realization of a number of things. First, he sees that thought is not a mode of extension; otherwise, it would not be possible for him to doubt that he is extended (has a body) while being certain that he is thinking, since it is impossible to conceive clearly and distinctly of a mode while doubting or denying that it is a mode of its attribute/substance. Second, extension is the principal attribute of body. Third, if thought is not a mode of extension, it must be a principal attribute in its own right. And fourth, every substance has only one principal attribute. From these premises Descartes can conclude that mind or thinking substance (the substance whose principal attribute is thought) is really distinct from body or extended substance.[63]

La Forge agrees that the real distinction between mind and body is fully established in the Second Meditation, and in the *Traité* he gives a good summary of Descartes's argument. However, this does not stop him from expanding on what Descartes had offered. Indeed, La Forge, at significant length—three whole chapters—both supplies additional proofs for the immaterial nature of the soul and addresses objections lobbed by materialists (primarily Hobbes) who deny the existence and even the possibility of immaterial substances, and by skeptics (such as Gassendi) who allow that there are both corporeal and spiritual substances but doubt whether it can be claimed with any certainty that their respective natures are as distinct as

110 THE GOOD CARTESIAN

Descartes made them out to be, and even suggest that minds are not the only substances to which thought might belong.

La Forge apparently does not require a divine guarantee of the truth of clear and distinct perceptions. His arguments for dualism make no appeal to what God can or cannot do and focus primarily and a priori on the nature of attributes and their modes. The concept of extension, which he defines as "simply having parts outside each other," is "in no way included" in the concept of thought, which, as we have seen, he defines as consciousness. Conversely, the concept of thought is not included in the concept of extension. Thought cannot be explained through extension, and extension cannot be explained through thought. These are absolutely distinct natures. But since no substance can have more than one attribute, it is impossible for both thought and extension to belong to—that is, constitute the fundamental nature of—one and the same substance. "That would be the same as saying that one and the same subject had two different natures, which is something that cannot be said without contradiction about a noncomposite, simple subject."[64]

The same conclusion follows if one turns from the attributes themselves and considers the diversity of the modes or properties which belong to substances. "Each thing has its essence which distinguishes it from all others, and since that essence can be known only through its properties, there could be no other way of knowing the distinction between two essences apart from the diversity of their properties."[65] Modes or accidents can be conceived only through the attribute which they modify. But the modes of thought cannot be conceived through extension and the modes of extension cannot be conceived through thought. There is no conceivable relation between ideas and volitions, on one hand, and, on the other hand, motion, shape, and divisibility; neither can extension play any role in understanding the former, nor thought play any role in understanding the latter. "There is no thought included in the idea of things which include extension and one finds no extension in the idea of those which include some thought."[66] La Forge concludes with as doctrinaire a statement of mind–body dualism as Descartes or any other Cartesian ever issued.

> Let us conclude, therefore, that thought and extension are not only two essential attributes but that they also constitute the essence of the thing to which they are attributed, and that they are even more incompatible and contrary than cold and heat which can easily occur in succession in

the same subject, whereas it is absolutely impossible that two essential attributes, such as thought and extension, could ever occur in the same subject either at the same time or successively.[67]

What to do, then, about those materialists who deny the possibility of immaterial (unextended) thinking substances and the (mitigated) skeptics who suggest that for all we know thought might be an activity of bodies? Hobbes, for example, vigorously remonstrated with Descartes in his Third Set of Objections to the *Meditationes* that "a thinking thing is something corporeal, for it seems the subject of any act can be understood only in terms of something corporeal or in terms of matter."[68] And Gassendi, in his Fifth Set of Objections, had argued both that nothing Descartes says proves that he "knows, either distinctly or indistinctly, what you are or what your nature is," and that, perhaps, as a thinking thing "you are a wind, or rather a very thin vapor, given off when the heart heats up the purest type of blood, or produced by some other source, which is diffused through the parts of the body and gives them life." Descartes, Gassendi insists, has not proven that "the power of thought is something so far beyond the nature of a body that neither vapor nor other mobile, pure and rarefied body can be organized in such a way as to make it capable of thought."[69]

Underlying La Forge's approach to both of these varieties of anti-dualism is the idea that those who allow that there are or may be substances other than immaterial minds that think are confused about what an attribute is and how modes or properties must relate, conceptually and modally, to their underlying nature. The burden of proof, in fact, is on those who would insist that thoughts (ideas, volitions, etc.) can belong to extended substance, since they would have to show that there is a connection between the concepts of such thinking modes and the concept of extension as an attribute—and it is a burden they cannot possibly bear. All would agree that thought and extension are not essential to substance *qua* substance, since any substance would then necessarily have to have both natures. In this way, thought and extension are not like the essential attributes that all substances must have, such as "existing by itself," "being the first subject of various properties," and so on. But La Forge says that even his opponents concede that bodies are extended and that minds think, that these are, respectively, the primary and distinguishing features that differentiate these two species of the genus "substance" from each other. Therefore,

112 THE GOOD CARTESIAN

they should also agree that it is impossible for a mind to be extended or for a body to think. For since all the properties which can be attributed to the mind and the body belong to them essentially, insofar as they are substances, except thought and extension and anything which depends on or follows from these, they can differ only in these two attributes and it would be a contradiction to claim that they could resemble each other in some respect in which they are formally contrasted. Therefore, no thought can be attributed to body nor any extension to mind without contradiction.[70]

The only way to attribute thinking to bodies would be to claim that thought must be an attribute of body. But aside from the fact that no substance can have more than one attribute, this would lead to the absurd conclusion—absurd, at least, to most seventeenth-century thinkers—that *all* bodies think.

As for Hobbes and other materialists "who say that everything is extended," La Forge addresses them in two steps. First, he establishes that there at least *can* be some beings without extension that think. After all, we can clearly and distinctly conceive of a thinking thing that does not have extension; the exercise of the Second Meditation certainly proves this (*pace* Hobbes's own protests in his objections). Therefore, immaterial substances are possible. Second, since a mode cannot be clearly conceived without its underlying attribute, and since it is not *necessary* to conceive of extension when conceiving of ideas or volitions—indeed, it is not *possible* to see a conceptual connection between ideas or volitions and extension, and it is even possible to see that there is *no* such conceptual connection—these acts of thought cannot be modes of an extended body. However, there are indeed thinking things in the world; this is perfectly evident (as the *cogito* argument shows). Therefore, there are non-extended thinking substances.

> I can easily conceive of [thought] without extended substance and I can conceive of the latter without thought. Thus, thought cannot be an accident or property of body, and it cannot be said that there are only bodily substances in the world, because we know there are things which think and that thought does not belong to body at all, either as its essence or as an accident. It must then constitute a distinct type of substance.[71]

La Forge's response to both the Gassendist and Hobbesian positions can thus be summarized as follows:

THE CARTESIAN MIND   113

1. There are things that think.
2. Thought cannot be an attribute of body, for then *every* body would think.
3. Thought cannot be a mode or accident of body, since thought can be conceived without body (the Gassendist position is false).
4. Therefore, there are thinking things that are not bodies (Hobbesian materialism is false).

*

If thought is the essence of the mind, the question naturally arises—for the Cartesian, at least—as to whether that means the mind is always actually thinking or only that the mind is or has the power or capacity to think. La Forge on at least one occasion identifies the mind with a faculty of thinking ("Since the nature of the mind consists in its faculty of thinking, it must be identical with it"), and this would seem to suggest the latter position: that the mind has the capacity to entertain thoughts but that this capacity may often lie dormant. However, he actually opts for the stronger position, and devotes an entire chapter of the *Traité* (Chapter 6: "Everything which thinks, thinks continuously as long as it exists") to defending it.

Descartes was perfectly willing to accept that the mind is always thinking—that there are never any moments when it is not engaged in some mental activity, whether it be perceiving, conceiving, sensing, imagining, dreaming, remembering, and so on. The topic does not arise in any of his treatises, but he does end up endorsing that position in his engagement with others, especially in light of his definition of thought as consciousness. Thus, in a 1642 letter to Gibieuf, Descartes says,

> I believe that the soul is always thinking for the same reason that I believe that light is always shining, even though there are not always eyes looking at it, and that heat is always warm though no one is being warmed by it, and that body, or extended substance, always has extension, and in general that whatever constitutes the nature of a thing always belongs to it as long as it exists. So it would be easier for me to believe that the soul ceased to exist at the times when it is supposed to cease to think than to conceive that it existed without thought.[72]

114   THE GOOD CARTESIAN

We do not have Gibieuf's missive to Descartes, and so do not know exactly how the issue came up. But from Descartes's response it seems that Gibieuf was wondering how such a thesis could be sustained when there are many occasions "when no memory of the thought remains with us afterwards."

This is precisely how Arnauld raises the question in his exchanges with Descartes. In the Fourth Objections, he asks whether, if as Descartes had claimed in the Third Meditation "there is nothing in him, in so far as he is a thinking thing, of which he is not aware," he can explain the fact that an infant is not aware of or remembers the thoughts it is having or had in its mother's womb. Arnauld says, "there are countless similar examples, which I will pass over," but perhaps he has in mind those extended periods in sleep where, once we are awake, we cannot remember having had any thoughts.[73] The young Sorbonne scholar's puzzlement is, at this point, directed not to the idea that the mind is always thinking—a topic which Descartes had not addressed in the *Meditationes*—but only to whether every thought is a conscious event.

Descartes's response to Arnauld's challenge is to point out that while we cannot have any thought in the mind "of which we are not [immediately] aware at the very moment when it is in us"—and he insists that this must apply as much to an infant in the womb as to an adult—we do not always subsequently remember having had the thought, usually because the impression it makes "does not remain in the memory" (which requires corporeal traces being left in the brain).[74] This could lead us to believe, falsely, that there was a moment at which no conscious thinking was taking place, whereas in fact, he says, "I do not doubt that the mind begins to think as soon as it is implanted in the body of an infant." Descartes does not seem here to be committing himself in any strong way to the claim that the mind is always thinking, much less offering an argument for that view. And if he were, his response would beg the question. Proving that the mind is always thinking would seem to require first establishing that the non-remembered thoughts did in fact obtain, or must have obtained, and only then offering a reason why one believes they did not. It will not do simply to say, "It was there, you just don't remember it."

Seven years later, Arnauld, in a new set of objections, some of which have to do with Descartes's account of memory, now pushes Descartes directly on the question of the mind's unceasing thinking activity. "It does not seem necessary that the mind always thinks, even if it is a thinking substance; for it is enough that there is always in it a power of thinking [*vis cogitandi*], just as corporeal substance is always divisible, even if it is not actually divided."[75]

THE CARTESIAN MIND   115

In his response, Descartes moves beyond references to memory and actually provides an a priori argument for his view: "It seems necessary that the mind should always be actually engaged in thinking; because thought constitutes its essence, just as extension constitutes the essence of a body. Thought is not conceived as an attribute which can be present or absent like the division of parts, or motion, in a body."[76] The comparison with extension might seem telling, since any existing body is actually and always extended; something cannot be a body without being extended in three dimensions. But, as Arnauld suggests, why not regard thought, insofar as it is the attribute of a thinking substance, as the power of thinking, a power of generating actual thoughts that may not always be actively doing so?

La Forge devotes a lot more attention than Descartes on this question. Once again, he elaborates both on what Descartes did say and what Descartes could have (and perhaps should have) said. As for what Descartes did say, La Forge refers to what he calls "the strongest objections which can be made against our position," namely, that if the mind were always thinking right from the moment of its union with the body, then we would remember the thoughts we had in our mothers' wombs. He stands by Descartes's response to this objection by laying the blame on the limitations of memory: "We have thousands of thoughts every day, while awake or asleep, of which nevertheless we have no memory."[77] He reserves discussion of this matter, however, to his complex but very Cartesian account of different kinds of memory; we will return to it in the next chapter, in connection with the mind's union with the body.

La Forge also adopts, and expands on, Descartes's analogy between the mind and its thinking and the body and its extension. The key here, for La Forge, is the Cartesian rejection of potentiality, a notion that was central to Aristotelian accounts of nature and activity. "Everything that exists," he insists, "must be something actually and not merely potentially, for, speaking truthfully, that which exists only potentially is nothing." It follows that

> just as we see no body which is not actually (and not just potentially) extended and which must not have some shape at present, and is not simply capable of acquiring the shape one might wish to give it, likewise the nature of the mind consists not simply in having a faculty of thinking; it must also always have some thought as long as it exists, to which it applies itself, which it entertains and which supports its life.[78]

116   THE GOOD CARTESIAN

Here La Forge, who no doubt had read Arnauld's follow-up objections from 1648 (published in French translation in Clerselier's second, 1659 volume of Descartes's correspondence[79]), provides an answer, on Descartes's behalf, to the suggestion that perhaps the mind is only a "power of thinking" that need not always be generating thoughts:

> You will tell me that it is enough for the mind to have the power of thinking even if it does not exercise it in any way. But have you noticed carefully that a body would be nothing if it were merely capable of being extended and were not actually extended? The same applies in the case of the mind which, since it is essentially a thing which thinks, would cease to exist immediately if it stopped thinking for a moment.

The analogy with body remains unsatisfying, however; or, rather, it suggests a way of turning the point back against La Forge (and Descartes) in just the way Arnauld did with his appeal to divisibility. Bodies, after all, are capable of motion, even when they lack motion and are at rest—they have mobility. Why might not the mind, as a faculty of thinking, have the capacity for generating actual thoughts, even when it is "at rest"?

La Forge offers what may be a coherent (if not entirely persuasive) answer to this objection. Assume that the mind is only a bare faculty of thought that is not always thinking. There must, he says, be a reason why a thinking substance is not, at some particular moment, actually thinking; and the reason for that state of affairs must be either (a) the mind is not able to produce a thought at that moment, or (b) the mind does not want to produce a thought at that moment. If (a), then at that moment the mind would lack the power of thinking, which is impossible; if (b), then at the moment that it is wishing not to have a thought it is having a thought, namely, the volition not to have a thought (he notes that "to will or to will not are ways of thinking"). Oddly, given his account of memory, La Forge does not consider the possibility that there might be at that moment some factor distinct from the mind—perhaps the state of the body—preventing the mind from having a thought. If the condition of the body (too weak an impression in the brain) can prevent the mind from remembering something, why cannot some other condition of the body interfere with the exercise of the faculty of thinking and the production of thoughts *tout court*?

La Forge was in good Cartesian company when it came to the topic of the mind's uninterrupted thinking. Régis, for example, uses the analogy with the extension of body to show that the soul does not have only thought in general as an essential attribute but must always have "some particular way of thinking [*quelque façon particuliere de penser*]."[80] Even Arnauld quickly came around.[81] Nor were the Cartesians alone in maintaining this bold thesis. Leibniz, despite his substantial departures from the Cartesian philosophy of mind—he allowed that a large number of the mind's perceptions are not conscious events (what he called *petites perceptions*)—agreed that the mind is always thinking. Not everyone in the century was on board, however. Locke, for one, demurred. While he agreed that the mind is a thinking thing, he rejected the idea that this capacity is always being exercised.[82]

Things are a little more complicated within the Cartesian camp when the question concerns what thoughts belong to the mind through its own essence as thinking substance. All parties agreed that many of the mind's thoughts—sensations, imaginings, and most memories—modify the mind only because it is united with a body. La Forge argued, however, that there are types of ideas that belong to the mind by virtue of its essence alone, independent of its union with a body in a living human being. Such thoughts will belong even to a disembodied mind—the immortal soul, for instance. As we shall see, in this respect he proves to be the better Cartesian than many of his peers.

6

The Union of Mind and Body

Readers of the first edition of Descartes's *Meditationes*, published in Paris by Michel Soly in 1641, must have been disappointed when they got to the end of the treatise. The subtitle of the work promised that in it "are demonstrated the existence of God and the immortality of the soul." The existence of God is well treated, with multiple arguments in both the Third and Fifth Meditations. But nowhere does Descartes explicitly address, much less prove, the immortality of the soul. Descartes does argue that an immaterial mind is "really distinct from my body, and can exist without it,"[1] and this would indeed seem to be a necessary condition for establishing the soul's post-mortem persistence. But immortality per se does not appear as a theme in the *Meditationes* itself.

The theological author(s) of the Second Set of Objections, most likely Father Mersenne, picked up on this lacuna: "You say not one word about the immortality of the human mind. Yet this is something you should have taken special care to prove and demonstrate, to counter those people, themselves unworthy of immortality, who utterly deny and even despise it."[2] Just because the soul is distinct from the body, it does not follow that it is immortal. "What if its nature were limited by the duration of the life of the body, and God had endowed it with just so much strength and existence as to ensure that it came to an end with the death of the body?"

Descartes knew that within the subtitle there was an unfulfilled promise. In his replies to the Second Objections, he notes, "I did provide an adequate proof of the fact that the soul is distinct from every body." He grants, however, that this is not sufficient for proving conclusively the soul's immortality. This is because "I cannot refute what you say" regarding the possibility that God has decreed that "its [the soul's] duration comes to an end simultaneously with the end of the body's life."[3] The reason is that knowledge of what God has or has not decreed cannot come from philosophy but only from revelation. "I do not take it upon myself to try to use the power of human reason to settle any of those matters which depend on the free will of God." The metaphysical dualism has the consequence that the soul is not subject to the decay and decomposition that inevitably affects the material body, and so it is

The Good Cartesian. Steven Nadler, Oxford University Press. © Oxford University Press 2024.
DOI: 10.1093/oso/9780197671719.003.0007

THE UNION OF MIND AND BODY 119

naturally capable of surviving the latter's demise. He thus concludes that "the mind, in so far as it can be known by natural philosophy, is immortal." But it is a different question as to whether the soul is truly immortal. "Absolutely all substances . . . are, by their nature, incorruptible," Descartes says in his prefatory Synopsis of the *Meditationes*, "and cannot ever cease to exist unless they are reduced to nothingness by God's denying his concurrence to them."[4] The only cause for a soul to perish, then, is that God, who created all souls, chose to limit its natural term or to actively destroy it. And that God has *not* so chosen is something that only faith and revelation, not philosophical reasoning, can determine. Descartes makes this same point in a letter to Mersenne from around the same time:

> You say that I have not said a word about the immortality of the soul. You should not be surprised. I could not prove that God could not annihilate the soul, but only that it is by nature entirely distinct from the body, and consequently is not bound by nature to die with it. This is all that is required as a foundation for religion, and is all that I had any intention of proving.[5]

In the second edition of the *Meditationes*, published one year later in Amsterdam by Elzevir, the promissory note about immortality is gone. The subtitle reads only: "in which are demonstrated the existence of God and the distinction between the human soul and the body."

La Forge did not share Descartes's scruples on this matter. Indeed, he is surprised at "those who make [the immortality of the soul] an article of faith rather than a conclusion of their reasoning." Oddly, given Descartes's explicit and repeated concession that he cannot prove immortality through reason alone, La Forge appears not to include him in this class. Perhaps it is because La Forge believes that the Cartesian philosophy, if not its author, does in fact do the job all by itself and without appeal to any revealed truths. "There is no school, ancient or modern, from whose principle this truth follows as necessarily and evidently as from our own." The absolute immortality of the soul, he insists, is "a conclusion which follows infallibly from his [Descartes's] principles," as "a conclusion of [his] reasoning."[6] The key lies just where Descartes should have found it: in the immateriality of the mind and its ontological distinction and independence from the material body. La

120 THE GOOD CARTESIAN

Forge believes that this is ultimately sufficient, when properly examined—and when supplemented by a universal premise about how things in nature can perish, as well as by evident principles about God's nature and *modus operandi*—for proving that the mind/soul is immortal.[7]

La Forge warns that the close and intimate union of mind and body, whereby so many of the mind's states and operations are determined and limited by the constitution of the body, should not mislead us into thinking that the fate itself of the mind is likewise constrained. He knows, however, that, even from a strictly philosophical perspective, a mere ontological distinction from body will not secure the soul's natural immortality. This is where he goes beyond Descartes. No matter how different from the body the soul may be, and while it is true that (a) the body's demise does not by itself imply the end of the soul that was united with it, and (b) immaterial thinking substances are not subject to the kind of decay and disintegration that affects material substances—and even putting aside any divine acts of annihilation—the soul, though a simple substance, might still be subject to some kind of natural breakdown or expiration of its own, albeit different from the kind of disintegration that the body suffers. Arnauld, in the Fourth Set of Objections, raises just this question when he asks "whether [the immortality of the soul] evidently follows from the fact that the soul is distinct from the body." At the very least, he says, "this by no means follows."[8] Something more is needed, as La Forge recognizes. Thus, where Descartes was content simply to say that the soul's distinction from the body means that "it is not bound by nature to die with it"—that the death of the body does not entail the death of the soul—La Forge goes on to argue, still on the basis of the soul's intrinsic nature, for the stronger claim that the soul does not die through any natural means whatsoever, bodily or spiritual.

He begins in a familiar way. As a simple substance, lacking parts, the soul is, in principle, not subject to the kind of decomposition to which bodies, as extended substances with parts, are subject. The soul cannot break down.

> Among things that cease to exist, some are composite and some are simple. Composite things lose their existence when the parts which compose them separate. But since [simple things] can perish only by annihilation, which, like creation, is beyond the power of all creatures, one can be sure that none of the changes which occur in nature is capable of making simple things perish. Therefore, since no one can fail to know, following what we said,

THE UNION OF MIND AND BODY 121

that the mind is simple, immaterial and has no parts, no one can doubt either that it is immortal and incorruptible.[9]

La Forge's assumption here is that *the only natural way* in which things can possibly come to an end is when they decay and fall apart. (He does not argue for this premise but seems to take it as an evident empirical fact.) Simple substances cannot decay and fall apart. Therefore, simple substances cannot naturally come to an end. La Forge thereby closes the loophole in Descartes's argument.

So far, so good. This rules out not just the soul being subject to the same kind of decay as the body suffers, but also any kind of natural expiration peculiar to spiritual substances by which they might die.[10] Still, there is nothing in the considerations for immortality that La Forge derives from the mind's simplicity that either Descartes did not say or is not implied (with the help of the additional premise) by his claims about the mind–body distinction and the soul not having parts.[11] La Forge, with just one additional premise about natural endings, has taken things only a bit further along than where Descartes had left them: we can securely know, via good philosophical reasoning, that the soul is *naturally* immortal.[12] But, again, is it, in fact, truly and absolutely immortal?

There remains the question of what God can or did do. "Someone might say," La Forge continues, "that I fail to prove that the Author who created these kinds of substances could not make them perish."[13] How can we be sure that God has not, in fact, set a term limit for the existence of the soul and decreed that it comes to an end either when the body dies or at some later time? After all, everything that exists exists by the grace of God's will.

This is where La Forge really strikes out on his own, going where Descartes himself would not go, but, he suggests, where Descartes certainly *could* have gone (and even *did* go in another context, his physics). La Forge argues, first, on roughly empirical and textual grounds, that there is no indication that God has decreed an end to the soul's life. "We see nothing which could make us suspect that he has such a will." No example of spiritual annihilation has ever been observed in nature. (We can pass over the fact that it is not clear what such an event would look like and how we would recognize it). And revelation certainly has not indicated any choice on God's part to cause or allow souls, or any substances for that matter, to go out of existence; on the contrary, "all religions which refer their origin to some divine revelation claim that He confirmed the contrary."[14]

122 THE GOOD CARTESIAN

But La Forge also offers an a priori argument against the divine annihilation of the soul. God, he says, is a perfect being, and thus his will is immutable. What this means is that "he will never annihilate the things which he has once created," since that would involve a change in God's mind, which in turn would imply a change in God's eternal nature, which is absurd. Therefore, God would never annihilate any human soul; therefore, once created, its everlastingness is preserved.[15] Why God could not have decreed, with an immutable will, that souls will exist only for a limited period of time is not a point that La Forge considers.

What is crucial here is a distinction between annihilation and destruction (or, better, deconstruction), which is just the flip side of a distinction (adopted by some Cartesians) between creation and generation.[16] Obviously, Scripture is full of stories in which God destroys something: a tower, a city, a population, almost all living creatures. In cases of destruction, organized parcels of matter are simply undone and their constitutive parts rearranged or dispersed. None of these destructive acts involve annihilation, a complete ceasing-to-be, which would involve the total elimination of a substance, whether extended substance or thinking substance. With annihilation, the quantity of matter or number of souls in the universe would be reduced, and this is just what the immutability of God will not allow.

In principle, there are two distinct questions here. It is one thing to claim that God, even if he should He want to, could never annihilate a material or immaterial substance. It is another thing to claim that God could never *want* to annihilate a substance. La Forge, it seems, opts only for the second position: God's immutability would never allow him to be of a mind to eliminate a created substance. The topic of the annihilation of substance is also addressed by a number of other Cartesians in the period, and some of them might appear to take the first, stronger position. In an early, unpublished treatise which, in some copies, bears the title *Traité de l'indéfectibilité des substances*, probably composed around 1649, Desgabets argues that substances, once created, "can in no way be annihilated, not even as one ordinarily says by the omnipotence of God."[17] However, it may be that this is misleading, and that the reason why God cannot destroy a substance—why substances are "indefectible"—has nothing to do with any *intrinsic* permanence of substance but with the permanence of God's will and the contradiction of having an eternal (that is, atemporal) God both will and not will that something exist.[18]

For Desgabets and others, the question of the indefectibility of substances is bound up with a host of issues, including the relationship between

THE UNION OF MIND AND BODY   123

mathematics and physics, the creation of the eternal truths and Eucharistic transubstantiation. Desgabets is well aware that he thereby goes beyond anything Descartes would allow. He says, however, that he is only amending Descartes—in light of Descartes's own account of divine omnipotence—and that Descartes (who did assert in the Synopsis that substances "are, by their nature, incorruptible") would have agreed with him that indefectibility is the best way to secure the immortality of the soul.[19]

What La Forge offers, then, even with his somewhat weaker theological principle, is a proof of the immortality of the soul based on reason—precisely what Descartes said could not be done. La Forge claims that everything he says here is but an extension of what Descartes does in his physics, where he uses divine immutability in the *Principia philosophiae* to establish his conservation principle and, by extension, other general laws of nature.[20] Just as an immutable God must preserve the same quantity of matter and motion in the universe that he created at the beginning, so (La Forge concludes) God will preserve the same number of souls that he has created and put in bodies.

There remains the question as to what this immortal soul, separated from the body, does or can do. Will it retain all the faculties that it had in this life? Or will it necessarily undergo the loss of some of its powers and operations? La Forge is clear that, like an embodied mind, the immortal mind will always be thinking. Such is its eternal fate as a substance whose essence is thought. But what about sensation? Imagination? Memory? In order to address these questions, we need first to examine what exactly *is* the nature of the mind's union with the body and what powers this confers on it.[21]

*

Descartes's view—or, rather, views—on the nature of the union of mind and body are a bit of a knot that generations of scholars have worked hard to untie.[22] His statements on the merger between two such metaphysically disparate substances in a human being, in various works (and sometimes within the same work), can appear to be inconsistent. Rather than try to cover this well-worn ground yet again, I will restrict my discussion to some salient features of Descartes's account that are relevant for understanding La Forge's approach to the problem.

One thing is perfectly clear, as Descartes reminds us several times: the mind's union with the body is not like the way in which a human being unites himself with, by making use of, some external object, like a tool or

124 THE GOOD CARTESIAN

instrument. His favorite and most well-known analogy on this point, which can be found in Aristotle, concerns a sailor's relationship to his ship.[23] In the Sixth Meditation, after showing that "there is nothing that my own nature teaches me more vividly than that I have a body," and that the sensations he experiences—such as pain, hunger, and thirst—indicate something about the condition and needs of that body, he insists,

> Nature also teaches me, by these sensations of pain, hunger, thirst and so on, that I am not merely present in my body as a sailor is present in a ship, but that I am very closely joined and, as it were, intermingled with it, so that I and the body form a unit. If this were not so, I, who am nothing but a thinking thing, would not feel pain when the body was hurt, but would perceive the damage purely by the intellect, just as a sailor perceives by sight if anything in his ship is broken.[24]

He had already drawn on this metaphor a few years earlier, in the *Discours de la méthode*:

> It is not sufficient for [the rational soul] to be lodged in the human body like a helmsman in his ship, except perhaps to move its limbs, but that it must be more closely joined and united with the body in order to have, besides this power of movement, feelings and appetites like ours and so constitute a real man.[25]

Descartes's point is that the union of mind and body is more intimate than the sailor's association with his ship. When something happens to the ship, the sailor can know it only by way of some intervening cognitive state— say, a perceptual belief about the condition of his vessel's mast. The mind's awareness of what is happening in its body, however, is more direct; it is not mediated by some propositional understanding. The latter may be the way in which God or angels perceive what is happening in bodies, especially those upon which they act, but therein lies the difference between the relationship these disembodied minds have to bodies and that of the embodied human mind. Sensations such as pleasure and pain, Descartes notes, "are not pure thoughts of a mind distinct from a body, but confused perceptions of a mind really united to a body. For if an angel were in a human body, he would not have sensations as we do, but would simply perceive the motions which are caused by external objects, and in this way would differ from a real man."[26]

THE UNION OF MIND AND BODY   125

While this may tell us what the mind–body union is not, it does little to clarify what precisely the union is. And this is something that Descartes has a bit of trouble with. Indeed, he tells Princess Elisabeth that we should not try to understand the union of mind and body through the clear and distinct "primitive notions" that we have of the mind and of the body; rather, there is a third, separate primitive notion of their union, but it does not, like the others, have its source in the "pure intellect."

> We have for the body in particular only the notion of extension, from which follow those of figure and motion; for the soul alone we only have the notion of thought, in which are comprised the perceptions of the under-standing and the inclinations of the will; finally, for the mind and body to-gether we have only the notion of their union, on which depends the notion of the force that the soul has to move the body, and of the body to act on the soul, causing its sensations and passions.[27]

He later warns Elisabeth that "what belongs to the union of the soul and the body is known only obscurely by the intellect alone or even by the intellect aided by the imagination, but it is known very clearly by the senses."[28]

He certainly does not mean to imply that the senses can provide us with as clear and distinct an understanding of that union as the intellect can provide separately of the soul and the body. Still, Descartes does his best to explain, for Elisabeth and others, how he understands mind–body union. Margaret Wilson famously identified what she considered two distinct accounts of union that she found in Descartes. What she called the "Natural Institution" theory is a fairly reductive account of the union of mind and body and consists only in an exclusive and regular causal relationship between the two substances. Moreover, the locus of that interaction is the brain—more precisely, the pineal gland. Thus, Descartes notes in the Sixth Meditation that

> the mind is not immediately affected by all parts of the body, but only by the brain, or perhaps just by one small part of the brain, namely the part which is said to contain the "common sense." Every time this part of the brain is in a given state, it presents the same signals to the mind, even though the other parts of the body may be in a different condition at the time.

The origin of the relationship does not lie in the nature of either the mind or the body. In keeping with the metaphysical dualism, there is no conceivable

126   THE GOOD CARTESIAN

natural relation between a mental state and a bodily state. Nothing about a mental state indicates that it should follow or be followed by this or that motion in the body. Rather, from a metaphysical standpoint the relationship is arbitrary and was established only by the providential will of God.

> It is true that God could have made the nature of man such that this particular motion in the brain indicated something else to the mind; it might, for example, have made the mind aware of the actual motion occurring in the brain, or in the foot, or in any of the intermediate regions; or it might have indicated something else entirely. But there is nothing else which would have been so conducive to the continued well-being of the body.[29]

Wilson finds this strictly causal account of union also in the *Principia philosophiae*, where Descartes explains that "the human soul, while informing the entire body, nevertheless has its principal seat in the brain; it is here alone that the soul not only understands and imagines but also has sensory awareness."[30] On this view, then, to say that mind A is united to body B and not to body C is only to say that certain changes in A are directly and immediately correlated with certain changes in B (that is, in the pineal gland in the brain in B) but not with any changes in C, and that this divinely instituted reciprocal correspondence between some of the states of A and some of the states of B is all there is to their union.

However, Wilson suggests as well that Descartes departs from this account when he claims, in the Sixth Meditation, that the mind is "intermingled [*permixtum*]" with the body and refers to "the union and, as it were, intermingling of the mind with the body."[31] What she calls the "Coextension" view is, she insists, inconsistent with the Natural Institution view insofar as it suggests that the union of mind and body is more than just a causal relationship between the two substances and amounts to a kind of extension of the mind *throughout* the body. In the Sixth Replies, Descartes encourages us to think of the mind's extension in the body along the lines of the (false) Scholastic conception of the way in which gravity is supposed to work. On this account, which Descartes says his younger, less sophisticated self once accepted, gravity is "scattered throughout the whole body that is heavy" and, though "remaining coextensive with the heavy body, could exercise all its force in any one part of the body." This, he says "is exactly the way in which I now understand the mind to be coextensive with the body—the whole mind in the whole body and the whole mind in any one of its parts."[32]

THE UNION OF MIND AND BODY   127

It is not entirely clear that the two models of mind–body union that Wilson finds in Descartes's texts are, in fact, inconsistent, or even that they are distinct. Since the extension of the mind in the body cannot be identical to the spatial way in which the material body is literally extended,[33] what Descartes has in mind here is not an "extension of substance [*extensio substantiae*]" but merely an "extension of power [*extensio potentiae*]," whereby the mind ultimately (if not directly) affects and is affected by parts throughout the whole body rather than just an isolated gland in the brain.[34] Descartes can thus describe the mind's power as being coextensive throughout the whole body in that all the parts of the body are potential causes of and (to a more limited extent) responsive to mental states: the sense organs (for sensory perceptions); the internal organs (for feelings of and appetites from thirst, hunger, aches and pains, etc.); even the skeletal, circulatory and nervous systems can be the occasion for some sensory event in the mind. And the mind through its volitions can move, if not all parts of its body, then very many of them. This is quite consistent with the claim that this extension of the mind's power, all of this interaction, is mediated by—must run through—states of the brain and pineal gland. Sensory states and appetites related to all those exterior and interior parts of the body arise only when motions are communicated through the nerves to the brain and lead to certain motions in the gland. The movement of even the most distal parts of the body—the toes, for example— have their start in the motion of the gland caused by the mind. This reading seems to work quite nicely with a set of passages from *Les Passions de l'âme*. Descartes notes, first, that "the soul is really joined to the whole body, and we cannot properly say that it exists in any one part of the body to the exclusion of the others." However, he adds in the next article that "we need to recognize also that although the soul is joined to the whole body, nevertheless there is a certain part of the body where it exercises its functions more particularly than in all the others," namely, the brain. From "the small gland located in the middle of the brain," the soul "radiates through the rest of the body by means of the animal spirits, the nerves, and even the blood."[35]

It is not my goal here to argue that this reading can make sense of all of Descartes's statements on mind–body union in his treatises and his correspondence. Rather than add to the voluminous literature on Descartes on mind–body union, I will focus on what I take to be the real question raised by these different passages: Does the union between mind and body in a human being consist solely in that divinely ordained reciprocal correlation between the states of one substance and the states of the other substance?

128   THE GOOD CARTESIAN

Or is that correlation grounded in some more fundamental kind of union? Is there nothing to mind–body union other than an exclusive causal relationship; or is there some deeper, unifying foundation that allows for the causal relationship between this particular mind and this particular body but not some other particular body? As Wilson explains the problem, is the "intermingling" of mind and body to be understood as "nothing but the arbitrarily established disposition of this mind to experience certain types of sensations on the occasion of certain changes in this body, and to refer to these sensations to (parts of this body)"? Or is it the case that "one has sensations of a certain sort, in response to changes in a certain body, *because* one its united with that body—not that having sensations of certain sort, etc., is what *it is* to be united to that body"?[36] After all, Descartes does say that "these sensations of hunger, thirst, pain and so on are nothing but confused modes of thinking which *arise from the union* and, as it were, intermingling of the mind with the body," and this suggests that mind–body union is something distinct from and the foundation for the correlations between mental states and bodily (brain) states.[37]

*

La Forge has definitely made up his mind on this set of questions. There is no union prior to or independent of the reciprocal dependence between some states of the mind and some states of the body. He also has no problem in explaining how to reconcile talk of the mind's being coextensive or united with the whole body with its having its "principal seat" in the brain. Nor is there any reason to think that, in his account of mind–body union, he does not take himself to be speaking faithfully on behalf of Descartes.

Undervaluing the "miracle" of union and failing to understand its true nature, La Forge warns, can lead to a host of errors, including materialism (whereby one attributes extension to the soul in order to explain its presence to the body) and Scholastic mysteries (such as substantial forms and real qualities). Echoing Descartes's appeal to the distinction between three different "primitive notions"—one for mind, one for body, one for body–mind union—La Forge insists, first, that the union of mind and body should not be conceived in the terms appropriate for understanding the union of two bodies. Local presence has no role to play here, since unextended mind cannot literally be present to and in contact with a body. Neither is it possible to think of mind–body union as being like the union of two minds, where

THE UNION OF MIND AND BODY   129

mutual love binds one mind to another. Finally, deploying (and expanding upon) Descartes's favored metaphor, La Forge says, several times, that it is not like the instrumental relationship between a sailor and his boat, or a rider and his horse.

> All other kinds of union that we can conceive, such as a pilot with his ship, a rider with their horse, ourselves with bodies other than our own, and other similar kinds of union, are very different from this. For, first, a pilot is usually united with their ship voluntarily. Second, they know clearly whatever good or damage happens to it. Third, the joy or sadness which they experience as a result is very different from the feeling of hunger, thirst, pain or tickling which the human mind has on the occasion of its body.[38]

He adds that, unlike the sailor or the equestrian, the soul's ability to move a part of the body simply by willing that it move is not mediated by any "distinct knowledge" of what has to be done, instrumentally and anatomically, to move that part.[39]

La Forge suggests that a lot of the trouble disappears if one thinks of the union as being not between an *unextended* substance and an extended substance, which on the face of it looks highly problematic if not impossible, but between a *thinking* substance and an extended substance. After all, what is essential to the mind is not its lack of extension but its thought.

Once the misconceptions about what *genus* of union is at issue have been cleared away, one can turn to the state of the union and the mechanism by which it is realized. La Forge rejects an idea that he attributes to certain unnamed "followers of Descartes," whereby there is "a certain mode which they call a union, which serves as some kind of link [*lien*] or cement to join the two substances."[40] There is no third item—whether itself a substance or a mode of a substance—that, like Leibniz's *vinculum substantiale*, acts as a bonding agent between the two substances.[41]

La Forge also rejects any kind of "substantial union" between mind and body. No new substance comes about as a result of their relationship. Here La Forge sets himself apart from Descartes's problematic disciple Regius, whose tortured views on mind–body union are part of what led to the falling out with his mentor. He also, it seems, sets himself apart from Descartes himself. In the early 1640s, Descartes became engaged in a rancorous dispute with Gisbertus Voetius, at the University of Utrecht. One of the firebrand rector's many concerns was that the Cartesian philosophy, by discarding the

130 THE GOOD CARTESIAN

Aristotelian-Scholastic view that the soul was the substantial form of the body, had so distinguished the mind from the body that the basic unity of the human being was undermined, taking with it some important doctrines of Calvinist theology. One of Regius's students, in fact, had defended a thesis in which he argued that in the human being mind and body enjoy only an "accidental union [*unum per accidens*]." This troubled Descartes, who saw, quite rightly, that it could raise problems with theologians. He tells Regius that "in your theses you say that a human being is an *ens per accidens*. You could scarcely have said anything more objectionable and provocative"[42]—objectionable, that is, to orthodox Reformed preachers. He thus counseled Regius to at least modify his language and confirm that the mind and a body united in a human being constitute an *ens* per se, a being in its own right. He even recommended that Regius adopt Scholastic usage and say that "the mind is united in a real and substantial manner to the body," that mind and body are connected "by a true mode of union, as everyone agrees though nobody explains what this amounts to, and so you need not do so either."[43]

His somewhat cynical advice to Regius in a polemical context aside, did Descartes see the human being, as a union of mind and body, as a substance in its own right? This point has been up for debate, with some scholars arguing that mind–body union in Descartes should be read hylomorphically: the human being is a composite substance with the soul as the substantial form of the body.[44] Others have gone so far as to suggest, albeit with some reservations, that Descartes is not a dualist but a "trialist," with the human being constituting a kind of third substance.[45] With La Forge, however, there is no ambiguity. The mind–body union is *not* a substantial union.

The composite of these two substances that is a human being certainly does not constitute a simple/singular substance. Given the radical difference in nature between thought and extension, and the fact that the concept of one is not included in the concept of the other,

> it is impossible that they could occur in one and the same subject. That would be the same as saying that one and the same subject had two different natures, which is something that cannot be said without contradiction about a noncomposite, simple subject.[46]

La Forge warns us "not to convince ourselves that this union, however close it may be, transforms these two substances into a simple substance and that the mind thereby becomes material or the body is spiritualized."[47]

THE UNION OF MIND AND BODY 131

Moreover, although La Forge does speak of the mind–body union as a composite, he refrains from calling it a composite *substance*, presumably because it lacks the ontological integrity—the unity and indivisibility—proper to substance. Mind and body "both remain after their union what they were before it, and they are no less two substances which retain everything which distinguished them from each other from the point of view of their absolute being." La Forge grants that union does introduce a new relational aspect to each substance, and a kind of unity results. "Every kind of union implies some kind of relation, resemblance or dependence by means of which we consider two things as in some sense constituting only one [*n'en faisant qu'une d'une certaine façon*]."[48] But the unity in question here is not that of a substance at all but of a "composite subject [*sujet composé*]." It is, as we shall see, a relational or functional unity, not a substantial one.

Ruling out any kind of substantiality to the mind–body union is one way in which La Forge clarifies—or, depending on how one reads Descartes, goes beyond—the Cartesian view on the relationship between the two substances in a human being. But some of Descartes's remarks, as we have seen, do suggest that mind–body union, whatever it may be, *and substantive or not*, is something antecedent to, and grounding of, the reciprocal causal relationship between mental states and bodily states. And this, too, is a thesis that La Forge explicitly rejects. He adopts the more reductive account of mind–body union—not unlike what Wilson calls the Natural Institution view—that consists only in a reciprocal dependence of modes or states, and absolutely nothing more.

La Forge begins his explanation by noting that any unifying relation between two substances, no matter what their respective kinds, must involve, at the very least, a reciprocity of action and passion. Without one subject serving as an agent and another subject serving as a patient, there can be no joining together. For two bodies, this causal reciprocity is made possible by proximity or contact, "which makes them capable of acting and being acted on while one is dependent on the other"; for two minds, the action/passion relation is grounded in love (the lover is active, the beloved passive). For a mind and a body, however, it seems that the reciprocal agency is all there is to the union, with each member of the relationship, agent and patient, exercising or acquiring its own proper modes, thoughts in the case of the mind and motion in the case of the body:

> We should say that a body and a mind are united when some movements of the first depend on thoughts of the second and, reciprocally, some thoughts

132   THE GOOD CARTESIAN

of the second depend on movements of the first, whether the cause of this dependence comes from the will of the mind which is united or derives from another will which is superior to its own. . . .

The union of a mind and body consists in a mutual and reciprocal dependence of thoughts of one of them on the movements of the other, and in the mutual interaction of their actions and passions.[49]

If the thoughts of a mind and the motions of a body do regularly exhibit this mutual dependence, then that mind and that body are as united as they can be. It need not be *all* thoughts of the mind and *all* motions of the body which are so reciprocal; in fact, such comprehensive dependency would undermine the ontological independence of each as a substance, at least for La Forge. "All the thoughts of the mind are not dependent on movements of the body, nor do all the movements of the body depend on thoughts of the mind."[50] (As we shall see, this is an important point on which La Forge and other Cartesians disagree, and on which he more closely follows Descartes.) But there must be at least a sufficient degree of reciprocal dependence, across a range of thoughts and motions, to identify this particular mind as united to this particular body, without threatening their independence as substances distinct in number and in nature. And the union comes to an end when this active/ passive reciprocity is at an end.

There are some thoughts of the mind and some movements of the body which so depend on each other that it is absolutely impossible for one to occur without the other and thus the union is as close as their natures could permit. . . . Just as the union of two minds will last as long as their love and that of two bodies does not cease until they cease being close together, likewise, the union of mind and body will not terminate until he who united them—that is, he who made the movements of one depend on the thoughts of the other—changes his mind, or until the body is no longer capable of producing the movements to which the thoughts of the mind are united.[51]

Thus, to say that mind A is united to body B and not to body C is only to say that there is a reciprocal dependence of thoughts in A with motions in B but not with motions in C. There is nothing more to the union than this perspicuous interactive relationship that anyone can experience for themselves. In particular, the reciprocity is not grounded in some antecedent relationship, such as an opaque and inexplicable "mind–body union." La Forge considers

THE UNION OF MIND AND BODY   133

the objection that "this mutual dependence and interaction between mind and body presupposes that they are already united, since it is impossible for the mind to have any thought on the occasion of its body if it is not already in the body and joined to it." His response is straightforward:

It is not necessary for [the mind] to be already in the body before it acts in it. For the mind considered in itself is not properly speaking in any place, or if one can say that it is in some place it is there only in virtue of its operation. But since its existence does not precede its operation in time, it is not neces-sary that it be in a body before it operates there.[52]

One question that arises at this point is whether La Forge means to say that the mind is united to the body *only* when such reciprocal action and passion is actually taking place. That would be an odd and counterintuitive position to take, and it is clearly not his. The union consists not in the occasional, oc-current acts of causal dependence but in tendencies or capacities for such occasions. As we see in one of the passages above, the union comes to an end not when there is no actual interactive production of modes but only when a certain capacity is gone—when the body "is no longer capable [*ne sera plus capable*] of producing the movements to which the thoughts of the mind are united." In an another passage, La Forge responds to the possible objection that if the union of body and mind is supposed to consist in the reciprocal dependence of some of their modes, then "as soon as the acts of the mind and body cease to concur and co-operate, as one could believe happens in leth-argy, ecstasy or very deep meditation, one would have to say that the mind is separated from the body." In reply, he says, "I do not locate the essence of the union of these two substances in the actual concurrence and interaction of their operations (although this is the view of the learned Clauberg), but in the reciprocal dependence of one on the other which does not cease to exist even when the actual interaction is interrupted for a short time," that is, "as long as the body is not incapable of having the movements with which the thoughts of the mind are immediately linked."[53] It is the general tendency of the states of this mind and the states of this body to be causally related that constitutes their union.

It is worth noting that La Forge's critical reference here to Clauberg, whereby he distances himself from the German thinker, is puzzling insofar as their views on union are quite similar. In 1664, the same year that Clerselier published Descartes's *Traité de l'homme* with La Forge's commentary,

134   THE GOOD CARTESIAN

Clauberg's *Corporis et animae in homine conjunctio* (The Union of Mind and Body in the Human Being) appeared. The goal of this short work, with which La Forge was familiar, is to understand how two such "heterogenous beings" are "able to be joined . . . so that they compose one animal, which we call a human being." Clauberg explains that the union consists not in anything that pertains to or follows from the essence of the two substances, but only "in something relational," namely, nothing more than the fact that "certain thoughts in the mind follow from certain motions in the body, or the way in which the motions of the [animal] spirits depend on the soul's will."[54] Perhaps it is all a matter of how La Forge is reading Chapter IX of Clauberg's treatise (the chapter is titled "This union consists not in the absolute substance of mind and body, but in the relative actions and passions of both [*Conjuntionem hanc non in mentis & corporis absoluta substantia, sed in relativis utriusque actionibus passionibusque consistere*]"), especially article 13, where Clauberg says that what is required for the relation of mind and body is that "something reaches from the one to the other or from this one to that one, or that one thing is given away to the other thing, or accepts something from the other [*aliquid ab illo ad hanc, vel ab hac ad ilud perveniat, seu, ut altera res alteri alquid largiatur, vel ab altera quid accipiat*]."[55] Or is La Forge, rarely one to promote his own originality, nonetheless trying to find a way to distinguish himself from someone—another Cartesian—who possibly influenced him on this subject?

*

The deeper question, of course, is what accounts for this ongoing tendency in mind and body to mutually act/react. La Forge has mentioned that, since the relationship is not grounded in the nature of either substance, its cause must be either "the will of the mind which is united [to the body] or derives from another will which is superior to its own." That it is not the will of the mind that belongs to the union is perfectly clear from everyday experience.

> It is certain that the human mind does not choose its body, nor the movements, the time, or which of its thoughts should be joined to a body; nor can it leave the body, change it, or associate another with it, nor change anything in the way bodies usually act on one another. Nor can it avoid perceiving objects which act on the senses strongly enough to carry the repercussions of their impact as far as the seat of the mind, nor perceive

THE UNION OF MIND AND BODY 135

them in a different way. Nor can the will avoid being moved by the thoughts which arise in the mind on the occasion of the body.[56]

This leaves only "the will of the Creator" whose "wisdom was so great that He arranged that our mind had no cause to complain about this union." God, that is, has "infused"[57] a mind into a body by establishing that there should be the regular correlations between motions in that body and thoughts in that mind.

The divine role here is to be understood at both the token level and the type level. It is one thing to ask why do the states of this body correlate with the states of this mind? But it is another thing to ask why do bodily states of a certain kind generally give rise to or follow from mental states of a certain kind? Now God unites a particular mind and a particular body by determining that there will be a "reciprocal, universal, immediate, stable, and involuntary" correlation between the token modes of the one and the token modes of the other. But the regularities constituting this particular union are simply an instantiation of a more general determination made by God that certain types of mental states will correlate with certain types of bodily motions. God does not just unite this mind with this (rather than some other) body by establishing that the states of one will be determined by the states of the other. He also establishes general laws of mind–body union—La Forge calls these "the articles of the union of mind and body"—such that when bodies of a certain type have motions of a certain type, there will be certain kinds of thoughts in minds, and vice versa. "God is the total and proximate cause of the union of the thoughts which are found united with the same movements in all human beings."[58] Thus, one such law specifies that "every particular configuration of the flow [of the animal spirits] when they come to leave the [pineal] gland in an unaccustomed way will be accompanied by a certain idea which will cause the mind to have a certain thought." Another law states that "each of these configurations will be joined naturally to only one idea or one thought which will always accompany it."[59]

As we have seen, some bodily motions do not give rise to any perceptions or answer to any acts of will in the mind, while others do. What regularities do exist in all human beings—for example, that a sensation of pain in the mind follows from the gland being moved in such and such a way—and what do not is an expression of divine providence. God has chosen an arrangement that "is most suitable for the implementation of his plans," one that also serves generally, if not always, for the well-being of both body and mind.

136 THE GOOD CARTESIAN

It is typically to our benefit that when some limb or organ is affected with motions that damage it we immediately feel a sensation of pain (as opposed to, say, having a propositional belief about the state of the body). When there is no real damage, or even no limb, but the nerves (and thus the gland) are agitated in the way they would be if there were such trauma, there will be no exception to the providential laws of mind–body union and the mind should still feel the appropriate sensation.

It is important to recognize, however, that this divine role in establishing mind–body union does not by itself commit La Forge to an occasionalist account of mind–body relations. God's uniting of a mind and a body in the way in which La Forge describes could, in principle, amount to granting to the substances, in their natures, real and highly determinate efficacious powers to cause in each other the appropriate modes (according to the relevant laws). Or it could mean that God arranged things so that the states of a substance unfold through its own intrinsic force but in correlation with how things are independently unfolding in the other substance, à la Leibnizian preestablished harmony. I return to this point in subsequent chapters.

*

For such a tiny piece of anatomy, the pineal gland does a remarkable amount of work in the (Cartesian) human being. Not only does it play an active and receptive role in the mechanical movements of the body "machine"—regardless of whether there is a soul united with the body—but as the "principal seat of the soul" in the center of the brain it is responsible for translating the mind's volitions into the body's voluntary movements and for serving as the material terminus of the externally and internally caused bodily affects which occasion sensory ideas in the mind. The pineal gland, one might say, punches well above its weight.

Descartes does not have much to say about the pineal gland in the *Meditationes*. He notes only that "the mind is not immediately affected by all parts of the body, but only by the brain, or perhaps just by one small part of the brain, namely the part which is said to contain the 'common' sense. Every time this part of the brain is in a given state, it presents the same signals to the mind."[60] In a letter to Mersenne from around the same time, he calls this "very mobile part of the brain" that is the "seat of the common sense" the *conarion*, making it clear by using this antiquated term that he is referring to the pineal gland. As we have seen, Descartes is more forthcoming in the *Traité de l'homme* and, especially, *Les Passions de l'âme*. In those texts, he explains that when the body is considered as simply a living organism engaged in automatic and instinctive behavior—whether it is the circulatory, respiratory, and other involuntary internal processes that keep the body functioning or the unthinking, reactive kind of behavior to external stimuli that the human body has in common with the bodies of non-human animals—the animal spirits that rise to the gland from the heart through arteries are directed by the gland from its pores into the openings of the nerve channels on the interior surface of the brain.

When there is a soul united with the body, this activity of the pineal gland, working as a kind of spout for the animal spirits, is the locus of a two-way intercourse.

> The small gland which is the principal seat of the soul is suspended within the cavities containing these [animal] spirits, so that it can be moved by them in as many different ways as there are perceptible differences in the objects. But it can also be moved in various different ways by the soul, whose nature is such that it receives as many different impressions—that is, it has as many different perceptions as there occur different movements in this gland. And conversely, the mechanism of our body is so constructed that simply by this gland's being moved in any way by the soul or by any other cause, it drives the surrounding spirits towards the pores of the brain, which direct them through the nerves to the muscles; and in this way the gland makes the spirits move the limbs.[61]

On the occasion of sensory stimulation, the spirits depart from the gland in a certain pattern, reflecting the pattern of the pores on the brain's inner lining into which they flow as these have been opened by the nerves connected to the sense organs. The pattern of the departing spirits leave an isomorphic material impression, a kind of image, on the gland's own surface and cause the gland to move in a particular way. This motion in the gland, in turn, is the occasion for the mind to give rise to a certain sensory idea or passion connected "by nature" with the way in which the body has been affected by the external object. For example, discussing the feeling of fear experienced on the occasion of the sight of a frightful object—an object, that is, whose motive effect on the optic nerve, when transferred to the brain, so agitates a set of the brain's pores to open—Descartes notes that "merely by entering into these pores, the spirits produce in the gland a particular movement which is ordained by nature to make the soul feel this passion."[62]

138 THE GOOD CARTESIAN

Conversely, when the mind wants the body to move in a certain way, whether on a small scale (for example, turning the eyes to the left or right) or in a larger way (moving a limb or walking in this or that direction), the volition in the soul causes a particular motion in the pineal gland which forces the spirits to depart the gland toward one set of nerve openings in the brain's lining and, ultimately, to the muscles responsible for the desired movement.

> The activity of the soul consists entirely in the fact that simply by willing something it brings it about that the little gland to which it is closely joined moves in the manner required to produce the effect corresponding to this volition.... When we want to fix our attention for some time on some particular object, this volition keeps the gland leaning in one particular direction during that time. And when we want to walk or move our body in some other way, this volition makes the gland drive the spirits to the muscles which serve to bring about this effect.[63]

I will return in a later chapter to the question of what exactly is the nature of the causal relationship between mind and body: Is it true efficient causation, preestablished harmony, or occasionalism? For now, the salient point is that for Descartes, the pineal gland, and in particular its role in directing the animal spirits that flow through its pores and thereby leave an image-pattern on its surface, is the primary and proximate locus for the mind's interaction with the body, whether it is a matter of passively experiencing sensations or actively initiating voluntary bodily movements, or, as we shall see, memory and imagination.[64]

Descartes never really provides empirical verification of the role the pineal gland is supposed to play in the human being's cognitive, volitional, and sensory life. When he mentions the gland and its relationship to the mind in the Sixth Meditation, he offers no argument for his account, saying only that "this is established by countless observations, which there is no need to review here."[65] How one might "observe" the gland's interaction with the mind is a bit perplexing, since neither the mind nor the animal spirits are something one can see. Even the tiny gland itself is hard to find, as he confesses to Mersenne in a letter of May 1640: "I found it impossible to recognize it, even though I looked very thoroughly, and knew well where it should be."[66]

The "argument," such as it is, that he offers in the Passions and his correspondence relies mainly on the location of the gland in the center of the brain, its uniqueness, and the fact that it is, if not an absolutely simple thing

THE UNION OF MIND AND BODY   139

(because it is an extended body), a unified whole without functionally different parts.

All the other parts of the brain, Descartes says, are double, and so they could not serve as the *sensus communis* where the multifarious data of the senses are united.

> Apart from this gland, there cannot be any other place in the whole body where the soul directly exercises its functions. I am convinced of this by the observation that all the other parts of the brain are double, as also are all the organs of our external senses. . . . But in so far as we have only one simple thought about a given object at any one time, there must necessarily be some place where the two images coming through the two eyes, or the two impressions coming from a single object through the double organs of any other sense, can come together in a single image or impression before reaching the soul, so that they do not present to it two objects instead of one.[67]

In a letter to Mersenne in which he responds to an objection from the anatomist Christophe Villiers, who had insisted that the soul can indeed make use of parts of the brain that are double, Descartes says that "to utilize a thing is not the same as to be immediately joined or united to it, and since our soul is not double, but single and indivisible, it seems to me that the part of the body to which it is most immediately joined should also be single and not divided into a part of similar parts. I cannot find such a part in the whole brain except this gland."[68]

We have seen how La Forge is fully committed to the pineal gland theory in its organic role of the body-machine. But he is no less steadfast in his account of the gland's role in human psychology. He does not regard the theory as "absolutely certain," but he is "certain that no other part could be found in the whole brain which satisfies all the conditions for being the [principal seat of the soul]," and grants that it is at least "the most probable and intelligible hypothesis . . . there is no theory which explains all these things as clearly as ours and in which there are not more serious difficulties."[69]

What are those conditions that the pineal gland theory satisfies so well?[70] First, the soul must have its "seat" in some part of the body that cannot move without the soul being affected; and there are many parts of the body whose motion has no impact whatsoever on the mind and is independent of the will. (Again, how one would verify empirically that it is the motion of the

140 THE GOOD CARTESIAN

gland that affects the mind is unclear.) Second, the "seat" must be located somewhere accessible to the nerves, since "we cannot doubt" that the only way we perceive things is when the nerve fibers are agitated. Third, it is clear from such things as paralysis, apoplexy, lethargy, "and a thousand other occurrences" that unless that agitation of the nerves is carried as far as the brain and leaves an impression there, there is no thought or feeling in the mind; and that the only way the soul can move the body is by making the animal spirits descend from the brain. Therefore, the seat of the soul must be either the brain itself or some part within it. That it is not the entire brain follows, fourth, from the fact so much of the brain (mainly its folds) is "the organ of memory," and so if the soul were joined "immediately and closely with the whole brain, it would have to have [the memory traces] almost continuously present before it and would have to think about all the objects which it is capable of remembering all the time," which is clearly not the case.

So the only viable candidate must be some part of the brain, but which part? The fifth condition is that it be a part of the brain from which the animal spirits flow, since any volition to move the body and any impression that an external object makes on the body lead ultimately, through the nerves, to those spirits being directed to the muscles that will move the appropriate bodily limb—for example, when we see something dangerous and flee. The sixth and final condition is that "this part be simple and unique," and here La Forge reprises Descartes's reasoning.

> Since all the organs of sensation are duplicated, there is no reason why the soul would not perceive two objects instead of one when some object makes an impression on both organs of the same sense simultaneously, unless these two impressions were carried to a certain part which is simple and unique and which re-unites them into a single impression.

The "seat," he adds, must also be rather mobile, so that the soul can move it with the immediacy necessary for the animal spirits to flow out of it toward the correct muscles.

There is, La Forge concludes, only one candidate that satisfies all of these conditions, and it is the pineal gland.

> For all other parts of the brain are duplicated or are not near to this source [of the animal spirits]. It is, therefore, the only part which we can most reasonably take as the principal seat of the soul, not only because it is simple

THE UNION OF MIND AND BODY 141

and unique . . . but also because it is movable and is surrounded on all sides by the arteries of the choroid plexus [i.e., the set of arteries from which the spirits flow from the heart].[71]

We have seen how La Forge, in his commentary on the *Traité de l'homme*, defends the pineal gland theory against the difficulties raised by Thomas Bartholin in his *Anatomia reformata*. By the time La Forge has written his *Traité de l'esprit de l'homme*, a new set of objections has emerged, from Bartholin's student, and fellow Dane, Niels Stensen (better known as Nicolaus Steno). During his years traveling throughout Europe on medical studies in the early 1660s, Steno first raised his concerns in a set of lectures at the Paris salon of Melchisédech Thévenot in 1665, just as La Forge was putting the final touches on his treatise. Though Steno's lectures were not published until some years later, in 1669 (after La Forge had died), he must have shared his concerns with La Forge, and perhaps even gave him a copy of his lecture, when he was passing through Saumur in October 1665.

Steno had great respect for Descartes's philosophy and favored the mechanical account of the human body as presented in *L'Homme*. At the same time, he notes, "we must not condemn Monsieur des Cartes if his system of the brain does not entirely conform to experience."[72] Based on evidence derived from dissections of the human body, Steno concludes that the pineal gland cannot do the work that Descartes would have it do.

> With regard to what Monsieur des Cartes says, that the gland can be used for actions although it leans now to one side and now to another, experience assures is that it is wholly incapable of this; for it shows us that it is so tangled up among all the parts of the brain and so attached with these same parts on all sides, that it cannot be given the least movement without forcing it and without breaking the links that keep it attached.[73]

As for the gland's placement in the brain, "it is easy to show the contrary of what Monsieur des Cartes tells us, for it is not plumb in the brain [*plomb sur le cerveau*] and facing forward"; rather, its point is turned always toward the cerebellum and makes a nearly 45-degree angle with its base. Finally, he adds, for good measure, that—again, contrary to what Descartes allegedly observed—there is nothing unique about the pineal gland; this *glande supérieure* is paired with a *glande inférieure*, the pituitary gland.[74]

142 THE GOOD CARTESIAN

La Forge does not name Steno in his *Traité*, but he clearly has his objections fresh in his mind. Given the timing of Steno's visit to Saumur, and the fact that the *Traité* was printed just one month later, these must have been late, quick additions to the text. In his response, La Forge rejects Steno's assertion that the pineal gland, like the other parts of the brain, is part of a pair. There is, he insists, only one gland in the brain permanently situated in the right spot in all animals to carry out the required functions, and it is the pineal. "Although other glands are sometimes found in the choroid plexus and elsewhere in the brain, it [the pineal gland] is still unique because there is none other apart from it which is attached to the part of the brain which is called the medullar trunk, from which, in the opinion of the most learned anatomists, all the nerves in general exit." Moreover, anyone who claims that the pineal gland is not in the internal surface of the brain ("in the ventricles") has simply been misled by their method of dissection. "When the whole membrane called the *mater dura* [a kind of sac that encloses part of the brain] is lifted from around the brain, if one lifts its extremities which lie on the cerebellum and then raises them up a little more one finds, without the slightest use of a scalpel, the tip of our little gland." When approached in this way, however, the gland will appear to be outside all of the ventricles, but this is only because the third and fourth ventricles cannot be seen from this angle.[75] As for Steno's claim that the pineal gland could not have the mobility that Descartes attributes to it, because it is "tangled up" among the parts of the brain, La Forge again refers to faulty experimentation. The problem, apparently, is that Steno dissected the head of a dead calf, and so did not investigate the situation of the gland in a living animal's brain, which "there is no reason to believe" is as compacted as that of a dead animal.[76]

As we have seen, one of the nagging questions about Descartes's account of mind–body union is how to reconcile his talk about the mind being "extended" throughout the body with his claim that the mind has its "principal seat in the brain." I suggested that we think of the mind's extension in the body as an extension of power—whereby the mind can affect and be affected by a great many parts of the body—but that the mind's immediate and most proximate locus for the exercise of this active power and passive capacity, which takes the mind throughout the body, is in the center of the brain, at the pineal gland. This seems to be precisely how La Forge wants us to understand the union. Referring to the intimate relationship between the soul's thoughts and the pineal gland's motions, he notes that

THE UNION OF MIND AND BODY   143

it is obvious that the soul is not joined in this way with the whole body. For we cannot doubt that we do not perceive anything—whether inside or outside the body—unless it has the power to agitate and shake the nerve fibers. Although we have said above that the mind or soul is united immediately with the whole body, that should be understood only in respect of its union with our body in contrast with the union by means of our body which it sometimes has with other bodies, and not in respect of all the individual parts of our body among themselves which, although they are all joined to the soul, are not all equally so.[77]

Another matter on which La Forge is able to add some clarification to Descartes's view.

*

As I mentioned in an earlier chapter, La Forge may be the world's last defender of the pineal gland theory. Among the first generation of Cartesians, Regius, though not a vigorous champion of the *conarion*, pretty much accepted its role as Descartes described it. By mid-century, however, even Cartesians are having second thoughts, and within just a few decades this small gland hanging in the center of the brain would be battered by philosophers from both within and outside the party.

In the same year that La Forge's *Traité* appeared at booksellers, his Cartesian colleague Cordemoy published his own treatise on the relationship between mind and body, *Le Discernement du corps et de l'âme en six discours*. While Cordemoy makes good use of animal spirits circulating in the brain and entering the nerves to travel to distal parts of the body, he does not mention the pineal gland at all.

> These spirits will, according to differences in their agitation, strike this or that part of the brain; and according to the disposition of the brain's pores, the spirits will then insinuate themselves into one nerve or another, which in turn leads them into the muscles of the arm, of the leg, or of any other part that corresponds to the places by which they have left the brain.[78]

Later Cartesians, perhaps in the wake of Steno's critique as well as attacks by the generally sympathetic Pierre Bayle and the extremely hostile

144　THE GOOD CARTESIAN

Pierre-Daniel Huet, also abandoned the theory.[79] Malebranche, the most important Cartesian philosopher of the final three decades of the century, seems to have hedged his bets in the first edition of his *De la recherche de la verité* (1674–75). He grants that there must be a "principal part" of the brain where the mind interacts with the body, and says that "even if [Descartes] were mistaken in this particular fact of the pineal gland, which I do not believe, even if it is not completely as he described it: this nevertheless could not basically invalidate his system." In the fourth edition of the work (1678), however, Malebranche has made a significant shift in his view: "For it must be remarked that *even when [Descartes] is mistaken, as seems probable* when he assures us that it is to the *pineal gland* that the soul is immediately united, this nevertheless could not basically invalidate his system."[80]

Régis, author of the important Cartesian *summa* and textbook *Cours entier de philosophie, ou Système générale selon les principes de Monsieur Descartes* (Complete Course of Philosophy, or General System According to the Principles of Monsieur Descartes, 1691),[81] agrees that there is an organ in the brain—or if there are two, they must be so dependent on each other that "they cannot act separately"—where the faculties of sensation, imagination, and voluntary motion operate. However, like Cordemoy, he never identifies this organ as the pineal gland. He calls it, rather, the "oval center" of the brain, and it is where all the nerves that travel from the sense organs terminate and where the animal spirits gather. "It is only the oval center that contains a sufficient quantity of spirits to awaken in the soul that infinite number of different imaginations that it experiences." Régis seems, in fact, to reject the identification of the seat of the soul (which is not a phrase he uses) with the pineal gland. Rather than being a homogeneous and relatively simple item, he indicates that the site of mind–body interaction is "a mass of small soft and flexible fibers which are not unified and polished, but which have small branches . . . that resemble in a way the trees in a thick forest."[82]

*

By the 1670s, then, most Cartesians have left the pineal gland behind. We, however, are not done with it. There remains the question raised earlier in this chapter as to what, for La Forge, the immortal soul, once separated from the body, does or can do. Will it retain all the faculties that it had in this life? Or will it necessarily undergo the loss of some of its operations? Understanding the pineal gland's function in sensation and memory, and

THE UNION OF MIND AND BODY 145

especially in grounding the ideas constitutive of each, is important for addressing this question.

The question "What is an idea?" would seem to be a simple one for a Cartesian. Descartes devoted a good deal of attention to the nature of ideas, both as modes of the mind and as representational beings. And yet just what ideas are and how they function in human knowledge and perception would prove a highly divisive topic for several generations of Cartesians in the seventeenth century. Some of these issues are ontological and regard an idea's "formal" or "material" reality. Are ideas acts of the mind or objects that it apprehends, or both? Are the ideas we perceive modes of the mind (mental items) or are they outside the mind (for example, in God, as Malebranche argued)? Are there ideas innate in the mind, as part of its natural endowment as thinking substance, or are all ideas derived from experience and related to the body? Then there is a further set of distinctions around the content of an idea, the idea's "objective" or "representational" reality. There are intellectual ideas and sensory ideas, clear and distinct ideas, and obscure and confused ones. (These two distinctions actually map onto each other, as intellectual ideas are clear and distinct while much of the content of sensory ideas tends to be obscure and confused.)

Even more basic is an equivocation in the reference of the term 'idea' itself that is left over from Descartes, an equivocation that La Forge is quick to eliminate. Descartes uses 'idea' to denote both mental states and images in the body (or, more precisely, motion patterns in the brain and on the pineal gland). In the *Traité de l'homme*, Descartes describes the kinetic "figures" that are imprinted on the sense organs by external objects; such images are, as we have seen, communicated to the brain via the nerves and leave a corresponding figure on the brain's internal surface among the openings there. He notes that "among these figures, it is not those imprinted on the external sense organs or on the internal surface of the brain which should be taken to be ideas, but only those which are traced in the spirits on the surface of the gland." That is, the image that arises on the pineal gland as the animal spirits flow from it to the corresponding figure composed by the now-active nerve openings is an "idea," albeit a *corporeal* idea. When a rational soul is united to the machine, it is this figure on the gland that it "considers directly when it imagines some object or perceives it by the senses."[83] These imagistic, corporeal ideas, however, should be distinguished from the purely mental ideas in the mind—that is, the ideas that are modes of thought. Though the latter are also "as it were images of things [*tanquam rerum imagines*],"[84] there is

146   THE GOOD CARTESIAN

nothing bodily about them, even if they are causally related to motions in the body.

La Forge very consciously departs from Descartes and reserves the term 'idea' to refer *only* to the mental phenomena. In his preface to the *Traité* he tells the reader that

> if any overly scrupulous Cartesian is shocked to see that I limited the term ['idea'] exclusively to the forms of thought of the mind, although Monsieur Descartes uses it also to signify the forms of animal spirits (with which these other forms of our thoughts are linked), I ask them to consider that, in a subject as obscure as this and in which misunderstanding was very much to be feared, I could not be too careful in the choice of words nor try too hard to avoid equivocations and disputes over words.[85]

La Forge, adopting Scholastic language, will refer to the corporeal figures in the sense organs, the brain and the pineal gland as "corporeal species"; 'idea' will be used strictly for "ideas or spiritual notions . . . as that form of all our thoughts by the immediate perception of which we know these same thoughts."[86]

Much of what La Forge has to say about the mind's ideas is standard Cartesian fare. Among ideas proper there are purely intellectual thoughts and sensory ideas and passions. The latter two are stimulated or occasioned in the mind by the motions of the pineal gland, which in turn is responding mechanistically to external and internal stimuli in the body. Sensory ideas and feelings generally do not resemble in any way their corporeal causes. While intellectual ideas are clear and distinct, "manifest and evident to an attentive mind," and present their content in a precise and informative manner, sensory ideas are typically "very obscure and confused." "Sensations of colors, sounds, odors, tastes, of heat and cold, dryness and humidity, of pain and tickling" say more about the condition of the individual's body than about real features of external things. Only when a sensory perception also includes a clear and distinct component—for example, "extension, shape, position, solidity and fluidity, and of other similar qualities of body"—does it resemble, to some degree, and tell us something about the item in the world that occasioned it.

> I claim that . . . when we have clear and distinct ideas we can well believe that there is something in objects which is similar to what they represent

THE UNION OF MIND AND BODY 147

to us; but when we have only confused perceptions, such as those of the senses, we have no reason to suspect that there may be anything in the object which corresponds to them.[87]

For the most part, sensory ideas are really nothing but the mind's natural response to a bodily state; the figures and corporeal motions in the pineal gland function as "natural signs" that the mind, in a sense, "reads" or interprets.[88]

In contrast with these ideas grounded in the mind's union with the body, there are also ideas that the mind has by virtue of its nature as a thinking substance, independent of any such union. These are ideas that do not derive, either directly or indirectly, from sense experience. Rather, La Forge says, they "originate from the mind alone."

> It is easy to see what we should think of the common axiom that there is nothing in the understanding which was not previously in the senses. Not only is it not true, if you mean corporeal species in the way we have defined them ... [these] are only accidents or modes of the body, none of which can be received in the mind; but even if one wished to say by this axiom that all our knowledge originates in sense observation, that would not be sustainable either.[89]

Now there is a sense, he grants, in which *all* ideas originate from the mind alone. It is precisely the sense in which Descartes had claimed that all of the mind's ideas are innate: all ideas, as mental states, are generated by the mind's faculty of thinking. Nothing literally passes from the body into the mind, not even in the case of empirically based sensory ideas. Bodily states, including sensory impressions, are nothing but matter in motion, and the mind cannot take on motion. As Descartes notes in his response to Regius in the *Notae in programma quoddam* (Comments on a Certain Broadsheet),

> If we bear well in mind the scope of our senses and what it is exactly that reaches our faculty of thinking by way of them, we must admit that in no case are the ideas of things presented to us by the senses just as we form them in our thinking. So much so that there is nothing in our ideas which is not innate to the mind or the faculty of thinking, with the sole exception of those circumstances which relate to experience.

148 THE GOOD CARTESIAN

In this broad sense, all ideas for Descartes, even perceptual data and sensations, are innate to the mind. However, there is a narrower sense in which a subset of the mind's ideas are more exclusively innate—not in the often and easily caricatured interpretation whereby the mind has always contained them as fully formed if not conscious thoughts somewhere in its recesses, but in the sense that there are inbred in the mind determinate powers or capacities or even propensities to think certain thoughts or have certain ideas independent of any kind of bodily stimulation, even if such stimulation happens to be the occasion for the occurrent actualization of the thought.

> I have never written or taken the view that the mind requires innate ideas which are something distinct from its own faculty of thinking. I did, however, observe that there were certain thoughts within me which neither came to me from external objects nor were determined by my will, but which came solely from the power of thinking within me. . . . This is the same sense as that in which we say that generosity is "innate" in certain families, or that certain diseases such as gout or stones are innate in others: it is not so much that the babies of such families suffer from these diseases in their mother's womb, but simply that they are born with a certain "faculty" or tendency to contract them.[90]

The mind, in other words, is hard-wired to think certain very particular thoughts, even if it never actually thinks them. The idea of God, for Descartes, is only the most obvious of such innate thoughts. In a well-known passage from the Third Meditation, he says, "it is no surprise that God, in creating me, should have placed this idea in me to be, as it were, the mark of the craftsman stamped on his work."[91]

La Forge adopts precisely this position, using the same language, in his *Traité*. Innate ideas are not "in the substance of the soul as in a reservoir, in the way one arranges pictures in a gallery to look at them when one wishes." Rather, they are innate "because it [the mind] is created with the faculty of thinking and of forming ideas and is the principal and proximate cause of them, in the same way in which one says that gout and stones are innate in certain families if those born into them carry dispositions towards those illnesses."[92] In the strict sense of 'innate,' then, some ideas are innate because their presence in the mind—their content, in particular—does not derive in any way from experience or other material circumstances; their origin lies in the mind's nature alone.

THE UNION OF MIND AND BODY   149

This account of innateness has an important consequence. One might hold that even such strictly innate ideas must have some bodily correlate, that only an embodied mind will actually think such thoughts and that their occurrence on this or that occasion must match up with some state of the brain and pineal gland. However, this is not the position taken by Descartes, nor by La Forge. On their account, there are ideas that are not connected with—causally or otherwise—anything that happens in the body, and thus are ideas that the mind would have even if it were not united with a body at all. Margaret Wilson has remarked on the fact that, compared to more recent "Cartesian dualist" analyses of the mind–body relationship, Descartes's version is rather extreme. While latter-day dualists recognize a second kind of "stuff" in the universe that is ontologically distinct from matter and insist that mental events are not identical with events in the body, they nonetheless generally maintain that every mental state has a corresponding or correlated type of physical occurrence—most proximately, some chemical and neurological process in the brain.[93] The feeling of pain is connected with the firing of certain nerve fibers, while one's thinking about a mathematical formula or remembering a lost love must correlate with some other neural activity. For Descartes, on the other hand, there is a broad range of ideas that do not causally depend on, or even require the presence of, the body. These are the thoughts that belong to "pure understanding." In his Fifth Replies, to the empirically minded Gassendi, he says that "the mind can operate independently of the brain; for the brain cannot in any way be employed in pure understanding [ad pure intelligendum], but only in imagining or perceiving by the senses."[94]

La Forge is completely with Descartes on this essential point. "I understand the pure understanding as that faculty by which the mind perceives its own thoughts and, in general, everything that it conceives without the assistance of a corporeal idea."[95] The ideas of the pure understanding—what he calls "intellectual ideas [pensées intellectuelles]"—are ideas or thoughts that do not depend in any way on the body and have no corporeal correlate. In this regard they differ from sensory and imaginative ideas and the ideas that come in memory. This is something that La Forge emphasizes a number of times in the Traité. If the "thing which thinks is really distinct from the body and therefore can exist without it," he notes, then, referring only to intellectual ideas, "the soul has no need of the body to exercise its thoughts."[96]

Here La Forge proves himself, once again, more faithful to Descartes than other Cartesians of the era. Regius, for one, had claimed that, from a strictly

150   THE GOOD CARTESIAN

philosophical perspective, it is an open question as to whether or not the mind, or that which performs the activity of thinking, is or can be a mode of a corporeal substance; only Scripture and revelation assure us that mind and body are distinct substances. He nonetheless seems to have been committed to denying that there are any ideas in the mind independent of the body when, in the "broadsheet [*programma*]" to which Descartes so vehemently objected, he says that "as long as [the mind] is in the body, it is organic in all its actions. Thus, as the disposition of the body varies, so the mind has different thoughts."[97] Desgabets, too, not only rejects the notion of innate ideas, but insists that there are no thoughts in the mind that are not connected with some state of the brain. The view that most clearly "bears the character of truth," he notes, is that according to which

> all our thoughts come originally from our senses, such that in the most abstract speculations, where the soul exercises its freedom, it always has commerce with the senses [*elle a toujours le commerce avec les sens*], at least with the interior ones, which are nothing other than species traced in the brain. But it does not in any way follow from this that our ideas are corporeal. . . . In every thought, without exception, there is something on the part of the body.[98]

Even "our most metaphysical thoughts," he notes—the ideas of God, of the soul, of angels, and of universal concepts—rely on this "commerce" with the body.

Then there is Régis, whose massive textbook is supposed to provide a thorough and systematic presentation of "the principles of Monsieur Descartes." Régis claims, straight out, that "the union of the mind and the body" consists in "the actual dependence of *all the thoughts* of the soul with some motions of the body, and of some motions of the body with some thoughts of the soul." He adds that "I say . . . 'of all the thoughts of the soul with some motions of the body' in order to signify that the mind insofar as it is united with the body cannot have any kind of thinking which does not depend on some motion of the body."[99] Does Régis want to leave open the possibility that when the mind is no longer united with the body it can still engage in some kind of thinking— perhaps thoughts that do not require temporal duration? Perhaps just the kind of thinking that Descartes had said does not require any bodily correlate?

THE UNION OF MIND AND BODY 151

This brings us back, finally, to La Forge on immortality. Will the mind, in its immortal disembodied state, retain all of the faculties that it had in this life? Or will it necessarily undergo the loss of some operations? Will it still have *any* of them? From what we have examined so far, it is clear that for La Forge the faculty of pure understanding is inseparable from the mind; even a disembodied mind/soul would have that faculty or power and thus would be capable of those intellectual thoughts it generates without any corporeal assistance or correlate. Given the nature of thought, he says,

the only [way of knowing] I find which I could believe is inseparable from the mind is pure understanding. For there is no other faculty of knowing which does not depend in some way on the body, and yet my concept of mind shows me that it can be separated from the body and that I could easily conceive of it without the body.[100]

La Forge is careful to note, though, that there is another faculty of the mind—the will—that also does not depend on the body, even though it is capable of exercising its power on the body. "These two faculties are not distinct from the mind or the power of thinking and, since they are two streams which are inconceivable apart from their source, they are not really distinct from each other either . . . these two faculties are just the thing itself which thinks, which sometimes knows and sometimes determines itself."[101] Thus, an immortal, disembodied soul will still have the faculties of pure understanding and of will.

La Forge returns to these points late the *Traité*, in Chapter 25, where he "draws out consequences from his [Descartes's] principles" as to what concerns "the state of the soul after death." He concedes that only faith and revelation can really tell us what faculties and powers the immortal soul will have. He cites Descartes's letter to Elisabeth, in which Descartes says that "as for the state of the soul after this life . . . leaving aside what faith tells us, I agree that by natural reason alone we can make many favorable conjectures and have fine hopes, but we cannot have any certainty."[102]

And yet, even within the constraints of philosophical reasoning, "by the natural light alone," La Forge finds much to say with great confidence. He notes that the character of the soul after this life is dependent on three factors: (1) What God freely grants to the immortal soul; (2) the way in which the soul after death is reunited with and makes use of the resurrected body; and (3) things that follow necessarily from the soul's essence, "when it

152   THE GOOD CARTESIAN

is considered on its own as a thing that thinks." Factors 1 and 2 are beyond our ken, since (absent revelation) we do not know what God has decided about the qualities of the post-mortem soul, and we can have no experience now of how the soul will exercise its functions in a resurrected body. That leaves only 3, the nature or essence of the soul itself, which apparently is not something subject to God's will.

Because the nature of the soul is to think, La Forge concludes, "it will always think." After the death of the body the soul will not have any of the thought functions that depend on the body (and especially on the pineal gland), such as sensation or imagination. But, he reiterates, it will have the faculties of understanding and volition. It will continue to think thoughts through the understanding alone, "which will furnish it with much clearer and more distinct ideas than all those it had by means of the senses in this life."[103] Moreover, the soul will be thoroughly active; it will no longer have any passive affects, since these belong to the soul only insofar as it is embodied. "It will be delivered from the passions and from the prejudices of the senses and will also be in control of its attention."[104] What this means, it seems, is that the immortal mind will be in total control of its thoughts. "[It] will no longer think of anything except what it wishes to think about."[105]

All of this must be problematic for Cartesians who, like Desgabets and Régis, insist that every durational exercise of the mind's power of thinking, every temporal idea or thought, bears some necessary correlation to a state of the body. Desgabets seems to regard a postmortem reunion between soul and a resurrected body as a necessary and "inestimable good" for the blessed, who will then enjoy the visible and passionate delights that heaven provides.[106] There are, to be sure, angelic minds, which are disembodied; but because their "pure thoughts" do not depend on motions, angels think without a succession of thoughts. Whatever takes place in their minds occurs "all at once," "indivisibly and irrevocably . . . without discourse, without composition, without division"—that is, as a single, fixed thought.[107] This, presumably, is how a disembodied human mind would think as well; only after its reunion with a body will it once again experience the kind of linear, discursive intellectual thinking and rich sensory experience that characterizes it in this life.[108]

Régis, too, argues that, on philosophical grounds at least, we must conclude that "separated souls do not retain, after death, any of the faculties that depend on the body." But because he also holds that *any* succession of thoughts in the mind are grounded in motions in the body, the disembodied

THE UNION OF MIND AND BODY   153

soul will lack pretty much every power it has in this life.[109] Régis does distinguish between the mind (*l'esprit*) and the soul (*l'âme*): the former "thinks of itself [*pense de luy-même*] and of everything it thinks about by its own nature," whereas the latter "thinks only of things that depend on the body that it animates." This means—and again, speaking only philosophically, by *la raison naturelle* alone and independent of what revelation may tell us—that after death the soul is deprived of *all* the faculties of thinking that it exercised while united with the body. Thus, Régis concludes, the post-mortem soul "will no longer have understanding and will," at least not in any way that resembles these faculties during the time of mind–body union. There will be no sensing, no imagining, no conceiving, no remembering, no passions, and no volitions. The disembodied human soul will not even be able to move bodies, the way angels do, since such a power is not essential to the mind as a thinking substance. This leaves the soul after death only with "all the advantages" it enjoys because of the nature of the mind as thinking substance. It is a rather short list, however: the immortal soul can "know and love God, and know and love itself."[110]

Descartes had likewise granted, as he must, that any faculties in the mind dependent on the body must be absent from the disembodied immortal soul. This includes sensation and imagination. While our sensory and imaginative ideas are modes of the soul, they are not modes that the soul would have were it not united with a body; sensation and imagination, that is, are not essential to the mind.

> I do not see any difficulty in understanding on the one hand that the faculties of imagination and sensation belong to the soul, because they are species of thoughts, and on the other hand that they belong to the soul only in so far as it is joined to the body, because they are kinds of thoughts without which one can conceive the soul in all its purity.[111]

The immortal soul will not feel pleasure or pain; nor will it experience, in a sensory or imaginative way, colors and visual shapes. All of these thought-modes require the pineal gland and the images that are made to occur on it either by the will (in imagination) or by the way it is affected by other parts of the body (in inner and external sensation). Descartes says (metaphorically, of course) that in both sensation and imagination the mind "turns toward" imagistic figures in the brain, whether in being determined to have this or that sensory idea or imagine this or that thing.[112]

154   THE GOOD CARTESIAN

The soul will, however, after the death of the body, have its faculty of pure understanding perfectly intact. In an August 1641 letter to Hyperaspistes, Descartes writes, "The essence of the soul consists in the fact that it is thinking. . . . Now nothing can ever be deprived of its own essence." Therefore, he concludes, although the mind when united to the body is extremely occupied by all the sensory and other ideas it has through that union, "nonetheless, it has in itself the ideas of God, of itself and of all such truths as are called self-evident." He adds, "I have no doubt that if it [the soul] were released from the prison of the body, it would find [these ideas] within itself."[113] Presumably this includes all the other truths of metaphysics, the truths of mathematics, and the most general principles of nature that follow from these.

*

The tricky item is memory. Immortality would be a poor and hollow condition if there were no connection between the self in the world-to-come and my self in the present life. It needs to be *me* who enjoys the fruits of heaven. Without the disembodied soul having memories of its time in this world, of its mundane thoughts and experiences—without that soul remembering *who* it *is*—there seems to be little chance of preservation of personal identity. But can a good Cartesian account for memory, and thus continuity of self, in the immortal, disembodied, postmortem soul?[114]

Descartes's view of memory—and it might be more appropriate to speak about his evolving views of memory—are scattered across a number of texts. These include his correspondence, when he is pushed to explain memory in response to the queries by Arnauld and Gassendi as to why a mind that is allegedly always thinking does not recall the thoughts it had in the womb.

Descartes distinguishes at least two, and possibly three kinds of memory. First, there is a purely corporeal memory. It does not require the presence of a mind, and it is something that human beings have in common with non-human animals. Memory in this sense, as described in the *Traité de l'homme*—where he calls the brain "the organ or the seat of the common sense, of the imagination, and of memory"—in *Les Passions de l'âme*, and in 1640 letters to Mersenne and Meyssonnier, is simply the acquired disposition of pores (nerve apertures) in the inner lining of the brain, having once been opened by sensory or voluntary stimulation, to reopen relatively easily on a subsequent occasion and have the figure that had been traced there before reappear. In *L'Homme* he compares it to the way in which the gaps in a

THE UNION OF MIND AND BODY   155

linen cloth punctured by needles or the points of an engraver's brush will be "very easy to open again" upon a second insertion of those sharp objects.[115] Or, as he says in a letter to Mesland, it is just like the way "the folds in a piece of paper or cloth make it easier to fold again in that way than it would be if it had never been so folded before."[116] In both humans and non-human animals, the result will be that the animal spirits will flow more easily into those neural openings in the same pattern as before, and then travel to the limbs. Thus, a dog once beaten with a stick will "remember" this and, when it sees a stick again, will react, strictly mechanically, in a similar way. It is, in both humans and animals, a kind of muscle memory. Descartes tells Mersenne in April 1640 that, beyond the pineal gland, "it is the other parts of the brain, especially the interior parts, which are for the most part utilized in memory. I think that all the nerves and muscles can also be so utilized, so that a lute player, for instance, has a part of his memory in his hands."[117] If there is a mind united with this body, then the reappearance of that figure in the openings of the brain and in the pattern of the spirits flowing out of the pineal gland will, by moving the gland once again in the same way as before, trigger the mind to produce the same idea.

There is no real remembering going on here, however. Even when the idea appears once again in the mind on the occasion of the repeated corporeal figure and gland motion, there is something missing. What is needed is that the mind somehow turns to the figure newly traced on the pineal gland and knows that that figure has been there before. Since the mind does not literally "look" at the gland,[118] this presumably means that the mind, as determined by nature, gives rise to the same idea that it caused on the first occasion *and* recognizes that the idea it is now experiencing has been in the mind once before. In response to Arnauld's objection that, if the mind were always thinking we would remember the thoughts we had as infants, Descartes says that

> I agree with you that there are two different powers of memory; but I am convinced that in the mind of an infant there have never been any pure acts of understanding, but only confused sensations. Although these confused sensations leave some traces in the brain, which remain there for life, that does not suffice to enable us to remember them. For that we would have to observe that the sensations which come to us as adults are like those which we had in our mother's womb; and that, in turn, would require a certain reflective act of the intellect, or intellectual memory, which was not in use in the womb.[119]

156 THE GOOD CARTESIAN

After being pressed further by Arnauld, Descartes, in a follow-up letter, explains that

> if we are to remember something, it is not sufficient that the thing should previously have been before our mind and have left some traces in the brain which give occasion for it to occur in our thought again; it is necessary in addition that we should recognize, when it occurs the second time, that this is happening because it has already been perceived by us earlier. . . . From this it is clear that it is not sufficient for memory that there should be traces left in the brain by preceding thoughts. The traces have to be of such a kind that the mind recognizes that they have not always been present in us, but were at some time newly impressed. Now for the mind to recognize this, I think that when the traces were first made it must have made use of pure intellect to notice that the thing which was then presented to it was new and had not been present before; for there cannot be any corporeal trace of this novelty. Consequently, if ever I wrote that the thoughts of children leave no traces in their brain, I meant traces sufficient for memory, that is, traces which at the time of their impression are observed by pure intellect to be new.[120]

Descartes describes this interpretive role of the mind to Mersenne (in August 1640) as the kind of memory "we mainly use." And because it requires an intellectual act, which in turn requires a soul, memory of this sort is unique to human beings. "There is also in our intellect another sort of memory, which is altogether spiritual, and is not found in animals."[121]

In both of these cases, the body is essential for memory. Without the traces in the brain, there is no remembering. He tells Gassendi that "so long as the mind is joined to the body, then in order for it to remember thoughts which it had in the past, it is necessary for some traces of them to be imprinted on the brain; it is by turning to these, or applying itself to them, that the mind remembers."[122]

Now this passage from the Fifth Set of Replies does at least raise the possibility of a memory faculty that does not require the body; for he says to Gassendi that these brain traces are needed "so long as the mind is joined to the body [*quandiu corpori est conjuncta*]." What, then, about when the mind is no longer joined to the body? Unfortunately, Descartes does not have very much to say about any kind of purely intellectual memory in a soul without a body. There are some suggestive passages, however. In a May 1644 letter to

THE UNION OF MIND AND BODY   157

Mersenne, he does note that while "the memory of material things depends on the traces which remain in the brain after an image has been imprinted on it ... the memory of intellectual things depends on some other traces which remain in the mind itself. But the latter are of a wholly different kind from the former, and I cannot explain them by any illustration drawn from corporeal things without a great deal of explanation."[123] There is no indication as to what these "traces ... in the mind itself" are.

Then there is the claim, in the August letter to Mersenne quoted above, that "there is also in our intellect another sort of memory, which is altogether spiritual, and is not found in animals." Can this intellectual or spiritual kind of memory, which recognizes an idea as having been there before, work totally independently of the body and thus remain as a faculty in the immortal soul? Or does it always involve the mind identifying an idea/brain trace combination as a recurrence? He does say, in the May letter, that "besides this memory, which depends on the body, I believe there is also another one, entirely intellectual, which depends on the soul alone."[124] And yet, that there is *no* memory involved when the intellect functions alone, without a body, is suggested by a remark that Descartes makes to Hyperaspistes in that August 1641 letter, to the effect that intellectual thoughts simply occur in the mind without any indication that they have been had before. "Where purely intellectual things are concerned, memory in the strict sense is not involved; they are thought of just as readily irrespective of whether it is the first or second time that they come to mind."[125] This would seem to imply that the disembodied mind does not recognize any idea as a reappearance.

All we are left with, in the end, is a comforting set of remarks that Descartes makes to Constantijn Huygens on the death of his friend's brother. Speaking of souls, he says that

> I know very clearly that they last longer than our bodies, and are destined
> by nature for pleasures and felicities much greater than those we enjoy in
> this world. Those who die pass to a sweeter and more tranquil life than ours;
> I cannot imagine otherwise. We shall go find them some day, and we shall
> still remember the past; for we have, in my view, an intellectual memory
> which is certainly independent of the body.[126]

A pious sentiment indeed, but one not backed up by any philosophical explanation.

158 THE GOOD CARTESIAN

It is thus up to La Forge, once again, to be the good Cartesian and take things a bit further and clarify what Descartes could have, or even should have, said. There is, first of all, the corporeal memory, precisely as Descartes had described it.

> By the term 'corporeal memory' here I understand only a certain facility to re-open which remains in those pores of the brain's ventricles which have already been opened by the spirits and in the fibers through which the spirits passed . . . for by means of this facility, these pores re-open sometimes of their own accord in the same way as they had been opened the first time and do not resist the flow of spirits towards them as much as other pores, and this can cause the same species to be retraced on the gland and the same idea to return to the mind.[127]

La Forge even reproduces the illustration from the *Traité de l'homme* showing the fabric being pierced by the engraver's tool. Corporeal memory, he notes, is what explains "most animals' actions" and allows us to understand "how animals are capable of being trained and how they remember so well the pathways they followed without us having to attribute any knowledge to them."[128] One difference between Descartes and La Forge here, though, is that La Forge had, in his commentary on the *Traité de l'homme*, argued that the corporeal traces that function in memory occur not only in the brain but elsewhere in the body; the "images" that are imprinted on the sense organs and their nerve pathways are also *figures de la memoire*, although ultimately all of these must relate to the "ideas" (here La Forge reverts to Descartes's term) that get traced on the pineal gland and in the openings of the brain.[129]

As in Descartes's account, however, this is not true remembering (*la réminiscence*).[130] Remembering something requires a recognition by the mind that the idea it is now having on the reappearance of the figure on the gland is an idea that it had once before. "For in order to remember [*se ressouvenir*] it is not enough simply to perceive a species which comes back again, if one does not know that this is a re-appearance and that it is not the first time one has had this thought."[131] Because bodily traces are necessary conditions both for corporeal memory and for remembering as we ordinarily experience it, neither of these two types of memory will be present in the disembodied soul.

If this were all La Forge had to say about memory, then he will have done nothing more than reproduce what Descartes had said in various contexts.

THE UNION OF MIND AND BODY   159

But now La Forge ventures forth into territory where Descartes did not. "I say confidently," he continues, that there are also two kinds of memory which do not require a body at all and thus which the disembodied immortal soul will retain. First, there is "an intellectual memory." La Forge, well read in Descartes's correspondence, has in mind here something that Arnauld brings up in the first of his 1648 letters to Descartes. This kind of memory is simply the ability of the intellect to engage in discursive reasoning by keeping in mind or recalling earlier ideas or thoughts in the process and linking them to subsequent ideas and the conclusion. Arnauld calls this a "purely spiritual" memory, to distinguish it from the memory that "requires a corporeal organ." He says to Descartes that

> Just as you yourself remarkably explain and prove that there are two powers of thinking, one in which it purely understands without any help from a bodily faculty, another in which it applies itself to images depicted in the brain. . . . For who can believe that the mind can understand without the help of the brain but that it cannot remember by the intellect without the help of the brain? Nay indeed, on this assumption the mind would not be able to think about spiritual and incorporeal things, such as itself and God, nor be able to reason, since all reasoning [*ratiocinatio*] consists in a series of multiple thoughts whose connection cannot be perceived by us unless we remember the prior ones while we are forming the later ones.[132]

Descartes does not directly address Arnauld's point here, but La Forge does and he concurs. If the mind could not remember without the aid of the body,

> we could not reason as we do about spiritual and corporeal things, for every reasoning is composed of a succession of many concepts, and we could not comprehend the link between them if, while we formed the second, we could not remember the first. However, there remains no trace of these first concepts in the brain because they are pure conceptions and not images. Therefore, it is established that we have an intellectual memory because our mind can recall some of its past thoughts without any traces of them remaining in the brain.[133]

Second, and more substantively, from the perspective of the continuation of personal identity in the immortal soul, there is what La Forge calls "spiritual memory." Here La Forge seems to be talking about the kind of

160   THE GOOD CARTESIAN

"remembering the past [*la souvenance du passé*]" that Descartes had used to comfort Huygens. Besides the strictly corporeal memory and the regular remembering that consists in the mind recognizing that brain traces and their corresponding ideas are re-appearances, "it is very probable," La Forge notes,

> that the mind also has a spiritual memory, not simply to store the traces of ideas which it once had perceived but to provide an occasion for the mind—at least when it is separated from the body—to recognize if the thought which occupies it, either voluntarily or otherwise, is a novel object or it knew it before. It seems very much to be the case that, just as the pores of the brain when they have once been opened have a greater facility to re-open a second time, likewise, when the mind has once had an idea, there remains in it a greater facility to conceive the same idea again. This facility can provide the mind with an occasion to notice that it had earlier perceived the idea which occurs to it again.[134]

There seems to be nothing about the recurring idea's content that indicates that it has been present to the mind before; rather, it is only the ease with which it reappears—something extrinsic to the idea itself—that alerts the mind to that fact.

Incidentally, this enables La Forge to provide an answer to an obvious question that should arise with respect to Descartes's account of the interpretive work that the intellect does in ordinary remembering. Descartes does not explain *how* the mind recognizes that the idea or brain trace has been there once before. One might then object that in order for the mind to recognize that the idea is a reappearance it would have to remember that the idea or figure was there once before, and so memory would be required in order to explain memory, which would generate an infinite regress. Although La Forge does not explicitly consider this objection, he can resolve it by pointing to the facility of the idea's (re-)appearance in the mind. Perhaps the ease with which the cerebral motions occur on the second occasion somehow gets encoded in the experience of the correlated idea itself; this phenomenological feature is what tells the mind that the idea (and, in the ordinary case, its brain trace) has been there before.

Descartes had told Hyperaspistes (in the August 1641 letter), "I have no doubt that if it [the soul] were released from the prison of the body," it would still find within itself the ideas of God, itself and self-evident truths.

THE UNION OF MIND AND BODY   161

However, Descartes also says in the same letter that the intellectual thoughts had by a disembodied soul simply occur in the mind without any indication that they have been there before. (Unlike La Forge's account, it seems that for Descartes previous experience of an idea does not lead to easier recall.) So it is hard to see how, for an immortal soul, continuity with the mental life in this world, and thus personal identity, would be preserved.

Although La Forge hedges his bets here somewhat ("it is very probable that . . ."), he is just as confident as Descartes that the soul will retain these ideas in the afterlife. "It would be ridiculous, in my opinion, to think that when the mind is separated from the body and can longer use the corporeal memory, it would have no way of remembering the thoughts it had during this life or those it will have in the afterlife."[135] But because La Forge also allows the immortal mind to recognize that the ideas it is now perceiving have been there before, he also goes beyond Descartes in stating that it would be a matter of true remembering. His clearest statement of this comes in Chapter 25, on "the soul after death." The soul, he says, "will be incomparably happier in this state [without the body] than it is at present." This is because

> although it will no longer have a corporeal memory and its first ideas will not return any more by chance in its thought, as they do now, it will be able instead to produce again the same ideas which it had in this life. The facility it will have then to produce them, together with the clarity with which it will conceive them, will make it remember that it had the same thoughts previously. It will even remember more distinctly and easily than it does at present because the activity of its intellectual memory cannot be interrupted as that of its corporeal memory is by the action of external objects.[136]

What was left to our speculation in the case of explaining ordinary, embodied remembering—the experience of the ease with which an idea comes (back) into the mind—is now explicitly offered as that which alerts the disembodied mind that the idea has been there before.

La Forge seems to be on better ground than Descartes in preserving personal identity in the afterlife.

7

Occasionalisms

What a crowded club occasionalism has become. From the literature, one might conclude that everyone who was anyone in the seventeenth century, at some point in their career, belonged: not just the usual suspects, Malebranche and fellow Cartesians, but Descartes, Boyle, Leibniz, and quite a few others.[1] In reality, the membership was relatively restricted, and some thinkers who have regularly, and perhaps with some reason, been identified as "occasionalists" were not true believers.

Seventeenth-century occasionalism is the doctrine according to which, in its fullest version, natural beings in the (Cartesian) cosmos—material bodies and immaterial minds—do not have any real causal powers or efficacy. God alone is a true causal agent, and all phenomena in nature—not just the continued existence of things but their properties, transitory and persisting states, and relationships—are brought about directly and immediately by God. When one moving body strikes another body at rest, the first body is not the true cause of the motion of the second body; rather, the impact is just an occasion for God, who was moving the first body, to move the second body. Damage to a human being's body does not itself cause the feeling of pain in the individual's mind or soul, but is just an occasion for God to cause the relevant sensory state. An individual's volition to raise her arm does not bring about the rising of the arm as an efficient cause, but provides only the occasion for God to raise the arm. Finally, even the human mind does not have any true efficacy to generate its own mental states; God is the cause of all thoughts and volitions. Most occasionalists agree that God's ubiquitous causal activity is not capricious or ad hoc but, with the possible exception of miracles, proceeds ordinarily in a regular (and thus predictable) manner according to laws, whether the relevant laws are those of physics covering body–body relations or some general, providential principles covering mind–body relations.[2]

Occasionalism is not a new phenomenon in the seventeenth century. Its roots can be traced back at least to the views of certain medieval theologians;

The Good Cartesian. Steven Nadler, Oxford University Press. © Oxford University Press 2024.
DOI: 10.1093/oso/9780197671719.003.0008

OCCASIONALISMS   163

the Asharite school of Islamic theology (which flourished in the tenth century), for example, adopted a particularly extreme version of the doctrine. Maimonides, writing in the twelfth century, describes their view as one according to which

> the wind does not blow by chance, for God sets it in motion; and it is not the wind that causes the leaves to fall, for every leaf falls through an ordinance and a decree of God; and it is He who causes them to fall now in this particular place . . . every motion and rest of animals has been decreed and man has in no way the ability to do or not to do a thing.[3]

A number of medieval Christian thinkers might also be described, plausibly, as having adopted an occasionalist position in one domain or another (for example, among bodies alone or between mind and body).[4] The doctrine was at least prominent enough for Thomas Aquinas to consider it one of three ways of understanding causal relations in the universe. He notes that either (a) creatures, once created by God, who "gives them the power of operating . . . in the beginning," are independent causal agents that require no additional divine effort other than that which sustains them in being; or (b) "God alone is the immediate cause of everything wrought" and "no creature works at all"; or (c), Thomas's own view, that God and creatures cooperate causally in the production of any effect. "God works sufficiently in things as a first cause, but it does not follow from this that the operation of secondary causes is superfluous."[5]

The first account (a) is now called "conservationism," and it limits God's causal role to creating things and maintaining them in existence with their natural causal powers, the exercise of which is due solely to the thing itself; it is a position most prominently held by the Dominican theologian Durandus de Saint Pourçain (c. 1275–c. 1332). The third account (c) is known as "concurrentism," and in the medieval and early modern period it generally took two main forms. On both accounts, God and creature each make a causal contribution to bringing about the effect. According to Thomas and his followers, "God works in every natural thing not as though the natural thing were altogether inert, but because God works in both nature and will when they work." Natural things have their own powers, but God is required in order for the thing's power to be activated or applied, much as a woodcutter is required for the sharp axe to bring about its effect on wood.

164 THE GOOD CARTESIAN

> A thing is said to cause another's action by moving it to act: whereby we do not mean that it causes or preserves the active power, but that it applies the power to action, even as a man causes the knife's cutting by the very fact that he applies the sharpness of the knife to cutting by moving it to cut. . . . God causes the action of every natural thing by moving and applying its power to action.[6]

On the Thomistic account, natural things function as God's instruments for bringing about effects. Having implanted in things their "natural forces" or powers to act (analogous to the sharpness of the axe or knife), God (like the axe- or knife-wielder) must act in order for a thing to exercise that power. "One thing causes the action of another, as a principal agent causes the action of its instrument; and in this way again we must say that God causes every action of natural things."

The Jesuit Francisco Suarez (1548–1617) adopts, as well, the general framework of divine concurrence, but offers a different order of mechanism to explain God's causal contribution. In contrast with the Thomistic account—whereby (as Suarez puts it) "the First Cause 'stimulates' the secondary cause to its action," with God's action thus preceding the causal activity of the natural substance and acting, as it were, "remotely and *per accidens*" from its effect—Suarez insists that God must be a "*per se* and immediate cause . . . of the secondary cause's effect and action." What this means is that both God and the natural thing contribute, concurrently and proximately, to the bringing about of the effect. God provides the general *esse* or being of the effect, while the creature contributes its determination to such and such a kind of thing. God's concurrence, by providing being, allows the secondary cause to have its effect, and thus in this sense God causes the action of that natural cause. "God is a per se and immediate cause not only of all the effects of creatures, but also of all their actions."[7] God does not stimulate the secondary cause to action, and thus God's action is not "prior" to the secondary cause's action but is simultaneous with it. The two causes—one infinite, one finite—constitute "one and the same action, and no genuine causality can exist between them."[8]

Both conservationism and concurrentism leave the efficacious powers of natural things intact, even though God is required on both theories to sustain things in existence and, on the concurrence view, cooperate with (either by stimulating or supplementing) the finite cause. Occasionalism in its thoroughgoing version, on the other hand, removes all causal efficacy from finite things and reserves it for God alone.

This is not to suggest that occasionalism in the seventeenth century was a monolithic doctrine, maintaining the same form among all philosophers or theologians who qualify authentically as occasionalists. There were differences, first, in the extent to which they employed an occasionalist solution to causal problems. Some thinkers (Cordemoy, Malebranche, possibly Geulincx) did use occasionalism across the board to explain body–body relations, mind–body relations (in both directions, body>mind in sensation and mind>body in voluntary motions), and all phenomena within the mind itself. Others, however—and I will argue that La Forge falls into this category—applied it in one or more domains but still allowed for true natural causal efficacy elsewhere.

Second, there were differences in the motivations and argumentation for the doctrine. Malebranche, an Oratorian priest, was moved primarily by theological principles in defense of Christian piety to demonstrate our complete and utter dependence on God, although his arguments for occasionalism also incorporate assumptions drawn from Cartesian metaphysics and natural philosophy. La Forge (a medical doctor) and Cordemoy (a lawyer), on the other hand, seem to be oriented less by religious faith than by those Cartesian philosophical commitments. The philosophy professor Geulincx, for his part, is, like Malebranche, foremost a moral and religious thinker; inspired by both Stoic and Christian conceptions of virtue, he sees occasionalism as the way to instill proper humility and obedience to God.

Some arguments are shared by a number of occasionalists—for example, the argument based on the premise that motion, as a mode of a body, cannot be transferred from one body to another; so, too, the argument grounded in God's continuous creation/conservation of finite substances, which appears in both La Forge and Malebranche. Other arguments, however, are peculiar to this or that thinker. Only Cordemoy, for example, employs the principle that an action can be continued only by the agent that begins it, and thus the First Mover of bodies must be the agent that, thereafter, continuously moves them. One might legitimately ask, then, as one scholar does, whether "one and the same term, 'occasionalism,' can be used for such different doctrines and authors."[9]

Despite these differences, though, a close reading of occasionalist texts shows—and as recent scholarship has established—the doctrine as held by

166   THE GOOD CARTESIAN

seventeenth-century Cartesians cannot be reduced to an ad hoc solution to a difficulty bequeathed by the dualist metaphysics. That is, contrary to the myth that generations of textbook accounts have propagated, Cartesian occasionalists were not simply engaged in using a *deus ex machina* to resolve a perceived mind–body problem, whereby God is introduced to mediate causally and constantly between mind and body because of the radical ontological difference between these two substances. God may be needed to bring about mental states on the occasion of bodily states, and vice versa; but the reasons for this go well beyond any concerns about the heterogeneity of Cartesian minds and bodies. What makes this particularly obvious is that, for these thinkers, first, God is an infinite mind and yet there seems to be no problem with *that* mind acting on bodies; and, second, God is required also to account for causal relations between bodies themselves.[10]

*

The term 'occasionalism' did not exist in the seventeenth century; it was used neither by the doctrine's partisans nor by its opponents. Philosophers did refer to "the system of occasional causes"—Leibniz, for example, in his *Système nouveau de la nature et de la communication des substances*, his correspondence with Arnauld, and elsewhere.[11] No one was called an "occasionalist" until the mid-eighteenth century, and the movement, if it can be called that, became "occasionalism" only in the early nineteenth century.[12]

The phrases 'give occasion' (*donne occasion, dare occasionem*) and 'occasional cause' (*cause occasionelle, causa occasionalis*), on the other hand, were current among seventeenth-century Cartesians. The term '*occasio*' to refer to a kind of cause has a medieval pedigree, and was used by Aquinas and others to refer to (in Aquinas's words) "something that acts on something but whose action does not reach all the way to the effect it is connected with." Aquinas says that such a contributing factor remains "a true cause *per accidens* . . . and it is rightly called an occasion."[13] The Cartesians, however, were most likely simply following Descartes himself. In the *Traité de l'homme*, Descartes notes that the way in which the animal spirits exit from the pineal gland will "give occasion to the soul [*donneroit occasion à l'âme*]" to have a particular sensation.[14] Similarly, in *La Dioptrique*, he says that motions caused in the brain by an external body "give occasion" to the soul to have sensory perceptions of various qualities of that body.[15] The first use of 'occasional cause' in a Cartesian context was apparently by Pierre Dorlix, a professor in the medical faculty at the University of Leuven who defended a thesis in 1662 in which he claimed that, as Descartes had shown in *L'Homme*, "the pores on the [pineal] gland, which are caused by the spirits coming immediately from this gland and the spirits issuing from it, are the occasional causes [*causae occasionales*] thanks to which the soul united with the gland has ideas of the things that happen to the body."[16] Just a few years later, La Forge would use the phrase in the *Traité de l'esprit de l'homme*, and do so in several contexts.[17]

Employing the language of occasional causes, however, does not make one an occasionalist. As I have argued elsewhere, one needs to distinguish between occasional causation and occasionalism, with the latter being just one variety of the former. Something is an occasional cause (also called a secondary, remote or accidental cause) of an effect when its contribution to bringing that effect about consists in inducing or eliciting another thing to exercise its own efficient causal power as primary cause of the effect. The relationship of occasional causation unites one thing or state of affairs with an effect wrought (through efficient causation, whether transeunt or imma- nent) by another thing. Thus, the term denotes the entire process whereby A occasions B to cause *e*. Even though it is B that A occasions or incites to produce *e*, the relation of occasional causation links A not just to B but also (and especially) to *e*. In other words, A is the occasional cause of *e*, not of B. Descartes gives as an example workers incited to do their work either by another's command or by the promise of payment. The command or promise of compensation is the occasional cause of the work that the laborers, through efficient causation, produce.

> Something can be said to derive its being from something else for two dif- ferent reasons: either the other thing is its proximate and primary cause, without which it cannot exist, or it is a remote and merely accidental cause, which gives the primary cause occasion [*dat occasionem*] to produce its ef- fect at one moment rather than another. Thus, workers are the primary and proximate causes of their work, whereas those who give them orders to do the work, or promise to pay for it, are accidental and remote causes, for the workers might not do the work without instructions.[18]

Without any additional claims, occasional causation does not amount to oc- casionalism. Occasional causation by itself does not include any essential limitations on the causal efficacy of finite beings. Indeed, given this general definition of occasional causation, if such a relationship is ever instantiated

168 THE GOOD CARTESIAN

by finite beings—and there is no a priori reason why it could not be—then they must have certain causal powers. If A is to occasion B to exercise its efficient causal power to produce *e*; and if A and B are both finite beings, then at least one finite being in this setup, B, has efficient causal efficacy. In other words, occasional causation does not require God to be the being, B, whose exercise of causal power is occasioned by A. The relationship between occasional causation and occasionalism is best framed as that between a genus and one of its species: occasionalism is that species of occasional causation in which the proximate and efficient cause whose operation is elicited by the occasional cause is God. But there may be other species of occasional causation, according to which the proximate and efficient cause whose operation is occasioned is some finite thing. This, at least, is how Descartes employs the concept; it is also, as we shall see, how La Forge uses it.

It is unclear whether the occasioning relation between the occasional cause (A) and the efficient cause (B) that produces the effect (*e*) should be classified as an instance of efficient causation. Is occasional causation itself a species of efficient causation? Does A act on B as a transeunt efficient cause?[19] On one hand, it seems that it does not. Rather, the occasional cause appears to function more as a *sine qua non* condition (or set of conditions), that without which the efficient cause B would not bring about *e*. The promise of payment or the command to work does not operate upon the laborers as a transeunt efficient cause, and thus it is not a remote efficient cause of the work that they, as the proximate efficient cause, perform. Moreover, if, as occasionalism demands, the desires or states of finite creatures can occasion God to bring about some effect, it certainly cannot be by operating upon God as efficient causes. This does not mean that occasional causation—the relation of occasioning that elicits the operation of efficient causal power in the primary and proximate cause of the effect—is not a real causal relation. The occasional cause is always noted as the secondary or accidental or remote or (to use Clauberg's term) "procatarctic" cause of the effect, and makes a necessary contribution to the process of bringing that effect about. Perhaps occasional causation should be considered a *sui generis* variety of transeunt causation, distinct from efficient causation. On the other hand, there is no reason why at least in some cases the occasional cause should not be a remote or secondary *efficient* cause, operating on the primary cause by virtue of some power or nature with which it is endowed. Be that as it may, the question as to whether or not occasional causation should be classified as a variety of efficient causation is immaterial to the point I want to make here: namely, that just because

OCCASIONALISMS 169

a philosopher is given to referring to one thing as being the occasion for some other thing to bring about an effect, or as being the occasional cause of that effect, does not mean that the philosopher is an "occasionalist" in that context, in the sense in which that term is properly used.[20]

*

So, who among seventeenth-century Cartesians *is* an occasionalist? And who was the first actually to employ an occasionalist account of causal relations, whether in a partial or a thoroughgoing way? Two major thinkers will serve as bookends for this discussion: Descartes, because it seems pretty clear that he was not an occasionalist, at least not by his own design; and Malebranche, because it is absolutely certain that he was.

There is a significant tradition, going back to the seventeenth century, according to which Descartes not only set the problems to which his followers responded with occasionalist solutions but was himself an occasionalist, at least when it comes to body–body relations, and possibly body>mind relations as well.[21] Bernard le Bovier de Fontenelle, writing in 1686 in his *Doutes sur le système des causes occasionelles*, holds Descartes directly responsible for the travesty that is occasionalism. "If the soul and the body are so disproportionate, how can the motions of the body cause thoughts in the soul? How can thoughts of the soul cause motions in the body? What connection can there by between two beings so different? Such is the difficulty that made Descartes invent occasional causes."[22] In Fontenelle's view, occasionalism was not just the legacy of Descartes's philosophy among some of his followers, but a core element in his own system.

To be sure, a number of passages from Descartes's works do, *prima facie*, lend themselves to an occasionalist reading. In article 36 of Part Two of the *Principia philosophiae*, Descartes calls God "the primary cause of motion." The article is intended only to establish that the quantity of motion in the universe is constant, just because an immutable God "merely by his regular concurrence, preserves the same amount of motion and rest in the material universe as he put there in the beginning."[23] However, in article 42, part of the demonstration of one of the laws of nature that follow from God's immutability—in this case, the law that states that if a body collides with another body that is stronger than itself, it loses none of its motion; but if it collides with a weaker body, it loses a quantity of motion equal to that which it imparts to the other body—Descartes argues that "it is clear that when he

170 THE GOOD CARTESIAN

[God] created the world in the beginning God did not only impart various motions to different parts of the world, but also produced all the reciprocal impulses and transfers of motion between the parts."[24] This suggests that all motions of all bodies, whether it is a matter of uniform movement or a change in motion or rest, are brought about by God.

Moreover, there are a number of fundamental principles in Descartes's philosophy that play an explicit role in the arguments employed by later occasionalists. First, there is Descartes's spare conception of matter. A Cartesian body is nothing but pure extension, a geometrical object made real, and so it can have only geometrical properties. A body cannot have any active force within it to move itself or act causally to modify the motion of other bodies, since such a force cannot be conceived as a mode of extension or space, which is absolutely passive. Such a consideration was used by some Cartesians in favor of body–body occasionalism, and so it seems but a small step to attribute the same conclusion to Descartes as well. Then there is the conservation as continuous creation doctrine, whereby the continued existence of any created finite substance requires the ongoing creative/causal activity of God. As we shall see in the next chapter, La Forge and Malebranche took this principle to imply that only God can be causally responsible for the motion of bodies (by conserving them from moment to moment in one relative place or another).

Still, if the question is whether Descartes *intended* an occasionalist account of causal relations throughout nature, the answer seems to me to be "no." First, Descartes clearly believes that God is not the sole cause of the motions of bodies, since finite minds also have the power to move the bodies with which they are united. A well-known passage from his correspondence with Henry More indicates as much: "The power causing motion may be the power of God himself preserving the same amount of transfer in matter as he put it in the first moment of creation; or it may be the power of a created substance, like our mind, or of any other such thing to which he gave the power to move a body."[25] In a slightly earlier letter, responding to More's worries about how an immaterial incorporeal substance could move a corporeal one, Descartes had framed things in less hypothetical terms:

> It is no disgrace for a philosopher to believe that God can move a body, even though he does not regard God as corporeal; so it is no more of a disgrace for him to think much the same of other incorporeal substances. . . . I must confess that the only idea I can find in my mind to represent the way in

which God or an angel can move matter is the one which shows me the way in which I am conscious I can move my own body by my own thought.[26]

In correspondence with Arnauld, Descartes seems to claim not only that the mind can affect the direction of pre-existing motions in the body—which, since Leibniz, has been one popular strategy for saving Descartes from occasionalism in light of God's role as the general and sustaining cause of the total quantity of motion[27]—but that the mind can actually generate motion in the body.

> That the mind, which is incorporeal, can set the body in motion is something which is shown to us not by any reasoning or comparison with other matters, but by the surest and plainest everyday experience. It is one of those self-evident things which we make obscure when we try to explain them in terms of other things.[28]

As for body–body and body>mind relations, one can find in Descartes's texts many instances where bodies are described as the genuine causes of changes in the motions of other bodies and of mental states like sensations. In the first part of *Le Monde* (*Traité de la lumière*), he notes that "God alone is the author of all the motions in the world in so far as they exist and in so far as they are rectilinear; but it is the various dispositions of matter which render them irregular and curved."[29] Once God has created bodies with motion, he notes in that work, "the various parts of matter . . . retain or transfer [motions] from one to another, according as they had the force to do so."[30] Likewise, in the *Principia philosophiae*, an article is devoted to explaining "the nature of the power which all bodies have to act on, or resist, other bodies"—a power that is accounted for by the fact that bodies, which are impenetrable, tend to persist in the same state, whether it be motion or rest. Thus, "what is at rest has some power of remaining at rest and consequently of resisting anything that may alter the state of rest; and what is in motion has some power of persisting in its motion."[31]

Meanwhile, the proof for the existence of the external world in the *Meditationes* involves attributing to bodies "an active faculty" which "produces" ideas in the mind. Descartes knows, however, that such a claim requires clarification, since bodies, which cannot have ideas as one of their modes, do not literally transmit them into the mind. Thus, in the *Notae in programma quoddam*, he tells Regius that "nothing reaches our mind from

172 THE GOOD CARTESIAN

external objects through the sense organs except certain corporeal motions," and that it is "on the occasion of [these] corporeal motions" that the mind itself generates the relevant sensory idea.[32] Now again, Descartes's use of the term 'occasion' here should not mislead one to think there is a kind of occasionalism going on. Rather, bodies are causing motions in other bodies (including the human body), and the human mind—by virtue of its nature as instituted by God—is, on the occasion of those motions in its body, causing the sensations within itself. (We will return to this process when discussing La Forge's account of body>mind causation.) Finally, there is Descartes's extended correspondence with Princess Elisabeth, where he is at pains to satisfy her concerns about the mind–body relationship and assure her that, though a metaphysical explanation of interaction between an unextended substance and an extended one is really of little help in understanding the *how*, still, she should have no doubt that "the soul moves the body and the body acts on the soul."[33]

Such, then, is the evidence *against* attributing occasionalism, either in whole or in part, to Descartes as his *intended and considered* view. As the case has been made at length by others, there is no need for me to review any further the considerations they have brought forward or the arguments that they have offered.[34] There are, to be sure, difficulties facing any attempt to attribute active causal power or force to Cartesian extended bodies, and those who would defend such a reading cannot agree among themselves how it is supposed to work; their complicated, even strained attempts can seem like the efforts of late Ptolemists introducing epicycle upon epicycle to save the geocentric model of the cosmos. Be that as it may, one point seems particularly salient: nowhere in his corpus does Descartes—who, as we have just seen, is not adverse to using the language of "occasions" in a causal context— say that God does this or that on the occasion of the condition of some finite substance or some state of affairs in the world. (It is, of course, a very different question as to whether Descartes's principles cannot but lead inevitably to occasionalism; and yet another question as to whether he *should* have opted for this doctrine in at least the body–body domain, for the sake of consistency and coherence. A compelling case has been made by some scholars for a positive answer to these two questions.[35])

As for Malebranche, there can be no doubt that occasionalism in *all* domains was his considered view, and so I will not review that case here. There has been a good deal of debate over how his occasionalism should be interpreted—for example, whether God causally operates in the world by discrete acts of will on particular occasions or does everything by a single, eternal volition that encompasses all the laws of nature.[36] But nobody, as far as I know, questions that for Malebranche God is the only truly efficacious causal agent in the cosmos, whether it is a matter of body–body or mind–body relations or even within the mind itself. To put it another way, if Malebranche is not an occasionalist, then nobody is.

But bracketing Descartes and Malebranche still leaves us with a number of Cartesian candidates active between 1650 (when Descartes died) and 1674 (when Malebranche published the first volume of his *De la recherche de la vérité*) for proposing an authentic occasionalist account of causal relations in at least one (and perhaps all) of the relevant domains, as well as for being the first to do so.

*

One name that typically comes up in quests for the origins of Cartesian occasionalism in the seventeenth century is Clauberg.[37] As we have seen, Clauberg paid a visit to Saumur between 1646 and 1648, after his studies in Groningen, but any serious intellectual contact with the adolescent La Forge at that time is unlikely.[38] More to the point, whatever La Forge might have learned from Clauberg, either *viva voce* or by later reading his works, would not have encouraged him toward occasionalism, for Clauberg was not an occasionalist, neither with respect to body–body relations nor in the mind–body domain.[39]

The union of mind and body, Clauberg insists, should not be modeled on the union of bodies (which requires contact or physical contiguity) or between two minds. A body and a mind are united only when there is a specific kind of causal relationship between them—namely, when the states of one correlate in a regular way with the states of the other. In his *Corporis et animae in homine conjunctio*, which appeared in 1664—just when La Forge was putting the finishing touches on his own treatise on mind and body—Clauberg notes that this *conjunctio* consists in

> something relative, in a certain relationship and respect, the reason and foundation for which is indeed found in the nature of the things themselves related to each other . . . the body and the soul relate reciprocally to each other through actions and passions, not that they exercise or undergo similar acts. The conjunction of body and soul is not set in the similarity and

174 THE GOOD CARTESIAN

agreement of actions and passions, such as occurs in the communion of minds among themselves, but in their relation, commerce, and reciprocity with each other.

He adds that the metaphysical dissimilarity, the "diversity in nature, however great," is not at all "incompatible with such a relation."[40] In this sense, his reductive view on union of mind and body is quite like that of La Forge: the union between this mind and this body simply *is* the law-like reciprocity in their respective states. Moreover, like La Forge, Clauberg holds that this reciprocity in modes between mind and body is not "natural"—that is, it is not grounded in the *essential* natures of the two substances (extension and thought)—but established by the will of God as he confers additional powers upon those natures.[41]

Now Clauberg says that "the body brings about [*efficere*] the kind of change in the mind of which it [the mind] is capable; and, vice versa, the mind produces [*producere*] the kind of change in the body that the body easily admits, that is, certain perceptions and volitions of the mind respond to local motions of the body."[42] At the same time, he asks "1. Whether and how the immobile mind itself can move a body, and 2. How a body can be able to produce thought, which it has neither formally nor eminently, in a soul." In addition, he notes that "God is the true efficient, originating and conserving cause of all motion." And in one of the articles of Chapter 16 he calls the motions in the human body "*procatarctic* causes, which give occasion to the mind as the principal cause to elicit from itself, at this time rather than another, these or those ideas which it always has in itself by a certain virtue and to bring its power of thinking into action."[43]

These questions about the essential differences between mind and body, the reference to God's causal role with respect to motion, and the language of occasional causes is probably what has led some to see Clauberg as an occasionalist. However, nowhere does Clauberg say that God is the only true causal agent, or that a state of the mind (such as a volition) is but the occasion for God to move the body, or that a state of the body is the occasion for God to cause a sensory idea in the mind. Neither does he ever suggest that bodies are without causal powers in the physical realm alone, with one body incapable of affecting the motion of another body. And he explicitly grants to the human mind a true causal power to generate its own states. In other words, there is no reason to think that Clauberg accepts either the positive or negative theses of occasionalism.

OCCASIONALISMS 175

God is indeed the "universal cause" of the motion of bodies, but only in the sense that, at creation, God introduced a quantity of motion into matter and subsequently sustains what he has created, including that quantity of motion, indefinitely. That bodies have a real causal efficacy to change the distribution of that motion among themselves is clear from Clauberg's remarks in his *Disputationes physicae*, where he notes that

> material things do not ever change, that is, they are not transformed with respect to any state, they do not pass from motion to rest, or from rest to motion . . . unless the change of this sort is induced by an external cause; and such an external cause, according to the order that God has established in nature, can be understood here as nothing unless other material things.[44]

When bodies interact with each other, they bring about changes in their kinetic states on account of their real properties as extended substances (their shape, size, solidity, and motion and rest), in conformity with the laws of nature. As for the mind's action on the body, Clauberg describes it as follows:

> The human mind is not a physical kind of cause of motions in human bodies, but only a moral cause, insofar as it only governs and reigns over some of those [motions] and makes it so that, through those motions, which are now in the body, at one time this and at another time that member is agitated.
>
> It is almost like the way in which the driver of a chariot is joined with the horse which he stimulates to motion, he bends here and there, and so governs the chariot's motion, which the horse truly produces as the physical cause. . . .
>
> If you insist that a new motion is indeed produced in the body by the soul, this would be contrary to the principles of physics, which proclaim that in the entire universe, which includes human bodies, there is perpetually the same quantity of motion.[45]

The human mind cannot add new motion to the body, but it can, efficaciously, change the direction of the motions already therein. This is the sense in which the mind is a "moral" cause, since the redirection of those motions (like the charioteer directing the horse), brings about real effects in, and exercises influence on, the world. The human mind, an active substance, thus has a direct efficacy on the human body.

176 THE GOOD CARTESIAN

When it comes to body>mind relations, Clauberg's account is a little murkier. He admits that, unlike the mind>body case—where the soul immediately affects the motions in the body—the motions in the body cannot directly cause thoughts in the mind. "Since the effect cannot be more noble than its cause, it is clear that a spiritual idea, such as what is in the mind whenever we sense or perceive something, cannot arise from a corporeal motion." Still, bodily motions serve as "procatarctic causes" that "give occasion to the mind" to act as the principal cause and "elicit from itself" the appropriate ideas. (What counts as "the appropriate idea" follows neither from the essential nature of the body, nor from the essential nature of the mind, but from God who providentially establishes this reciprocal relationship in the first place and grounds it in their respective natures as a kind of supplement to their essences.)

One question about Clauberg's account that has arisen in the literature concerns whether the body, acting procatarctically, operates as an efficient cause upon the mind to stimulate it to produce an idea. Clauberg does say that the bodily motions serving as procatarctic causes are "sufficiently powerful on our soul."[46] While the language of procatarctic causes comes from earlier medical literature, especially in the Galenic tradition, Clauberg's source for this notion is likely to have been one of his Cartesian contemporaries, albeit a rather eclectic one who sought to combine the new philosophy with Scholasticism. When he was not drinking heavily, Heereboord was teaching philosophy in Leiden precisely when Clauberg was studying there. Heereboord defines a *causa procatarctica* as the "extrinsic cause that impels the efficient cause to act."[47] Burgersdijk, another Dutch Scholastic, who preceded Heereboord at Leiden, explicitly categorizes procatarctic causation as a species of efficient causation—namely, that cause that (efficiently) causes another cause to exercise its own efficient causality to bring about an effect.[48] (We can thus regard procatarctic causes as functioning in the way I have described occasional causes as functioning.)

However, on another reading of Clauberg, adopted by some scholars, the relationship between mind and body involves no efficient causation at all in play between the two substances (or at least not from body to mind). On this interpretation, the mind–body relationship for Clauberg is supposed to be more like the parallelism of Leibniz's preestablished harmony, with each substance acting as it has been programmed (by God, at creation) to do.[49]

Fortunately, for our purposes here, we do not need to resolve this dilemma. What is relatively clear is that Clauberg is no occasionalist, neither with respect to body–body relations nor with respect to mind–body relations. Bodies truly affect the motions of other bodies; minds causally affect the motions of the bodies with which they are united; and bodies stimulate the minds with which they are united to exercise their own proper causal efficacy. And for what it is worth, La Forge read Clauberg as a non-occasionalist interactionist. He notes that "I do not locate the essence of the union of these two substances [mind and body] in the actual concurrence and interaction of their operations (although this is the view of the learned Clauberg)."[50]

By contrast, Geulincx—another Cartesian philosopher in Leiden and thus, for a brief time, a colleague of Heereboord (who died just a few years after Geulincx's arrival in 1658)[51]—was indeed a true occasionalist, if not a thoroughgoing one. He published the first part of his *Ethica* in 1665, one year after Clauberg's *Conjunctio* and Clerselier and La Forge's edition of Descartes's *Traité de l'homme*.[52] As the title of the work indicates, it is primarily a contribution to moral philosophy, not metaphysics. Virtue, as Geulincx defines it (following Descartes), is the love of, and therefore obedience to, reason, as opposed to the passions; and freedom is a matter of doing what reason dictates, not in order to promote one's self-interest but out of service to God (although virtue so understood is also what is in one's own best interest). In the course of his moral investigations, Geulincx takes up some metaphysical topics as he addresses the ancient Stoic question as to what exactly is within one's control and what is not. Among the things that are not within one's control—which Geulincx understands as the things upon which one has no causal efficacy—is, in addition to all those "external" bodies, one's own body.

> Now it is indeed the case that my body moves in accordance with my will. When I want to speak, my tongue flaps about in my mouth; when I want to swim, my arms splash about; when I want to walk, my feet are flung forward. But I do not make that motion. I do not know how such a thing is brought about, and it would be impudent of me to say that I do what I do not know how to do. I do not know how, and through which nerves and other channels, motion is directed from my brain into my limbs; nor do I know how motion reaches the brain, or even whether it reaches the brain at all.[53]

There is an epistemological principle at work in Geulincx's analysis of causation here, as he elaborates in one of his annotations to the treatise. "What

178 THE GOOD CARTESIAN

I do not know how to do is not my action [*ego non facio id quod quomodo fiat nescio*]."[54] In order to be the true cause of something, one must know what needs to be done in order to do it; and knowing what needs to be done includes knowing all the intermediate causal factors that bring about the final effect and how to put them into operation. Because I do not know what needs to be done in order to move the parts of my body, I am not the true cause of those motions. "If you do not know how motion is made in the organs of your body while being nevertheless quite sure that you made it, you could say with equal justification that you are the author of Homer's *Iliad*, or that you built the walls of Ninevah, or the Pyramids."[55] The upshot is that the human mind is not the true cause of movements of the human body, since one is ignorant of what motions in what parts of the body are required and how to bring them about. It must be some other "Mind" that moves the body's limbs when a person wills to move them. My body moves, that is, "because another wishes what I wish."[56] Geulincx compares this to the rocking of a cradle: the cradle rocks when the baby wants it to be rocked not because the baby's will efficaciously rocks the cradle but because the mother or nurse, knowing the baby's desire, efficaciously fulfills it.

Geulincx then generalizes this conclusion to include relations between bodies. Because they are mindless substances and thus devoid of any cognition whatsoever, inanimate bodies *a fortiori* lack the requisite causal knowledge. "Since we readily concede that those things we do not know how to do are beyond our power . . . it is remarkable that we do not apply the same argument to these brute things," to such "natural things" as the sun, fire, and all such bodies. It is not the sun that makes light, nor is it fire that causes heat, but "a Mover [*Motor*] who produces all these things . . . by impressing various motions on this or that part of matter."[57] God moves bodies around "as if they were his instruments."

Body–body and mind–body relations are thus, for Geulincx, accounted for in an occasionalist manner. In the *Metaphysica vera*, composed in the late 1660s but not published until 1691, after Geulincx's death, the epistemological principle that sets the condition for causal efficacy is framed in this way: "What you do not know how to do, you do not do [*Quod nescis quomodo fiat, id non facis*]."[58] It is used again to rule out any causal efficacy that the human mind might be assumed to have over the body ("parts of my body are frequently moved about, though not by me but by the real mover") and that one body might exercise over another. But Geulincx now supplements this argument for occasionalism with other considerations drawn from the radical ontological distinction between mind and body, or what has been called the "heterogeneity problem." He notes that "nothing can be attributed to body beyond mass and extension, which have no capacity to arouse thoughts. . . . There is no conformity of bodies, as they spin endlessly about, colliding and rebounding, with even the most insignificant thought in my mind." As for whether the mind can directly affect the body, he says, "I do not, properly speaking, interact with bodies; I have no place with them, and occupy no space."[59] Once again, causal efficacy is reserved for God's will alone.

Is Geulincx a thoroughgoing occasionalist? It all depends on whether he allows the mind itself to have some causal efficacy with regard to its own states: its ideas and volitions. He notes that while one's body is "a part of the world," the "I" or self, as a thinking substance, is not. Thus, despite the fact that I am accustomed to call this body "my" body, I, as mind or soul, stand independently apart from it and the domain of bodies generally. "If I do not make motion in my body, how much less do I make motion outside my body."[60] Geulincx insists, "I am defined by consciousness and will alone."[61]

Now he has established that certain mental states—sensory ideas—are generated in the human mind by God on the occasion of motions in the body.

> My consciousness has certain modalities, such as when I see purple, when I hear a melody, or when I enjoy spicy food, that do not depend at all on my will . . . nor do these and other such modalities just come to me. . . . My consciousness, then, has certain modalities that do not depend on me, which I do not arouse in myself.[62]

Geulincx does not avail himself of an active faculty of the mind for producing its own sensations and other perceptual ideas on the occasion of bodily motions, as Clauberg does (and, as we shall see, Descartes and La Forge do). However, there does seem to be at least one domain where the human mind can exercise true causal efficacy: the will. The mind, apparently, has a real power to generate its volitions, desires, and judgments. In the *Metaphysica vera* he notes, "I do not truly act on my body, but only on the judgment of my will [*ad arbitrium voluntatis meae*]."[63] In the *Ethica*, he states, "it is clear that I do nothing outside myself; that whatever I do stays within me; and that nothing I do passes into my body, or any other body, or anything else." He calls "the command of my will" an "action that is within me," and says, "my every action, insofar as it is mine, remains within me." But any "diffusion"

180 THE GOOD CARTESIAN

of my action outside of myself, into the realm of bodies—including my own body, such as "the flapping of my tongue"—is due not to my power but to God's.[64]

There is also a cryptic passage that suggests (but only suggests) that Geulincx allows the human mind some causal power over at least some of its intellectual thoughts, and not just in the generation of its volitional acts. The mind, it seems, has the power to combine, separate, and revise its ideas. "With all that was in me, I made great things small, turned them upside down, and mixed them together."[65] This may, however, simply be an extension of the will's power insofar as such mental activity is voluntary. In the end, much remains unclear in Geulincx's account. But if it is indeed the case that Geulincx leaves intact a power in the mind over its volitions and at least some of its ideas, then Geulincx's occasionalism, though somewhat extensive, will still be but a limited one.[66]

*

At this point, we return to France—to Paris and the Montmor circle. Cordemoy is arguably our best candidate for a complete occasionalist before Malebranche, although it takes some work to see this. Given Cordemoy's importance and (unlike Geulincx) influence in the history of occasionalism, and the fact that comparison between him and La Forge is unavoidable— both because they published their major works within months of each other and because they make many of the same claims—he warrants a more extended treatment.

There is some debate among scholars as to how systematic Cordemoy is with respect to his claims about God's causal role in the world, and with good reason.[67] He comes nowhere as close as Malebranche in providing occasionalism with an extensive and elaborate account of causal relations generally, much less in doing so in a single text.[68] On the other hand, although he is certainly no Malebranche, Cordemoy does not merely use occasionalism in a limited or ad hoc way, merely to solve this or that problem.

The domains in which Cordemoy's occasionalism is most clear and forthright are that of body–body and mind>body relations. There is no mistaking Cordemoy's view in his *Le Discernement du corps et de l'âme en six discours* (1666). For Cordemoy, bodies are not the causes of the motions of other bodies. Neither is the human soul the true cause of the motion of the body

OCCASIONALISMS   181

with which it is united. Only God is the genuine cause of the motions of bodies.

Cordemoy begins his demonstration of this conclusion with five axioms:

1. A thing does not have from itself (*de soy*) that which it might lose without ceasing to be what it is.
2. Every body can lose some its motion, to the point of not having any at all, without ceasing to be a body.
3. Only two kinds of substances can be conceived, namely, *mind* (or that which thinks) and *body*. That is why they ought to be considered the causes of everything that happens. What does not come about by means of one must necessarily be attributed to the other.
4. *To move*, or to cause motion, is an action.
5. An action can be continued only by the agent that began it.[69]

Premise one says that the only states or properties of a thing that derive from its own nature, that it has "from itself," are its essential states or properties. If a property belongs to a thing in such a way that the loss of that property entails no change in the thing's nature, if it is not an essential property, then possession of that property is not due to the thing's nature and thus does not come from its own resources. Cordemoy then argues that no body has its motion *de soy*, from its own nature or resources. This follows immediately from axioms one and two. Since any body can lose its motion without ceasing to be a body, the essence of which is simply extension, no body is the source of its own motion. But if no body has motion from itself—that is, if no body can put itself in motion—then neither can any body be a first cause of the motion of bodies, since any such bodily first cause of motion or bodily prime mover would have to be able to put itself in motion. Therefore, any first mover of bodies must be a mind, since (by axiom three) there are only minds and bodies.

Cordemoy's next step is to show that not only is some mind (or minds) a *first* mover(s) of bodies, but also that all subsequent motions in bodies are caused by that same mind (or those same minds). This is supposed to follow from axiom four, which states that moving something is an action, and axiom five, which seems to derive from an intuition about the identity conditions of an action. Axiom five says that any single action, to remain the same action, must continue to be generated by the same agent that began it; any change in agency implies a change in action. Cordemoy is assuming

182 THE GOOD CARTESIAN

that the subsequent moving of bodies is continuous with the initial moving of bodies, and thus that the two constitute an identical action (and therefore require the same agent). This part of the argument is intended to rule out the possibility that, a mind/first mover having once initiated motion in bodies, bodies themselves are subsequently responsible for continuing that motion and also, therefore, for causing the changes in motions among themselves. Bodies thus have no motive force whatsoever. They have no efficacy to move themselves or to be the true cause of motions in each other. Only minds can move bodies.

Cordemoy grants that sense experience appears to contradict all this and to tell us that one body moves another. But, he insists, in an argument that foreshadows Hume (and appears in La Forge as well), upon closer examination we discover that, in fact, all that sense experience reveals is a succession of events. What we really see is that following the impact of two bodies, one of which is in motion and the other at rest, the motion of the first body ceases and the motion of the second body begins; we do not, however, witness the one actively causing the other.

> Consider again what body B does to body C when it is said that it moves it from its place. All that is evident in this case . . . is that B was moved, that C is now moved, and that the former remains in the place that the latter occupied before it. We see only this; everything else is a matter of conjecture.[70]

Moreover—and Cordemoy, recalling a point made by Henry More in correspondence with Descartes, seems to offer this as an independent argument against body–body interaction—motion is a state (*état*) of a body, or (to put it in Cartesian terms) a mode of its substance.[71] A state or mode of one finite substance just *is* that substance existing in a certain way, and thus cannot be communicated to another finite substance. Therefore, one body could not be the cause of motion in another body, presumably because any real transeunt causal relationship between distinct things could only be explained in terms of such transference of properties (that is, of motion).[72]

Thus, the same mind(s) that first moves bodies is (are) responsible for continuing the motion of those bodies. "However accustomed we may be to believe the contrary," Cordemoy insists, we must nonetheless admit that that which first moves a body is what always moves it, "since that which produces also conserves, and the same action that began the motion must continue it."

To regard one body as the real cause of the motion of another body is to mistake "the occasion for the cause."[73]

The question remains, however, as to the identity of the mind(s) which is (are) the source of motion in bodies. What mind or minds serve as the first and continuous mover(s) of bodies in general, and thus of any particular body? Nothing Cordemoy has said so far either necessitates or rules out a plurality of minds, of different sorts, moving bodies. His argument implies only that when a body moves, there must be some mind moving it. Taking our cue from the way the motions of our bodies follow so closely the volitions of our minds, we tend to believe that it is our own minds that move our bodies. But this belief, Cordemoy argues, is no better grounded than the belief that one body is the cause of the motion of another.[74] This brings us to the question of the causal efficacy of the human soul and occasionalism in the domain of mind–body relations.

Cordemoy shares credit with La Forge, as we shall see, for making what, in the seventeenth century, is an important and remarkable discovery—namely, that the causal relationship between mind and body is not necessarily *more* opaque than the causal relationship between bodies. "It is undoubtedly no more difficult to conceive the action of minds upon bodies or that of bodies upon minds than to conceive the action of bodies upon bodies."[75] The point here is not to show that mind–body causal relations are as perspicuous as body–body causal relations might seem to be (at least, to the philosophically untutored), but, on the contrary, that in neither case do we truly comprehend true efficacy. Real causal interaction is inconceivable in *both* domains. "I dare say that when what occurs [*ce qui se rencontre*] in the action of one body upon another body is carefully examined, it will not be found any more conceivable [*plus concevable*] than what occurs in the action of minds upon bodies."[76]

Cordemoy argues that a number of considerations count against the human mind's being the real cause of the motions of the human body. He is evidently struck by what he sees as the general independence of the body from the mind (and the will in particular) and the mind's overwhelming lack of control over the body's movements. Such impotence is clear from the involuntary motions in the body that both precede that body's being animated by a soul and cease before the soul has abandoned the body in death. This shows that these and other motions in the body do not depend upon the will. This conclusion is reinforced by the fact that, even after the union of soul and body, we cannot stop many of the body's motions even if we wanted to

184 THE GOOD CARTESIAN

(and certainly not *just* by wanting to). There are many motions in the animated body—for example, the beating of the heart and the circulation of the blood—that bear no relationship to the will whatsoever. Simply by willing these motions to stop or change we can do nothing to affect them.

> If sometimes our unhappiness is such that it leads us to desire death, it would be in vain for us simply to will these motions in us to come to an end. They depend so little on us that, if we simply willed them to stop, they would not, for all that, stop. But were we to use some weapon upon ourselves and make the life-giving blood flow out of the body's vessels, we would then see those same parts whose motion serves to move our bodies exhaled like smoke. If our despair allowed us still to philosophize, we would see that, since our blood exits from us without our will causing its motion, it is not our will that makes it move in us. . . . All those convulsive motions and those subtle and fatal transports that assail our brain fully demonstrate that our will does not provide motion to these particles (which, because of their subtlety, are called 'spirits'), and that the will is not even the master of the course they take, since on these occasions the will cannot prevent the particles from flowing wherever their impetuosity takes them.[77]

More generally, Cordemoy argues that a person simply does not have that control over the motions of his body, even the voluntary motions, that he would have if the mind, through the will, were truly the cause of those motions. Old age, exhaustion, and other conditions make this perfectly clear. "It is in vain that an old man wills to walk quickly, or that a drunkard wills to walk a straight line, and it is useless for anyone whose hand is frozen to will to move his fingers." Sleep overcomes us in spite of ourselves, and we often hiccup or shiver no matter how hard we will to cease. In other words, "our weakness [*faiblesse*] teaches us that it is not our mind that causes motion." From the previous argument, however, we know that it must be *some* mind that moves our (and any) body. Cordemoy concludes that it is "another Mind, one to which nothing is lacking, that does it, and does it through its will."[78] The cause of the body's motions is an all-powerful mind, the same one that *first* introduced motion into matter and that moves all bodies.

A second, somewhat subsidiary consideration that Cordemoy brings forward against the human mind being the cause of motion in the body derives from physics. Cordemoy, like Clauberg, is committed to the Cartesian conservation principle, according to which the total quantity of motion in the

OCCASIONALISMS 185

universe is constant. Now, he argues, if we *could*, at will, initiate new motions in our bodies, it would follow that motion would be added to the universe, since such new motions would not necessarily be compensated for by the loss of motion in some other body. A real causal influence of the human mind upon the body to which it is united would therefore result in a "disruption of the order of nature."[79] This consideration does not rule out some higher mind being the cause of motions in all bodies, however, as long as that mind is the original and sustaining source of those motions and as long as it acts in accordance with the laws of nature, adjusting the motions of bodies in corresponding ways to insure a constancy in the overall quantity of motion. "We must admire [this Mind], above all, on this point, namely, that . . . it established laws among bodies, following which it moves them in various ways, according to the diversity of their collisions [*leurs rencontres*]."[80]

The conclusion of Cordemoy's argument is that God—the "First Mind" that is the source of its own being—is the first and continuous and only cause of motion in bodies.[81] All material and mental events are only occasions for this "Sovereign Mind" to exercise its causal activity upon bodies.

> If there is any way of saying that the soul moves the body, it is in the same sense in which it can be said that one body moves another body. For just as it is said that one body moves another when, because of their collision, it happens that whatever was moving the first now moves the second, so it can be said that a soul moves a body when, because it so wishes, it happens that whatever was moving the body now moves it to where this soul wants it to be moved. Still, it must be admitted that it is convenient to explain things in the ordinary manner, that is, to say that a soul moves a body and that one body moves another. Since we do not always seek the origin of things, it is often more reasonable, given what has already been noted, to cite the occasion rather than the cause of some effect.[82]

For Cordemoy, one body is not the real cause of the motion of another body, nor is the human mind the real cause of any motions in the human body. Neither, he argues, is the body the real cause of any event in the human mind. Lacking the causal power even to move another body, the human body certainly cannot exert a real and efficacious influence upon the human mind. Besides, how could motion in a body genuinely bring about an effect in a mind? "If a body acts upon a mind, it cannot be by causing in it any change of motion, shape, or parts, since this mind does not have any of these things."[83]

186 THE GOOD CARTESIAN

The union of mind and body in a human being cannot, therefore, consist in any real causally interactive relationship between the two, but only in a law-like correlation in their respective states, a correlation brought about and maintained by God.

All the elements seem to be in place in Cordemoy for a full-blown occasionalism. Bodies do not cause effects in other bodies or in minds, and minds do not cause motion in bodies. God causes all motions in nature. This is the conclusion of the Fifth Discourse in *Le Discernement du corps et de l'âme*:

> To consider the matter precisely, it seems to me that the action of minds upon bodies should not be found more inconceivable than that of bodies upon bodies.[84] For we recognize that, if our souls cannot move our bodies, neither can bodies move other bodies. And just as we ought to acknowledge that the collision of two bodies is an occasion for the power that was moving the first body to move the second, so we ought to have no difficulty in conceiving that our will is an occasion for the power that already is moving a body to direct the motion in a certain way corresponding to this thought. (CG 151)

Still, one question seems to be left unanswered by Cordemoy's argument in the treatise. Bodies may, by their nature, lack all causal efficacy; as pure extension, they are capable only of passively receiving motion. But what about finite minds? They are not, we now know, the cause of motions in the human body. But there are two things to notice about what Cordemoy has established with his arguments to this effect.

First, even though the human mind is not in fact the cause of motions in the body, nothing Cordemoy has said implies that it is not the cause of motions because it lacks causal power *tout court*. Most of Cordemoy's argumentation against mind–body causation is based on empirical data that is intended to persuade us that the mind is not, *de facto*, the cause of the involuntary or even the voluntary motions of the body. But none of the empirical considerations about bodily control that he brings forward establish that it is in principle impossible for the mind to move the body. Only the secondary argument from the principle of the conservation of motion establishes this. But—and this is the second thing to notice—even here what is demonstrated is only that a law of physics disallows mind–body causal action. What is not demonstrated, and what cannot be demonstrated by a law of physics alone, is that the soul is *by its nature* causally inert.

OCCASIONALISMS   187

Related to this is the fact that none of Cordemoy's arguments in *Le Discernement* explicitly addresses the issue of the mind's causality with respect to its own internal properties. Is the mind the real cause of its own ideas, volitions, and other mental states? He does not in this work expressly argue against this position, and nothing he has said in it rules it out. None of his arguments imply that the mind has no immanent causal powers—not the argument from physics against mind>body causation, nor the argument based on the non-transference of modes or states that is used against body–body interaction. This latter argument does rule out the mind causing motion in the body, if all transeunt causal interaction is to be understood on the model of such transference—just as much as it rules out one body causing motion in another body, and perhaps even more so, since the mind does not have any motion to transfer to the body in the first place. But the non-transference argument would seem to apply *only* to cases of transeunt causation between numerically distinct things, and not to any case of immanent causation, whereby a thing brings about changes in its own states.

What about the central argument in *Le Discernement* against body–body causation, and especially the part directed against a body being the cause of its own motion—that is, the argument based on what properties a thing can have *de soy*? Can this line of reasoning be used to eliminate causal powers in the soul? Does it imply that the soul cannot possibly be the cause of its own thoughts—its ideas and volitions—since the soul might lose its thoughts (just as a body can lose its motion) without ceasing to be what it is, a thinking substance?

The answer to this question is clearly "no." For a Cartesian like Cordemoy, there is an important difference between the way in which a body is related to its motion and the way in which a mind is related to its thoughts. Both motion and ideas are modes of their respective substances. But while a body can indeed lose its motion and remain a body (at rest), a mind cannot lose its thoughts and remain a thinking substance. The mind can, of course, lose any particular thoughts it might have, but it cannot *not* have *some* thoughts. There is in the mental realm no state corresponding to rest, no property that stands to actual thoughts in the way in which rest stands to actual motion. As we have seen La Forge argue, the Cartesian mind, simply by virtue of being a thinking substance, is always modified by thoughts, while a Cartesian body is not modified by motion simply by virtue of being an extended substance. Cordemoy, in fact, in another work—his *Discours physique de la parole*—seems explicitly to rule out such a parallel application to the mind itself of

188   THE GOOD CARTESIAN

the argument used in *Le Discernement* with respect to bodies. He brings up the will as his example: "Just as the body is a substance to which extension naturally belongs, so much so that, as for physical effects, it would cease to be a body if it ceased to be extended; in the same way the mind is a substance to which the power of determining itself belongs so naturally, that it would cease to be a mind if it ceased to will."[85] Thus, the argument provides no impediment to Cordemoy saying that a mind does indeed have its thoughts "from itself."

Even an attempt to turn Cordemoy's main argument against human mind>human body causation—the argument based on our evident lack of control over our own bodies—against the mind and its own states would not succeed, and would not demonstrate the mind's immanent causal impotence. For example, one could easily marshal empirical considerations on Cordemoy's behalf to the effect that frequently ideas and sensations occur in the mind involuntarily and beyond the control of the will, similar to the considerations he brings forward in the context of the human body's motions. Perceptions, pains, and pleasures all appear in the mind independently of any volitions. Does this not show that the mind is not, therefore, the cause of those mental states?

However, there is again an important difference between the two cases, one that forestalls using the argument in this way. The will is regarded by Cartesians as the sole locus of causal control that the mind has over the body's motions; if the mind moves the body, it can only be through its volitions. This explains why Cordemoy believes that to show that the body does not, in fact, answer to the soul's volitions is to show that the soul is not the cause of the body's motions. In the realm of the mind alone, however, there is no assumption that mental causation of mental events must always occur through the will. No Cartesian would argue that if the mind causes its own states, it is through the will alone. Indeed, as we saw in the case of Clauberg, Cartesians generally believe that often the mind does cause its own states but with no involvement of the will. Thus, to show that mental states do not always answer to the soul's volitions would not, in a Cartesian context, confirm that the soul is not the cause of its own states.

The arguments from *Le Discernement*, then, appear to leave the causal powers of the soul intact. All that he says on this matter is that "[the soul] can receive new thoughts through the motions of the body, according to the relation and dependence that God has established between them."[86] This is a fairly neutral and non-committal remark. It is compatible with God having created the soul in such a way that, on the occasion of certain motions occurring in the body (in particular, in the brain), the soul causes specific ideas within itself, much as Descartes and Clauberg (and, as we shall see, La Forge) believe.

A causally active human soul generating its own ideas is also suggested by some of Cordemoy's statements in the *Discours physique de la parole*. He notes that "it should not be difficult to conceive that the Author of nature, in forming a human being, has so well united certain thoughts in his soul to motions in his body that as soon as these motions are excited in the body, these thoughts are excited in the soul."[87] He later says that there is a "natural correspondence" between events in the body and events in the mind, according to which "certain sensations always arise [*naissent*] in the soul as soon as certain motions are excited in the brain."[88] He does not say that God causes the sensations on the occasion of the brain motions, but only that they "arise" in the soul—perhaps from the soul's own causal resources and as a result of some kind of natural or divine institution.

Finally, there are Cordemoy's remarks on the will in the *Discours physique* already mentioned, which likewise hint at a human soul endowed with genuine causal efficacy.

> Our souls which depend on [God] for their being and for their conservation do not in any way depend on Him in the employment of their will, whose determination he has left completely free. I will even propose, as something that will seem evident to all men of good sense who will consider it attentively, that just as the body is a substance to which extension naturally belongs, so much so that, as for physical effects, it would cease to be a body if it ceased to be extended; in the same way the mind is a substance to which the power of determining itself belongs so naturally, that it would cease to be a mind if it ceased to will.[89]

Cordemoy, in other words, seems *prima facie* to allow for real causal powers in the human soul. He does not appear in these passages to be willing to rule out genuine causation in finite thinking substances. But this, along with the causal inertness of bodies, is precisely what is required for a thoroughgoing occasionalism.

In the end, however, this picture of Cordemoy as only a limited occasionalist will not withstand scrutiny. Cordemoy is not willing to grant causal efficacy even to the human soul, although his occasionalist account of

190   THE GOOD CARTESIAN

the generation of ideas in the mind and of the operation of the will appears outside *Le Discernement*. The notion that the soul causally generates its own ideas on the occasion of bodily motions is, in fact, eliminated right where it seems to begin, in the *Discours physique de la parole*. "It is," Cordemoy says—and he apparently proceeds here without any argument whatsoever—"just as impossible for souls to have new perceptions without God as it is for bodies to acquire new motions without him."[90] The parallel with God's role in causing bodily motions is there to make it clear that the correlation between motions in the brain and sensory ideas in the mind is due not to the soul's own, albeit God-given cognitive causal resources, but directly to the constant causal activity of God. He makes this point just as strongly in the second of his two *Traitez de métaphysique*:

> The only thing that God did to unite this body and this mind was to make the body move not only on the occasion of other bodies, as he made those of beasts move, but also on the occasion of the volitions of this mind; and *to give sensations and inclinations to this mind on the occasion of motions of this body.*[91]

What, then, about the will? The soul causing its own sensory ideas was really never more than a veiled suggestion, a possible way of reading some ambiguous lines. But Cordemoy does at least seem to be explicitly committed to a soul that is causally active in its volitions. The mind's adventitious ideas may be brought about by God on the occasion of external material events, but does not the human being's freedom require the capacity on the part of the soul to will something through its own inner powers, "to determine itself toward one thing or another"? As Cordemoy says in the *Discours physique*, "all the soul's action consists in willing . . . our mind has the power to determine itself."[92] Does not the mind generate its own volitions?

Alas, even here Cordemoy ultimately resorts to occasionalism.[93] But to discover this, we need to go again to the second of the *Traitez de métaphysique*, which is titled "That God does everything that is real in our actions, without depriving us of freedom."

Human beings, Cordemoy claims, universally strive for happiness, and they do so through an inborn tendency toward the good in general. This tendency (*pente*) should be understood as a primordial urge or desire at-large toward what we believe will benefit us. All of our actions derive from this spiritual force. As soon as we alight upon something that seems to be a means

OCCASIONALISMS 191

toward happiness and well-being—and we sometimes make this judgment on the basis of the pleasure it occasions in us—our desire is naturally attracted to it. The will toward "good in general" now becomes focused on a particular good, either because we consider it to be itself the supreme good or because we believe it to be a genuine means toward the supreme good. We need to be careful, though, lest we direct our will toward a thing that is not, in fact, a true good. The will needs to be guided by understanding and clear and distinct ideas in order to ensure that it is properly directed.

The will, this inborn inclination toward the good in general, is nothing but a divine force, a kind of sustained push that God communicates continually to created souls. The mind's own "action" is limited to either allowing or withholding its consent when the will becomes focused on some particular thing. When the mind is unsure whether or not the object is a true good, then it can suspend judgment and refuse consent, allowing the inclination to move on to another object; when it believes the object to be a true good—and only God *is* the true good—it consents to the will's urge toward that object.

God ceaselessly impels minds toward this end. They have a constant desire for it. They cannot even prevent themselves from wanting to arrive at it. And as long as nothing obscures their understanding and they know perfectly the means for achieving it, all the activity of their will is a striving for it. But as soon as their understanding is obscured and presents to them various things whose appearance is such that they no longer know what to choose, this is when they suspend this activity. While God ceaselessly impels them toward their end, and even impels them to choose one of the means that are available to achieve this end, since they often do not know how to choose, they remain in suspense, and this is an action. For they resolve not to choose, and this resolution is an action; while it truly would not be in them without God, it is their action and not God's.[94]

God provides "all that is real [*tout ce qu'il y a de réel*]" in the human will. The will just is the spiritual impulse continually generated in a soul by God. All that human beings can "do" is suspend or provide their consent to allowing the will to rest on one particular thing or another that they perceive to be good. Cordemoy does want to say that this suspension or provision of consent is an "action." After all, it is a Cartesian mind that he is discussing, and Cartesian minds are by their nature active; some of their modifications—in particular, their volitional modalities—are actions. But Cordemoy also wants

192 THE GOOD CARTESIAN

to distinguish between something being an action or active and something being a cause. What he has in mind for the human soul's decisive attitude regarding the direction of the divine impulse is a non-productive activity. It is an activity presumably because it is followed by some continuation or alteration in the circumstances: depending upon whether the soul gives its consent or not, its striving rests upon or moves past some particular thing.[95] Cordemoy does not want to say that it is a true and efficacious causal activity, however, since, he insists, it produces nothing real. No new and positive mode arises either in the soul's substance or in any other thing.[96]

Unfortunately, Cordemoy does not present any argument for this view of the will, and so we are left wondering why exactly it is that the human mind does not have even the power to generate its own volitions. For Malebranche, the total causal inefficacy of the soul is established from general (and argued-for) principles regarding the inefficacy of finite creatures, as well as from specific arguments against causal powers in the soul. But no such global or particular causal considerations appear in Cordemoy's works to lend support to his occasionalist account of volition and freedom. Indeed, as we have seen, Cordemoy nowhere offers any real arguments against any causal powers in the soul (including the power to generate its own ideas). No in-principle claims about the causal (in)efficacy of the mind appear in either of the *Traitez de métaphysique*. Neither do any such claims follow from the theses and arguments he offers in *Le Discernement* and the *Discours physique*; nor does Cordemoy indicate therein that he believes there to be any claims that do so follow. At best what he offers in the second of the *Traitez de métaphysique* is a simple and unexamined premise to the effect that "God is the cause of all that is [*Dieu est cause de tout ce qui est*]" and from this it is supposed to follow immediately that "all minds derive their being and their thoughts from Him" and that "God causes the actions of minds."[97] That is the extent of the support he provides for his account. To put this another way, Cordemoy does not argue for the claim that the mind lacks real causal power with respect to its volitions (and other states) as a step on the way to an occasionalist conclusion; rather, he moves instead from an occasionalist account of the will to the inefficacy of the mind with respect to its volitions.

*

If we are looking for the first philosopher in the Cartesian camp to adopt a full-blown occasionalism in published writings, then the award must go to

Cordemoy.[98] Clauberg was no occasionalist, and Geulincx's occasionalism seems to have been only partial (although there is plenty of room for dispute in his case). On the other hand, if we are looking for the first Cartesian to use occasionalism at all in a published work, even if in just a limited way, then Geulincx, in his *Ethica* of 1665, earlier in the same year that La Forge had his *Traité de l'esprit de l'homme* printed and a year before Cordemoy brought out his own treatise on mind and body, appears to be the best candidate.[99]

However, there may be reason to give La Forge and Cordemoy equal credit for being the first Cartesians to offer, at least in conversations if not in writing, occasionalist accounts of causation in one domain or another. There is good evidence that both men were defending occasionalism with respect to body–body and mind–body relations already in 1658.[100]

Right at the beginning of the Fifth Discourse in *Le Discernement*, where Cordemoy takes up the question of "the union of mind and body," he provides some background to the occasionalist ideas he is presenting in this chapter:

> This marvelous relationship between our motions and our thoughts gives me occasion to speak about the union of our body and our soul and the manner in which they act on one another. These two things have long been admired without being explained. I dare not say that I have discovered their secret, but it does seem to me that I leave nothing more to be desired on this score. *Some of my friends to whom I have communicated my thoughts on this subject several times over the past seven or eight years want to persuade me that they are true.*[101]

If Cordemoy was defending his ideas on causation, and perhaps even circulating a draft of his treatise, "seven or eight years" earlier, that dates his "discovery" to around 1658.

Coincidentally—or perhaps not—1658 is reportedly the same year that La Forge was propounding, in conversation and in a manuscript, his own occasionalist view of the world. Was the good doctor from Saumur among those "friends" to whom Cordemoy was communicating his thoughts?

8

The World of Bodies

When Jacques Gousset, still in his early twenties, was a philosophy and theology student at the Protestant Academy in Saumur, he became good friends with the slightly older La Forge. The two men met often to talk about various matters, with Gousset coming to La Forge's home and La Forge visiting Gousset's "childish bedroom." He says La Forge's interests were in "the Romans"—presumably he means classical and secular literature—while Gousset calls himself "religious." The two men performed experiments together, including breaking chicken eggs to determine the circulation of the blood, and Gousset later helped La Forge with his illustrations for Clerselier. "We labored over devising the figures that he was making for Descartes's *L'Homme*."[1]

At some point the conversations turned to what Gousset calls "the present disagreement concerning secondary causes":

> Whether they themselves have a real and proper efficacy; or whether, truly, all causality that really influences [*influat*] the effect in a subject belongs to the First [Cause] alone, doing it at the presence of secondary causes as either an occasion or a *sine qua non* condition, on account of its disposition, here and now, and on account of the reason and requirement of the laws imposed by the First Cause by itself in its proper decrees by which it constituted nature and made itself governor of it.[2]

According to Gousset, the true "parent" of the new doctrine of occasional causes was "Louis de la Forge, a medical doctor living in Saumur, when I used to listen to the professors of philosophy and theology." La Forge, he claims, was the first to come up with this opinion about causality, and "opened up" to him about it in 1658. It is worth quoting at length Gousset's "faithful" recollection of their first conversation about this matter, not least because it has never been translated from the Latin.[3]

The Good Cartesian. Steven Nadler, Oxford University Press. © Oxford University Press 2024.
DOI: 10.1093/oso/9780197671719.003.0009

THE WORLD OF BODIES   195

The learned man came to me unexpectedly in my cubicle leaning against books, made a brief greeting, and I quickly greeted him in return. He said that he is writing a new book. When I asked for the argument, he replied with a smile, and instead of a response he answered with a question. What is the cause, he asked, why one thought is able to follow another in your mind? A power, I said, implanted in the mind by the creator for forming every now and then new and new thoughts, and so bringing about a passage from one thought to another. This I am sure of. But that man was waiting there for me to make his attack.

Gousset then reviews La Forge's reasoning:

Try to conceive such a natural power of the mind as being different from the essence itself of the mind. Indeed, what is the mind according to its essence? A thinking thing: this idea of it is simple and whole. But it is truly thinking, wholly thinking, by a present act of thinking. Therefore, one singular thought constitutes the essence of the mind, and satisfies what the essence of the mind requires, such that it both exhausts the mind's active power absolutely and with respect to its essence. The power of forming another thought, and a third, and a fourth, and so on, is more than the power of having one thought. Just as, certainly, number is more than unity: a faculty of transitioning from one to another is something more than remaining on one. Therefore a second thought comes from no cause and arises *ex nihilo*, as if through a kind of creation, or it receives existence as if from itself. Indeed, he added, the first thought present at this moment is related to the mind, just as a present motion or figure is related to the body, for it is a modification of [the mind], just as motion [of a body]. And just as a body will certainly and constantly maintain one figure, and with the same quantity and determination of motion, if it is left untouched to itself and its nature, with no other cause arriving: so, too, will the mind remain occupied by one singular thought in perpetuity, unless some agent, different from it, introduces a new one, which will inform this mind in a new way. There is a law common to all things: *Everything, insofar as it is simple and undivided and left to itself, always remains in the same state, nor will it ever change except through an external cause.* And although it is generally used by Descartes for motion, nevertheless, it is connected with the word *thing*.[4]

196 THE GOOD CARTESIAN

Gousset wanted there to be a natural power in the mind to bring about successive thoughts, to be able to do this "by the exercise of its vital acts." La Forge replied that this power would have to be something besides the essence or nature of the mind, since "I have given proof that it would exceed the essence."

> What then would be this power? A mode? But a mode of the mind is an actual thought, by which it is clearly modified. Or is it a thing conjoined with the mind? Then the question will again arise, is it corporeal? But in a body there is nothing that desires to give rise to thoughts, which would be so absurd that it is not worth being refuted by reasons, however strong they may be. Therefore it would be spiritual? Indeed, how would this spiritual thing differ from the mind itself? In number? Species? Kind? Or even categorically, since we have seen that this power cannot be a mode, is it therefore a *real accident*? Finally, says this sharp man, no matter whether that power is a substantial thing or rather a real accident, some *bond* will be needed by which that power can connect to the mind. Is therefore that bond itself a substance? or is it a real accident? Choose. And if it should be such an accident, choose whether it is to be spiritual or corporeal. At least say what is the nature of that by which this bond is affixed to each of the bonded things, that is, to the mind and the power to be connected. Say how much that bond contributes so that those things that, by its work, are brought more closely together than without it. Say why this bond is more apt to be applied to those things immediately than those things are to each other. Finally, say how that bond conveys from the natural power into the mind new thoughts generated in the natural power. These things, he [La Forge] said, are unsolvable [*inextricabilia*], and therefore useless and must be abandoned. Therefore, he concluded, there remains one thing by which any new thought might exist in the mind. And that thing is nothing other than God, who, according to the laws established by him in all things and to execution of which he committed himself, efficaciously substitutes one thought to follow a prior one at a given moment.[5]

To Gousset's objection that God would therefore have been responsible for the first humans' sin, since God would have caused their minds to move from pure thoughts to vicious thoughts—"just as if there was a wax figure with the most beautiful form of a girl, and someone with his fingers changed it into a monstrous form"—La Forge responded, "I am a philosopher, not a

THE WORLD OF BODIES   197

theologian, and am concerned, with all my soul, to draw conclusions from premises, and leave other matters to others."[6]

The conversation then turned to the question of the body and how a body might be moved either by another body or by a mind. To Gousset's response that that power of moving was instilled in those created things by the creator, La Forge "denied not only that that was true, but that it was even possible."

> First he rejected, on one hand, that it was by the migration of the numerically same motion from one body into another, and on the other hand by contact between body and mind. He then opposed by reasoning very similar to those mentioned concerning spiritual things, by which he inferred that one body cannot bring about anything in another body by impressing motion upon it; and that neither is a finite spirit more capable of this power of doing something; but that God alone does this by a real action—namely, according to the laws which he prescribed to himself when constituting the nature of things and establishing himself as its director, and he willingly took on the role of executing [the laws].[7]

Gousset was unhappy with the theological implications of La Forge's position. "If things are as you say, then God is awarded a glory that is neither his nor can be his." Think of God as the builder of an automated machine, he suggests.

> [God] carefully gave properly adapted form to parts of the world, dimensions, textures, exchanges, seams, hinges, numbers, reciprocal proportions and applications, mutually consequential motions, responding to each other in speed and determination according to weight. He distributes his tasks to agents and patients. He wanted constant laws to be followed in these things. He took care that good ends should appear to be obtained in operations, and means prudently chosen for them. Finally, he displayed all observable things, which arose so that they might persuade us that this world is an automaton machine made by him . . . and thus he hoped that the praise would redound to him.[8]

But, Gousset insists, that praise would be false and unearned if La Forge's opinion were true, insofar as on that view

> the world is not an automaton machine, because its parts do not in fact exercise any efficacy or operation or any reciprocal impression of motions.

198   THE GOOD CARTESIAN

> Rather, all this which appears to be brought about by them, the Creator himself assiduously brings about with his hidden finger. Indeed, this glory that God wanted to receive [from the machine he made] is such that he does not deserve it . . . since you deny that it is possible that he gives to any body a real power of acting on any body, which nevertheless would be required in a machine. Since your opinion carries with it an absurd thought about God, clearly it is false and for that reason ought to be repudiated by you.[9]

La Forge's reply, as reported by Gousset, is that his opinion gave greater glory to God than the common opinion.

Incidentally, Gousset is not the only one among La Forge's contemporaries who credited him with being the "inventor" of occasionalism.[10] Pierre de Villemandy (1636–1703) was a professor of philosophy at the Protestant Academy in Saumur (before he, like Gousset and many others, left for Holland in the wake of the revocation of the Edict of Nantes in 1685). He and Gousset must have known each other. He was also—like Gousset, who would later write a book defending Descartes's philosophy[11]—partial to Cartesianism, but primarily insofar as it offered a solid response to skepticism. In 1686, De Villemandy published in Leiden his *Traité de l'efficace des causes secondes* in which he opposes those who "remove [efficacy] from the creature" to give it solely to God. While he does not consider Descartes himself to have been an occasionalist, he does hold him responsible for "having furnished the occasion for some of his disciples to promote this new opinion."[12] Most prominent among those disciples is the late Saumur resident, Louis de La Forge, "the first among [Descartes's disciples] that I know to have put forth and openly sustained" this thesis.[13]

*

From Gousset's narrative we learn several things. First, in 1658, La Forge held a view that pretty much qualifies as a thoroughgoing occasionalism. He denied any true causal efficacy to natural substances, both bodies and minds, and made God the immediate cause of all changes of motion in bodies and thoughts in the mind. Second, La Forge was already putting his views down in writing—"he said he is writing a new book," and this is two years before he agrees to work with Clerselier on Descartes's *L'Homme!*[14] In the end, though, La Forge would, in his book, back off from this extreme position, as will become clear as we review in this and the following chapters his account of

THE WORLD OF BODIES 199

body–body and body–mind relations and the causal power of the mind over its own thoughts.

Now 1658, when La Forge and Gousset are talking about causal powers in Saumur, is, as we have seen, precisely when Cordemoy, based in Paris, was communicating his own thoughts on causation "to some of my friends." There is no documentary evidence that La Forge and Cordemoy ever met, or even knew of each other. And yet, in the same year both men are propounding a complete occasionalism, albeit most likely with different arguments. A mere coincidence?[15] Or was La Forge among those "friends" to whom Cordemoy was communicating his thoughts—if not in person then by correspondence, perhaps through the mediation of Montmor or Clerselier?[16]

There is yet more circumstantial evidence to consider. Both La Forge, writing no later than 1664, and Cordemoy, no doubt finished with his composition by late 1665, expressed their views on the perspicuity of causal relations among bodies and between minds and bodies in very similar terms—indeed, using a nearly identical turn of phrase that, as far as I know, appears in no other work of the period. Here are Cordemoy's statements, both appearing in *Le Discernement* (Discourse 5):

It is undoubtedly no more difficult to conceive the action of minds upon bodies or that of bodies upon minds than to conceive the actions of bodies upon bodies [*Sans doute il n'est pas plus mal-aisé de concevoir l'action des esprits sur les corps, ou celle des corps sur les esprits, que de concevoir l'action des corps sur les corps.*]

The action of bodies upon bodies is no better known to us than that of minds upon bodies or bodies upon minds . . . when what occurs in the action of one body upon another is carefully examined, it will not be found any more conceivable than what occurs in the action of minds upon bodies. . . . The action of minds upon bodies should not be found more inconceivable than that of bodies upon bodies. For we recognize that, if our souls cannot move our bodies, neither can bodies move other bodies. And just as we ought to acknowledge that the collision of two bodies is an occasion for the power that was moving the first body to move the second, so we ought to have no difficulty in conceiving that our will is an occasion for the power that is already moving a body to direct the motion in a certain way corresponding to this thought. [*L'action des corps sur les corps ne nous soit pas mieux connuë, que celle des esprits sur les corps, or des corps sur les esprits. . . . Quand on aura bien examiné ce qui se rencontre dans l'action d'un*

200 THE GOOD CARTESIAN

corps sur un corps, on ne trouvera pas qu'elle soit plus concevable, que celle des esprits sur les corps. . . . On ne doit plus trouver l'action de esprits sur le corps plus inconcevable, que celle des corps sur les corps; car nous reconnoissons que, si nos ames ne peuvent mouvoir nos corps, les corps ne peuvent aussi mouvoir d'autres corps. Et, comme on est obligé de reconnoître que la rencontre de deux corps est une occasion à la puissance qui mouvoit le premier, de mouvoir le second; on ne doit point avoir de peine à concevoir que nôtre volonté soit une occasion à la puissance qui meut déja un corps, d'en diriger le mouvement vers un certain côté répondant à cette pensée.][17]

And here are La Forge's versions of exactly the same sentiment in almost exactly the same words:

It is no more difficult to conceive how the human mind, without being extended, can move the body and how the body without being a spiritual thing can act on the mind, than to conceive how a body has the power to move itself and to communicate its motion to another body. Yet there is nothing more true. . . . It [is] no more difficult to conceive how the mind moves the body than to know how one body moves another because, in fact, one must have recourse to the same universal cause in both cases. [*Il n'est plus difficile de concevoir comment l'Esprit de l'Homme sans estre estendu, peut mouvoir le Corps, & comment le Corps, sans estre une chose Spirituelle, peut agir sur l'Esprit, que de concevoir commen un Corps a la puissance de se mouvoir & de communiquer son mouvement à un autre corps. . . . Cependant il n'y a rien de plus veritable. . . . Il [n'est] pas plus difficile de concevoir comment l'Esprit meut le Corps, que de sçavoir comment un Corps en meut un autre; car en effet dans l'un & dans l'autre il faut recourir à la mesme cause universelle.*][18]

Neither philosopher is claiming that both mind–body relations and body–body relations are equally clear and distinct, equally easy to conceive and understand. On the contrary—and here is the irony in their respective "it is no more difficult" locutions—the two cases are on an equal footing because neither relation is clearly and distinctly understood at all. As both Cordemoy and La Forge see it, we ordinarily believe that there is a particular difficulty with conceiving mind–body causation—the so-called heterogeneity problem—that does not arise in the body–body case, where experience is taken to reveal motion and rest between bodies being affected by contact. In fact, we no more understand how one body affects the motive state of

THE WORLD OF BODIES 201

another than we understand how mind can move body or body can cause thoughts in the mind. As La Forge puts it, in a way strikingly like what we saw was Cordemoy's pre-Humean warning that we not mistake "the occasion for the cause,"

> There is a big difference between the obviousness of the effect and that of the cause. The effect is very clear here, for what do our senses show us more clearly than the various movements of bodies? But do they show us the force which carries heavy things downwards, light things upwards, and how one body has the power to make another body move? Do our senses teach us how motion can pass from one body to another? ... The cause of motion is not therefore something which is as obvious as one might think.[19]

It is one thing to perceive how one body touches another. It is an entirely different thing to perceive "how one body could move another."

Of course, the claim that body–body causality is, in fact, no better understood (or clearly and distinctly conceived) than mind–body causality does not, by itself, lead necessarily to occasionalism. But it does complicate the causal picture, much more so than Descartes, for one, was willing to admit.

*

La Forge was certainly an occasionalist of some sort. But what kind of occasionalist was he? In what domains did he opt for occasionalism to account for the modes of substances and the correlations between the modes of different substances?

There are scholars who have argued that he was not in fact committed to any manner of occasionalism, and that to believe otherwise is to misread his claims about causes and powers. One such interpretation attributes to La Forge a kind of pre-established harmony *avant la lettre* (that is, *avant Leibniz*). On this reading, La Forge's talk of God as the primary cause of all motions and thoughts is to be taken to mean only that God set up at creation correlations grounded in the natures of things.[20] Another interpretation simply has La Forge granting to bodies and minds real causal efficacy, albeit a causal efficacy that needs to be accounted for in such a way that it is consistent with certain Cartesian principles (for example, that a mode cannot literally be transferred from one substance to another).[21]

202   THE GOOD CARTESIAN

The more common interpretation in the literature, however, is that La Forge was a partial occasionalist.[22] What this usually involves is accepting that La Forge is an occasionalist when it comes to body–body relations but that he grants to the human soul, as an active substance, genuine causal powers—at the very least an "internal" power to generate its own ideas and volitions (including sensory ideas on the occasion of bodily motions)[23], and on some readings a real causal capacity to move the body as well.[24]
Finally, there are those who, while tempted to see La Forge as only a partial occasionalist, simply throw up their hands and confess that they are unable to determine with any certainty what exactly La Forge's view is, that they find his account of causal relations "opaque" and his occasionalism "unstable."[25]

In this and the following two chapters, I argue that the reading according to which La Forge adopts only a partial occasionalism is correct—at least if the question concerns what he intended his position to be. Things might become murkier when we push a bit further and ask what position La Forge is ultimately committed to, *malgré lui*. In the end, however, I believe it all works out and his partial occasionalism can be shown to be coherent after all.

*

One thing does seem perfectly clear about La Forge and occasionalism. Bodies, understood as Cartesian bodies—individual parcels of pure extension in a plenum and distinguished from each other only by relative internal and external motions—are causally inert. They have no real causal efficacy or active powers to cause effects in themselves or in other bodies. When it comes to the material realm alone, God is the only true efficient causal agent. God alone is responsible for the motion and rest of bodies—both the existence per se of motion in the world, and the particular speeds and directions of the motions instantiated in bodies. (As I will discuss, La Forge also allows that the explanation as to why a body is moving such as it is on any given occasion must include reference to the size, motion, and rest of other bodies as *sine qua non* conditions for God to exercise that efficient causality). In other words, in the case of body–body relations, La Forge is a true occasionalist. "It is God," he says, "who is the first, universal and total cause of motion," and the local contact of one body with another body is only an occasion for God to modify the motion or rest of those bodies, as dictated by the laws of nature.[26] This reading of La Forge on body–body relations is, for the most part, uncontroversial and supported by his arguments to the effect that bodies have no

THE WORLD OF BODIES 203

motive force, no power to cause or sustain motion either in themselves or in other bodies.

In Chapter 16 of the *Traité de l'esprit de l'homme* ("How the Mind and Body act on each other, and how one Body moves another"), La Forge introduces a double division. First, he distinguishes the motion of a body from the determination of that motion (primarily its direction). Second, and following Descartes, he distinguishes the motion of a body from the cause of that motion, that is, the force that makes something begin to move and keeps it in motion (which he calls both *la force de mouvoir* and *la cause motrice*).[27] The motion itself is a mode of the body, just like its shape and size, and is simply the body's transfer from the vicinity of those that are in immediate contact with it to the vicinity of other bodies, just as Descartes (whom La Forge quotes on this point) had defined it.[28] The motive force, on the other hand, is that active power "which transports a body from one vicinity to another." Such a force must therefore be distinct both from the motion it causes and from the body to which it is applied.

One might object that there is something missing in La Forge's reasoning here. All he seems entitled to claim from what he says so far is that moving force (cause) is distinct from motion (effect), not that moving force is distinct from the body that is moving. Motion is a mode of the body. But why cannot the moving force also be a mode of the body, just as long as it is not identified with that other mode of the body that is its motion? This would mean that the causal power that brings about the body's motion belongs to the body itself.

However, the claim that moving force must be distinct from the body itself (as well as from its motion) follows not merely from the difference between motion and its cause, but also from the fact that such a force cannot be conceived as a mode of a body. "The notion of this force would have to include in its concept the idea of extension, as the other modes of body do."[29] Shape, for example, cannot be understood without appealing to extension, since any particular shape just is a way of being extended. However, no such conceptual containment exists in the case of motive force; the concept of what that force is includes no necessary reference to extension. On the contrary, any conceptual relationship between force and extension is excluded on the grounds that the essence of extension is incompatible with having a causally active mode. Our idea of extension, La Forge says, "in which the nature of body in general consists . . . is not active."[30] No examination of the clear and distinct idea of extension would reveal that a Cartesian body could possibly have as one of its modes an active power (something like what the

204 THE GOOD CARTESIAN

Aristotelians in "the Schools" attribute to bodily substances by virtue of the forms or real qualities that are supposed to inhere in them).

But if motive force is not and cannot be a mode of the body being moved, then no body can move itself. And if a body cannot move itself, then it certainly cannot move another body.

> Now if the force which moves is distinct from the thing which is moved and if bodies alone can be moved, it follows clearly that no body can have the power of self-movement in itself. For if that were the case this force would not be distinct from the body, because no attribute or property is distinct from the thing to which it belongs. If a body cannot move itself, it is obvious in my opinion that it cannot move another body.[31]

Even if motive force *were* a mode or property of bodies, that would not help explain how one body moves another. The mode of a body is not distinct from the body of which it is a mode, since it just is that body existing in a certain manner; and on the Cartesian metaphysics of substance, a mode cannot pass from the substance to which it belongs to some other substance. Thus, one body cannot move another by transferring its motive force, either in whole or in part, to the other body. (This likewise rules out one body causing motion in another through real transeunt causation, whereby one body would communicate its motion to another body.[32]) Nor could one body put another body in motion by producing a new motive force in it. This would be tantamount to attributing to bodies a power of creation *ex nihilo*, which La Forge considers an obvious absurdity; only God can truly create something.[33]

Because motive force cannot be a mode of body, La Forge concludes, "every body which is in motion must be pushed by something which is not itself a body and which is completely distinct from it"[34]—that is, it must be moved by the only other kind of substance there is: mind. But what mind would that be?

This is where La Forge turns to what might be his most important and powerful argument for his occasionalist thesis: the so-called argument from "divine conservation as continued creation." La Forge, like Descartes and so many philosophers and theologians before him, claims that God's causal activity is required not just to create the world and its contents, but also subsequently to sustain everything in existence. This divine conservation, moreover, happens through what is tantamount to a continuation of the original creative action. Were God to cease conserving the world he has

THE WORLD OF BODIES   205

created, it would reduce to nothing. Descartes's presentation of this principle in the *Meditationes* and the *Principia philosophiae* concerns the creation and persistence of himself as a thinking thing or soul, but the reasoning is supposed to apply to all finite substances:

> From the fact that we now exist, it does not follow that we shall exist a moment from now, unless there is some cause—the same cause which originally produced us—which continually reproduces us, as it were [*veluti*], that is to say, which keeps us [*conservet*] in existence. For we easily understand that there is no power in us enabling us to keep ourselves in existence.[35]

Thus, no created body or mind persists in being unless God continues actively to preserve it in being—or, as Descartes puts it in the *Meditationes*, "as it were [*quasi*], creates [it] afresh."[36]

It is important to note that—as Descartes's use of the qualifiers *veluti* and *quasi* indicates—continuous creation as adopted by Cartesians and other early modern philosophers does not imply a literal *re*-creation of things from moment to moment. It is not that time consists of discrete atomistic moments and things cease to exist after each such moment and are immediately created anew, brought back in to existence from nothing.[37] One does find such a radical version of the principle—a kind of "cinematic" view of the world, where the apparent spatio-temporal continuity of things really just is, at a deeper, metaphysical level, an uninterrupted series of discrete "frames"—at work among some medieval Muslim theologians, particularly the occasionalist followers of al-Ashari mentioned earlier.[38] But a philosophically less problematic scenario, from the perspective of identity over time, is that God's initial act of creation is sustained. In this way the activity of conservation does not differ in reality or even numerically—as an exercise of power—from the creative act but is just a prolonging of it. As Descartes puts it in the *Meditationes*, "the same power and action are needed to preserve anything at each individual moment of its duration as would be required to create that thing anew if it were not yet in existence. Hence the distinction between conservation and creation is only a conceptual one."[39] The presumption is that the thing does *not* need to be created anew since it already is in existence. Malebranche, who, like La Forge, uses the divine conservation principle to argue for occasionalism, is even more clear on this point: "The conservation of creatures is, on the part of God, nothing but their continued creation. . . . In essence the act of creation does not cease, because in God

206 THE GOOD CARTESIAN

creation and conservation are but a single volition which, consequently, is necessarily followed by the same effects."[40]

La Forge's introduction of the principle of divine conservation as continuous creation itself is somewhat succinct. All he really says, referring to the body, is that "it is a creature, that is, a being which is nothing on its own and which subsists only when, and how, and to the extent that it pleases Him who created it."[41] Nonetheless, the principle provides the foundation for La Forge's argument that only God can move a body.

> Let us assume, for example, during the first moment of [matter's] creation, that it was produced at rest. If that were the case, since God is immutable and acts in a way which he never changes, how could we believe that this formless mass—which even lacks the power to continue to exist on its own for a single moment—could in its entirety move itself by its own power a moment later or could force one of its parts to change place? But not only can it not change its condition by its own power; I also claim that there is no creature, spiritual or corporeal, which can cause change in it or in any of its parts, in the second moment of their creation, if the Creator does not do so himself.[42]

When God creates or sustains a body at any given time, God must do so in some relative place or other, in some specific relation of distance to other bodies; God cannot just create or conserve a body *in abstracto*, without creating or conserving it *somewhere*, relative to other bodies.

> Since it was He who produced this part of matter in place A . . . not only must he continue to produce it if he wishes it to continue to exist, but also, since he cannot create it everywhere or nowhere, he must put it in place B himself if he wishes it to be there. For if he puts it anywhere else there is no force capable of removing it from that location.

As I read this, a body is at rest if it is being sustained by God from one moment to the next in the same relative place, and it is in motion just in case it is being sustained by God from one moment to the next in different successive relative places. The force that moves that body, therefore, is and can be only the will of God.

> Let us conclude . . . that God is the first, universal and total cause of motion, and that just as he had to use his omnipotent word to draw the whole

THE WORLD OF BODIES 207

of nature out of nothingness, it is also by means of this word that he drew this same nature out of chaos by producing motion in it. And just as nature would revert to nothingness if he ceased drawing it out from [nothingness] at every moment in which he conserves it, it would likewise return to its pristine confusion if He did not maintain the motion which he produced.

La Forge explains that "the force with which God initially moved the various parts of matter . . . is identical with God because everything which is in God is God himself, and, when considered from this point of view, is indivisible and cannot increase or decrease." The total quantity of motion that an immutable God introduces into matter must remain constant. Nevertheless, he continues,

> Because of the way he [God] applies [this force] and the various subjects to which it is applied, it seems to be subdivided; and although it never increases nor decreases in the whole of nature, it increases and decreases from the perspective of the various bodies on which He exercises it.[43]

God is the cause of motion not only in the sense that God has introduced motion into the world and preserves its overall quantity, but also because all local determinations of that motion—increases and decreases in speed and changes of direction among particular parts of matter—are due to God's efficient causal activity as he conserves bodies over time in different spatial relationships (not arbitrarily but in specific ways on certain occasions "to satisfy the laws which he prescribed for himself").[44]

This line of reasoning, which appears in Malebranche in even clearer terms, should, I believe, be read as an exceptionally strong argument for the claim that bodies have no power to move themselves or other bodies, and that God is the primary and sole cause of the motion and rest of bodies and of any changes therein.[45] To be sure, as Leibniz understood and recent commentators have pointed out, the doctrine of divine conservation as continued creation does not, by itself, imply occasionalism.[46] In his *Theodicy*, Leibniz, after casting doubt on the radical version of the divine conservation doctrine—whereby "God resuscitates, as it were, all things outside himself at each moment: falling away as they do at each moment, they must ever have one who shall resuscitate them"—notes that

> What can be said for certain on the present subject is that the creature depends continually upon divine operation, and that it depends upon that

208 THE GOOD CARTESIAN

no less after the time of its beginning than when it first begins. This dependence implies that it would not continue to exist if God did not continue to act.[47]

But Leibniz certainly does not think that it follows from this that creatures lack causal efficacy. Indeed, among his objections to occasionalism is that the doctrine, by removing all activity and power from finite substances, thereby robs of them of their substantiality.[48] Plenty of good concurrentists—including Aquinas and Suarez—are committed to the divine conservation doctrine as well.[49] One could claim that the creatures whose continued existence is dependent on the continuation of God's creative act are also endowed and sustained by God with their own true causal powers.[50] However, it does seem, from La Forge's framing of the argument, that he, at least—along with Malebranche—most certainly intends it to lead to an occasionalist conclusion with respect to body–body relations.[51]

*

La Forge does want to preserve a sense in which bodies play a causal role in the scheme of things, and even have a "force" to move other bodies. But any such force is to be understood in a purely reductive manner. In an important passage immediately after presenting his arguments for God's ubiquitous and exclusive role as efficient cause of motion, he says that

> Although God is thus the universal cause of all the motions which occur in the world, I also recognize bodies and minds as the particular causes of these same motions, not really in producing any "impressed" quality in the way the Schools explain it, but in determining and forcing the first cause to apply his force and motive power to the bodies to which he would not otherwise have applied it, according to the way He decided to govern himself in relation to bodies and minds; that is, for bodies, according to the laws of motion which are so well explained in Book Two of Monsieur Descartes's *Principles*; and for minds, according to the scope of the power which He chose to give to their wills.[52]

Some commentators have taken the opening phrases of this passage to mean that, while God alone introduces motion into the world at creation, La Forge allows bodies efficaciously to determine the distribution of and changes in

THE WORLD OF BODIES 209

that motion among themselves, and thus that there is a real power in bodies to affect the modes of other bodies. But the rest of the passage makes it clear that bodies function only as occasional causes or *sine qua non* conditions, not true efficient causes. Their role is limited to prompting God to bring about some change or other in the particular motions of bodies. Thus, any "force" or "motive power [*vertu motrice*]" in bodies is to be understood in this very attenuated sense. To make that clear, La Forge ends the paragraph by saying that "the power [*vertu*] of bodies and minds to move [bodies] consists in that alone," that is, in occasioning "the first cause to apply his force and motive power" to bodies.

One can even continue to speak of force or motion being "transferred" from one body to another, but all this amounts to is that God causes some change in the distribution of motion on the appropriate occasions.

> He also had to arrange that this force would pass successively from one body to another, that is, that it would be applied successively to the various parts of matter to satisfy the laws which he prescribed for himself.[53]
>
> God conserves the same quantity of motion in the whole of nature because he uses the same force all the time without increasing or decreasing it, and . . . this force passes from one body to another because God applies it successively to different parts of matter.[54]

(It is worth noting that La Forge ends his paragraph about "minds and bodies as the particular causes" by repeating his claim that "therefore it is no more difficult to understand how a mind can act on a body and move it, than to conceive how one body pushes another." As we shall see in the next chapter, La Forge will—or, since things are not entirely clear, at least should—be treating the "force" or power of the mind to move the body in the same reductive way as he treats the force or power of one body to move another.)

*

La Forge insists that nothing he is saying here about body–body relations is a departure from "the thought of Monsieur Descartes" or from "the principles of Monsieur Descartes." On the face of it, this is somewhat cagey. Does La Forge mean that what he is saying is what Descartes actually had in mind, whether or not he expressed himself adequately on the topic? Or does he mean that what he is saying is consistent with Descartes's principles, even if

210 THE GOOD CARTESIAN

Descartes himself did not see fit to take things in this direction, and perhaps would not have approved of it?

La Forge quotes from the *Principia philosophiae* (II.36) the passage examined in the previous chapter where Descartes introduces God as "the first and more universal cause, which produces all the motions in the world in general." But he also brings up Descartes's letter to More of August 1649, and provides an extensive excerpt, in Latin, from it.

> The transfer which I call motion is no less something existent than shape is: it is a mode in a body. However, the power causing motion may be the power of God himself preserving the same amount of transfer in matter as he put there in the first moment of creation; or it may be the power of a created substance, such as our mind or any other thing to which he gave the power to move a body. In a created substance, this power is a mode of the substance, but it is not a mode of God. . . . You observe correctly that "motion, being a mode of body, cannot pass from one body to another." But that is not what I wrote; indeed, I think that motion, considered as such a mode, continually changes. For there is one mode in the first point of a body A in that it is separated from the first point of a body B; and another mode in that it is separated from the second point; and another mode in that it is separated from the third point, and so on. But when I said that the same amount of motion always remains in matter, I meant this about the force which impels its parts, which is applied at different times to different parts of matter.[55]

Now La Forge has already established that there cannot be in body an active power to affect the motion of another body; force understood in this sense cannot be in body as "a mode of the substance." But what *can* be a mode of a body is force in the attenuated sense, that is, the extended body's actual properties functioning as the occasion for God's causal activity as moving force. By bringing in a proof text from Descartes in which "the power causing motion . . . is a mode of the substance" without explicitly excluding body from among the items to which God might give such a power as a mode, La Forge may be read as suggesting that his own reductive view of motive force in body, and thus his account of God's role in moving bodies, is precisely what Descartes intended.

Then there is the fact that when La Forge provides a paraphrase French translation of this passage from Descartes's original Latin, he inserts his own

THE WORLD OF BODIES   211

interpretative remark. To complete the sentence in which Descartes says "it may be the power of a created substance . . . to which he gave the power to move a body," La Forge adds, in parentheses, "not by producing a new motion in the universe, but in merely determining the first cause to exercise its force on a given subject." He seems to want this to be read merely as a clarification of what Descartes was saying.

As we have seen, there are textual reasons, presented by commentators, for thinking that Descartes was not an occasionalist, not even in the body–body case. But what matters here is not how we are to read Descartes, but how La Forge read Descartes. And when La Forge concludes by insisting that "I do not think these passages [from Descartes] allow one to doubt whether what I said about the cause of motion and its nature agrees with the thought of Monsieur Descartes," it is tempting to take him to mean that his view *is* Descartes's view. Now he may indeed mean that, and he may want *us* to believe that Descartes was, likewise, an occasionalist on body–body relations. But I think that La Forge must also know that it is not true. I will return to this question in the book's Conclusion.

It is worth noting, though, that even if La Forge knows very well that Descartes is not an occasionalist but grants to bodies the capacity to affect, as efficient causes, the motive states of other bodies—by virtue of their modes or properties as extension (such as shape, size, divisibility, and impenetrability), along with their divinely caused tendency to persist in the same state[56]—still, La Forge's reductive conception of force can be drawn from Descartes's physics. To be sure, no active power distinct from other modes of extension can be a mode of a Cartesian body, for just the reasons that La Forge offers. However, force is an equivocal notion for Descartes, as it is for La Forge. On one hand, it can refer to that causally efficacious power which moves a body (or, as Descartes puts it in the letter to More, "which impels its parts"), in which case it "can be considered as belonging to God" or to "our mind or any other thing to which he gave the power to move a body." But what Descartes describes in his *Principia* as "the power of any given body to produce or resist motion" is represented by the product of the bulk or mass of the body and its speed (mv).[57]

> To enable us to determine . . . how individual bodies increase or diminish their motions or change direction as a result of a collision with other bodies, all that is necessary is to calculate how much force there is to move or to resist motion.[58]

This quantity that constitutes the force of a body either to move another body or to resist that other body's motion—a quantity which *is* a mode of a body (being but a function of the body's size and speed)—determines the distribution of motion upon collisions between bodies. It does not include any kind of active power that actually moves the bodies, but it does play a role in the explanation of the outcome of those collisions.[59]

*

For La Forge, then, bodies are the efficient causes neither of motion in the world of bodies nor of the changes that motion constantly undergoes. God alone causes and distributes motion among inanimate bodies, acting always on the occasion of some state in or between bodies, as determined by the laws of physics. La Forge's body–body occasionalism is fairly clear cut, and prefigures, in several ways, the account that Malebranche will defend a decade later.

There is, however, a noteworthy and rather fundamental difference between the case that La Forge builds against the true causal efficacy of bodies and the concerns that lie behind Malebranche's occasionalism. Both thinkers are Cartesians, of course, and both seek to demonstrate their Augustinian *bona fides* as well. But Malebranche and La Forge come to the question of causation from very different orientations. Malebranche is a Catholic theologian, La Forge is a medical doctor. For La Forge, withholding causal efficacy from natural bodies is primarily a philosophical and scientific affair. For Malebranche, while sharing those philosophical and scientific interests, it is primarily a matter of Christian piety.

This is no mere secondary concern for Malebranche, an afterthought or *pro forma* expression of religious sentiment. It is right at the forefront of this thinking, something he proclaims when he first introduces the problem of causation in his writings. To believe that those things in the world around us are endowed with real causal powers—including the power to affect us with pleasures and pains and thus to contribute to or detract from our happiness—leads the mind away from God and to a kind of pagan idolatry of nature. What Malebranche calls "the most dangerous error of the philosophy of the ancients" consists in believing that "[bodies] are the true or major causes of the effects we see." The idea of what a cause or power is

THE WORLD OF BODIES   213

represents something divine. For the idea of a sovereign power is the idea of a sovereign divinity but a genuine one. . . . We therefore admit something divine in all the bodies around us when we posit forms, faculties qualities, virtues or real beings capable of producing certain effects through the force of their nature.[60]

Because we will love and fear what we regard as the true cause of good and evil, the belief in causally efficacious natural bodies will lead us, like the ancient pagans, to worship these bodies in the heavens and on earth and "render sovereign honor to leeks and onions." Only the realization that all natural things are not true causes but mere occasions that "determine the Author of nature to act in such and such a manner in such and such a situation" can foster the proper worship of "the one true God."

Now it is hard to accuse a thinker who claims that God is the first, universal, total, and sole cause of the motion of bodies of not being sufficiently pious. La Forge is, to all appearances, a good Catholic (despite Gousset's claim that La Forge's taste ran more toward "the Romans"). Still, we do not find in La Forge—nor, for that matter, in Cordemoy—the kind of principled religious considerations that play so central a role when Malebranche addresses the topic of natural causation.

*

Thus runs La Forge's occasionalism in the strictly physical world of bodies. Descartes, however, in his letter to More, raises the possibility that God may have given "the power to move a body" to the human mind. Is this something that La Forge is willing to countenance? And conversely, while bodies may not be able to cause or affect motion in other bodies, does he allow that a body—more precisely, motions in the human body—may cause thoughts and other mental states in the mind? These are the questions to which we now turn.

9

Mind and Motion

Writing to Descartes in May 1643, Elisabeth of Bohemia is having some difficulty understanding how, if Descartes is right about the radically different natures of thinking substance and extended substance, mind and body can causally interact in a human being, as Descartes appears to maintain.

> So I ask you please to tell me how the soul of a human being (being only a thinking substance) can determine the bodily spirits, in order to bring about voluntary actions. For it seems all determination of movement happens through the impulsion of the thing moved, by the manner in which it is pushed by that which moves, or else by the particular qualities and shape of the surface of the latter. Physical contact is required for the first two conditions, extension for the third. You entirely exclude the one [extension] from the notion you have of the soul, and the other [physical contact] appears to me incompatible with an immaterial being.[1]

In his reply later that month, Descartes acknowledges that "the question which Your Highness poses seems to me the one which can most properly be put to me in view of my published writings." He cautions her not to try to understand mind>body interaction on the model of body–body interaction; this would be to use concepts proper only to the physical realm and the union of bodies among themselves to understand the union of mind and body. "If we try to solve a problem by means of a notion that does not pertain to it, we cannot help going wrong." This happens when "we try to conceive the way in which the soul moves the body by conceiving the way in which one body is moved by another."[2] We have by our intellects (aided by the imagination) a clear and distinct idea of what a body is and, he insists, how one body moves another. We also have a clear and distinct idea of what the soul is and how it gives rise to thoughts. As for the mind–body relationship, we know from experience that the soul, through its volitions, moves the body and that the body causes sensations in the soul. Even though the mechanisms by which such exchanges take place between disparate substances are opaque

The Good Cartesian. Steven Nadler, Oxford University Press. © Oxford University Press 2024.
DOI: 10.1093/oso/9780197671719.003.0010

MIND AND MOTION 215

to us—and cannot be grasped through the clear and distinct ideas of the intellect—we should have no doubts about the facts themselves.

In his Fifth Set of Objections to the *Meditationes*, Pierre Gassendi raises a difficulty similar to Elisabeth's. How, he asks, can the soul "set up motions in the [animal] spirits without being a body or having a body that would allow you to be in contact with them and make them move." More generally,

> How can there be effort directed against anything, or motion set up in it, unless there is mutual contact between what moves and what is moved? And how can there be contact without a body when, as is transparently clear by the natural light, "naught apart from body can touch or yet be touched"?[3]

In a letter to Clerselier appended to Descartes's Fifth Replies that appeared in the authorized French translation (1646), Descartes tells his friend that Gassendi's concern is based on a false assumption. "The whole problem contained in such questions arises simply from a supposition that is false and cannot in any way be proved, namely that, if the soul and the body are two substances whose nature is different, this prevents them from being able to act on each other."[4]

Descartes seems rather unconcerned about any supposed metaphysical obstacles standing in the way of mind and body acting on each other as efficient causes. In his view, the so-called heterogeneity problem simply does not arise.[5]

Not all later Cartesians were so sanguine. As we have seen, Geulincx has trouble understanding how mind and body, as radically different as they are, can interact. "Nothing can be attributed to body beyond mass and extension, which have no capacity to arouse thoughts. . . . There is no conformity of bodies, as they spin endlessly about, colliding and rebounding, with even the most insignificant thought in my mind." As for whether the mind can directly affect the body, he says, "I do not, properly speaking, interact with bodies; I have no place with them, and occupy no space."[6]

Clauberg is a bit less worried. As discussed in Chapter 7, he insists that the union of mind and body in a human being consists in "a certain relationship" whereby "the body and the soul relate reciprocally to each other through actions and passions," and that "no diversity in nature, however great, is incompatible with such a relation." After all, there is no greater diversity in nature than that between an infinite thinking substance and a finite extended one, and yet "God is able to act on a created thing."[7] Clauberg recognizes

216   THE GOOD CARTESIAN

that the causal correlation between mind and body cannot come about naturally. "The acts of the mind and the body in the human being are connected not by any natural relationship but only by the will of God." To an extent, Descartes would not disagree with this, in so far as he too attributes the close and intimate (and, to the human being, beneficial) connection between specific motions in the body and particular sensory effects in the mind—for example, fire burning the body and a feeling of pain in the mind—to God's providential will.[8] Still, Clauberg does at least see something problematic here that needs to be addressed:

> If you insist that a new motion is indeed produced in the body by the soul, this would be contrary to the principles of physics, which proclaim that in the entire universe, which includes human bodies, there is perpetually the same quantity of motion. . . . As to the doubt [that the body cannot cause thoughts in the mind], since the effect cannot be more noble than its cause, it is clear that a spiritual idea, such as what is in the mind whenever we sense or perceive something, cannot arise from a corporeal motion.[9]

Clauberg's conclusion, we saw, is that the mind, as a "moral cause," can only redirect motions already in the body. And in the body>mind case, he says that

> the motions of our body are only procatarctic causes, which give occasion to the mind as the principal cause to elicit from itself, at this time rather than another, these or those ideas which it always has in itself by a certain virtue and to bring its power of thinking into action.[10]

Again, it is unclear whether a bodily procatarctic cause—as well as any "occasional cause"—is simply a remote efficient cause of an idea, or some other, *sui generis* kind of cause. But, as before, there is no need for me to resolve this question here; in either case, the body>mind causal correlations come about only because God has willed that things be such as they are.

More to the present point, there seems to be nothing in Clauberg's account of body>mind causality that Descartes would not accept. On the contrary, it is pretty much his view. In the *Principia philosophiae/Principes de philosophie*, he notes that it is the "various kinds of motions in our nerves <which are required to produce all the various sensations in our soul>."[11] But, as he clarifies to Regius in the *Notae in programma quoddam*, he does

MIND AND MOTION 217

not mean that the motions are the direct and principal cause of those ideas in the mind. Nothing literally gets transmitted into the mind by the body; certainly not motion, which is not something that the mind can take on. Rather, there is a sense in which all the mind's thoughts are "innate" insofar as, with regard to both their formal reality as modes of the mind and their objective reality/representational content, they are the product of the mind's own causal power. He reminds his wayward disciple that

> nothing reaches our mind from external objects through the sense organs except certain corporeal motions . . . the ideas of pain, colors, sounds and the like must [like the ideas of motion and figure] be all the more innate if, on the occasion of certain corporeal motions, our mind is to be capable of representing them to itself, for there is no similarity between these ideas and the corporeal motions.[12]

Drawing on the distinction between a "proximate and primary cause" of some effect and a "remote and merely accidental cause which gives the primary cause occasion to produce its effect at one moment rather than another"—this is where Descartes provides the analogy of workers who are the primary and proximate cause of their work and the promise to pay them which counts as the remote and occasional cause of the work—Descartes locates the proximate and primary cause of ideas in the mind's own faculty of thinking.

This explanation that bodily motions are the "occasion" for the mind to causally generate an idea from its own resources will be the standard orthodox Cartesian account of the body>mind causal relationship. In no way does it amount to occasionalism, despite the use of the notion of occasional causation and the appeal to God as the ultimate source of the relationship.

*

On the face of it, La Forge appears to agree with Descartes when it concerns any alleged homogeneity problem. He allows that causal relations can occur both between things that are of the same nature or essence and between things that are not. Using terminology that has a fine medieval pedigree, he labels the former "univocal causation" and the latter "equivocal causation."[13]

218 THE GOOD CARTESIAN

Now among causes, some are univocal, when the effect resembles the cause, and others are equivocal, when the effect does not resemble the cause. It is obvious that the mind cannot act on the body as a univocal cause by forcing it to produce some thought, and that the body likewise does not act on the mind by communicating some motion to it, because the mind cannot be moved nor can the body think. It must therefore be as an equivocal cause that the mind, by its thoughts, forces the body to move and that the body, by moving, provides an occasion for the mind to produce some thought.[14]

Immediately following this, La Forge insists that

However it does not follow that the body is not the cause of the thoughts that arise in the mind on its occasion, nor that the latter is not equally the cause of the movements which occur in the body as a result of its thoughts, just because they are only equivocal causes. For God is no less the Creator of all things, and workmen are no less the authors of their workmanship, despite the fact that they are all merely the equivocal causes of these effects.

It would seem, then, that La Forge believes that bodily motions are re-mote (equivocal) efficient causes of sensory states in the mind—with the mind being the proximate (univocal) efficient cause of those states—and that the mind is the (equivocal) efficient cause of voluntary motions in the body. At one point he says that "the motions of the body bring [*portent*] their sensations to the soul instantaneously [*en un instant*]."[15] Elsewhere he claims that the mind "has the power [*le pouvoir*] to move our limbs directly [*directement*] by willing to move them"[16]—although this requires the mind also to turn the pineal gland in one way or another and thereby direct the an-imal spirits into certain openings in the brain's interior lining.

And yet, all may not be what it seems. True, La Forge insists that "it is no more difficult" to conceive of mind–body causation than it is to conceive or know body–body causation. But remember, first of all, that this is because it is not in fact as easy as we think to know how one body moves another, and thus mind–body causality is really just as opaque.

Moreover, we have seen that the "force" that one body has to move another is to be understood reductively, in terms of a law-like relationship whereby the states of one body are an occasion or *sine qua non* condition for God, as the only efficacious cause in play, to affect the motion of the other body. Might it not be the case, then, that the body's power to occasion the mind

MIND AND MOTION 219

to generate an idea and the mind's power (*pouvoir*) to move the body by changing the motion of the pineal should all be understood in the same reductive way, without attributing to the mind a truly efficacious causal power to affect the body or vice versa?

When it comes to identifying La Forge's brand of occasionalism, then, and especially its scope, things are not as clear-cut in the case of the reciprocal relations between minds and bodies as they are in the realm of bodies.

We begin with the body>mind case. There is that undeniable correspondence between certain bodily motions and certain thoughts (*pensées*) in the mind. More particularly, when an external material object communicates motions through a material medium, these motions eventually strike the sense organs. The sense organs, in turn, communicate the motions, via the nerves and the animal spirits, to the brain and ultimately to the pineal gland in its center. All of this takes place via divine efficacy in an occasionalist manner, since it involves only matter and motion. When the motions reach the gland and move it in particular ways, certain ideas and sensations occur in the mind. This correlation between bodily states and mental states is constant, universal, and involuntary.

But what explains the correlation? What is the relationship, in causal terms, between the motions in the body and the corresponding thoughts in the mind? As we have just seen, La Forge can talk as if the bodily motions directly and efficaciously cause the sensations. On the other hand, it is tempting, on the basis of some texts, to read La Forge as a body>mind occasionalist, and not just because of his use of the term 'occasion.' While discussing the correlation between motions in the body and ideas in the mind that constitutes the union of a mind and a body, he notes that "He who willed to join them in this way had to resolve at the same time to give to the mind the thoughts which we observe it acquiring on the occasion of motions of its body, and to determine the motions of its body in the way they should be in order to be subject to the mind's will."[17]

However, this passage, taken by itself and out of context, is misleading. La Forge's considered view seems definitely to be a non-occasionalist one, but *not* because the motions operate as direct and proximate efficient causes bringing about ideas. Just as Descartes does in the *Notae in programma quoddam*, La Forge distinguishes between two kinds of causes of ideas in the mind: the

220 THE GOOD CARTESIAN

principal and efficient (*effective*) cause, and the remote (*éloignée*) and occasional cause. The principal and efficient cause of any idea is the mind itself. The mind is an active substance and has the power to produce thoughts through its *faculté de penser*. "There is," he says, "an active power [*une puissance active*] in the mind which produces and forms ideas."[18] Sometimes, the mind produces ideas voluntarily, as occurs in pure rational thinking and imagination. More typically, thoughts are present to the mind without any volition. Sensations and ideas of the real features of extended bodies occur involuntarily when the human body's senses are at work, normally on the occasion of the presence of some external material object. What happens, according to La Forge, is that the motions communicated to the brain by the object, which motions are the remote and occasional cause of the sensible idea, give the principal and efficient cause—the mind—occasion to produce that idea.

> Although one could say that the bodies which surround our body and, in general, everything which can make us think of bodies—or even of minds, when such thinking is not initiated by our will—are in some sense the cause of the ideas we then have, because we would not have them in all the circumstances in which we have them if they had not acted on our body. However, because these are material substances, the action of which does not extend to the soul insofar as it is simply a thing which thinks but insofar as it is joined with a body . . . they cannot be more than their remote and occasional cause which, by the union of mind and body, causes our faculty to think and determines it to produce the ideas of which the faculty of thinking itself is the principal and effective cause.[19]

Two things are perfectly clear in this passage. First, motions in the body are *sine qua non* causes or occasions for sensations in the mind. As he says elsewhere: as a consequence of the divinely ordained union, "if the body had not had such a movement, the mind would never have had such a thought."[20] Second, the mind is the proximate efficient cause of its own sensory ideas. As a thinking substance functioning as an immanent cause—a cause whose effects inhere in it, as opposed to a transeunt cause, whose effects are in some other thing—it has a true efficacy and power for generating thoughts.

This becomes especially evident when La Forge turns to voluntary thinking, such as when we call up our intellectual ideas of God, the soul and other such metaphysical items.

It is only our power of willing and of determining ourselves which is the efficient cause of the ideas we form of spiritual substances and their properties when, without stopping at all the images of painters, we apply our understanding to examining them exclusively as things which think, and it is not on the occasion of some bodily object but by a simple effect of our will that we bring ourselves, of our own accord, to think of them.[21]

La Forge continues by explaining that "all our ideas, considered in themselves insofar as they are merely different ways of thinking, have no need—no more than all our other thoughts—of any other cause to produce them apart from our mind." The mind, with its faculty of thinking, contains within itself (and he insists that he is speaking here of something *dedans l'Ame*) the sole efficient cause of its ideas, "which has the power to determine its thought, to give it a form and thereby to represent to it the object which the faculty of perceiving thinks about in all cases of knowing."

There is, La Forge notes, a relevant distinction between the efficient cause of an idea and the exemplary cause of an idea. He emphasizes that he is interested mainly in the former. "The cause that we are looking for here is the efficient cause, that is, that which gives to our thoughts the form by the perception of which we are sure that we have such a thought."[22] That cause is none other than the mind itself, although the mind has been created by God such that it does generate certain (sensory) ideas on the occasion of certain bodily motions. It is in this sense that "the Author of the union of body and soul" has a causal role to play "for all the ideas that we have without the cooperation of our will on the occasion of species which are traced on the gland by some cause or other." But once the mind's union with the body has been established in the natures of things, God's primary work is done. The motions in the brain do not occasion *God* to do any immediate and direct causal work; rather, they serve the mind or soul itself.

(The exemplary cause of any idea, on the other hand, would be the external object that the idea is *of*—or, more accurately, it would be the isomorphic image of that body on the surface of the pineal gland corresponding to an image caused by the nerves on the interior surface of the brain. This material object or image is exemplary in the sense that its form occasions the mind to have an idea representing a particular object or features of an object. It provides, in other words, the information that directs the mind to "give our thoughts their forms" and cause this rather than that idea.[23])

222 THE GOOD CARTESIAN

La Forge knows that he is using, almost verbatim, the same explication of the origin of ideas that Descartes offers in his response to Regius in the *Notae in programma quoddam*; indeed, he cites just those passages from the *Notae*, which had been published in 1648, discussed above. To his mind, it is the orthodox Cartesian explanation of the causation of ideas. It appears, for example, in *La Logique, ou l'Art de penser* (the so-called Port-Royal Logic), composed by Arnauld, along with his Jansenist colleague Pierre Nicole, and published in 1662. In *La Logique*, a widely disseminated treatise on language and reasoning with which La Forge was no doubt familiar, its authors offer a brief paraphrase of Descartes's claim in the *Notae*:

> It may be affirmed that no idea has its origin in the senses, except by occasion, in that the movements that are made in the brain, which is all our senses can do, give occasion to the soul to form different ideas that it would not have formed without them.[24]

La Forge's view of body>mind relations, with the mind causally responsible for producing its own sequence of thoughts, is a remarkable departure from what Gousset tells us was his friend's view in 1658. Gousset, as we have seen, reports that according to La Forge "there remains one thing by which any new thought might exist in the mind. And that thing is nothing other than God." Yet, here is La Forge, in 1665, arguing that the mind is the efficient cause of its own ideas—both singular ideas and their sequential appearance. Why the change (assuming that what La Forge was proposing to Gousset was his true view)? We can only speculate, but perhaps it was La Forge's reading of Descartes's *Notae*, or Arnauld's *Logique*? Or, a more likely candidate, it was his collaboration with Clerselier, as of 1660, on the *Traité de l'homme*, in which Descartes says that

> When God unites a rational soul to this machine [i.e., the human body] . . . he will place its principal seat in the brain and will make its nature such that the soul will have different sensations depending on the different ways in which the nerves open the entrances to the pores in the internal surface of the brain.

The images thereby traced on the brain's surface, he explains, "give the soul occasion to sense movement, size, distance, colors, sounds, smells, and other such qualities."[25] Working on the *Traité* must have opened La Forge's eyes to how Descartes envisioned the body>mind relationship in the generation of ideas.

*

At this point, an old question comes back to haunt us. When La Forge says that the motions in the body occasion the mind to cause an idea, does he mean this occasioning relation to be a matter of real efficient causation? Is an occasional cause a true, if remote or "secondary" or "accidental," efficient cause? For Scholastics like Burgersdijk and Heereboord, the answer should be "yes," at least if (as seems likely) they would understand *occasional* causes (a term they do not use) to be *procatarctic* causes, which they explicitly identify as a species of efficient causes. It could be argued that this is also the view of Clauberg, who does refer to bodily motions both as what "give occasion" to the mind and as procatarctic causes of ideas.

For Descartes, it is just not clear whether, when the body "gives occasion" to the mind to cause an idea, it is to be understood as doing so as an efficient cause.[26]

In La Forge's case, however, there are good reasons for thinking that giving occasion is *not* a matter of efficient causality but a *sui generis* species of causation. First, if efficient causation requires an active power grounded in the nature of a thing, then it is hard to see how such an active power upon the mind can be grounded in the nature of an extended body, especially when the nature of body will not allow even for an active power to cause motion in another body. Moreover, consider the body–body case, where the state of one body gives occasion for God to affect the motion of another body: here it is absolutely clear that the occasional cause is not an efficient cause, since no finite creature could possibly exercise efficient causality upon God. This suggests that for La Forge occasional causation operates quite well without being a species of efficient causation. Why think, then, that the body can or is needed to exercise efficient causality upon the mind when it occasions the mind to produce an idea? Finally, to the extent that La Forge often describes bodily motions *qua* occasions as only *sine qua non* conditions for the primary cause to exercise its efficient causality, he appears not to regard this relationship as involving efficient causation. If I may import the paradigmatic example used by Descartes, it really does not seem correct to see the promise of payment as an efficient cause of the laborers doing their job, especially as that promise is neither necessary nor sufficient for the workers to exercise

224 THE GOOD CARTESIAN

their labor; they could certainly do the work without the offer (though they are not likely to); and, if they do not feel like working that day or have some more pressing matter to attend to, they can ignore the offer.[27]

In connection with this, it is also worth considering La Forge's remarks in his preface to the *Traité de l'esprit de l'homme*, where he emphasizes the agreement of his (and Descartes's) views with those of Saint Augustine. "This wise doctor" says in a passage approvingly quoted by La Forge that "all the bodily accidents that appear before our bodies and which external objects send to our senses, do not act on the soul," and that "it seems to me that the soul does not suffer anything from the body when it senses, but that it only pays more attention to its activity when the body suffers something from objects."[28]

While none of this is absolutely conclusive, it does seem to point to the fact that La Forge does not regard the operation of an occasional (*sine qua non*) cause to be an instance of efficient causation. The body does not act on the mind as an efficient cause when it occasions the mind to cause sensory ideas.

*

We now turn to the other side of the relationship between mind and body, mind>body causation and the voluntary movements of the body. Here, too, although La Forge's various statements across chapters of the *Traité* regarding the agency of the mind on the body can, when taken together, be somewhat confusing, he *seems* to be promoting a non-occasionalist account by granting to the mind a true causal efficacy upon the body, by way of the will.

In several contexts La Forge attributes to the soul "a power to move the body," alternately referred to as *une force* and *une puissance*,[29] and grants to the will "the power [*le pouvoir*] to join our thoughts to movements which do not resemble them."[30] The mind moves the body by exerting this power over the position of the pineal gland, which in turn controls the direction or course (but not the speed) of the animal spirits exiting it toward openings in the interior lining of the brain and, then, to the muscles. "Nothing follows from the will to move some limb except that it causes the animal spirits to exit in the way which is appropriate for carrying them to the muscles which can move it."[31] There is usually no indication that this is anything but a real efficacious activity, with the mind being the efficient cause of the movement of the gland and the flow of the spirits and thus, ultimately, of the motion of the body's limbs. "[The will]," he notes, "can well be the efficient cause of all those things that we notice depend immediately on it in this union."[32] It

MIND AND MOTION   225

may be a particularly telling difference in language when, in his explanation of equivocal causation, La Forge says, on one hand, that "the body, by
moving, provides an occasion for the mind to produce some thought," but
that, on the other hand, "the mind, by its thoughts, forces [oblige] the body
to move."[33]

Because La Forge's Cartesian soul is an active substance, it may not be
thought surprising that it can act on and move the body. Still, because the
soul is not extended or spatial, there are the old concerns about a heterogeneity or mind–body problem, and thus, once again—despite La Forge's
appeal to equivocal causation—some *prima facie* credibility to Elisabeth's
question to Descartes as to how the unextended mind can "push" or move an
extended body. La Forge, like Descartes before him, basically assures us not
to worry about such things. He says that he is explaining the matter the way
he does

> to remove from many people's minds the unfortunate tendency to believe
> that unless their soul were corporeal, it would not have the power to move
> the body because, they say, it could not do so without touching it and, ac-
> cording to the words of the poet, "Nothing except a body can touch or be
> touched." As if motion could be communicated only by impact or as if it
> were as easy to perceive how one body could move another as it is to see
> how it touches it.[34]

While the situation is muddied by La Forge's comparison once again, in
this passage, of mind>body causation with the difficulty of body–body
interaction—since "the cause of the motion of bodies is not something which
is as obvious as one might think"—it at least *seems* to be the case that La
Forge's occasionalism does not extend to the mind>body relation.

*

This "force to move the body" that La Forge grants to the human soul, however we end up reading it, is yet another instance of his fealty to Descartes,
although La Forge's position is actually more restricted than that of his
mentor. In numerous places, Descartes willingly concedes that the soul has
the power both to cause and to affect movement in the body, "to excite, or
resist or change [motions] in some manner," as he puts it in the *Traité de
l'homme*.[35] There is his reference in a letter to Elisabeth to "the power that

226 THE GOOD CARTESIAN

the mind has to move the body [*la force qu'a l'ame de mouvoir le corps*]" and "the soul's power to act on the body."[36] To Arnauld, he says, "that the mind, which is incorporeal, can set a body in motion [*corpus possit impellere*] is something which is shown to us not by any reasoning or comparison with other matters, but by the surest and plainest everyday experience."[37] And there is Descartes's claim in the letter to More cited earlier that "the power [*vis*] causing motion may be the power of God himself preserving the same amount of transfer in matter as he put in it in the first moment of creation; or it may be the power of a created substance, like our mind, or of any other such thing to which he gave the power to move a body."[38] For those who have trouble conceiving of how the mind can move the body, such as Elisabeth and Gassendi, he recommends once again—just as he does when it comes to understanding the mind's extension throughout the body—a comparison with the (false) conception of gravity. In this case, the analogy is with how gravity operates causally on a body. On the Aristotelian-Scholastic model, heaviness (*gravitas*) is supposed to be an immaterial "real quality" inhering in a solid body that, by acting on its matter, causes it to move downward. As he tells Elisabeth, such an explanation of gravity, though based on a misapplication of the "primitive notion" of the soul's power to act on the body, is nonetheless useful "for the purpose of conceiving the manner in which the soul moves the body."[39]

Clauberg was not the only member of this second generation of Cartesians to point out that Descartes has a problem if he believes, as these passages suggest he does, that the mind can really cause (initiate) or put an end to motion in a body. Cordemoy, too, saw that this would be inconsistent with the principle of the conservation of the quantity of motion in the universe, in so far as the mind would be adding to or decreasing the quantity of motion in the world.[40] He notes that "if we were able at will to make new motions, it would follow that the quantity of motion in nature could increase, and thus the order of nature would be disrupted."[41]

La Forge, as well, is too good a Cartesian not to know that the mind cannot move the body by adding motion to it. Unlike Descartes, then, La Forge—despite some language that suggests that the mind's "power" allows it to put the body into motion—actually limits the mind's influence to redirecting motions already there. This follows both a priori, from the conservation of motion principle, and empirically, from the fact that were we able to initiate, increase, or decrease the body's motions, we would have much more control over the condition of the body than we actually do.

> The soul does not have the power either to increase or decrease the motion of the spirits which exit from the gland; it has the power only to determine them, that is, to turn them in the direction in which they must go in order to execute its will. That seems clear from what we have already said, that God conserves the same quantity of motion which He had put in nature without increasing or decreasing it, and also from the fact that if the will had the power to increase or decrease the motion of the animal spirits as it pleases, we would not be subject as we are to an infinity of accidents to which we are subject; for example, we would be able to wake or sleep when we feel like it and in that way we would be able to escape an infinity of irritating inconveniences.[42]

It may be that what brought La Forge to this solution of how to reconcile the mind's causal power over the body and the conservation principle was an exchange he had with Clerselier in late 1660, during their collaboration on the 1664 edition of Descartes's *L'Homme*. In a letter that Clerselier wrote to La Forge on December 4, Descartes's literary executor appears to be disagreeing with something that La Forge had said in his original missive, now lost. Clerselier begins by acknowledging that "I see very little difference between what you think about the manner in which the soul and the body act on one another and what I told you was my view on that."[43] Since La Forge's letter is no longer extant, we do not know for certain what his position was; we can only guess from what Clerselier has to say in this letter. And despite Clerselier's conciliatory opening, it does seem as if, at this point, there was at least one very significant difference between their respective views on mind–body interaction.

Clerselier notes that he and La Forge agree that "the force that moves [a body] and even that which only determines motion at will and as it pleases has nothing corporeal about it . . . the principle of motion is outside bodies." The cause of motion, that is, must be a spiritual being, since "the essence of the body consists only in extension in length, breadth and depth." But what spiritual being would that be—an infinite one or a finite one? Or do both have some role to play? Clerselier argues that only an infinite being can cause or introduce motion into matter (*imprimer le premier mouvement au corps*), since it involves bringing something out of nothing and thus requires the power of creating *ex nihilo*. By contrast, "the human soul is only capable of determining the motions that already exist [*peut seulement capable de determiner le mouvement qui est deja*]."[44]

228　THE GOOD CARTESIAN

What La Forge must have been claiming in his letter—and here I believe he would have been taking himself merely to be following Descartes, who, as we saw, allows the mind to introduce or reduce motion in the body—is that the soul, in addition to redirecting pre-existing motions, can also cause motion itself. This is suggested by Clerselier's framing of a hypothetical response on La Forge's part:

> Perhaps you will say to me that because motion is only a mode of matter, which presupposes its subject . . . it does not require so great a power to introduce; matter, being divisible by its nature and having no repugnance to receiving it [motion].

But, Clerselier replies,

> Before matter existed, God's omnipotent word [*voix*] was required to make it come out of the nothingness in which it was. Similarly, to move or animate this matter and to bring out of nothingness the general and universal principle of all its forms [i.e., motion], this requires nothing less than the same word.

What the soul *can* do, Clerselier adds, is determine the motions by changing their direction, "which adds nothing real to Nature, and which involves nothing more than motion itself, which cannot be without determination." This is the position that La Forge ultimately adopts in his book, albeit (I will argue) with an occasionalist twist.

If La Forge had indeed been saying to Clerselier in 1660 that the human mind can introduce motion into the body, then this would seem to be yet another departure from what we know of his views in the late 1650s. According to the narrative provided by Gousset, at the time of their conversation La Forge was a thoroughgoing occasionalist who did not recognize in the mind a power to affect the motion of a body or even to cause its own sequence of thoughts. In the body>mind case, as we have seen, by the time he writes the *Traité de l'esprit de l'homme*—and possibly as a result of his work on the *Traité de l'homme*—La Forge has modified his view to accept the more orthodox Cartesian opinion that the mind causes its own ideas on the occasion of bodily motions. It may be, then, that we find La Forge by 1660 having changed his mind also on the mind>body case likewise simply to hew more closely to what he realized was Descartes's considered view and allow for the

MIND AND MOTION 229

mind to put the body into motion. However, the exchange with Clerselier enlightens him as to what a properly consistent Cartesian position should be (even if it is a departure from Descartes himself). It is a tight timeframe, since in the space of just a few years (1658 to 1665, the period when we know he was working on his *Traité*) we see La Forge swinging from the position that the mind cannot do anything, to the equally extreme view that it can introduce motion into the body, and finally to his moderate view that the mind can only change the direction of the body's motions.

It is worth noting that, in the *Traité* at least, La Forge dismisses one assumption that we have seen Geulincx, a thoroughgoing occasionalist, use to reject the mind as the true (as opposed to the occasional) cause of the body's movements. The epistemological principle behind Geulincx's so-called *quod nescis* argument requires that in order to be the cause of x one must know how to bring about x—one must know what causal factors mediate the occurrence of x and how to manipulate them so that they do bring it about. La Forge says that "we experience in ourselves that neither our will nor the knowledge of parts of the body which we acquire from anatomy make us either more disposed or more competent than we are naturally."[45] There are movements of the body that "depend directly on the soul and of which it is absolutely the mistress when the body is well disposed, such as those movements which are called voluntary."[46] Everyone knows that in order to move our legs to walk, all we need to do is will to move the legs. "It is enough to wish to walk in order to do so, when the paths are not blocked." The efficacy of the will in such cases does not require any knowledge of the pineal gland, the animal spirits, the nerves, or the muscles. In this respect, the soul's relationship to its body is, once again, not like the relationship between a sailor and his ship. A sailor will not successfully navigate his vessel to his desired destination simply by willing that the ship go there; nor will he succeed even if he knows what the route is. He must also have some understanding of the parts and instruments of the ship and how to use them. No such requirement holds for the mind's control over the body.[47]

*

What do we have so far, then? La Forge is an occasionalist when it comes to the realm of bodies alone, but he seems *not* to be an occasionalist when it comes to the reciprocal relationship between mind and body. God is the sole efficient cause of the motion and rest of a body on the occasion of its

230 THE GOOD CARTESIAN

encounter with another body in motion or at rest. The mind is the sole efficient cause of its sensory ideas on the occasion of certain motions in the body
with which it is united. And the mind, apparently—and, I will argue, *only*
apparently—is the true efficient cause of voluntary movements of the body
by causing (via re-direction) the requisite internal motions that make that
happen. God may be the foundational cause of the setup between mind and
body, such that the state of the body serves as a *sine qua non* condition for the
mind to exercise its faculty of thinking to produce sensations, and that the
mind has the power to move the body through the will; but God's causal role
in this scenario is, one might reasonably conclude, limited to establishing the
relationship in the nature of things.

There is, however, a problem with this highly restrictive picture of La
Forge's occasionalism which limits it to the realm of bodies alone. There may
be a serious tension between La Forge's depiction of the human soul efficaciously moving parts of the human body (even if only by determining the
directions of the motions already there) and his account of the divine conservation of bodies. There may also be a tension between divine conservation
and a human mind being the efficient cause of its own ideas and volitions. We
will consider the first potential difficulty here, and the second one in the next
chapter.

La Forge has established through his particular use of the divine conservation
as continuous creation doctrine that no created thing can move a body—only
God can move a body, by conserving it in different successive relative places.
But it would seem to follow, *a fortiori*, that no human soul can move a body,
any body, not even the body with which it is united. And because the motion of
a body, on La Forge's argument, is nothing but God conserving it in one place
rather than another, the soul would not be able even efficaciously to redirect a
body already in motion, since this would require it to change the place of a body.
La Forge's particular use of the continuous creation argument, in other words,
should preclude granting to the soul any ability to cause or modify motion in the
parts of its body. Even if the soul is an active substance and *does* have some real
causal powers—for example, to cause its own mental states—the exceedingly
strong argument for occasionalism with respect to bodies that La Forge employs
would render the body immovable by anything except God. Consider his conclusion of the divine conservation argument for the motion of bodies:

> Not only can [a body] not change its condition by its own power; I also
> claim that there is no creature, spiritual or corporeal, which can cause

MIND AND MOTION   231

change in it or in any of its parts, in the second moment of their creation, if the Creator does not do so himself.[48]

Now it is certainly possible to read this passage, and especially the final clause, in a concurrentist and not occasionalist manner. In that case, La Forge would be saying that the human mind does have a true power to affect the motions of its body but that it cannot exercise that power without God's concurrent causal contribution.[49] We have seen that divine continuous conservation per se does not entail occasionalism. Still, it is difficult to reconcile the mechanics of motion implied by the divine conservation argument as La Forge frames it with any kind of efficacious capacity in the mind to affect the motions in the body. Basically, Malebranche gets it right: if you use divine continuous creation to prove body–body occasionalism (as La Forge does), then you are also committed to occasionalism in the context of mind>body relations.[50]

La Forge's considered and metaphysically informed position may thus very well be that the mind has no more power to move a body, even by redirection, than any body has to move another body. It is hard to believe that La Forge himself did not recognize the difficulties raised for mind>body causation by his version of the divine continuous creation argument. Of course, one must be careful not to read the history of philosophy backward and anachronistically. It was only *with* and *after* La Forge that the continuous creation argument took on its importance among Cartesians as a powerful argument for occasionalism with respect to the motion of bodies; it is not as if there were a precedent in the form of the thoroughgoing occasionalism that we later find in Malebranche with which La Forge would have been familiar. Still, La Forge was no philosophical slouch, and the fact that the way he uses divine continuous creation has implications for minds moving bodies could not have escaped him.

There are, admittedly, statements about the mind>body case which are sufficiently ambiguous to be read in both an occasionalist and non-occasionalist manner. La Forge says that

the force which the mind has to move the body and that which the body has to stimulate various thoughts in the mind are necessary consequences of this union [of mind and body]. For having shown that this union consists in the interaction and reciprocal dependence between the movements of the body and the thoughts of the mind, it is easy to see that He who willed to join them in this way had to resolve at the same time to give to the mind

232 THE GOOD CARTESIAN

the thoughts which we observe it acquiring on the occasion of motions in its body, and to determine the motions of the body in the way they should be in order to be subject to the mind's will.

On one way of reading this, God's "resolution" consists only in setting things up once and for all so that the mind and the body have reciprocal modifications. God gave to the mind both the faculty for generating thoughts on the occasion of bodily motions and a causal power to move the body, and he gave to the body the (passive) capacity to be moved in the ways in which the mind would want it moved. What makes this reading plausible is the fact that—despite the occasionalist-like language whereby "[God resolved] to give to the mind the thoughts which we observe it acquiring on the occasion of motions in its body"—La Forge clearly does allow that in fact God gave to the soul a real efficacious power to generate its own thoughts on those occasions. Thus, the parallel he draws here with what God "resolved" with respect to the mind and its thoughts and what God resolved with respect to the mind determining the motions of the body suggests that the latter is an equally real and efficacious power. Still, it is hard to rule out another reading, one that, in light of the divine conservation argument and what we saw to be its ramifications for the motions of bodies, takes seriously that occasionalist-like language in the case of the mind>body relation. On that reading, what God resolves is that he would "determine the motions of the body" directly on those occasions when the mind wills it to move in some particular way.

Now one might raise the following, perfectly legitimate question: If La Forge *is* an occasionalist about mind>body relations, what are we to make of his regular use of the terms 'power [*puissance*]' and 'force [*vis*]' to describe the soul's causal capacity with regard to the body? But recall that La Forge uses this language also to describe the capacity of one body to move another, although it is certain that for him this bodily "power" is not a real causal efficacy grounded in the nature of body. What this suggests is that the "power" or "force" of the mind to move or affect the motion of the body is on the same metaphysical plane as the "power" or "force" of one body to move another. And, as we have seen in my reductive reading of 'force' in the case of bodies, what this "power" or "force" must amount to is nothing more than the regular, law-like correlation between the states of one and the states of the other, a correlation maintained by the efficacious and ubiquitous causal activity of God. La Forge makes this fairly explicit in the *Traité* in a passage we have already considered, in which he once again explains that the cases of body–body relations and mind>body relations are on a par:

> Although God is thus the universal cause of all the motions which occur in the world, I also recognize bodies and minds as the particular causes of these same motions, not really in producing any "impressed" quality in the way the Schools explain it, but *in determining and forcing the first cause to apply his force and motive power to the bodies to which he would not otherwise have applied it, according to the way He decided to govern himself in relation to bodies and minds*; that is, for bodies, according to the laws of motion which are so well explained in Book Two of Monsieur Descartes's *Principles*; and for minds, according to the scope of the power which He chose to give to their wills. *The power of bodies and minds to move consists in that alone.* Therefore it is no more difficult to understand how a mind can act on a body and move it, than to conceive how one body pushes another.[51]

On a natural reading of this text, the *pouvoir* or *puissance* that the soul, via its will, has to move the body is reducible to the fact that God moves the body on the occasion of a volition that the body should move. The reason why it is "no more difficult" to understand how the mind can act on the body than to understand how one body can act on another is because "one must have recourse to the same universal cause in both cases."[52]

Similarly, right after noting that God is the origin of the reciprocal relations between mind and body, La Forge warns us that "you should not say that it is God who does everything and that the body and mind do not really act on each other." This might look like a concession that the mind and the body are real efficacious causes, albeit because of the way God has set things up. However, he immediately explains that when natural substances "really act [*agissent veritablement*]" upon each other, this "action" consists only in the relationship of counter-factual dependence or *sine qua non* conditionality between the states of one substance upon the states of the other, just as in the body–body case.[53] "For if the body had not had such a movement, the mind would never have had such a thought, and if the mind had not had such a thought the body might also never have had such a movement."[54] It is God, it seems, who, at least in the body–body and mind>body cases, actually and causally brings about the relevant consequent states when the appropriate conditions obtain. (In the body>mind case, the *sine qua non* conditionality between body and mind can leave the active mind causally efficacious with

234 THE GOOD CARTESIAN

respect to its own ideas.) The sense in which God does not do "everything," then, is that minds are still causally relevant insofar as any full explanation of why a body is moving in a certain way in a case of voluntary movement must make reference to the mind and its volitions.

La Forge's deflationary strategy here appears contemporaneously with Cordemoy's claim that, though God is the only causal agent actively moving bodies with an efficacious power, minds and bodies can still be regarded as playing some kind of causal role.

> We perceive that as soon as the mind wills the motion of the body to be directed in a certain way, it happens. Why, then, can we not equally say that the mind acts upon the body, since, while it is not effectively our mind that causes motion, it is nonetheless certain that the motion of our body depends upon our will to the same degree and in the same way as the motion of a body depends upon collision with another body.

As Cordemoy explains,

> Just as it is said that one body moves another when, because of their collision, it happens that whatever was moving the first now moves the second; so it can be said that a soul moves a body when, because it so wills, it happens that whatever was moving the body now moves it to where this soul wants it to be moved. Still, it must be admitted that it is convenient to explain things in the ordinary manner, that is, to say that a soul moves a body and that one body moves another. Since we do not always seek the origin of things, it is often more reasonable, given what has already been noted, to cite the occasion rather than the cause of some effect.[55]

I believe La Forge is making precisely this same point.

It is useful in this context to bring up, once again, La Forge's long excerpt from Descartes's August 1649 letter to More, which he enhances with his own editorial intervention. La Forge quotes Descartes as saying that

> The transfer which I call motion is no less something existent than shape is: it is a mode in a body. However, the power causing motion may be the power of God himself preserving the same amount of transfer in matter as he put there in the first moment of creation; or it may be the power of a

created substance, such as our mind or any other thing to which he gave the power to move a body.

To clarify this last sentence, La Forge, all on his own, adds in parentheses: "not by producing a new motion in the universe, but in merely determining the first cause to exercise its force on a given subject."[56]

Finally, there is a later passage in which La Forge inquires as to whether the mind, once separated from the body after death, will retain "its power of moving some body." He explains that such a power in this lifetime "is not a necessary result of the essence of a finite mind, and its will has not power to do that except to the extent that it pleased its Creator to give it to it; that is"—and here La Forge explains what that "power" actually consists in—"to the extent that He decided to use his motive force according to the determination of his will."[57] So the essence of the mind does not include a power to move the body—unlike, say, its power to have a thought. But neither, it seems, does God grant to the soul any such real power when establishing its union with a body. Rather, the union—and the power—is nothing but the fact that God moves the body in a certain way when the mind has the relevant volition. La Forge can still stand by his final position as this appears in the *Traité*: that the mind, while it cannot introduce new motions into the body, can redirect motions already there. But this "power" in the mind to redirect motion must be reduced to the fact that its volitions serve as occasions for God, not to add or subtract motion, but to carry out any such vectoral changes.

Unlike the body, the Cartesian soul is an active substance. Thus, not all talk of the soul's powers needs to be understood in this deflationist way. But just because the soul does have causal efficacy—in particular, with respect to its own modes—it does not follow that it also has any true efficacious power to move the body. Ultimately, then, it seems that La Forge's position on mind>body relations, like his view of body–body relations, is an occasionalist one.[58] It is hard not to conclude, as well, that, in the mind>body case at least, he is knowingly modifying, in a significant way, Descartes's own views.

10

Ideas and Volitions

Thoroughgoing occasionalists like Cordemoy and Malebranche face a vexing conundrum. If God is the only efficacious cause and literally does everything, including generating all ideas in the mind and all volitional acts of the will, then human freedom would seem to be an illusion. And without at least *some* degree or kind of human freedom there will be serious moral and theological repercussions. Unless human beings do what they voluntarily do freely (however 'freedom' is to be understood), whether the action is virtuous or vicious, then arguably they cannot be held morally responsible for their actions. And if God is the sole true cause of our intentions and volitions, then it would seem that God is also the true author of our sinful thoughts and the actions that follow from them.

The challenge of reconciling human freedom with divine foreknowledge is one thing. If an omniscient God knows infallibly and from eternity what a person will choose to do, then it would seem to follow that that choice of action is destined to occur—that it happens necessarily—and therefore is not free, or so the argument goes. Theologically inclined philosophers, of course, have long wrestled with this problem. But the problem runs significantly deeper when God not only knows what a person shall will but also brings it about that she wills it. Even a compatibilist will disallow that a volition is free if its proximate efficient cause lies outside the mind, in some external agent—such as God.

In one of his letters to Elisabeth, Descartes, responding to some of her concerns about divine providence, concedes to God a more extensive causal role in the world than what one would conclude from most of his other writings. In the *Meditationes* and the *Principia philosophiae*, we learn that the omnipotent God who created and sustains the world and its constituents is also a perfect, non-deceiving deity whose goodness guarantees the reliability of our faculty for clear and distinct perception. God, Descartes says, also endowed us with a free will that is "infinite" in its capacity for choice and is thus the respect in which we "bear in some way the image and likeness of God." To Elisabeth, however, he goes even further:

The Good Cartesian. Steven Nadler, Oxford University Press. © Oxford University Press 2024.
DOI: 10.1093/oso/9780197671719.003.0011

IDEAS AND VOLITIONS   237

I must say at once that all the reasons that prove that God exists and is the first and immutable cause of all effects that do not depend on human free will prove similarly, I think, that he is also the cause of all the effects that do so depend. For the only way to prove that he exists is to consider him as a supremely perfect being; and he would not be supremely perfect if anything could happen in the world without coming entirely from him. . . . Philosophy by itself [i.e., without the aid of faith] is able to discover that the slightest thought could not enter into a person's mind without God's willing, and having willed from all eternity, that it should so enter. . . . God is the universal cause of everything in such a way as to be also the total cause of everything; and so nothing can happen without his will.[1]

Philosophy may be able to tell us that God is the universal cause of all things physical and mental. However, Descartes admits elsewhere, what it cannot do is tell us how consistently to accept both such an extensive conception of divine omnipotence and providence, on one hand, and, on the other hand, human freedom. Article 41 of the *Principia* is headlined "How to reconcile the freedom of our will with divine preordination." In it, he writes that

We shall get out of these difficulties if we remember that our mind is finite, while the power of God is infinite—the power by which he not only knew from eternity whatever is or can be, but also willed it and preordained it. We may attain sufficient knowledge of this power to perceive clearly and distinctly that God possesses it; but we cannot get a sufficient grasp of it to see how it leaves the free actions of men undetermined.[2]

As we shall see, and despite what this passage may suggest, Descartes does not believe that freedom requires a complete absence of determination; it only requires an absence of determination from something *outside* the mind, which the Cartesian God surely is.

Some occasionalists were willing to boldly go where Descartes feared to tread. Geulincx was not one of them; he left the mind alone, as the efficient cause if not of its own ideas then at least of its volitions. "My consciousness has certain modalities that do not depend on me, which I do not arouse in myself." Sensory ideas and other thoughts come from God. What *is* at my command, though, is "my will."[3] Cordemoy and Malebranche, on the other hand, were not so generous. Both of them denied any real causal efficacy in

238 THE GOOD CARTESIAN

the mind to generate its own volitions, and both struggled, in a very similar way, to reconcile this with human freedom.

Though Cordemoy appears, at first glance, to allow the mind this small corner of causal efficacy and autonomy—"All the soul's action," he says in the *Discours physique de la parole*, "consists in willing . . . our mind has the power to determine itself"[4]—appearances are ultimately deceiving. As we saw in Chapter 7, in the analysis of his position in the *Traitez de métaphysique*, the human will—the mind's universal striving for happiness, its inborn tendency toward the good in general—is but a spiritual impulse or shove continuously generated by God. God provides "all that is real [*tout ce qu'il y a de réel*]" in the will. As soon as we alight upon something that seems to be a means toward happiness and well-being, our desire is naturally attracted to it. The impulse toward "good in general" now becomes focused on a particular good. Nothing here derives from any kind of causal efficacy in the mind. All that human beings can "do" is suspend or provide their consent to allowing the will to rest on one particular thing or another that they perceive to be good.

What constitutes human freedom for Cordemoy just is the deliberation and choice behind our suspension or non-suspension of consent, and he insists that this is sufficient to relieve God from moral responsibility for what we do and place it in us. If a person consents for the will and desire to rest upon some inferior good rather than upon God, the true good, and thus ends up pursuing that inferior good, then that person bears full responsibility for his moral lapse. "If minds have chosen badly, it is because of a lack for which they alone are responsible. God made everything that was from Him and that sufficed for acting well, and minds did not use the power that He put in them. . . . The upshot is that whatever is evil or defective in this comes purely from the man and not from God."[5]

This is very much like Malebranche's mature theory of the will and its freedom—that is, Malebranche's view once he has moved beyond his early but quickly abandoned claim that the human mind can actually and actively "determine" or direct the divine impulse, much as one directs the trajectory of water by moving the hose from which it flows.[6] After noting that "just as the Author of nature is the universal cause of all motion found in matter, so is He also the general cause of all inclinations found in minds," Malebranche defines the will as "the impression or natural impulse" given to the soul by God "that carries us toward general and indeterminate good." The freedom of the will consists only in the fact that, when the mind is not fully convinced that a particular thing is a true good worthy of devotion, "it can suspend

IDEAS AND VOLITIONS 239

its judgment and love" and withhold its consent to allowing the divinely generated inclination to rest with that thing.[7]

Malebranche, too, sees this modicum of freedom as a quasi-power to suspend or not suspend consent to the divine force that (as it runs in the human mind) is the will as sufficient to address any concerns about freedom and responsibility and related theological issues.[8] God is always pushing us toward the true good. If we fall short in that endeavor and, by refusing to suspend consent, allow desire to rest on some inferior good or even on an evil, the fault is all our own.

> It is clear from all this that God is in no way the author of sin, and that man in no way gives himself new modifications. God is not the author of sin because He constantly impresses the impulse to continue on whoever sins or stops at some particular good, because He gives the sinner the power of thinking of other things and of proceeding to goods other than the one that is actually the object of his thought and love, because He commands him not to love whatever he can refuse to love without being troubled by remorse, and because He unceasingly reminds him of Himself through the secret reproaches of his reason.[9]

Cordemoy and Malebranche are unorthodox Cartesians—Cordemoy because of his atomism; Malebranche for his Vision in God doctrine and, well, quite a few other things. Their essentially shared account of the will as a directly sourced divine force is, likewise, a departure from Descartes. Despite what Descartes says to Elisabeth about God doing everything—and it is, admittedly, a puzzling remark, which some commentators have taken as an indication of his commitment to concurrentism[10]—there is no hint in his *oeuvre* that he denies to the human mind a true efficacy with respect to its volitions. On this topic, La Forge, once again, proves himself to be the more faithful Cartesian. Indeed, much of the chapter on the will in the *Traité de l'esprit de l'homme* is occupied with long quotations from Descartes, taken from both his treatises and his correspondence.

*

As we seek the full picture of La Forge's occasionalism, and having considered body–body and mind–body relations, we arrive at the final causal arena: the mental realm alone. So far it is clear that, at the very least, La Forge allows the

240 THE GOOD CARTESIAN

mind, with its faculty of thinking, an efficacious power to cause its own ideas. Sensory perceptions are caused by the mind on the occasion of bodily motions. But there are also ideas that are not related to motions in the body at all. These include intellectual concepts of extended bodies and other mathematical items, as well as ideas of "spiritual natures," such as God, angels, and the soul. Token thoughts of such ideas are typically voluntary and arise from "an active power in the mind which produces and forms the ideas which it freely perceives."[11]

That active power to generate thoughts spontaneously—one of "the principal causes which determine our mind to produce the idea which should represent one thing rather than another in a particular temporal context"—is the will. La Forge describes (but does not define) the will (*la volonté*) as "[the cause] of all the ideas which we think about only because we decide to think about them." Even if God, as "the author of the union of body and soul," is the ultimate cause of the mind's innate capacity to have this or that thought, by virtue of creating the mind with a particular nature and certain inborn powers—not just to think, but to think of particular items—still, it is the will that is the cause of any episode of voluntarily thinking of something. In such cases, La Forge says, "the will is the principal and proximate cause of the idea."

In the same chapter, La Forge also calls mind's faculty of thinking "the principal and proximate cause" of all of the mind's ideas. Any confusion is quickly dispelled, however, by the fact that he regards the will as a part of the mind's thinking understood in the broad sense. "These two faculties [understanding and will] are not distinct from the mind or the power of thinking [*puissance de penser*], and, since they are two streams which are inconceivable apart from their source, they are not really distinct from each other . . . these two faculties are just the thing itself which thinks, which sometimes knows and sometimes determines itself."[12] A more precise description of what happens, then, is that the will, acting as an efficient cause, stimulates the understanding to form a particular thought on a given occasion (not unlike the way the bodily motions, albeit serving only as occasional causes, incite the faculty of thinking to form a sensory idea[13]). This, at least, is suggested by La Forge's explanation that the mind "forms an idea of something at exactly the same time as the will determines itself and applies the understanding to think about such a thing." The appearance of voluntary ideas in the mind is thus a collaborative affair, with two active powers of the mind at work.

So, sensory ideas are generated by the mind on the occasion of bodily motions, and intellectual or imaginative ideas are generated by the mind when it wills to think of something.

As for the willing itself, any act of volition, like any idea, comes from the mind's own causal power or resources. Volitions are not modes of the mind that God causes directly, either by generating some ongoing power running through the mind (such as Cordemoy and Malebranche conceive it) or by causing on this or that occasion a particular act of affirmation or rejection. La Forge identifies "the essence" of the will itself as being

> the active faculty of all the mind's actions which chooses from itself and by itself [*de lui mesme et par lui mesme*] and determines itself to accept or reject what the understanding perceives or to remain suspended when something is not yet perceived clearly enough.[14]

The will, as part of the active faculty of thinking, is an efficacy essential to the mind. Unlike the mind's "power" to move the body, its power to cause ideas and to choose, judge, affirm, etc., is inseparable from it.

There is thus no occasionalism at work here. As De Villemandy points out in his 1686 treatise, La Forge may have removed causal efficacy from bodies acting on one another, bodies acting on minds, and even from a mind acting on a body. "But he stops there, and does not deny that a mind can act on itself, and that, by the principle of freedom, which is natural to it, determines itself now to one action, and now to another, according to what it judges to be convenient."[15]

Moreover, there is nothing in La Forge's account of the will that does not come right out of Descartes's conception of the mind's faculties and the relationship between will (which Descartes calls "the faculty of choice" and "the faculty of judgment") and understanding. The understanding, as the source of ideas—both clear and distinct ideas and obscure and confused ones— "proposes" items to the will for its action, either as something that is true or as something that is good. The will then either affirms or denies the idea, that is, either accepts or rejects the content of the idea as true or as presenting something that is in fact good and thus worthy to be pursued. "The will," Descartes notes in the *Meditationes*, "consists simply in our ability to do or not do something, that is, to affirm or deny, to pursue or avoid" whatever the intellect puts forward for affirmation or denial or for pursuit or avoidance.[16]

*

That "principle of freedom" to which De Villemandy refers in his account of La Forge's occasionalism raises a number of questions. What kind of freedom

242 THE GOOD CARTESIAN

does La Forge envision for the will? In what sense does it "determine itself"? Does La Forge in fact, as he insists in the chapter of the *Traité* titled "The Will," really only "borrow [Descartes's] ideas and provide a supplement to what he would have said about the nature of the mind at the end of the *Traité de l'homme* if death had not prevented him from completing it"?[17]

Descartes's views on freedom are notoriously complex, and a good deal of scholarship has been devoted to trying to untangle them.[18] Trouble lies especially for those who would categorize Descartes in contemporary (but anachronistic) terms as either a libertarian or a compatibilist/soft determinist. A few things, however, are quite clear.

First, Descartes does not see freedom of the will as compatible with external determination. But then again, he insists that our acts of will never are and *cannot* be externally determined or constrained (despite his pious remarks to Elisabeth about the extent of God's causal role). In his definition of the will as "our ability to do or not do something," Descartes adds that when we make those mental affirmations or denials or pursuits or avoidances, "our inclinations are such that we do not feel we are determined by any external force."[19] It does not follow, however, that freedom requires an absolute lack of determination and an indifference such that, all things being the same, one could just as well have decided or chosen otherwise. There are many instances of judgment in which one could *not* have done otherwise, and yet, he claims, these represent the highest grade of freedom. In a crucial passage from the Fourth Meditation, Descartes notes that

> In order to be free, there is no need for me to be inclined both ways; on the contrary, the more I incline in one direction—either because I clearly understand that reasons of truth and goodness point that way, or because of a divinely produced disposition of my inmost thoughts [i.e., via grace], the freer is my choice. Neither divine grace nor natural knowledge ever diminishes freedom; on the contrary, they increase and strengthen it. But the indifference I feel when there is no reason pushing me in one direction rather than another is the lowest grade of freedom; it is evidence not of any perfection of freedom, but rather of a defect in knowledge or a kind of negation. For if I always saw clearly what was true and good, I should never have to deliberate about the right judgment or choice; in that case, although I should be wholly free, it would be impossible for me ever to be in a state of indifference.[20]

IDEAS AND VOLITIONS 243

In the presence of an obscure and confused idea, where the representational content does not provide enough epistemic justification or evidence for certain judgment—where, Descartes says, "the intellect does not have sufficiently clear knowledge at the time when the will deliberates"—the mind is not rationally drawn one way or the other. The sensory idea of cold, for example, is so opaque and indistinct in its content that it does not allow one to judge with evident reason whether cold is a positive quality or an absence of heat. In the face of such a "materially false" idea, there will be no spontaneous urge to assent to what it purports to say about what cold actually is.[21] This kind of indifference, characteristic of what a libertarian account might demand, consists, if not in a perfect equilibrium between options, at least in an absence of irresistible determination.

The highest grade of freedom, on the other hand, involves the will determined to give its assent to the clear and distinct evidence in front of it. This is not a matter of external determination, strictly speaking, since the two faculties at work here are both a part of the mind. But neither is it correct to regard the idea of the understanding as operating on the will as an efficient cause. Rather, the will is of such a nature that, in the presence of the clear and distinct idea, it spontaneously assents. One experiences a kind of inner compulsion whereby the will, by its own nature, practically cannot *not* assent to the idea's content.

> I could not but judge that something which I understood so clearly was true; but this was not because I was compelled to do so by any external force, but because a great light in the intellect was followed by a great inclination in the will, and thus the spontaneity and freedom of my belief was all the greater in proportion to my lack of indifference.[22]

A will determined by reasons alone is as free as the will can be, even though it really cannot act otherwise than as it does.

In Chapter 11 of his *Traité*, La Forge quotes all of these passages at length, and agrees wholeheartedly with their lesson. A second part of the will's essence, as La Forge defines it, consists in "being such that at the same time that the understanding proposes to it, distinctly and without obscurity, a truth or falsehood, a good or evil, it determines itself infallibly to accept one and reject the other."[23] When the will is so moved by the clarity and distinctness of the intellect's ideas, it is not "forced [*violenté*]" in its judgments. Rather, this

244 THE GOOD CARTESIAN

condition represents perfectly "the power which it has to produce by itself...
all the actions and thoughts which involve some choice and discrimination."

Nor, La Forge says, does the will's determination in the face of the intellect
represent any loss or diminution of that "positive power which we have to act
or not act, which [Descartes] recognizes is exercised by the will in all its action." What he means is that a power to choose remains the two-way power
it is even if, on a given occasion, when prompted by the understanding, it
determines itself infallibly to a particular exercise of that power. (One might
compare it to the mind's faculty of thinking, which, despite being determined
to think about one thing on a particular occasion, is still a power to think of
many other things.) Being a two-way power is essential to *the will* as a faculty; as Descartes puts it, "the will consists in the ability to do or not do something." Even when the will moves irresistibly in one particular way because of
the clear and distinct content of an idea, it retains the "hypothetical" power
to do otherwise insofar as it could have done otherwise if things had been
different.[24] However, being able indifferently and without determination to
exercise that power in either of two ways on any given occasion is not essential to *freedom*; or, in Descartes's words again, "in order to be free, there is no
need for me to be inclined both ways."

La Forge notes, too, that the mind's freedom also consists in the fact that
"despite following and infallibly accepting the good it knows clearly, nevertheless, by means of this faculty it always does so freely and it could (absolutely speaking) not do so." La Forge is here bringing up something that
Descartes himself had claimed—not in the *Meditationes*, however, but in a
1641 letter or memorandum, possibly for Mesland but directed at the views
of Mesland's fellow Jesuit Denis Petau.[25] This letter is the source of some of La
Forge's longest quotations from Descartes, and what Descartes says therein
about what the will can "absolutely" do has led some recent commentators to
see him as making a non-trivial concession to libertarianism.[26]

After explaining in the 1641 piece that indifference in the will comes in
degrees, depending on how many reasons "impel [a person] to choose
one side rather than another," Descartes addresses the question as to the
conditions under which one can in fact suspend judgment.

> It seems to me certain that a great light in the intellect is followed by a great
> inclination in the will; so that if we see very clearly that a thing is good for
> us, it is very difficult—*and, on my view, impossible, as long as one continues
> in the same thought*—to stop the course of our desire.

IDEAS AND VOLITIONS 245

That is, while one is actually attending to a clear and distinct idea, one cannot refrain from assenting to it. But, he continues,

> The nature of the soul is such that it hardly attends for more than a moment to a single thing; hence, as soon as our attention turns from the reasons which show us that the thing is good for us, and we merely keep in our memory the thought that it appeared desirable to us, we can call up before our mind some other reason to make us doubt it, and so suspend our judgment, and perhaps even form a contrary judgment. . . . I call free in the general sense whatever is voluntary, whereas you [Mesland] wish to restrict the term to the power to determine oneself only if accompanied by indifference.[27]

The fact that one cannot help but assent to a clear and distinct idea does not detract from the freedom of the will in doing so. True indifference only appears when one is not in the presence of a clear and distinct idea. This can happen either when one's idea is obscure and confused, or when, subsequently remembering that one did have a clear and distinct perception but no longer attending to it, one now entertains some reason or another to suspend judgment about its content (much as Descartes does in the First Meditation, when he subjects even his most evident beliefs to skeptical doubt).

In a later letter to Mesland, Descartes returns to the question. He reiterates that the freedom of indifference that consists in the will "not impelled one way rather than another by any perception of truth or goodness" is the "lowest grade of freedom." He then adds that there is another meaning of 'indifference,' namely, "a positive faculty of determining oneself to one or other of two contraries, that is, to pursue or avoid, to affirm or deny. I do not deny that the will has this positive faculty." Even when the will is compelled by a clear and distinct idea to give its assent, it maintains this faculty to choose between two contraries. Being determined to exercise that faculty toward one of the contraries does not destroy the power it has to have chosen the other.

> The will has this positive faculty . . . not only with respect to those actions to which it is not pushed by any evident reasons on one side rather than on the other, but also with respect to all other actions; so that when a very evident reason moves us in one direction, *although morally speaking we can hardly move in the contrary direction, absolutely speaking we can.* For it is always open to us to hold back from pursuing a clearly known good, or from

246 THE GOOD CARTESIAN

admitting a clearly perceived truth, provided we consider it a good thing to demonstrate the freedom of our will by so doing.[28]

It is the distinction between what is "morally" possible and "absolutely" possible that Descartes brings up here that has caused much distress among commentators. Is Descartes saying that even when we are determined, before a clear and distinct idea, to give our consent, we can still, absolutely speaking, withhold it? If that were the case, then he apparently would be trying to preserve at least some degree of (libertarian) indifference *qua* capacity to act otherwise in the same circumstances. But this is not what Descartes is saying. What he means, it seems, is precisely what he says in the earlier letter or memorandum about Petau. If I am attending solely to the clear and distinct idea, I cannot withhold judgment. But then consider two other scenarios. First, I am no longer attending to the idea: in this case, I am not compelled to give it my assent, and so can suspend judgment. Second, I am attending to the idea but also attending to some other, equally or perhaps more pressing reason to suspend that judgment—for example, that "it is a good thing to demonstrate the freedom of our will."[29] In this latter case, I suspend judgment, but (assuming that the reason to suspend is itself clear and distinct) am just as determined to do so as I was determined to give my assent when attending only to the original clear and distinct idea.[30] Descartes is not reintroducing some kind of libertarian indifference through the back door.[31]

La Forge, quoting from these texts, says that "when indifference is understood as [a] neutral condition of the soul, when it does not know to what to determine itself," Descartes was "surely correct" to say that freedom does not consist in indifference. "For who can deny that we do nothing as freely and voluntarily as those things where we do not find the least reason to hesitate or doubt."[32] At one point he describes the effect that ideas have upon the will as the will being "pushed and incited [*poussez & incitez*] to judge or suspend our judgment in proportion to the clarity or obscurity of our ideas."[33] When the will is so determined in the face of clear and distinct reasons, it remains self-determining insofar as "the will attaches itself of its own accord [*s'attache d'elle mesme*] and joins itself infallibly to this truth or goodness."[34] The only thing that could keep it from doing so is a lapse of attention, the discovery of something obscure in the idea—both of which would leave the will indifferent in the sense that it is not irresistibly drawn by its nature to make a particular judgment—or attending to some more compelling reason (such as "considering the exercise of its freedom as the highest good"), which, far

IDEAS AND VOLITIONS 247

from leaving the will indifferent, sees it determined in a new direction. But, he insists, even as the will acts in one particular way, and thus cannot be said to have maintained at that moment the possibility of acting in another way, it retains its "indifference" understood as its "positive power which we have to act or not act." He compares the will to someone who has come in from the cold and infallibly moves toward the fire that he sees. La Forge insists that while that choice of bodily motion is certain to happen, "absolutely speaking, they would be able not to do so." The person who makes such a (determined) decision does so because he is endowed with an absolute capacity to choose one way or another. "The infallibility of an action does not destroy the power of doing the contrary," he says, even if that power to do the contrary most certainly will not, indeed cannot, be exercised in the circumstances.[35]

There is one other text from Descartes that La Forge cites in his discussion of freedom of the will, and that is the letter to Elisabeth examined above in which Descartes declares that God is "the cause of all those [effects] which do depend on human free will," insofar as "God is the universal cause of everything in such a way as to be also the total cause of everything." La Forge says that this represents "the biggest difficulty which is introduced by those who doubt their freedom." And yet, he claims, a recognition that, while all things depend on God, they do so in different ways is sufficient to address the problem.[36]

> For in the production of effects to which neither our own will nor that of any other free agent contributes, one could say that God consulted his own will alone, by which he unconditionally determined to produce them in a certain way and at a certain time; but in the case of effects to which our will contributes, God did not consider his own will alone but he also included the consent of our will in his decree, and it was only after having foreseen how our will would determine itself in such and such circumstances that he consequently willed absolutely that such effects would result.[37]

It is tempting to read this as a classic concurrentist account (in the Suarezian mode) with respect to the causal efficacy of the will in the external world. The human mind wills that such and such a thing happen—for example, a movement of my limbs—but the will does not have that bodily effect unless God, seeing what the mind wills, also wills concurrently that the effect should occur. A better reading, though—one in keeping with what I have argued is La Forge's occasionalism with respect to the motion of bodies—is

248   THE GOOD CARTESIAN

that God brings about these external effects on the occasion of the mind's volition. In either case, there is no indication that God's causality extends to the
volition itself. God does not will *that* I will. Rather, the willing arises from the
mind's active and efficacious faculty and the will "determines itself." Indeed,
La Forge's claim here about divine foreknowledge of my willing would make
no sense if God was required first to will that I will.[38]

Thus, even in the shadow of divine omnipotence, the mind maintains an
independent power to generate its own volitions. As La Forge writes about
the mind's autonomy in his dedicatory letter to Montmor, "threats, torture,
and the cruelest tyrrany could not constrain its desires nor force its decisions,
and even God, from whom it got its existence and on whom it depends completely for its conservation, has left it complete freedom in its actions."[39]

*

So far, so good. La Forge may be an occasionalist when it comes to the motion of bodies—whether they stand in relation to each other or to a willing
mind. But there remains one arena where a finite substance has true causal
efficacy. The mind retains a capacity to cause its own thoughts, its own ideas
and volitions. This is something that neither Cordemoy nor Malebranche
allows.

Now La Forge might seem to be in a bit of a philosophical bind. If the mind
is supposed to be the true and efficacious cause of its own ideas and volitions,
one could legitimately wonder whether there is a problem of consistency internal to his system. As we have seen, La Forge uses the strong "divine conservation as continuous creation" argument to demonstrate an occasionalist
thesis about the motions of bodies. It is natural then to ask: Does the continuous creation thesis apply to the soul as much as to the body? The answer is: Yes, of course—it applies to all created natural substances. Descartes,
La Forge's mentor in all things philosophical, explicitly says in the Third
Meditation that God's continuous activity is required to conserve him, as a
thinking thing, in existence from moment to moment. La Forge follows him
on this point:

> As regards duration, it is indubitable that it applies to the body and mind
> in the same way, because neither of them is anything of itself and they both
> need the Supreme Being to produce them, not only at the first moment of
> their creation but also during all the moments in which they continue to

exist, and therefore their duration must be a continuous reproduction by which they persevere in their existence as long as it pleases the Creator to conserve them.[40]

On this basis, I once argued that La Forge is not entitled to claim that the mind is or can be the active and efficacious cause of its own ideas (whether sensory ideas on the occasion of bodily motions or intellectual ideas in voluntary thoughts) or volitions.[41] Can the Cartesian who employs the doctrine of divine conservation in arguing for body–body occasionalism as La Forge does consistently hold, at the same time, that the soul, unlike the body, is active with real causal efficacy? If that doctrine renders bodies inert, why should things be any different with the soul? God, it would seem, must, through his activity of conserving all finite substances, be the cause of all mental states, as much as he is the cause of all bodily motions.

Recall that God gives bodies their kinetic modifications precisely through his activity as their sustaining cause. He brings about the motion and rest of bodies by conserving them in particular spatio-temporal modalities. At each moment God must sustain ("recreate") a body in some particular relative place; if the body is conserved in the same relative place from one moment to the next it is at rest, and if it is conserved in different successive relative places it is in motion. It would seem, moreover, that God's causal activity in sustaining his creation should account for the all the other modes or properties of bodies as well. Just as God brings about the particular motive properties of a body merely by conserving it in the same or different relative places, so God cannot conserve a body without conserving it with some particular shape—either the same continuous shape or some change in shape from moment to moment. God's continuous activity of sustaining a body thereby gives it not just its specific place(s) and thus its motion or rest, but presumably its other modalities as well.[42]

Should not this same argument carry through to the case of the soul? Just as only God can cause a body to be in motion or at rest, so only God can cause a soul to have the particular thoughts it has, by conserving it in this or that mental state. The divine *modus operandi* as conserver of things—whereby God does not (re)create things in abstraction, without regard to their particular ways of being—would apparently have to work the same way with minds as it does with bodies. But then God must be responsible for bringing about the mental properties of a soul just by conserving it in one thinking state or another. The modes of a mind are its ideas and volitions. As a body undergoes

250 THE GOOD CARTESIAN

from moment to moment a series of modes, each of which consists in spatial contiguity to other bodies, so a mind over time undergoes (or experiences) a series of ideas and volitions. What would bring it about that one idea or volition either persists through a time segment or succeeds and is succeeded by another is simply that at each moment God sustains/recreates a soul either with the same particular idea or volition from the previous moment or with a different idea or volition. Thus, the soul would be no more active with respect to its modes than the body is with respect to its modes. In both cases God's conserving activity would extend, so to speak, through the substance to its modes. How, then, can the soul really be the true efficient cause of its ideas on the occasion of bodily motions or of its volitions? This extreme view seems, in fact, to be precisely the position that La Forge was defending to Gousset back in 1658.

It is interesting to note that Malebranche takes things in just this direction. Among his arguments for occasionalism with respect to the soul's modalities is one based on his divine conservation principle. In the *Traité de morale* (1684), he writes that

> Glory and honor belong to God alone. Toward Him alone all the movements of all minds ought to tend, because only in him does power [*puissance*] reside. All willing by creatures is inefficacious by itself. Only He who gives being could be able to give the ways of being, since the ways of being are nothing but beings themselves in this or that fashion [*façon*]. . . . For what is more evident than that if God, for example, keeps a body always in one place, then no creature could move it to another? Or that no man could even move his own arm unless God wills to concur in doing that which the ungrateful and stupid man thinks he is doing by himself? *And the same goes for the ways of being of minds.* If God keeps or creates a soul in a way of being which afflicts it, such as with pain, no mind can deliver itself therefrom, nor make itself to feel pleasure thereby, unless God concurs with it to carry out its desires.[43]

La Forge seems, then, to be caught in a conundrum. He wants to reserve to the human mind some element of causal efficacy, at least with regard to its own thoughts. However, given his commitment to that strong version of the doctrine of divine continuous creation, he may not be entitled to any such power in the mind. The same argument that renders a body causally inert, incapable of causing motion in itself or in another body, and that reserves all

IDEAS AND VOLITIONS 251

causal efficacy for God, would appear also to render the soul causally inert, incapable of causing its own mental states. Or so I once argued.[44]

However, as several scholars have rightly pointed out, there are relevant differences between God's conserving a body from moment to moment and God's conserving a mind.[45] At least one of these differences derives from the nature of the item being conserved. Bodies, as mere extension, are passive, and so, as La Forge argues at length, are incapable of putting themselves into motion, or indeed of generating any modification of their substance. God is therefore required to do the necessary causal work. In the case of the mind, however, we are dealing with something that, by its nature, is active—a finite substance that, La Forge also argues (as any Cartesian would), is endowed by God with the power to cause its own thoughts and volitions. This, I agree, should effectively block the divine conservation argument—which in the case of bodies extends to their modes—from also reaching the modes of the human mind.

La Forge's account of the mind's causal powers with respect to its own modes is thus best read as a kind of conservationism. The mind or soul must be sustained in existence by the God who created it. But the spiritual substance thus conserved escapes the clutches of La Forge's occasionalism and remains the efficacious master of its own domain.

Conclusion

How Important Was La Forge?

Louis de la Forge passed away sometime in 1666. He did not live to witness the celebration one year later of the repatriation to Paris of (most of) Descartes's remains from Stockholm, where the philosopher had died in the service of Queen Christina.[1] The casket containing the bones was buried in the Church of Saint Geneviève, part of an abbey which no longer exists but which stood at the site now occupied by the Pantheon (which was constructed in the late 18th century). This was "the most elevated place of the capital," Baillet reports, "and at the summit of the first university of the kingdom."[2] Descartes's return to his native land was to be carried out with all due ceremony, including a banquet and speeches. The chancellor of the University of Paris, Father Pierre Lallemant, was engaged to deliver a funeral oration, aided by notes supplied by Clerselier.

With everything in place, and the *Messieurs de Sainte Geneviève* having prepared their church in magnificent fashion, the cortège began its march from the Church of Saint Paul, where the remains were being stored, to what would be Descartes's final resting place. Bells were rung, prayers and a Mass were said, and a large crowd gathered to hear the encomiums. At the eleventh hour, however, a royal order came down forbidding Lallement from going through with his speech. According to the chancellor's diary, he was told that there was no way the university could be seen giving public approval to Descartes's philosophy.[3]

We can imagine that La Forge, were he still among the living, would have made the journey from Saumur to Paris for the event. No matter, though. His work was done. While the prohibition against the eulogy was but the beginning of a long period of censorship of Descartes's philosophy in France by civil, academic, and ecclesiastic authorities—a formal condemnation by the University of Paris and the city's archbishop would be issued four years later—Cartesianism would dominate the philosophical scene there and elsewhere in Europe for the rest of the century. And a good deal of credit for that

The Good Cartesian. Steven Nadler, Oxford University Press. © Oxford University Press 2024.
DOI: 10.1093/oso/9780197671719.003.0012

CONCLUSION: HOW IMPORTANT WAS LA FORGE? 253

goes to La Forge. His impact was both subtle and, given how short his life was and how little he actually wrote—one commentary on Descartes's physiology and one treatise of his own—well out of proportion.

The question of La Forge's importance has been broached before. Prost, in his groundbreaking *Essai sur l'atomisme et l'occasionalisme dans la philosophie cartésienne* (1907), notes that La Forge saw himself as but "a modest continuer of the great philosopher whom he presents in general terms," and yet grants him a central role in the development of Cartesianism.[4] Pierre Clair, likewise, in both his article "Louis de la Forge et les origines de l'occasionalisme" and his introduction to La Forge's *Oeuvres complètes* (which, unfortunately, is long out of print), acknowledges La Forge's significance for the use of the phrases *donner occasion* and *cause occasionelle*.[5] There is also Seyfarth's short 1887 study *Louis de la Forge und seine Stellung im Occasionalismus*; and fine discussions of La Forge and occasionalism in broader contexts in Rainer Specht's *Commercium mentis et corporis: Über Kausalvorstellungen im Cartesianismus* (1966) and Jean-François Battail's *L'Avocat philosophe Géraud de Cordemoy* (1973). Of course, quite a few books on Malebranche give a nod to La Forge, starting with Gouhier's *La Vocation de Malebranche* (1926). And then there are important recent essays on La Forge by Andrea Sangiacomo, Delphine Antoine-Mahut, and Emanuela Scribano, among others, as well as studies of Cartesianism by Tad Schmaltz, Sandrine Roux, and Andrew Platt in which La Forge plays a substantial role. So we cannot say that La Forge has been totally ignored.

At the same time, when one mentions that one is working on a book on La Forge, the typical response, including from philosophers and sometimes even from scholars in the history of modern philosophy, is "Who?"

How important, then, *was* La Forge?

He was no Descartes, of course. Even other Cartesians far exceeded him in boldness and originality, although often at the expense of ending up with highly unorthodox brands of Cartesianism. La Forge was, by comparison (and here Prost is right), a more modest thinker. He was, in meaningful ways, more faithful to Descartes—or, at least, more concerned to remain faithful—than practically all of his French Cartesian contemporaries, including Desgabets, Rohault, Cordemoy, Régis, and, especially, Malebranche. La Forge was the good Cartesian. But he was not an uncritical or uncreative one, and therein lies his importance. Baillet, for one, gives him a great deal of credit:

It can be said as to the glory of this work [*Traité de l'esprit de l'homme*] that the disciple has surpassed the master through his own industry. M. de la Forge has gathered there everything fine and beautiful that M. Descartes has said in various places of his writings. He has even gone much further. He has explained in detail many things that Descartes touched on only in passing, and what he says about them is found explained in so clear and natural a manner that it seems that he has illuminated [*rendu plus sensible*] the knowledge of our mind better than that of our body.[6]

What so impresses Baillet is the fact that La Forge has demonstrated much more clearly than Descartes did his claim in the *Meditationes* that the mind is better known than the body.[7]

La Forge's contribution to the fortunes of Cartesianism in the seventeenth century consists mainly in three tasks he undertook with respect to the philosophy he inherited.

First, in both his *Remarques* to Descartes's *Traité de l'homme* and his own *Traité de l'esprit de l'homme*, La Forge was an expert and generous expositor of Descartes's views. As he examines the workings of the human body, the nature of the mind, and the relationship between the two substances, along with a host of other topics, La Forge delves into greater detail than Descartes did. Where Descartes, for example, is content in the *Principia philosophiae* to tell us that "all the modes of thinking that we experience within ourselves can be brought under two general headings: perception, or the operation of the intellect, and volition, or the operation of the will,"[8] La Forge devotes separate chapters in his *Traité* to sensation, understanding, imagination, the will, and memory, and demonstrates how the "faculty of thinking" operates in each case. Similarly, his analysis of the distinction between motion and motive force is more precise and edifying than what Descartes provides, and more consequential in terms of the metaphysics of the motion of bodies.

Second, La Forge corrects and updates Descartes, pushing the system toward both greater internal consistency and greater compatibility with the most up-to-date developments in natural philosophy. We saw La Forge do this quite explicitly in his commentary on *L'Homme*, in which he brings Descartes's general doctrines and detailed explanations into line with experimental advances in anatomy and physiology. It is also, I believe, what he takes himself to be up to in his occasionalism, which he sees as the only consistent position for a Cartesian to adopt. La Forge is not shy about letting us know when he thinks his philosophical mentor contradicts himself or simply gets

CONCLUSION: HOW IMPORTANT WAS LA FORGE? 255

it wrong, although he is also confident that had Descartes recognized the problems or had access to the latest ideas he would have modified his views accordingly.

Third, La Forge completes Descartes's grand philosophical project by covering those topics that Descartes intended to discuss at greater length but never did. Descartes tells us that he was planning to write more—perhaps two additional parts for the *Principia*—about the nature of the soul and its relation to the body. This is precisely the material that La Forge supplies with his *Traité*. We can assume that La Forge would have regarded his undertaking as unnecessary had Descartes lived longer.

But *how* faithful, really, *is* La Forge as he carries out Descartes's plans? We have seen him insist, several times in the *Traité*, that what he says "agrees with the thought of Monsieur Descartes." Fair enough, and this leaves him a bit of interpretive latitude. We can read this in a minimalist way as asserting that nothing in the book is contrary to Descartes's general principles. Then there is his statement that his account of the mind and its relationship to the body "follows so clearly from the first truths which Monsieur Descartes demonstrated that, even if I could not locate all of them in the books which he left us, there would still be no room to doubt that they are consequences drawn from his principles."[9] This, too, though a little bit of a stronger constraint, would still leave him free to enter speculative terrain, saying not only things that Descartes did not actually say but also, perhaps, things Descartes was not going to say (and possibly things Descartes would not have said), just as long as they are, again, either implied by his doctrines or consistently within Cartesian parameters.

But La Forge also says that all he is doing is "borrow [Descartes's] ideas and provide a supplement to *what he would have said* about the nature of the mind at the end of his *Traité de l'homme*, if death had not prevented him from completing it." He also insists that "I argue according to his principles and *do not stray from his views*,"[10] and that no one should suspect that he "departs from [the footprints of M. Descartes] even minimally [*tant soit peu*]."[11] This seems quite a bit stronger than claiming that what he says is merely consistent with or even implied by Descartes's principles and views. He is claiming that what he says in his book is exactly what Descartes would have said and how he would have completed his own project.

For much of what the *Traité* covers, this is arguably true. But what about La Forge's occasionalism? For better or for worse, it is mainly on this that his reputation in the historiography of philosophy rests. When La Forge argues that

256   THE GOOD CARTESIAN

God is the sole efficacious cause of the motion of bodies—both the motion per se and its directional modifications—and that not even human minds cause bodies to move except in the same deflationary (occasionalist) sense in which one body causes another body to move—does he take himself, once again, merely to be clarifying what Descartes really *did* say? Is he reviewing what Descartes *would* have said, had he lived longer? Or is La Forge intentionally going beyond Descartes and telling us what the philosopher *should* have said, if only he had seen where his principles ultimately lead? One question, of course, is whether Descartes would have sanctioned the occasionalism. I have my doubts. But my query here is, rather: Does *La Forge* believe Descartes would have sanctioned it?

At least one scholar thinks not. Referring to La Forge's account of the union of mind and body, Sandrine Roux notes that, on one hand, "things . . . have lost the element of obscurity which characterizes them in Descartes." On the other hand,

> If there is no doubt, for La Forge, that the analyses in his *Traité* are in every way Cartesian, and that they could have been developed by Descartes himself in response to objections that were addressed to him, nonetheless, it is clear that we are no longer dealing either with the response that this latter saw fit to provide nor with exactly the same notions and the same facts.[12]

I am not sure if this is correct with respect to La Forge's account of mind–body *union*; here it seems that he truly does not regard himself as departing from Descartes's own views but only clarifying them. However, when it comes to the causal relationships among bodies and at least one dimension of the interaction between mind and body (mind>body action), La Forge, with his occasionalism, has taken things in a novel direction—and he knows it, or so I believe. He admits that he says more than what Descartes actually "saw fit to provide"; his whole project is predicated on the untimely incompleteness of Descartes's project. And when La Forge claims that his views "agree with the thought of Monsieur Descartes," we can grant him that Descartes *could have* developed things in the way in which La Forge does—that nothing La Forge says is inconsistent with the most basic tenets of Descartes's philosophy. However, La Forge must be aware that he is saying more than what Descartes *would have* said, or would even have allowed.

Descartes seems never to have wavered from his view that, while God is the universal creator and sustaining cause of motion in the physical world,

CONCLUSION: HOW IMPORTANT WAS LA FORGE? 257

the properties of extended bodies (their size, shape, divisibility, solidity, impenetrability, and motion or rest) do really causally modify the motions of other bodies without any additional divine help, whatever difficulties such a position may have faced within his system.[13] Nor did he ever back away from the claim that the human mind can actually put a body in motion (and not just redirect the motions that are already there). Descartes had plenty of opportunity—in his treatises, in his responses to objections, in his correspondence—to clarify the nature of causal relations (including God's role therein) in the way in which La Forge did. He could have explained just what the force of one body to move another consists in; he could have addressed concerns about "the power of the mind to move the body," especially in light of the conservation law; and he could have drawn out any implications for body–body causal interaction generated by the conservation as continuous creation doctrine. In short, Descartes could have brought God in just where La Forge (and others) saw he was needed. But he did not. And this is not something that La Forge, given his deep familiarity with Descartes's *oeuvre*, could have mistaken.

Despite La Forge's claim that *je ne m'éloigne pas des sentiments de Monsieur Descartes*, then, I believe he does in fact, with full awareness, go beyond not just anything Descartes actually said but anything he would have said, at least when left to his own devices and without further, and compelling, prompting. However, La Forge does so in a way that he regards as perfectly consistent with Cartesian metaphysical and physical principles, and in this sense he does not stray. Any changes he makes to Descartes are in the service of a grander cause—namely, Cartesianism. This is not something that can be said about the radical modifications that, say, Malebranche introduces.

Perhaps, if we are to be generous, we can say that when La Forge proclaims that he is only giving us an account of "what Descartes would have said," he sincerely believed that even the occasionalist elements of his *Traité* are something with which Descartes, once sufficiently alerted to their necessity, might eventually be brought to agree.

*

La Forge's "modest" contributions to Cartesian philosophy—its development and its fortunes—should not be underestimated. The 1664 edition of Descartes's *Traité de l'homme* that he produced with Clerselier, to which he contributed illustrations and his long commentary, is among the most

258 THE GOOD CARTESIAN

important works of natural philosophy in the period. Along with the rest of *Le Monde* and Descartes's *Principia philosophiae*, it helped set the agenda for the mechanistic science, especially the study of the human body as a kind of "machine." As the book circulated widely, La Forge's *Remarques* would not have passed without notice.[14] And, as we have seen, the *Traité de l'esprit de l'homme*, appearing at the end of 1665 and so at least a few months before Cordemoy's *Le Discernement*, represents the first systematic presentation of occasionalism (however limited) published in the seventeenth century, going well beyond what we find in Geulincx's *Ethica*, which came out the same year. A Latin translation of the *Traité* appeared in 1669, produced in Amsterdam by Descartes's Dutch publisher Daniel Elzevir; and an English version was reportedly circulating in manuscript.

A more difficult question concerns La Forge's actual influence. Parisian intellectual society immediately took notice of his *Traité de l'esprit de l'homme*. On May 3, 1666, shortly after the book was available in bookstores, the *Journal des sçavans* gave it a brief notice:

> Death having prevented M. Descartes from completing the treatise on Man,
> of which he has left us only the first part which considers only the body,
> M. de la Forge, in order to supply the second part, has composed this book,
> in which, following the same principles, he explains what the mind is.[15]

The review provides only a short summary of the contents of the book, however, and nowhere mentions La Forge's views on causation.

The book received more careful consideration within the salons and academies of the city, especially those in which Cartesianism was the preferred topic of conversation. Writing around 1673, Jean Corbinelli, a friend of Madame de Sévigné and Madame de Grignan and frequent attendee of their gatherings, after expressing his "devotion to the philosophy of Descartes," reports that La Forge's *traité de l'Esprit de l'homme . . . m'a paru admirable*.[16] There are indications, as well, that *les deux Madames* matched him in their admiration for the work.

In terms of philosophical impact, seventeenth-century discussions like Gousset's and De Villemandy's award La Forge an important role in the dissemination of occasionalism—a theme taken up by many later studies, beginning with Seyfarth and Prost. It is hard to disagree with this assessment.

We can begin chronologically, with La Forge's older contemporary Clauberg. Though the two men likely never met, they may have corresponded.

CONCLUSION: HOW IMPORTANT WAS LA FORGE? 259

If there was any influence here, however, it would have been from Clauberg to La Forge, who we know studied the former's works. La Forge cites Clauberg approvingly on the modes of union between substances, and his reduction of mind-body union to a law-like "causal" reciprocity in their states is very much like the view that Clauberg defends. Clauberg, however, as we have seen, was no occasionalist.

Cordemoy is a more interesting case. Christian Henkel has made the very plausible suggestion that La Forge was an inspiration to Cordemoy, especially with regard to the "non-transference of modes" argument for occasionalism.[17] But we are a bit stuck in explaining how any kind of influence, one way or the other, would have come about, since there is no evidence that the two men ever met, or even corresponded with each other. On the other hand, there is the fact, circumstantial as it may be, that they came to their respective occasionalist resolutions at around the same time, c. 1658, and published them six years later within months of each other. Moreover, what we find in those writings, expressed in practically identical terms, is the totally unprecedented claim that mind-body interaction is on a par with body–body interaction, mainly because they are equally difficult to conceive or understand. Both La Forge and Cordemoy insist that the sense in which it can be said that the soul moves the body is the same sense in which it can be said that one body moves another body, namely, by occasioning God to move the body. Was all this merely a coincidence, or had the two men, part of a national Cartesian network, compared notes at some point, perhaps with the help of Clerselier, who was in touch with both of them?

With Malebranche, we are on firmer ground. No one contributed more than this Oratorian priest to the fate of Cartesianism, for better or (some other Cartesians would say) for worse. He was not only the leading, if highly unorthodox, representative of that philosophy, but arguably the most famous philosopher in the second half of the century. It seems fair to say that his conversion to Cartesianism owed something to La Forge.

First, we have the story from Malebranche's earliest biographer, Father Yves André, of how his friend discovered his philosophical vocation. Writing around 1710, while the philosopher was still alive, André reports that one day, likely in the late 1660s, Malebranche came across a copy of Clerselier's and La Forge's edition of Descartes's *Traité de l'homme* in a bookstall along the Seine, on the Quai des Augustins. He was, Father André reports, "ecstatic . . . the joy of learning so great a number of new discoveries caused him such violent palpitations of the heart that he had to put the book down right

260 THE GOOD CARTESIAN

away and interrupt his reading in order to calm himself."[18] In his *Remarques* in the book, which an excited Malebranche no doubt read, La Forge refers to his own *Traité de l'esprit de l'homme*. We can be confident that Malebranche would not have wasted any time before going out to find a copy of this other text explaining the marvelous new philosophy. Gousset, in the narrative of his conversations with La Forge, agrees, saying that "I do not doubt that he [Malebranche] read the book of La Forge."

> It was a famous work, as famous as his other work about Cartesian man [i.e., *L'Homme*], and there was such a connection between them that it would be unbelievable if Malebranche, so engaged in similar studies, did not know about or neglected that book. I therefore believe that he was, at one and the same time, both excited and corrupted by his reading of La Forge.[19]

While we can ignore the remark about "corruption," Gousset must be right. And indeed, La Forge's *Traité de l'esprit de l'homme*—along with quite a few works by Descartes, Clauberg, and other Cartesians, including De Villemandy's book on "secondary causes," but, oddly, not Descartes's *Traité de l'homme* with La Forge's commentary—is to be found among the many items in Malebranche's library.[20]

Malebranche must have been no less impressed by his reading of La Forge than by his reading of Descartes (though perhaps without the heart palpitations). The Oratorian's use of the "continuous creation" argument for his occasionalism, which makes its most rigorous appearance in Book VII of the *Entretiens sur la métaphysique* (1688), essentially replicates, albeit at greater length and detail, what La Forge wrote. Having noted that "the conservation of creatures is, on God's part, simply a continuous creation, a single volition subsisting and operating continuously," Malebranche puts this principle to work to deny any causal efficacy to finite creatures.

> Now God can neither conceive nor consequently will that a body exist nowhere, nor that it does not stand in certain relations of distance to other bodies. Thus, God cannot will that this armchair exist, and by this volition create or conserve it, without situating it here, there, or elsewhere. It is a contradiction, therefore, for one body to move another. Further, I claim, it is a contradiction for you to be able to move your armchair. Nor is this enough; it is a contradiction for all the angels and demons together to be able to move a wisp of straw. . . . It is a contradiction that God will this

CONCLUSION: HOW IMPORTANT WAS LA FORGE? 261

armchair to exist unless he wills it to exist somewhere and unless, by the efficacy of His will, He puts it there, conserves it there, creates it there. Hence, no power can convey it to where God does not convey it, nor fix nor stop it where God does not stop it, unless God accommodates the efficacy of His action to the inefficacious action of his Creatures.

The motion of a body, then, is nothing more than "the efficacy of the will of God, who conserves it successively in different places."[21] We have seen, too, that Malebranche uses the same argument to deny to the human mind any efficacy to generate its own sensory ideas and volitions. To say that God "communicates his power to creatures" means only that, as a consequence of the general laws he has established, the states of bodies and minds serve as occasional causes for the exercise of the divine will.

Can there be any doubt that Malebranche was inspired here by La Forge? Unfortunately, he never cites La Forge anywhere in his writing. But then again, like Descartes, Malebranche is rather stingy in giving credit to others for influence on his own ideas. (It is tempting to speculate that Malebranche was able to engage La Forge in conversation during his extended visit to the Oratorian house of study in Saumur in 1661. However, this would have been several years before Malebranche became a "philosopher," much less inspired by Cartesianism, and so it seems unlikely that he would have sought out the local physician who was himself already discussing Cartesian matters, committed to some form of occasionalism and working on his treatises.)

This brings us to Leibniz. Here, too, the documentary record is thin. But at least Leibniz does acknowledge La Forge as an important player in the game of causal relations. When Leibniz sets his pre-established harmony in opposition to occasionalism, he clearly has Malebranche in mind, but La Forge is part of the picture as well. La Forge, he notes, is among those who "remove true and proper action from created things. . . . They think that things do not act but that God acts in the presence of things and according to their aptitude, and therefore things are occasions, not causes, and receive but do not effect or elicit. Which doctrine Cordemoy, La Forge and other Cartesians have proposed, Malebranche especially."[22] Whether or not Leibniz actually read La Forge, we do not know; this, as far as I know, is Leibniz's only reference to him.

However, if we turn to the prominent quasi-Leibnizian Christian Wolff, we find a more generous acknowledgment of La Forge's influence. In a letter to Leibniz, from April 4, 1705, Wolff says that among those authors whom he has consulted "in metaphysics" are *Cartesio, Ludovico de la Forge, Malebranche*.[23] Henkel sees an influence of La Forge (and Cordemoy) on Wolff with respect to the claim that mind-body relations are no more difficult to understand than body–body relations, just because the latter are not as clearly understood as people ordinarily think.[24]

A thorough examination of La Forge's importance will have to look beyond the social spaces of Paris and the obvious candidates like Cordemoy, Malebranche, and Leibniz and go deep into the Cartesian bench. What was La Forge's reception among people who gave some thought to causal relations in a Cartesian context—philosophers like Rohault, Régis, Nicolas Poisson (author of *Commentaire ou remarques sur la méthode de Mr. Descartes* [1671]), and Bernard Lamy (who also lived in Saumur for a time)? Unfortunately, it is difficult to find in any of their texts explicit citations of La Forge. Still, the more empirically oriented Rohault and Régis must have been struck by La Forge's careful experimental work in revising Descartes's anatomy in the *Traité de l'homme*.

At a more general level, La Forge's critical and creative project as a Cartesian was duly acknowledged by other members of the party. Desgabets, for one, seems to have found some inspiration in La Forge's efforts. Consider, once again, what the Benedictine monk says in his *Supplément à la philosophie de Monsieur Descartes* (1675), where he presents himself as something more than a mere expositor of Descartes's philosophy.

> I will take the occasion to mark the places where he [Descartes] failed to push things as far as he should. I will uncover the contradictions that are to be found between the things that he has proposed and how he sometimes ceased to be himself a good Cartesian. . . . I will show that it is almost through his own doctrine that one corrects his faults and that it is he himself who provides the remedy for whatever mistake he has made.[25]

He sees himself as working in the same vein as La Forge, along with Cordemoy, Rohault, and Clauberg, "in the fine works that they have given to the public." What they are all doing is "rectifying his [Descartes's] own thoughts on matters in which he seems to me that he veered off the correct path that leads to truth."[26]

Gallery of Figures

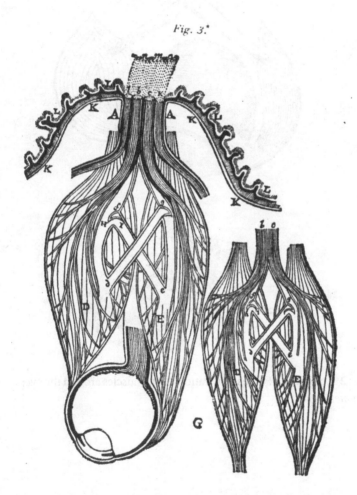

Figure 1 Gerard van Gutschoven's illustration of the muscles around the eye; from Clerselier's edition, *L'Homme de Rene Descartes* (Descartes 1664).

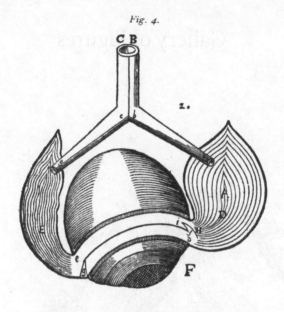
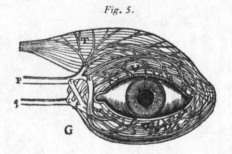

Figure 2 Louis de La Forge's illustration of the muscles around the eye; *L'Homme* (1664).

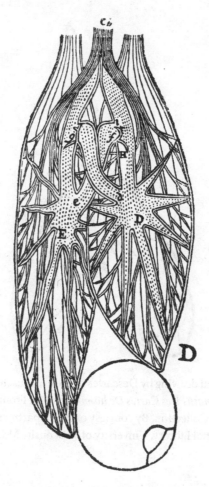

Figure 3 Descartes's illustration (re-drawn by Clerselier) of the muscles around the eye; *L'Homme* (1664).

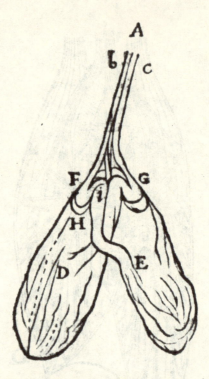

Figure 4 An original drawing by Descartes of the eye muscles; from Florent Schuyl's edition, *Renatus Des Cartes De homine* (1662). From the Daniel and Eleanor Albert Collection. By courtesy of the Department of Special Collections, Memorial Library, University of Wisconsin-Madison.

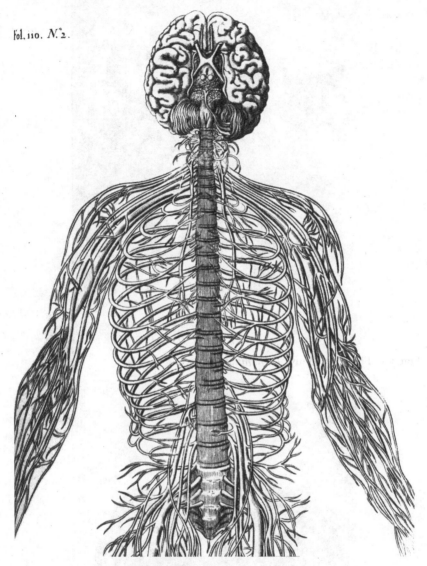

Figure 5 Figure by Schuyl, *De homine* (1662).

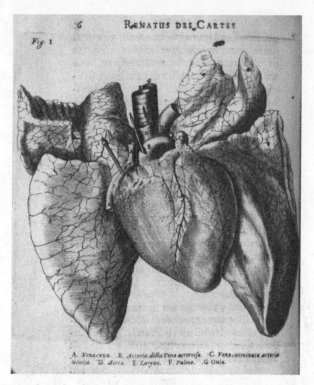

Figure 6 Figure by Schuyl, *De homine* (1662).

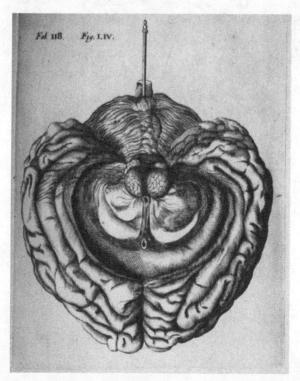

Figure 7 Figure by Schuyl, *De homine* (1662).

Figure 8 Figure by Schuyl, *De homine* (1662).

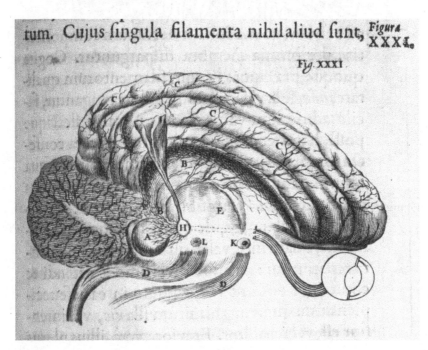

Figure 9 Figure by Schuyl, *De homine* (1662).

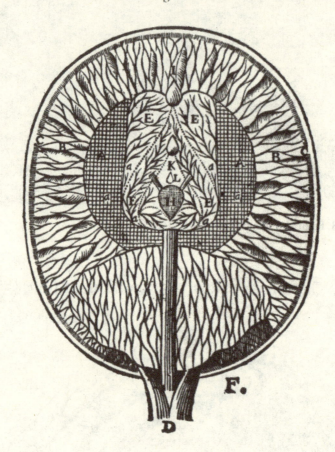

Figure 10 Figure by La Forge, from *L'Homme* (1664).

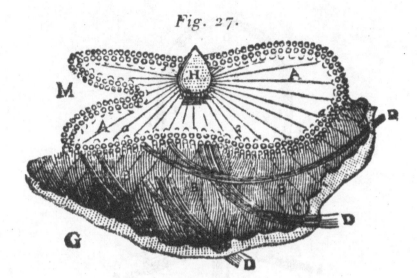

Figure 11 Figure by Gutschoven, from *L'Homme* (1664).

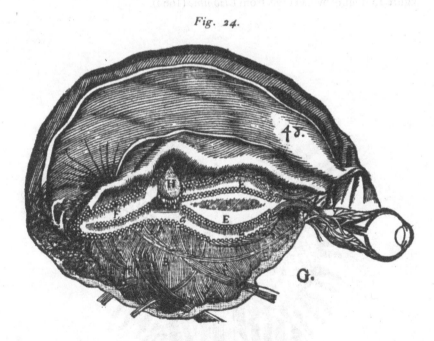

Figure 12 Figure by Gutschoven, from *L'Homme* (1664).

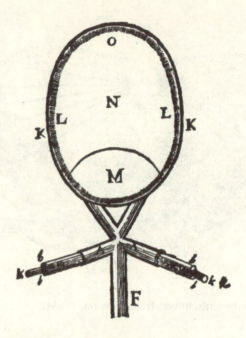

Figure 13 Figure by La Forge, from *L'Homme* (1664).

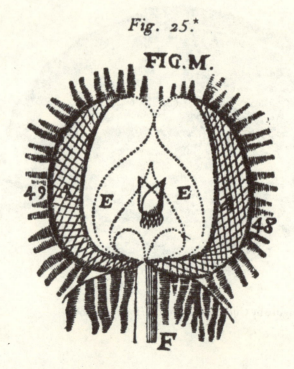

Figure 14 Figure by La Forge, from *L'Homme* (1664).

Figure 15 Figure by La Forge, from *L'Homme* (1664).

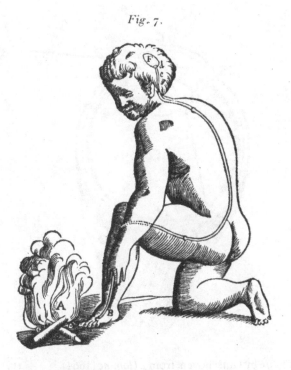

Figure 16 Figure by Gutschoven, from *L'Homme* (1664).

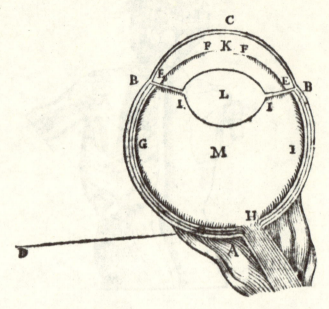

Figure 17 Figure by Schuyl, *De homine* (1664).

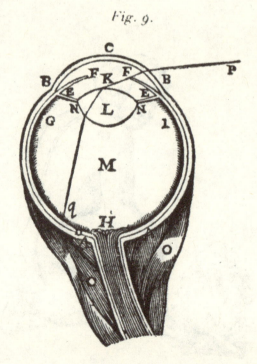

Figure 18 Figure by Gutschoven, from *L'Homme* (1664).

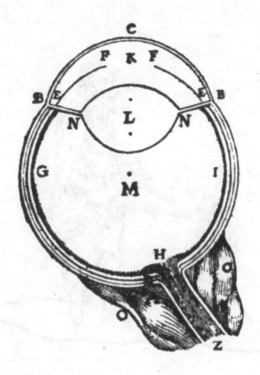

Figure 19 Figure by Frans van Schooten the Younger, from Descartes, *La Dioptrique* (Leiden: Maire, 1637).

Figure 20 Figure by Gutschoven, from *L'Homme* (1664).

Figure 21 Figure by Van Schooten, from Descartes, *La Dioptrique* (1637).

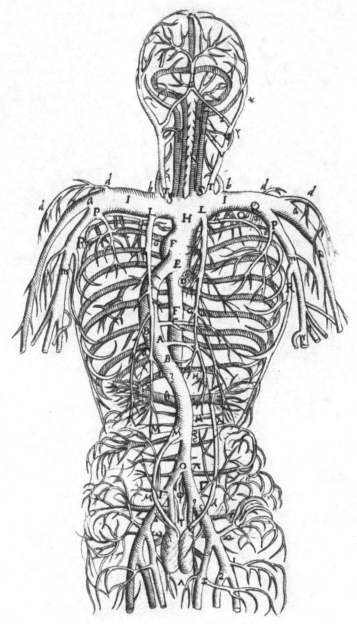

Figure 22 From Caspar Bauhin, *Theatrum anatomicum* (Frankfurt: Moenem, 1605). Courtesy of Ebling Library, Rare Books & Special Collections, University of Wisconsin-Madison.

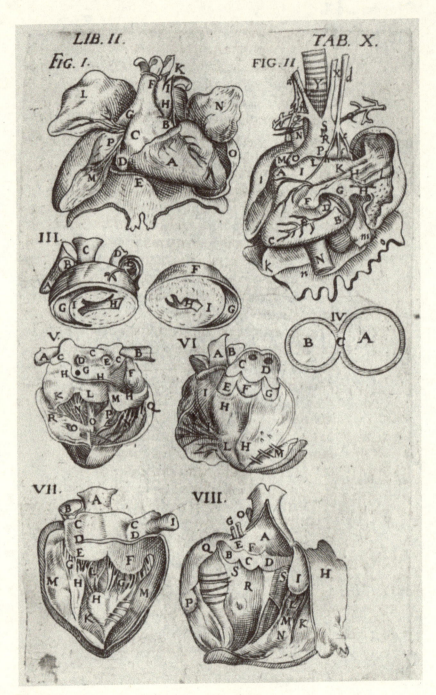

Figure 23 From Bauhin, *Theatrum anatomicum*.

Notes

Introduction

1. The text of this order is in Bouillier 1868: I.469.
2. The propositions and their censure are in Babin 1679: 96. On this episode, see Garber 2002.
3. Babin 1679: 5. In this document the relationship with the 1624 censure is made explicit.
4. For a study of the controversies around Desgabets's treatise, see Schmaltz 2002.
5. Bouillier 1868: I.474–5.
6. I borrow the term from Schmaltz 2002.
7. Desgabets 1983–85: V.152.
8. This is from Clerselier's *Préface* to volume 3 of Descartes's correspondence, 1667, AT V.780.
9. A Latin translation had been published in 1662, in Leiden, by Florent Schuyl.

Chapter 1

1. The most up-to-date and critical biographical study of La Forge is Clair 1974. See also Prost 1904, Chassagne 1938, and Isolle 1971.
2. There was apparently a child born in 1631 while the family still lived in Lude; the name of this child is not extant, and he or she, though baptized, probably did not survive infancy; see Clair 1974: 21.
3. This information on Noël is drawn from Romano 1999 and a biographical entry on Noël by Theo Verbeek to appear in his forthcoming edition of Descartes's correspondence.
4. AT I.383–4. The identity of the recipient of this letter to a *Reverend Père* who, Descartes says, taught him philosophy at La Flèche *il y a vingt-trois ou vingt-quatre ans* and of the *Discours* has been disputed; but Noël, at this point rector of the *collège*, does seem the most likely candidate.
5. AT IV.585–6.
6. Farrell 1970: 62. This is a complete translation of the text of the *Ratio Studiorum*.
7. Farrell 1970: 43.
8. Farrell 1970: 40.
9. Chassagne 1938: 26; Clair 1974: 25.
10. As Clair argues (1974: 27). Clair thus suggests that the title page of Clerselier's 1664 edition of Descartes's *Traité de l'homme*, which refers to La Forge as *demeurant à La Flèche* in that year, must be an error.

280 NOTES

11. This is the dating favored by Clair (1974: 27). Isolle, following Chassagne, prefers the rather implausible date of 1664 for the move to Saumur (1971: 107). This seems to me way too late.
12. Prost 1907b: 9.
13. Prost 1907b: 3.
14. Prost 1907b: 6.
15. Prost 1907b: 79. Gootjes (2013: 589) wisely urges caution about seeing this request as an attempt to introduce Cartesianism into Saumur.
16. Prost 1907b: 79.
17. Prost 1907b: 74; Isolle 1971: 108–9.
18. Prost 1907b: 96.
19. Prost 1907b: 93.
20. Quoted in Gootjes 2013: 584.
21. Gootjes 2013: 591.
22. Quoted in Clair 1974: 38.
23. La Forge 1974: 76/La Forge 1997: 5.
24. Clair (1974: 40), for example, says, "Le 'presque' indiquerait quelques déplacements à Paris."
25. The letter is quoted in Clair 1974: 59.
26. It is also possible that Chapelain was simply unaware that La Forge and Montmor were acquainted.
27. Baillet 1691: II.161.
28. To Mesland, 2 May 1644, AT IV.111/CSMK 231.
29. See Clerselier's *Préface* to the *Traité de l'homme*, in Descartes 1664: x–xi/La Forge 1999: 20.
30. Gousset 1716: 6–7.
31. Gousset 1716: 4.
32. La Forge 1999: 384–6.
33. In his *Préface* to volume 3 of Descartes's correspondence, AT V.780.
34. AT V.780.
35. Gousset 1716: 4.
36. Gousset 1716: 4.

Chapter 2

1. On the Académie Bourdelot, see Brown 1934: 231–53. Clair (1978: 59), however, puts its beginning in 1635.
2. Clair 1978: 59–60.
3. On the dating of Rohault's *mercredis*, see Clair 1978: 43–4.
4. From Clerselier's "Preface" to volume 2 of Descartes's correspondence (1659), AT V.758. As Harth (1992: 81) notes, for women the salon was an "intellectual haven."
5. Le Gallois 1672: 48.
6. On the Scudéry salon, see Adam 1997: 40–46.

NOTES   281

7. See Clair 1990: 48–9.

8. Buffet 1668: 265.

9. On Thévenot, see Sophie Roux 2014: 66–7. On Carnavalet, see Bouillier 1868: I.440. It should be noted that not all of these academies and salons were contemporaneous, although all of them were active between the late 1650s and 1664. For example, the conferences hosted by Denis and Thévenot did not begin until 1664, by which point the Montmor Academy was coming to an end. The Scudéry salon, meanwhile, was over by 1661 (Adam 1997: 45).

10. *Pensées diverses ecrites à l'occasion de la comete*, Bayle 1737: III.157.

11. Bouillier 1868: I.430.

12. Bouillier 1868: I.437.

13. Sorbière's document is presented in Brown 1934: 75–6.

14. Huet 1810: 231.

15. Roux 2014: 67; Clair 1978: 58.

16. Huet 1810: 232.

17. Boulliau to Nicolas Heinsius, Letter DXVIII, February 1658, Burmann 1724: 592–3.

18. Boulliau to Huygens, 6 December 1658, Huygens 1889: 287.

19. Boulliau to Huygens, 17 January 1659, Huygens 1889: 320. There was no love lost between Roberval and Descartes; what were initially mathematical differences soon led to a rancorous personal falling-out.

20. Clerselier, *Préface*, in Rohault 1690: n.p. (vii–viii).

21. Clair 1978: 50–56. Clair's essay is the most thorough analysis available of all conceivable aspects of Rohault's *mercredis*, including the furniture in the room.

22. Clerselier, *Préface* to volume 2 of Descartes's correspondence (1659), AT V.758.

23. Clerselier, *Préface*, in Rohault 1690: n.p. (v).

24. Clerselier, *Préface*, in Rohault 1690: n.p. (ix). On experimentalism at Rohault's conferences and other Cartesian venues, see Sophie Roux 2014: 74–6.

25. A Latin edition had been published in Leiden in 1662.

26. Du Roure seems also to have been the editor of that 1664 edition of *Le Monde* that included Cordemoy's treatise on motion and rest; the introductory material bears the initials 'DR.'

27. Quoted in Schmaltz 2002: 40. How faithful Desgabets was to Descartes's explication of transubstantiation has been debated; Dilucia (2022) argues, for example, that it is a mistake to take Desgabets as "a 'champion of Cartesian transubstantiation' and loyal proponent of the *theologia cartesiana*."

28. Bouillier 1868: I.430.

29. La Forge 1974: 73/La Forge 1997: 4.

30. On Philippi, see Collacciani 2016.

31. Baillet 1691: II.522.

32. On Dutch Cartesianism, see Thijssen-Schoute 1989, Verbeek 1992, and Schmaltz 2017.

33. The best studies of Descartes's troubles in Utrecht, Leiden, and elsewhere in the Dutch Republic is Verbeek 1988 (which contains the related documents) and 1992.

34. Quoted in Collacciani 2016: 110–11.

282 NOTES

35. On Spinoza vs. Cartesianism, see Nadler 2019.

36. On "the two problems" for Descartes, see Schmaltz 2017: 17–63.

37. Fourth Set of Objections, AT VII.217–18/CSM II.152–3.

38. In fact, it is a little more complex than this. The human body itself is a substance whose matter is informed by the substantial form that makes it a living human body; that human body substance then takes on the substantial form that is the human soul, which endows it with rationality and the other human psychic functions.

39. See, for example, Thomas Aquinas, *De ente et essentia*, sections 17–18.

40. To Mersenne, 11 November 1640, AT III.232/CSMK 156.

41. See Madeira Arrais 1650: 1–19.

42. Collegium Conimbricense, *In octo libros physicorum Aristotelis*, VIII.4.i.3.

43. On this subject, see Armogathe 1977.

44. Fourth Set of Replies, AT VII.253–254/CSM II.176.

45. It was Mersenne who cut the relevant paragraphs from the first (Paris, 1641) edition of the *Meditationes*. Descartes himself knew that he had to be cautious in responding to Arnauld on this topic. He tells Mersenne in the spring of 1641 that "I am not yet sending you the last sheet of my Reply to M. Arnauld, where I give an explanation of transubstantiation according to m principles, because I want first to read the Councils [of the Church] on this topic, and I have not yet been able to obtain them" (To Mersenne, 18 March 1641, AT III.340/CSMK 177).

46. Fourth Set of Replies, AT VII.251/CSM II.175.

47. Descartes to Mesland, 9 February 1645, AT IV.163–9.

48. For the text of the Leuven condemnation, see Armogathe and Carraud 2003: 104–7. For a discussion of this episode, see Collacciani 2016.

49. For the texts of the two Vatican censors, see Armogathe and Carraud 2003: 73–89.

50. For the text of the Congregation's decree, see Armogathe and Carraud 2003: 109. As Armogathe and Carraud show, many of the objections by the Vatican's censors focus on philosophical rather than theological problems, and the censors indeed show some admiration for Descartes as a thinker.

51. On this, see Sophie Roux 2013: 73.

52. Lennon and Easton 1992: 1.

53. Sophie Roux 2013: 317–18.

54. Descartes, *Principia philosophiae* I.51, 53, 56, AT VIII-A.24–6/CSM I.210–11.

55. *Principia philosophiae* I.51–52, AT VIII-A.24–5/CSM I.210.

56. *Principia philosophiae* I.60, AT VIII-A.29/CSM I.213.

57. See *Principia philosophiae* I.53, II.4.

58. See, for example, Hobbes, *Leviathan* I.v.5; Gassendi, Fifth Set of Objections, AT VII.273–4/CSM II.191; Locke, *An Essay Concerning Human Understanding*, IV.3.vi.

59. Descartes himself calls the laws of nature "secondary and particular causes of the various motions we see in particular bodies" (*Principia philosophiae* II.37). But how exactly laws are "causes" for Cartesians is rather unclear; on this, see Garber 1992: 197–204, and Schmaltz 2008: 105–21.

60. Janiak (2008) argues that no matter how one construes the "mechanist" picture of matter, Newton rejects essential components of it.

NOTES 283

61. Making allowance, of course, for Malebranche's view whereby clear and distinct ideas are in God's understanding but perceived by the human intellect.
62. *Principia philosophiae* I.43, AT VIII-A.21/CSM I.207.
63. Ariew 2007: 401.
64. *Principia philosophiae* II.20.
65. *Principia philosophiae* II.11, 16.
66. Cordemoy 1968: 95–6.
67. Cordemoy 1968: 102.
68. Cordemoy 1968: 103.
69. See Descartes to More, 5 February 1649, AT V.272–3/CSMK 363.
70. Schmaltz 2002.
71. On these various departures from Descartes, see Schmaltz 2002: 4–19.
72. The letter is unpublished, but quoted in Prost 1907a: 158.
73. Sixth Set of Replies, AT VII.435/CSM II.293–4.
74. To Mersenne, 27 May 1630, AT I.151–152/CSMK 25.
75. To Mersenne, 15 April 1630, AT I.146/CSMK 23.
76. On this, see Schmaltz 2002: 16.
77. That is, to be a Cartesian in a meaningful sense of the term, as opposed to being labeled a "Cartesian" by intellectual conservatives/reactionaries of the time, who often used the term as an all-purpose epithet for anyone who opposed the Scholastic-Aristotelian philosophy (much in the way the term 'communist' has been, and continues to be, used in the United States by the political right to demonize anyone whose political principles, communist or not, are too left of center).
78. Letter to Oldenburg, Ep. 68, Spinoza 1925: IV.299.
79. *Supplement à la philosophie de M. Descartes*, in Desgabets 1983–85: VI.156.
80. Schmaltz 2002: 11.
81. Schmaltz 2017: 6–7. On the Wittgensteinian analogy, see also Sophie Roux 2013: 316.
82. At least according to the editor of *J. Claubergii opera* (1691), cited in Prost 1907a: 153.
83. Prost 1907a: 103.
84. In his preface to volume 3 of Descartes's correspondence, AT V.780.

Chapter 3

1. See Clerselier's chronology leading up to the publication of his edition of the *Traité de l'homme* in his preface to the 1664 volume *L'Homme de René Descartes et Un traitté de la formation du foetus du mesme autheur, avec les Remarques de Louis de la Forge* (Descartes 1664).
2. In fact, there is reason to believe that, despite what he says, Clerselier did *not* have an autograph original of the *Traité de l'homme*; see Matton 2005: 148–9. Theo Verbeek has suggested to me that what Clerselier possessed was a copy that was no less removed from an original than the copy used by Florent Schuyl for his 1662 Latin translation. For the provenance of Descartes's posthumous papers, including those found in the

284 NOTES

"Leiden suitcase" and those listed in the Stockholm inventory, see Bos, Verbeek, and Van de Ven 2003: xvi–xxiii. See also Meschini 2011 and Van Otegem 2002: 541, who seem to leave open the possibility, and even favor the view, that Clerselier did have an autograph original.

3. For the dramatic but unconfirmed story of their delivery in Paris, see Baillet 1691: II.428.

4. Descartes 1659: xii.

5. Descartes 1667: i.

6. It is not entirely clear *how* or when Clerselier came into possession of *L'Homme*. It may have been among the items conveyed to him by his brother in-law, Descartes's friend, and French ambassador to Sweden Pierre Chanut, who in turn got it from either (a) the Leiden or Stockholm inventories of Descartes's effects, although it is not listed in the latter (see AT X.5–12); or (b) some other source, as the document published in Matton 2005 implies. Or the manuscript may have been given to Clerselier by Tobias Andreae (Bos, Verbeek, and Van de Ven 2003: xxi–xxii). Andreae is also identified as Clerselier's source by Van Otegem 2002 (490). It is also possible that Clerselier received several copies of the manuscript, from all these different sources.

7. To Mersenne, 8 October 1629, AT I.23.

8. There is some difference of scholarly opinion over whether the title *Le Monde* applies to the whole composed of both treatises together, or only to the *Traité de la lumière*. The earliest editions of these works all use *Le Monde* only with respect to the *Traité de la lumière*. Florent Schuyl's 1662 Latin edition of the *Traité de l'homme—De Homine*—and Clerselier's 1664 French edition of that work do not have *Le Monde* in the title. (There was a 1664 edition of *Le Monde de Mr. Descartes ou le Traité de la lumière* published by Jacques du Roure [according to Sophie Roux 2021].) Moreover, Clerselier's 1677 edition containing both treatises has the following title: *L'Homme de René Descartes . . . a quoy l'on a ajouté Le Monde ou Traité de la lumière du mesme auteur*. In Clerselier's view, then, only the *Traité de la lumière* is *Le Monde*. The editors of CSM, the standard English edition of Descartes's writings, follow his lead, and reserve *The World* only for the *Treatise on Light*. It seems clear from Descartes's correspondence, however, that the work he refers to as *mon Monde* includes both parts. For example, he tells Mersenne that "my discussion of man in *Le Monde* will be a little fuller than I had intended, for I have undertaken to explain all the main functions in man" (AT I.263/CSMK 40)—which is precisely what he does in the *Traité de l'homme*. The editors of AT, still the standard critical edition of Descartes's writings, include both treatises under *Le Monde*, as have I.

9. See the summary in *Discours de la méthode*, AT VI.40–44/CSM I.131–4.

10. An edition of the *Traité de la lumière* did appear in 1664, but it was based on an unreliable copy of a manuscript.

11. To Mersenne, November or December 1632, AT I.263. Though the first part, the *Traité de la lumière*, was published as *Le Monde de Monsieur Descartes* in 1664, probably by Du Roure (see Sophie Roux 2021), this was based on only a copy of the original manuscript. Clerselier published his edition, based on the original manuscript, in 1677, when he brought out both parts of *Le Monde* together in a single volume. Andrault (2016) and Antoine-Mahut (2016: 22), with good reason, dispute

NOTES 285

categorizing *L'Homme* strictly as a work on human anatomy; in this respect they apparently take a different approach from Bitbol-Hespériès (1996). See also Antoine-Mahut 2018, where she presents the "patchwork" constitution of *L'Homme*.

12. There was some dispute on this matter among Scholastic Aristotelians, however. Thomists, for example, argued that there is only one substantial form in the human body, the rational soul, with all nutritive and sensory powers deriving from it rather than from additional forms.

13. *Traité de l'homme*, AT XI.120/G 99.

14. While Descartes rejects the Aristotelian and Galenic accounts of the heart as the source of life in the body, the notion that the heart has a "faculty" by which it heats and expands the blood does go back to Aristotle and Galen.

15. *Traité de l'homme*, AT XI.201–2/G 169.

16. *Traité de l'homme*, AT XI.130/G 107.

17. *Traité de l'homme*, AT XI.143/G 119.

18. *Traité de l'homme*, AT XI.145–6/G 120.

19. *Le Monde*, AT XI.3–4/CSM I.81.

20. *Le Monde*, AT XI.64–9/G 41–5. The diagrams in the work make the heliocentrism perfectly clear.

21. *Le Monde*, AT XI.48/G 32.

22. *Le Monde*, AT XI.31–2/G 21.

23. Schmaltz (2020b) argues that the use of a "fable" may also have been a way to avoid having to engage with alternative Scholastic accounts of nature.

24. Descartes to Mersenne, November 1633, AT I.271/CSMK 41.

25. Descartes to Mersenne, December 1640, AT III.258/CSMK 160.

26. *Préface*, Descartes 1664: v–vi (there is no pagination in the original text, but these are the page numbers that would be there).

27. In the end, the Elzevirs' plan never came to fruition. If Huyberts did in fact produce illustrations for their planned *L'Homme*, he must have had access to one of several manuscript copies of the treatise that were apparently circulating in the Netherlands among a small coterie of Cartesian devotés.

28. *Préface*, Descartes 1664: xvii.

29. *Préface*, Descartes 1664: vi.

30. To Elisabeth [of Bohemia], March 1647, AT IV.626/CSMK 315.

31. *Préface*, Descartes 1664: vii–viii.

32. Whether Clerselier did in fact receive the manuscript from Chanut (or exclusively from Chanut) is open to question; see note 6 above.

33. *Préface*, Descartes 1659: xiv.

34. *Préface*, Descartes 1664: xi.

35. *Préface*, Descartes 1664: xi.

36. We have a letter from Clerselier to La Forge in December 1660 (it appears as the final entry in Clerselier's third volume of Descartes's correspondence, published in 1667), in response to at least one letter from La Forge, and so their arrangement must have been concluded before that.

37. *Préface*, Descartes 1664: iv.

286 NOTES

38. See the final paragraph of Schuyl's *"Ad lectorem,"* in Descartes 1662 (n.p.): *Additis duabus figuris a Des Cartes rudi Minerva exaratis.*

39. *Préface*, Descartes 1664: v.

40. La Forge was, as I discuss in subsequent chapters, completing Descartes's project, since the treatment of the human body in the *Traité de l'homme* was, as Descartes says in the opening paragraph of the treatise, supposed to be followed by a description of "the soul on its own [*l'âme aussi à part*]" and then an account of "how these two natures must be joined and united." In 1661, however, Clerselier felt that there was enough work to be done on *L'Homme* without taking on the project of publishing La Forge's treatise as well. Moreover, he felt that La Forge's work was not quite ready, that it needed a bit more work (*il luy faut encore quelques coups de lime pour la mettre à sa perfection* [*Préface*, Descartes 1664: xii]).

41. Clerselier says in his preface to the 1664 edition that if not for Van Gutschoven's delay, the book could have been published two years earlier.

42. Clerselier had Van Gutschoven's illustrations before Schuyl's book appeared in 1662, because he says that he when he received *le présent que Monsieur Schuyl m'avoit fait de son livre*, presumably just after the book's publication, he already possessed *toutes les figures de ce Traité, que chacun de ces Messieurs avoit faites* (*Préface*, Descartes 1664: v).

43. AT XI.31.

44. AT XI.119–20/CSM I.99.

45. *Préface*, Descartes 1664: xv.

46. AT XI.201.

47. Zittel 2011: 221.

48. *Préface*, Descartes 1664: xx–xxi.

49. *Préface*, Descartes 1664: xiii–xiv.

50. *Préface*, Descartes 1664: xx.

51. *Préface*, Descartes 1664: xxv.

52. *Préface*, Descartes 1664: xviii. Baigrie (1996: 96) has argued that Descartes, at least, did not see the role of illustrations in his works as "to clarify the meaning of the text" but rather "are meant to play an important role in the creation of new knowledge." I am not sure, however, what the difference is supposed to be, since the former would represent a contribution to the latter.

53. Zittel 2011: 221.

54. *Préface*, Descartes 1664: xxv. For a discussion of one contemporary critique (by Nicolaus Steno, in 1664) of what Descartes is doing in *L'Homme* in contrast with an anatomy book, see Andrault 2016. One could, in fact, say that the treatise is both less and more than an anatomy book: less, because it lacks the empirically based descriptive account of the body's constituent organs, and more because it includes much speculation about hidden and invisible parts and processes.

55. *Préface*, Descartes 1664: xvii–xviii.

56. *Préface*, Descartes 1664: xxv. Clerselier notes that the reader's imagination is especially required both when it comes to filling in the details that cannot be captured in woodcut printing and for supplying the motions that are to take place in the body, which he says *lequel on ne sçauroit representer* (xxvi).

NOTES 287

57. *Préface*, Descartes 1664: xx.
58. *Préface*, Descartes 1664: xiv–xv.
59. *Préface*, Descartes 1664: xix–xx.
60. *Préface*, Descartes 1664: xv.
61. See the insert following AT XI.634.
62. *Préface*, Descartes 1664: xviii.
63. *Préface*, Descartes 1664: xviii.
64. *Préface*, Descartes 1664: xviii.
65. *Préface*, Descartes 1664: xviii.
66. I am grateful to Annie Bitbol-Hespériès for sharing her insights on this with me through correspondence. She is skeptical about the discovered *brouillon*, especially given that what Clerselier says about this alleged autograph drawing (*je le garde pour le faire voir à ceux qui en auront la curiosité* [*Préface*, Descartes 1664: xviii]) is just like what he says about the autograph original of *L'Homme* he claims to have possessed (*l'original que j'ay, et que je feray voir quand on voudra* [*Préface*, Descartes 1664: iii]), a claim about which many scholars are dubious (see note 2 above). Her view is that when Clerselier re-drew Descartes's drawing, he was influenced both by the crude figure by Descartes published by Schuyl and by Van Gutschoven's rendering.
67. *Préface*, Descartes 1664: xix.
68. Wilkin (2003) has argued, on the other hand, that these items in fact play a role in the overall philosophical message conveyed by Schuyl's illustrations, although she claims that, with their realism and worldliness, they function as a kind of *memento mori* and reminder of the transience of things human and thereby undermine Descartes's dualist project.
69. *Préface*, Descartes 1664: ii.
70. *Préface*, Descartes 1664: iv.
71. *Préface*, Descartes 1664: ii.
72. *Préface*, Descartes 1664: xiv.
73. In fact, the resulting image appears to be a side-angle view of the figure produced by Schuyl for the same text, suggesting that either Clerselier or Van Gutschoven referred to Schuyl's work for guidance; compare the figure in *De homine* (Descartes 1662: 14) with the figure in *L'Homme* (Descartes 1664: 9).
74. *Préface*, Descartes 1664: xix.
75. *Préface*, Descartes 1664: xx. La Forge explains his departure from Descartes on this point in his commentary (Descartes 1664: 228/La Forge 1999: 230). Interestingly, the crude and barely understandable drawing by Descartes that Schuyl used [fig. 4], unlike the one reproduced by Clerselier, seems to show the nerves discharging the animal spirits into the muscle, as La Forge's illustration does.
76. As far as I can tell, this is the only instance in which one of the illustrations "corrects" Descartes's text. Thus, Zittel (2011: 221) may be exaggerating a bit when he says that Van Gutschoven and La Forge, as trained medical doctors, made an effort "to bring Descartes's book up to date with the latest scientific knowledge. As a consequence, their main objective in drawing the images was often not the exact reconstruction of what Descartes might have intended, but the reflection of current scientific knowledge."

288 NOTES

77. Descartes 1664: 225–8/La Forge 1999: 228–30.
78. Here is how Clerselier describes La Forge's various contributions: *Il n'y a point de difficultez qu'il n'ait resolües, point de scruples qu'il n'ait levez, point d'obscuritez qu'il n'ait éclaircies* (*Préface*, Descartes 1664: xxiii–xxiv).
79. Descartes 1664: 225/La Forge 1999: 227.
80. AT XI.138/G 114.
81. AT XI.138–9/G 115.
82. AT XI.137/G 113.
83. Descartes 1664: 259/La Forge 1999: 257.
84. AT VI.106.
85. Van Schooten's image is at AT VI.135–6. On this borrowing from Van Schooten, see Bitbol-Hespériès 1996: xlviii.
86. *Préface*, Descartes 1664: ii.
87. Bitbol-Hespériès 1996: xxiv–xxvii; and Bitbol-Hespériès 1990.
88. *Préface*, Descartes 1664: xxvi.
89. Interesting and compelling analyses of the illustrations for *L'Homme*, especially comparing Van Gutschoven and La Forge vs. Schuyl, are offered in Zittel 2011 and Wilkin 2003, although they disagree on a central issue. According to Wilkin, Schuyl's worldly illustrations subvert Descartes's scientific project, and especially the mind–body dualism, by underscoring human mortality and the transience of bodily things, whereas the more abstract and spare figures by Van Gutschoven and La Forge "perpetuate the philosopher's project of postponing death by diverting the reader's attention from the corruptible nature of the body" (45). Zittel, on the other hand, insists that Van Gutschoven's and La Forge's illustrations go beyond Descartes's own project by prioritizing "the reductionist notion of man as a machine," and represent Clerselier's ideal (and that of other latter-day Cartesians) more than Descartes's. Zittel insists that "from the point of view of Descartes's supposed intentions, . . . the arguments in favour of Schuyl's visual language would definitely be stronger" (230).
90. Descartes 1664: 325/La Forge 1999: 314.
91. *Journal des sçavans*, 5 January 1665, 9–11 (11). Accessible online: (https://gallica.bnf.fr/ark:/12148/bpt6k56523g/f13.item).

Chapter 4

1. Descartes 1664: xii/La Forge 1999: 21.
2. Descartes 1664: xxiii–xxiv/La Forge 1999: 29–30.
3. Descartes 1664: xix/La Forge 1999: 26.
4. Descartes 1664: 226/La Forge 1999: 228.
5. Descartes 1664: 171/La Forge 1999: 181.
6. See *Discours de la méthode* V, AT VI.45–6/CSM I.133–4.
7. Descartes 1664: 173/La Forge 1999: 182–3.
8. AT XI.127/G 104.
9. Descartes 1664: 204/La Forge 1999: 209.
10. Descartes 1664: 218/La Forge 1999: 222.

NOTES 289

11. Descartes 1664: 223–4/La Forge 1999: 226.
12. AT XI.123/G 101.
13. Descartes 1664: 187/La Forge 1999: 194–5.
14. *Discours de la méthode* V, AT VI.50/CSM I.136; see also *La Description du corps humain*, AT XI.239/G 179.
15. *Discours de la méthode* V, AT VI.48–9/CSM I.135.
16. Descartes 1664: 183–4/La Forge 1999: 191–2.
17. These three objections, and La Forge's responses, are in Descartes 1664: 184–6/La Forge 1999: 192–4.
18. See AT I.522–3/CSMK 80.
19. Descartes 1664: 186/La Forge 1999: 194.
20. Descartes 1664: 228–9/La Forge 1999: 230–31.
21. Descartes 1664: 229–31/La Forge 1999: 231–3.
22. AT XI.196–7/G 165.
23. Descartes 1664: 395–6/La Forge 1999: 375.
24. Descartes 1664: 331–2/La Forge 1999: 319–20.
25. Descartes 1664: 312–13/La Forge 1999: 302–3. See also Descartes 1664: 323–4/La Forge 1999: 312–3. For Bartholin's objections, see Bartholin 1651: 336–7. On La Forge's response to Bartholin, see Grigoropoulou 2018: 126–7. Antoine-Mahut shows how La Forge, in his response to Bartholin, appropriates several critical responses to Bartholin by Henry More in his *Immortality of the Soul* (1659), though More ultimately rejected the pineal gland theory; see Antoine-Mahut 2021: 147–66.
26. On this, see Schmaltz (Forthcoming).
27. AT XI.120–21/G 99–100.
28. Descartes 1664: 175–6/La Forge 1999: 184–5.
29. Descartes 1664: 195/La Forge 1999: 202.
30. Descartes 1664: 196–8/La Forge 1999: 202–4.
31. Descartes 1664: 209/La Forge 1999: 214.
32. Descartes to Plempius, 15 February 1638, AT I.524–6/CSMK 81–2.
33. AT XI.123/G 101.
34. AT I.523/CSMK 80. La Forge makes use of this letter at Descartes 1664: 187/La Forge 1999: 194.
35. Descartes 1664: 190–91/La Forge 1999: 197–9. I find this passage somewhat confusing and apparently inconsistent. On one hand, it says that for Descartes the moment of systole (when the blood is forced out of the heart) occurs while the heart elongates (vertically?); on the other hand, it says that for Descartes the blood leaves the heart when the heart contracts (which would mean that it occurs at diastole rather than at systole).
36. Descartes 1664: 180–81/La Forge 1999: 189.
37. Descartes 1664: 226/La Forge 1999: 228.
38. Descartes 1664: 227–8/La Forge 1999: 230.
39. AT XI.179
40. Descartes 1664: 347–8/La Forge 1999: 333–4.
41. AT XI.185/G 157.
42. Descartes 1664: 357/La Forge 1999: 342.
43. Descartes 1664: 359–60/La Forge 1999: 344. For a discussion of La Forge's comments on this topic, see Drieux 2016.

290   NOTES

44. Descartes 1664: 362/La Forge 1999: 346.
45. Descartes 1664: 406–7/La Forge 1999: 384–5.
46. Descartes 1664: 407/La Forge 1999: 385.
47. For the inventory, see AT X.9.
48. On this question of title, see Bitbol-Hespériès 2016.
49. Descartes 1664: 408/La Forge 1999: 386.
50. Descartes 1664: 229/La Forge 1999: 231.
51. AT XI.143/G 119.
52. Descartes 1664: 278–9/La Forge 1999: 273–4.

Chapter 5

1. The phrase literally means "some cuts with a file."
2. Descartes 1664: xii–xiii/La Forge 1999: 21–2.
3. Due credit should be given to Jacques du Roure, whose Cartesian treatise *La philosophie divisée en toutes ses parties* was published in 1654.
4. This is evident, as we shall see, from Jacques Gousset's report on La Forge showing him a manuscript of his "new book" in 1658.
5. See Sixth Set of Replies, AT VII.436–7/CSM II.294–5.
6. Descartes 1664: 262/La Forge 1999: 260.
7. Descartes 1664: 278/La Forge 1999: 273. See also Descartes 1664: 299, 315, 334, 335, 399/La Forge 1999: 292, 305, 322, 323, 378.
8. Chapelain to La Forge, 31 July 1665, quoted in Clair 1974: 58–9.
9. Descartes 1664: 334/La Forge 1999: 322.
10. AT XI.119–20/CSM I.99.
11. AT XI.200–202/CSM I.107–8.
12. *Discours de la méthode* V, AT VI.59/CSM I.141.
13. *Principia philosophiae* IV.188, AT VIIIA.315/CSM I.279.
14. La Forge 1974: 105–6 /La Forge 1997: 33–4.
15. La Forge 1974: 186/La Forge 1997: 100.
16. La Forge 1974: 322–3/La Forge 1997: 212.
17. La Forge 1974: 78, 106 /La Forge 1997: 7, 34.
18. La Forge 1974: 76–7/La Forge 1997: 6.
19. La Forge 1974: 77/La Forge 1997: 7.
20. *Principia philosophiae/Principes de philosophie*, Preface to the French translation, AT IX-B.8/CSM I.182–3.
21. Act 3, third interlude, lines 58–66.
22. La Forge 1974: 78–9/La Forge 1997: 8.
23. La Forge 1974: 77/La Forge 1997: 6–7.
24. La Forge 1974: 78/La Forge 1997: 8. In the full sentence, La Forge adds, for good measure, that Descartes's thought is also "completely consistent" with the doctrines of "Marcilio Ficino, and of some other authors of antiquity."
25. AT VII.197–8/CSM II.139.

NOTES   291

26. AT VII.219/CSM II.154.
27. November 1640, AT III.247.
28. For a comparison of "the Cartesian *cogito*" and "the Augustinian *cogito*," see Matthews 1992: 11–38. For a general study of Descartes and Augustine, see Menn 1998.
29. See Moreau 1999. For general studies of Cartesianism and Augustinism in the seventeenth century, see Gouhier 1978a and Faye 2000.
30. La Forge 1974: 89–90/La Forge 1997: 19.
31. La Forge 1974: 94, 96/La Forge 1997: 23, 26.
32. La Forge 1974: 106–7/La Forge 1997: 34.
33. La Forge 1974: 108/La Forge 1997: 35.
34. La Forge 1974:126/La Forge 1997: 50.
35. La Forge 1974: 135–6/La Forge 1997: 58.
36. La Forge 1974: 112/La Forge 1997: 39.
37. *Principia philosophiae* I.9, AT VIII-A.7/CSM I.195.
38. Fourth Replies, AT VII.246/CSM II.171.
39. Chalmers 1995.
40. AT X.523–4/CSM II.417–18.
41. AT V.149.
42. AT V.149.
43. Sixth Replies, AT VII.422/CSM II.285.
44. Compare, for example, Wilson 1978 (160–61) with Radner 1993 (451).
45. Beyssade (1979: 244–9) agrees that there is a distinction in Descartes between conscious awareness and reflective consciousness. See also McCrae 1976: 8–16, and Glauser 2011. Not all scholars who agree on this, however, also concur that conscious awareness occurs through a first-order act reflecting *on itself* (for example, Lähteenmäki 2007).
46. Radner 1993: 446. Lähteenmäki (2007) suggests, by contrast, that for Descartes consciousness within first-order adult (but not infant) perceptual awareness occurs through a "second perception" (albeit not a deliberately willed second-order act). "What we have here is an intellectual perception of a logically prior but temporally simultaneous perception which occurs as a byproduct of the initial perception" (189). On the other hand, the consciousness of volition for Descartes *does* occur, Lähteenmäki insists, by the reflexivity of the first-order act of volition itself. Thus, on his reading, consciousness occurs differently in adult perception and volition; this strikes me as a serious problem for his reading.
47. To Mersenne, 28 January 1641, AT III.295.
48. AT XI.343/CSM I.335.
49. The debate over ideas was in fact not an end-in-itself, but mainly a preliminary to the more important (for them) debate over the nature of grace and God's *modus operandi*.
50. Arnauld 1775: XXXVIII.184–5.
51. Arnauld 1775: XXXVIII.204.
52. Arnauld 1775: XXXVIII.204.
53. La Forge 1974: 134/La Forge 1997: 57.
54. La Forge 1974: 134/La Forge 1997: 57.
55. La Forge 1974: 80/La Forge 1997: 10.

292 NOTES

56. La Forge 1974: 112 /La Forge 1997: 38.
57. Manning (2012) argues that, in fact, La Forge was a more extreme dualist than Descartes. He claims that while Descartes was willing to subsume at least part of the study of the mind in "natural philosophy" (physics)—namely, its relationship to the body in sensation—La Forge took a more "exclusionist" approach and isolated the "un-natural" study of the mind in metaphysics. I do not agree with this assessment, however, insofar as La Forge is just as interested as Descartes in studying, as an integral science, the union and interactive relationship between mind and body in sensory, imaginative, and memory experience.
58. AT VI.33/CSM I.127.
59. *Principia philosophiae* I.53–63, AT VIII-A.25–31/CSM I.210–15.
60. Wilson, for one, argues that the Second Meditation only offers "preparations for the argument for mind–body distinctness, finally presented in Meditation VI" (1978: 76). Rozemond, on the other hand, and taking issue with Wilson's reading, argues (convincingly, in my opinion) that "the real distinction argument" is effectively completed in the Second Meditation, where the "thought experiment" Descartes runs is sufficient to establish dualism (1998: Chapter 1).
61. AT VII.223/CSM II.157.
62. AT VII.78/CSM II.54.
63. See Rozemond 1998: 35.
64. La Forge 1974: 115/La Forge 1997: 41.
65. La Forge 1974: 112–3/La Forge 1997: 39. This passage seems, in part, to be inconsistent with La Forge's proof based on the distinction between the natures of the attributes themselves.
66. La Forge 1974: 116/La Forge 1997: 42.
67. La Forge 1974: 116/La Forge 1997: 42.
68. Third Set of Objections, AT VII.173/CSM II.122. Hobbes also proclaims in *Leviathan* (1651) that "*substance* and *body* signify the same thing; and therefore, *substance incorporeal* are words which, when they are joined together, destroy one another, as if a man should say an *incorporeal body*" (*Leviathan*, III.xxxiv.2). The Latin edition of *Leviathan* came out only in 1668, after La Forge's death. Unless La Forge read English, which seems unlikely, his familiarity with Hobbes's materialism could have come only through the Third Set of Objections (1641) and the Latin work *De corpore* (1655).
69. Fifth Set of Objections, AT VII.261–2/CSM II.182–3.
70. La Forge 1974: 120/La Forge 1997: 45.
71. La Forge 1974: 127–8/La Forge 1997: 51.
72. 19 January 1642, AT III.478/CSMK 203.
73. Fourth Set of Objections, AT VII.215/CSM II.150.
74. Fourth Replies, AT VII.246/CSM II.171–2.
75. [Arnauld] to Descartes, 3 June 1648, AT V.188.
76. For [Arnauld], 4 June 1648, AT V.193/CSMK 355. See also the "Conversation with Burman," AT V.150.
77. La Forge 1974: 138/La Forge 1997: 60.
78. La Forge 1974: 137/La Forge 1997: 59.

NOTES 293

79. See Descartes 1659: 15–21.

80. Régis 1690: I.132.

81. Arnauld tells Descartes, "I greatly approve what you say, that the mind always actually thinks" (Arnauld to Descartes, July 1648, AT V.213). However, he then right away questions the claim that thought constitutes the essence of the mind; since thoughts are constantly changing, does that mean that the mind's essence constantly undergoes change?

82. For Leibniz, see the *New Essays on Human Understanding* II.i.9; for Locke, *An Essay Concerning Human Understanding*, II.I.10.

Chapter 6

1. Sixth Meditation, AT VII.78/CSM II.54. Descartes to Elisabeth, 6 October 1645, AT IV.314–5/CSMK 272.

2. AT VII.127–8/CSM II.91.

3. AT VII.153/CSM II.108–9.

4. AT VII.14/CSM II.10; on this, see Gueroult 1953: 107–18. Since an individual body is subject to decay, this suggests that for Descartes, strictly speaking, individual bodies are not substances and only matter itself, the extension of the cosmos, is a substance.

5. Descartes to Mersenne, 24 December 1640, AT III.266/CSMK 163.

6. La Forge 1974: 139/La Forge 1997: 61.

7. "I could be content with this demonstration [that these are two substances that are not only distinct but even completely different] if I only wanted to prove that the mind is immortal" (La Forge 1974: 140/La Forge 1997: 62).

8. AT VII.204/CSM II.143–4. Arnauld points out that "the souls of brute animals" are ordinarily conceived to be distinct from their bodies but "nevertheless perish with them."

9. La Forge 1974: 140–1/La Forge 1997: 63.

10. La Forge's argument also serves to elucidate Descartes's assertion in the Synopsis that substances "are, by their nature, incorruptible." When a body dies by decomposing into its constituent parts, no substance is lost—matter is not destroyed, only rearranged. If decomposition is the only way in which things naturally come to an end, then no such option for disappearing is available to a simple substance.

11. See Sixth Meditation where he notes that the mind, unlike the body, "is utterly indivisible" (AT VII.85–6/CSM II.59); and *Les Passions de l'âme* I.47: "There is within us but one soul, and this soul has within it no diversity of parts" (AT XI.364/CSM I.346).

12. As I read La Forge, I suspect he would say that Descartes was justified only in claiming that the soul, not being subject to material decay, is to that extent naturally *capable* of surviving the body's demise; but that without the additional premise about the only way in which natural things can die, Descartes was *not* justified in concluding that "the mind, in so far as it can be known by natural philosophy," *is* in fact immortal.

13. La Forge 1974: 141/La Forge 1997: 63.

14. La Forge 1974: 141/La Forge 1997: 63.

294 NOTES

15. La Forge 1974: 141/La Forge 1997: 63.

16. See, for example, Régis's *Système général*, I.1.xii (Régis 1690: I.101).

17. Desgabets 1983–85: II.21. On Desgabets and indefectibility, see Schmaltz 2002 and Easton 2005. The doctrine of substance indefectibility is also adopted by Rohault and Régis. Rohault insists, as one of his self-evident "axioms," that "no thing or substance can be completely annihilated [*anéantie*]" (*Traité de physique* I.5, 1671: 29–30). Unlike Desgabets, however, Régis, in his *Système général*, takes the weaker position, that God can never will to destroy a substance: "I say that body and mind are two indefectible substances; not by their own nature . . . but because God, who produced them, acts by an immutable will. This means that to ask if body and mind are indefectible is the same as asking whether the will of God is immutable" (I.1.xii, 1690: I.101).

18. This, at least, is Easton's reconstruction of what Desgabets would respond to questions raised by the Cardinal de Retz (2005: 32–3).

19. See Easton 2005: 32.

20. See *Principia philosophiae* II.36–42.

21. Delphine Antoine-Mahut has argued, correctly I think, that "l'objectif principal" of the *Traité* is an understanding of mind–body union, to preserve "l'empire de l'Esprit sur le corps" by considering exactly the nature of each; for La Forge, she argues, "on ne saurait penser de 'vrai homme,' au sens cartésien, sans prendre au sérieux l'union de l'âme et du corps, donc aussi les diverse formes de dépendance qui s'exercent sur la première" (2021: 187–8).

22. See Gilson 1976: 433–4; Gueroult 1953: II.123–57; Wilson 1978: Chapter 6; and, more recently, Rozemond 1998: Chapter 6, and Carriero 2009: Chapter 6. According to Gouhier, however, Descartes himself recognized no such problem of union: "Descartes, semble-t-il, s'expliquait aisément l'union vécue de l'esprit au corps: le fait que l'un fût res extensa et l'autre, res cogitans, ne paraissait pas le gêner" (1978b: 352).

23. See Aristotle, *De anima* II.1, 413a8–9.

24. AT VII.80–81/CSM II.56.

25. *Discours de la méthode* V, AT VI.59/CSM I.141.

26. Descartes to Regius, January 1642, AT III.493/CSMK 206.

27. Descartes to Elisabeth, 21 May 1643, AT III.665/CSMK 218.

28. Descartes to Elisabeth, 28 June 1643, AT III.691–2/CSMK 227.

29. AT VII.88/CSM II.60–61.

30. *Principia philosophiae* IV.189, AT VIII-A.315/CSM I.279–80.

31. AT VII.81/CSM II.56.

32. AT VII.442/CSM II.298. Rozemond suggests that the gravity analogy via "coextension" and the "intermixture" analogy are in fact put to different purposes: the former for understanding how the mind acts on the body in voluntary motion, and the latter or understanding how the body causes sensations in the mind (1998: 178).

33. See, for example, Fifth Replies, AT VII.388–90/CSM II.266–7.

34. Letter to More, 15 April 1649, AT V.342/CSMK 372. On this, see Rozemond 1998: 180; and Schmaltz 2008: 167–71.

35. *Les Passions de l'âme*, I.30–34, AT XI.351–4/CSM I.339–41.

36. Wilson 1978: 211.

NOTES 295

37. Sixth Meditation, AT VII.81/CSM II.56, emphasis added.
38. La Forge 1974: 223/La Forge 1997: 132–3. See also 1974: 218/1997: 128, where La Forge claims that if the mind's relationship to its body were like a pilot in his ship, "this mind would have much more reason to think of itself as something with completely separate interests which is distinct from the body, rather than at present when it is joined from the first moment of its creation without being able to separate from it."
39. Scribano (2016b) has shown how La Forge uses this analogy—demonstrating that knowledge is never necessary to produce movements in the body—against materialists (who attribute some form of knowledge and thought to body, especially in instinctive movements by humans and animals) and vitalists (like Campanella).
40. La Forge 1974: 206/La Forge 1997: 119. Both Clair (1974: 379n139) and Clarke (La Forge 1997: 119n128) note a similar reference by Desgabets, but are unable to come up with any candidates in the Cartesian camp.
41. Leibniz employs the notion in his correspondence with Des Bosses to explain the reality of corporeal substance, especially in the context of Eucharistic transubstantiation.
42. Descartes to Regius, December 1641, AT III.460/CSMK 200.
43. Descartes to Regius, January 1642, AT III.493/CSMK 206. He even suggests that Regius refer to the soul as "the true substantial form of man" (AT III.503–5/ CSMK 207–8). On the Utrecht crisis and Descartes's relationship with Regius, see Verbeek 1992.
44. See Hoffman 1986.
45. Cottingham 1985. Cottingham says that his reading does not imply that Descartes recognized a third kind of *substance*. "At least one of the categories involved in the trialistic scheme is to be understood attributively, not substantivally" (229). However, given the identification of substance and its principal attribute, it is hard to see how the trialist reading can avoid identifying a third kind of substance in Descartes. For a critique of the trialist reading, see Rozemond 1998: 192–203.
46. La Forge 1974: 115/La Forge 1997: 41.
47. La Forge 1974: 207–8/La Forge 1997: 120. By "simple substance," La Forge cannot mean here the kind of simplicity that characterizes the soul as a simple substance— that is, being non-composite and lacking parts.
48. La Forge 1974: 208/La Forge 1997: 121.
49. La Forge 1974: 209–10/La Forge 1997: 121–2.
50. La Forge 1974: 216/La Forge 1997: 127.
51. La Forge 1974: 210/La Forge 1997: 122.
52. La Forge 1974: 210/La Forge 1997: 122.
53. La Forge 1974: 211/La Forge 1997: 123. I do not think this is a fair reading of Clauberg, however.
54. *Corporis et animae conjunctio*, IX.1–3, XIV.8–9, Clauberg 1968: I.215, 219. As Platt notes, "So (like Clauberg) La Forge holds that the human mind and body are united by a 'reciprocal dependence' between their modes" (2020: 225).
55. Clauberg 1968: I.215. I have not found any passage in Clauberg which implies that the union consists only in occurrent acts of mind–body causation.
56. La Forge 1974: 218–9/La Forge 1997: 129.

296   NOTES

57. "A philosopher should not be any more ashamed to acknowledge God as the author of this union than as the cause of the creation of the soul and of its infusion [*infusion*] into the body; for in fact the infusion and union are just the same thing" (La Forge 1974: 227/La Forge 1997: 136).

58. La Forge 1974: 227/La Forge 1997: 136.

59. La Forge lists these "articles" or laws at the beginning of Chapter 15 (La Forge 1974: 224–5/La Forge 1997: 134).

60. Sixth Meditation, AT VII.86/CSM II.59–60.

61. *Les Passions de l'âme* I.34, AT XI.354–5/CSM I.341.

62. *Les Passions de l'âme* I.36, AT XI.357/CSM I.342.

63. *Les Passions de l'âme* I.41, 43, AT XI.360, 361/CSM I.343, 344.

64. Bos (2017) discusses a subtle change in Descartes's writings, from *La Dioptrique* to *Les Passions de l'âme*, on the way in which the pineal gland is alleged to function relative to the animal spirits, especially in sensation, from "inverse transmission" (where the focus is on the way the spirits leave the gland) to a picture in which the spirits travel from the nerve openings in the brain *to* the gland to move it. He concludes, however, that when all the relevant texts are taken into account, Descartes is consistent.

65. AT VII.86/CSM II.60.

66. To Mersenne, 1 April 1640, AT III.49/CSMK 146.

67. *Les Passions de l'âme* AT XI.352–3/CSM I.340.

68. To Mersenne, 30 July 1640, AT III.124/CSMK 149. For a discussion of this passage and argument, see Schmaltz (Forthcoming).

69. La Forge 1974: 234–5/La Forge 1997:142.

70. These conditions are laid out in Chapter 15 of the *Traité*, La Forge 1974: 227–30/La Forge 1997: 136–9.

71. La Forge 1974: 232–3/La Forge 1997: 141.

72. Steno 1669: 13.

73. Steno 1669: 20.

74. Steno 1669: 30–31.

75. La Forge 1974: 233–4/La Forge 1997: 141–2.

76. La Forge 1974: 134/La Forge 1997: 142. On Steno's objections and La Forge's responses, see Andrault 2009 and 2016, Grigoropoulou 2018, and Schmaltz (Forthcoming).

77. La Forge 1974: 229/La Forge 1997: 137.

78. *Le Discernement du corps et de l'ame* VI.3, Cordemoy 1968: 164/Cordemoy 2015: 120.

79. Huet, for example, had this to say in his *Censura philosophiae cartesianae* (1689): "What Descartes says about the *conarion* controlling the flow of the animal spirits in the ventricles of the brain, besides being just silly, is entirely at odds with the discoveries and teachings of the recent anatomists, and was long ago refuted by Galen" (Huet 2003: 152).

80. See Malebranche 1972–84: I.194/Malebranche 1980: 89 (first emphasis is mine). For discussion of Malebranche's attitude toward the pineal gland, see Schmaltz (Forthcoming). I am indebted to Schmaltz for bringing this change in the passage from Malebranche to my attention.

81. This is the retitled second edition of Régis's 1690 *Système de philosophie*.

82. Régis 1690: I.293–6.

NOTES 297

83. AT XI.176–7/CSM I.106.

84. Third Meditation, AT VII.37/CSM II.25.

85. La Forge 1974: 76/La Forge 1997: 6.

86. La Forge 1974: 158/La Forge 1997: 77; see also 1974: 167/1997: 84. Chapter 10 of the *Traité* is titled "Corporeal Species and Intellectual Ideas or Notions." Antoine-Mahut (2017) argues that La Forge is concerned that the use of the term 'idea' to refer to both corporeal figures and mental states could encourage a Hobbesian-type materialism.

87. La Forge 1974: 163–4/La Forge 1997: 81–2.

88. La Forge 1974: 166–70/La Forge 1997: 84–8. This is similar to how Descartes describes the process, as well, in *La Dioptrique*, Discourse 4.

89. La Forge 1974: 171/La Forge 1997: 88.

90. AT VIII-B.357–61/CSM I.303–5.

91. AT VII.51/CSM II.35.

92. La Forge 1974: 181/La Forge 1997: 96.

93. Wilson 1978: 180.

94. AT VII.358/CSM II.248.

95. La Forge 1974: 146/La Forge 1997: 68. Here La Forge does use 'idea' (rather than 'species') to refer to a corporeal impression.

96. La Forge 1974: 139/La Forge 1997: 61. See also 1974: 216/1997: 127.

97. AT VIII-B.344/CSM I.295. Regius's wording here at least seems to allow, in principle, that when the mind is *not* "in the body" there is a range of ideas it can still have.

98. *Supplément à la philosophie de Monsieur Descartes* I.3, Desgabets 1983–85: 181. On this, see Schmaltz 2002: 179–82.

99. Régis 1690: I.122–3; the emphasis is mine.

100. La Forge 1974: 146/La Forge 1997: 68.

101. La Forge 1974: 148/La Forge 1997: 69.

102. To Elisabeth, 3 November 1645, AT IV.333/CSMK 277.

103. La Forge 1974: 324/La Forge 1997: 213.

104. La Forge 1974: 325/La Forge 1997: 214.

105. La Forge 1974: 324/La Forge 1997: 213.

106. *Supplément à la philosophie de Monsieur Descartes* I.9, Desgabets 1983–85: 187–8.

107. *Supplément à la philosophie de Monsieur Descartes* I.5, Desgabets 1983–85: 176.

108. My thanks to Tad Schmaltz for discussing this with me.

109. *Système général* I.3.1–3, Régis 1690: I.265–9. He does grant, though, that it is possible that revelation will confirm for us that immortal souls will still have many of these powers; but until such a revelation occurs, "we must suspend our judgment" (269).

110. *Système général* I.3.2–3, Régis 1690: I.269–70.

111. To Gibieuf, 19 January 1642, AT III.479/CSMK 203.

112. On imagination, see Sixth Meditation, AT VII.72–3/CSM II.50–51; and *Les Passions de l'âme* I.43, AT XI.361/CSM I.344.

113. To Hyperaspistes, August 1641, AT III.424/CSMK 190.

114. Régis, for one, takes the extreme view and says that, on philosophical grounds, we must conclude that death, by destroying the mind–body union, "destroys everything modal in a human being, without touching what is substantial, which is effectively incorruptible" (*Système générale* III.1.iii, 1690: I.270–71). But he also says that "it is

298 NOTES

only the modes that determine [the soul] to be such and such a soul, for example, the soul of Peter, of Paul, of John, etc., who are destroyed (1690: 267). Once again, then, only faith and revelation can assure us of what we want to know.

115. AT XI.177–8/G 150.

116. To Mesland, 2 May 1644, AT IV.114/CSMK 233. See also *Les Passions de l'âme* I.42, AT XI.360/CSM I.344.

117. To Mersenne, 1 April 1640, AT III.48/CSMK 146. See also To Meyssonnier, 29 January 1640, AT III.20–21/CSMK 143–4.

118. In *La Dioptrique*, Descartes ridicules the notion that the mind literally looks at the brain motions, "as if there were yet other eyes within our brain with which we could perceive it" (AT VI.130/CSM I.167).

119. For Arnauld, 4 June 1648, AT V.192–3/CSMK 354.

120. For Arnauld, 29 July 1648, AT V.220/CSMK 356.

121. To Mersenne, 6 August 1640, AT III.143/CSMK 151. For an illuminating discussion of these texts on memory, see Scribano 2016a: 140–47, and Clarke 2003: 78–105.

122. Fifth Set of Replies, AT VII.356–7/CSM II.247.

123. To Mesland, 2 May 1644, AT IV.114/CSMK 233.

124. To Mersenne, 1 April 1640, AT III.48/CSMK 146.

125. To Hyperaspistes, August 1641, AT III.425/CSMK 190.

126. To Huygens, 13 October 1642, AT III.580/CSMK 216. As Clarke notes, "the reality of an 'intellectual memory' is a tentative conclusion from a theological doctrine about the afterlife . . . rather than a conclusion derived from the Cartesian theory of mind" (2003:101).

127. La Forge 1974: 280–81/La Forge 1997: 178.

128. La Forge 1974: 284/La Forge 1997: 182.

129. Descartes 1664: 346/La Forge 1999: 332. This is a point nicely noted by Scribano (2016a: 147).

130. As Scribano notes, La Forge uses the term 'reminiscence' for what Descartes had called 'intellectual memory', most likely under the influence of Pierre Chanet's 1649 text *Traité de l'esprit de l'homme et de ses fonctions* (2016a: 149).

131. La Forge 1974: 284/La Forge 1997: 182.

132. Arnauld to Descartes, 3 June 1648, AT V.186–7.

133. La Forge 1974: 291/La Forge 1997: 187.

134. La Forge 1974: 290/La Forge 1997: 186–7.

135. La Forge 1974: 291/La Forge 1997: 187. On this see Watson 1987.

136. La Forge 1974: 324/La Forge 1997: 213. Scribano (2016a: 153) raises an interesting point when she notes that there is no discussion of the fact that mind would be tasked with remembering thoughts that, during this life, were grounded in brain traces.

Chapter 7

1. On Descartes, see Garber 1992, 1993, and 2001, and Hatfield 1979; on Boyle, see McGuire 1972; on Leibniz, for whom a more plausible case can be made for his early, post-Paris years, see Kulstad 1993.

NOTES 299

2. Malebranche also extends occasionalism into the realm of grace, whereby thoughts in the mind of Christ are the occasion for God's to distribute grace among human beings; see his *Traité de la nature et de la grace*. Even miracles for Malebranche are in accordance with the divine "Order," and thus in a sense are law-like as well.

3. *Guide of the Perplexed* III.17, in Maimonides 1963: II.466–7. On Islamic occasionalism, see Fakhry 1958.

4. Three names that typically come up are Gabriel Biel, Pierre d'Ailly, and Nicolas of Autrecourt. Although all three argued against necessary connections in nature, it is difficult to read any of them as a committed occasionalist.

5. *Summa theologiae*, Part One, Q. 105, art. 5.

6. *Questiones disputatae de potentia dei*, Q. 3, art. 7.

7. *Disputationes metaphysicae*, Disp. 22, sect. 3, n. 4.

8. *Disputationes metaphysicae*, Disp. 22, sect. 3, n. 10. For an illuminating discussion of conservationism and concurrence, especially Suarez's version, see Freddoso 1991 and 2002.

9. Kolesnik 2006: 42.

10. For a more accurate analysis of the motivations and arguments for occasionalism, see Lennon 1974, Nadler 2011, Sandrine Roux 2018, and Platt 2020, among others.

11. See, for example, *Système nouveau*, in Leibniz 1960–61: IV.483.

12. Platt 2020: 21–2.

13. *In quattuor libros sententiarum*, Book 1, disq. 46, question 1, article 2.

14. AT XI.181/G 153. Unfortunately, Gaukroger translates this simply as 'causes.'

15. AT VI.114/CSM I.166. See also *Notae in programma quoddam*, AT VIII-B.359/CSM I.304.

16. Quoted in Collacciani 2016: 122.

17. On *occasio* and related concepts in Cartesian thought, see Specht 1972.

18. *Notae in programma quoddam*, AT VIII-B.360/CSM I.305.

19. In Nadler 1994, I argue that occasional causation is not a species of efficient causation, but rather a *sui generis* causal relation. Schmaltz (2008: 145–62) and Platt (2020: 37–42) have argued that it should indeed be classified as efficient causation, at least in those cases in which the relation is grounded in the (divinely instituted) natures of things. I would agree that sometimes it can be read as a species of efficient causation, but that in some cases (and, as we shall see, in the case of La Forge) it should not be so read. Gouhier (1926: 86) seems to opt for treating it as efficient causation, though his language is ambiguous; what he says is that "ce qui est curieux, ce n'est pas que le corps agisse sur l'âme, mais c'est *ce que le corps produit dans l'âme*. Descartes a senti la nécessité d'expliquer non pas la possibilité d'un rapport causal, mais le contenu des termes de ce rapport. Le mot *occasion* ne remplace pas le mot *cause*."

20. Despite this, many scholars have conflated occasional causation with occasionalism, and taken philosophers who employ only the former to be representatives of the latter. See, for example, Balz 1951 and Baker and Morris 1996: 138–62.

21. See, for example, Prost 1907a, Hatfield 1979, and Broughton 1986. Ott (2009: 64–78), too, argues that while in his early works Descartes did hold that bodies have efficacious causal powers, tensions within his physics led him toward the occasionalist position. Garber's considered interpretation is a bit more hesitant, having grown more nuanced over time. In Garber 1992 and 1993, his Descartes is definitely an occasionalist with respect to body–body relations. Garber says (1993: 12) that "it seems to me as clear as

300 NOTES

anything that, for Descartes, God is the only cause of motion in the inanimate world or bodies, that bodies cannot themselves be genuine causes of change in the physical world of extended substance." However, in Garber 2001, he is less sure of this. "While many of Descartes' followers drew this conclusion [that bodies are strictly speaking passive, and contain no genuine causal efficacy of their own], it is not at all clear how he himself stood on the issue" (74). Even the conservation as continuous creation doctrine, Garber notes, was not envisioned by Descartes as establishing that bodies are causally inefficacious and that God alone is the efficient cause of their motions. "I see no reason to believe that Descartes ever saw such consequences as following out of his doctrine of continual recreation" (302). Garber allows that, at most, this doctrine *"would seem to commit him* to the view that God can be the only cause of change in the world" (my emphasis). At the same time, while admitting that "it is not absolutely impossible that [Descartes] meant to include bodies among the finite substances that can cause motion," he also says that "it is highly unlikely," mainly because Descartes, writing to Henry More, does not explicitly include bodies among those items to which "God gave the power of moving a body" (August 1649, AT V.403–4/CSMK 381). If he did believe they had such a power, it would have been "too important a fact to pass unnoticed" in that letter. Garber concludes that "[Descartes] does seem to agree with his occasionalist followers in denying that bodies are genuine causes of motion" (2001: 304).

22. Fontenelle 1825: III.86.
23. AT VIII-A.61/CSM I.240.
24. AT VIII-A.66/CSM I.243.
25. To More, August 1649, AT V.403–4/CSMK 381.
26. To More, 15 April 1649, AT V.347/CSMK 375.
27. On this, see Garber 1983 and Favaretti Camposampiero 2018.
28. To Arnauld, 29 July 1648, AT V.222/CSMK 358.
29. AT XI.46/CSM I.97.
30. AT XI.43/CSM I.96.
31. AT VIII-A.66–7/CSM I.243–4.
32. AT VIII-B.358–9/CSM I.304.
33. To Elisabeth, 28 June 1643, AT III.692/CSMK 227.
34. See, for example, Gouhier 1926: 83–8; Gabbey 1971; Hattab 2001 and 2007; Schmaltz 2008; and Platt 2020: 87–136, among others. They do not all offer the same arguments against an occasionalist reading; nor do they all agree on just how to understand Descartes's views on causation. Schmaltz, for example, opts for a conservationist reading, while Platt regards him as a concurrentist.
35. As Ott (2009: 64) puts it, "Descartes's positions on laws and force seem to push him toward some version of occasionalism," by which he means a "limited" occasionalism— limited, that is, to body–body relations.
36. Compare, for example, Nadler 1993a and Black 1997.
37. See, for example, Balz 1951, Loeb 1981, and Garber 1993, who all regard Clauberg as an occasionalist to some degree. Bouillier (1868: I.298) regards Clauberg as a one-sided occasionalist, since he allows that the soul can move the body; but even in the body>mind case Bouillier is misled by the term 'occasional cause.' Lucarini (2007),

NOTES 301

likewise, says that Clauberg "non può essere ritenuto un 'classical occasionalist'" because he maintains the causal efficacy of the mind over its own thoughts and ideas. Favaretti Camposampiero (2018: 201) says that "Clauberg does not aim to deny every kind of interaction between mind and body, but rather to establish a sort of restricted interactionism."

38. La Forge was familiar with Clauberg's writings, though, as he quotes him a couple of times in the *Traité* (115, 123).

39. This is the conclusion reached by most scholars; see Bardout 2002a, Schmaltz 2017: 176–81, Platt 2020: 137–66, and Hamid 2022. Weir (1981) does find an "implicit occasionalism" in Clauberg, given his commitment to the doctrine of continuous creation.

40. *Corporis et animae in homine conjunctio* IX.2, 11, 12; Clauberg 1968: I.215–6.

41. Thus Clauberg's reference in the text quoted above to "found in the nature of the things themselves."

42. *Corporis et animae in homine conjunctio* XVI.1; Clauberg 1968: I.221.

43. *Corporis et animae in homine conjunctio* XVI.4, 10; Clauberg 1968: I.221.

44. *Disputationes physicae*, Disp. XIX, art. 4; Clauberg 1968: I.104. It was Platt's discussion of this passage that brought it to my attention (Platt 2020: 255, where he argues that Clauberg was not an occasionalist in the body–body realm).

45. *Corporis et animae in homine conjunctio* XVI.5, 6, 7; Clauberg 1968: I.221.

46. *Corporis et animae in homine conjunctio* XVI.12; Clauberg 1968: I.221.

47. Heereboord 1665: 242.

48. See the *Tabula secunda* at the end of the *Institutionum logicorum libri duo*, in Burgersdijk 1634: 417.

49. Platt (2020) opts for real efficient causation in both directions of the mind–body relationship and sees procatarctic causes as efficient causes; likewise, Schmaltz 2017. Hamid (2022), on the other hand, says that there is no real interaction but a kind of parallelism, with body and mind each causally efficacious in its own domain.

50. *Traité de l'esprit de l'homme* XIII, La Forge 1974: 211/La Forge 1997: 123.

51. Geulincx was giving private lessons in philosophy by 1659, before formally joining the Leiden faculty in 1662.

52. The rest of the work would not appear until 1675, after Geulincx's death, but Part One includes the occasionalist material.

53. *Ethica* I.2.2.iv, Geulincx 1891–93: II.32/Geulincx 2006: 33.

54. Geulincx 1891–93: III.205/Geulincx 2006: 225. The annotations were not added until the 1675 edition of the *Ethica*. For a discussion of the *quod nescis* principle, including its possible historical sources and various applications, see Scribano 2011, Sangiacomo 2014a, and Sandrine Roux 2018 (where the discussion extends to Malebranche, who also helps himself to this principle).

55. Geulincx 1891–93: III.206/Geulincx 2006: 226.

56. Geulincx 1891–93: III.211/Geulincx 2006: 232.

57. Geulincx 1891–93: III.205/Geulincx 2006: 225.

58. *Metaphysica vera* I.5, Geulincx 1891–93: II.150/Geulincx 1999: 35. As Scribano (2011) shows, La Forge rejects the *quod nescis* principle, on the grounds that it leads ultimately to materialism.

302 NOTES

59. *Metaphysica vera* I.8, Geulincx 1891–93: II.153/Geulincx 1999: 40.

60. *Ethica* I.2.2.ii, Geulincx 1891–93: II.32/Geulincx 2006: 33.

61. *Ethica*, Annotations, Geulincx 1891–93: II.207/Geulincx 2006: 226.

62. *Metaphysica vera* I.4–5, Geulincx 1891–93: II.149–50/Geulincx 1999: 34.

63. *Metaphysica vera* I.9, Geulincx 1891–93: II.154/Geulincx 1999: 41.

64. *Ethica* I.2.2.vi–vii, Geulincx 1891–93: II.33/Geulincx 2006: 33–4.

65. *Ethica* I.2.2.xiii, Geulincx 1891–93: II.36/Geulincx 2006: 36.

66. Seyfarth (1887: 58) calls Geulincx a "complete occasionalist [*vollendeter occasionalist*]." Stein (1888) also seems to attribute to Geulincx a complete occasionalism, although in his view Geulincx's occasionalism did not achieve "systematic form" until the *Metaphysica vera*. Prost (1907a), Specht (1966), and Schmaltz (2017: 205–209), too, see Geulincx as a thoroughgoing occasionalist. Bardout (2002b), meanwhile, does not appear to address this particular question. The fullest study of Geulincx's philosophy, and especially his occasionalism, is De Lattre 1967.

67. On Cordemoy's occasionalism, see Battail 1973, Ablondi 2005, and Nadler 2005. Battail insists that for Cordemoy "cet universe tout entier [est] passif et inerte . . . il n'y a en son sein aucune liaison effective entre les causes et les effets. . . . La puissance [est] tout entière concentrée en Dieu" (140, 136). Similarly, Specht (1966: 148) says that "bei Cordemoy is der occasionalismus in seinem vollen Sinne erreicht." Prost (1907a: 69), on the other hand, sees a more limited occasionalism and believes that Cordemoy grants to the human soul a degree of causal efficacy, particularly the power to generate some of its own internal states, such as volitions and desires. Balz (1951: 16) declines to take a stand on the issue: "Whether Cordemoy's doctrine is a complete occasionalism . . . is not a question that need detain us." Similarly, Platt (2020: 285), who agrees that Cordemoy is an occasionalist when it comes to body–body and mind>body relations, concludes that "it is unclear whether Cordemoy is an occasionalist" when it comes to body>mind or intra-mental causation. See also Bardout 2002b: 148, and Gouhier 1926: 101. For a more extended discussion and adjudication of this issue, see Nadler 2005.

68. See Battail 1973: 150. See also Gouhier 1926: 95–107, 120. Carraud (2002: 376, 380) insists that Cordemoy begins from difficulties regarding causation, not (like Malebranche) from "l'adoration . . . de la gloire de Dieu et de sa puissance . . . pour le dire autrement, la pensée de l'efficace divine, chez Malebranche, est antérieure à la solution occasionaliste. À la difference d'un La Forge ou d'un Cordemoy, Malebranche n'est pas d'abord occasionaliste."

69. Cordemoy 1968: 135–6/Cordemoy 2015: 92–3.

70. Cordemoy 1968: 150/Cordemoy 2015: 106.

71. See More's letter to Descartes, 5 March 1649.

72. Cordemoy 1968: 138/Cordemoy 2015: 95.

73. Cordemoy 1968: 139/Cordemoy 2015: 96.

74. Cordemoy 1968: 139, 142/Cordemoy 2015: 97, 99.

75. Cordemoy 1968: 149/Cordemoy 2015: 106.

76. Cordemoy 1968: 150/Cordemoy 2015: 106.

77. Cordemoy 1968: 140–41/Cordemoy 2015: 97–8.

78. Cordemoy 1968: 141–3/Cordemoy 2015: 98–100.

79. Cordemoy 1968: 140–41/Cordemoy 2015: 98.

NOTES 303

80. Cordemoy 1968: 144/Cordemoy 2015: 101.
81. As Platt has shown (2020: 274), Cordemoy must also assume, for his argument to go through, that "the various states of motion or rest in different bodies at different times are the action of a single agent ... that they are a single action." That is, all motions in all bodies are initiated at creation by one and the same action and thus continued by one and the same agent, as opposed to there being multiple minds as first (and thus continuing) causes of motions in different bodies.
82. Cordemoy 1968: 142/Cordemoy 2015: 99.
83. Cordemoy 1968: 149/Cordemoy 2015: 105.
84. I have corrected for an apparent error in the text here, one that is noted by Clair and Girbal in their modern edition (see note c at Cordemoy 1968: 151). The text of the first, third, and fourth editions reads *celle des corps sur l'esprits*. But what Cordemoy should say here is that the action of minds upon bodies is no more inconceivable than the action of bodies upon bodies. The second edition has (apparently correctly) *celle des corps sur les corps*.
85. Cordemoy 1968: 225.
86. Cordemoy 1968: 148/Cordemoy 2015: 104.
87. Cordemoy 1968: 210.
88. Cordemoy 1968: 238.
89. Cordemoy 1968: 225.
90. Cordemoy 1968: 255.
91. Cordemoy 1968: 279/Cordemoy 2015: 147 (emphasis added). Battail (1973: 149) recognizes that the occasionalist account of sensory ideas lies only outside *Le Discernement*: "Sa thèse, c'est que les idées sont produites en nous par Dieu toutes les fois que cela est nécessaire." See also Prost 1907a: 91.
92. Cordemoy 1968: 253–4.
93. We do not know when the *Traitez de métaphysique* were composed, and thus it is certainly possible that Cordemoy initially (in *Le Discernement* and the *Discours physique*) believed the soul to be active with respect to its volitions, but then (in the *Traitez*) changed his view under the influence of Malebranche's *Recherche* (and especially Éclaircissement I, published in the third edition of the work in 1678). But Battail argues, on the basis of biographical and textual evidence, that it is likely that the *Traitez* were composed between 1668 and 1670, which would put them before the publication of Malebranche's work (Battail 1973: 18).
94. Cordemoy 1968: 284/Cordemoy 2015: 151.
95. Radner (1993: 358) says that what makes the mind active (but not causally efficacious) for Cordemoy is the fact that the volitional "movement" in the mind is an action that, while caused by God, belongs to the mind as its modification. But it would seem to follow from this way of reading the argument that bodies, too, would be active, since they too have divinely caused movement as a modification; and surely Cordemoy does not want to say that bodies are active.
96. What Cordemoy offers here is very much like Malebranche's mature theory of the will and its freedom (see *De la recherche de la vérité*, I.1.2 and IV.1, and *Traité de la nature et de la grace*, III.1). I return to this in Chapter 10.
97. Cordemoy 1968: 283/Cordemoy 2015: 150.

304 NOTES

98. Stein 1888, Prost (1907a: 137), Specht (1966: 148), Battail (1973), and Carraud (2002) agree.

99. The second of the six discourses of Cordemoy's *Le Discernement* had previously been published on its own in 1664, as part of the first published edition of Descartes's *Le Monde* (an edition *not* overseen by Clerselier). Cordemoy had originally presented the essay to a gathering at Montmor's academy, and it appears in the 1664 volume under the title *Discours . . . touchant le mouvement et le repos*. However, there is no hint of occasionalism in this text.

100. De Vleeschauwer claims that "les grands linéaments" of Geulincx's doctrines were already in place during his Louvain period and "déja arrêtés en 1652" (1978: 396); however, he offers no evidence for this statement.

101. Cordemoy 1968: 145/Cordemoy 2015: 103 (emphasis added).

Chapter 8

1. Gousset 1716: 4.

2. Gousset 1716: 3–4.

3. Gousset's memories about La Forge appear in his *Causarum primae et secundum realis operatio rationibus confirmatur et ab objectionibus defenditur*, which was published in 1716.

4. Gousset 1716: 7.

5. Gousset 1716: 7–8.

6. Gousset 1716: 9.

7. Gousset 1716: 11–12.

8. Gousset 1716: 12.

9. Gousset 1716: 12–13.

10. As far as I can tell, De Villemandy (unlike Gousset) probably did not know La Forge personally. He did not take up his position at the Protestant Academy in Saumur until 1669, when he succeeded Jean-Robert Chouet as professor of philosophy.

11. *Dissertatio philosophica. Ostendens cartesianum mundi systema non esse . . . periculosum* (1696).

12. De Villemandy 1686: 21.

13. De Villemandy 1686: 21. De Villemandy says, however, that La Forge was not a complete occasionalist, that he did not "push things to extremes, where they ended up" (21). And yet, he also notes that La Forge did not allow bodies to efficaciously interact nor minds and bodies to act on each other; thus, the "extreme" La Forge apparently avoided was removing the mind's causal power to generate its own thoughts and volitions.

14. What this means is that La Forge found his philosophical vocation even before he signed on with Clerselier on *L'Homme*.

15. We can rule out any influence by Geulincx, since that first part of the *Ethica* would not be published for several more years.

NOTES 305

16. That this was the case is suggested by Prost (1907a: 102n1) and Clair (1976: 64). Stein (1888: 56–7) claims that Cordemoy most likely shared his thoughts with La Forge directly in 1658.

17. Cordemoy 1968: 149–51/Cordemoy 2015: 106–7.

18. La Forge 1974: 235–6/La Forge 1997: 143. Sandrine Roux (2018: 94n17) rightly finds La Forge's change of language between these two passages (substituting *savoir* for *concevoir* in the case of body–body relations) significant, in that it suggests that for La Forge body–body causation is indeed more conceivable than mind–body causation but that we still do not know how it is supposed to take place.

19. La Forge 1974: 235–6/La Forge 1997: 143.

20. Seyfarth 1887: 56–7; Stein 1888.

21. Gouhier 1926: 101; Carraud 2002: 350–51. If I read him correctly, Clarke also denies that La Forge is an occasionalist in any domain, although he notes that "La Forge's theory of causal interaction is sufficiently ambiguous to leave room for a number of alternative interpretations" (La Forge 1997: xx–21, and Clarke 2000). Clarke's own view, however, is ambiguous as well, insofar as he identifies La Forge as an occasionalist in Clarke 1989 (106–7) and Clarke 2016 (124).

22. One exception is Prost 1904: 212, and 1907b: 133–5, where La Forge is portrayed as a full and thoroughgoing occasionalist who does not allow for any true causal efficacy outside of God.

23. Radner 1993; Sandrine Roux 2022.

24. Bouillier 1868: I.513; Bardout 2002b; Sangiacomo 2014b; Schmaltz 2017: 195–8; and Platt 2020. This was also a reading I defended in Nadler 1993b and 1998; although now I am pretty certain that it is not correct.

25. Bardout 2002b; Drieux 2019.

26. La Forge 1974: 241/La Forge 1997: 147.

27. See Descartes, *Principia philosophiae* II.25: "And I say [motion] is 'the transfer,' as opposed to the force or action that brings about the transfer, to show that it is always in the moving body, as opposed to the thing that brings about the motion. The two are not normally distinguished with sufficient care" (AT VIII-A.54/CSM I.233, translation modified to better capture the original).

28. *Principia philosophiae* II.25.

29. La Forge 1974: 238/La Forge 1997: 145.

30. La Forge 1974: 240/La Forge 1997: 146.

31. La Forge 1974: 238/La Forge 1997: 145.

32. Descartes himself, in a letter to More (August 1649), denies that body–body interaction would require such a communication or transfer (AT V.404–5/CSMK 382).

33. La Forge 1974: 238–9/La Forge 1997: 145–6.

34. La Forge 1974: 238/La Forge 1997: 145.

35. *Principia philosophiae* I.21, AT VIII-A.13/CSM I.200.

36. *Meditationes* III, AT VII.49/CSM II.33–4.

37. Garber (2001) argues that this is not Descartes's view, and Anfray (2019) agrees that neither La Forge nor Malebranche adopts the "strong" (re-creation) version of the doctrine.

306 NOTES

38. See Fakhry 1958. I owe the term 'cinematic view' to Garber 2001.

39. *Meditationes* III, AT VII.49/CSM II.33.

40. *Entretiens sur la métaphysique et sur la religion*, VII.7, Malebranche 1972–84: XII.156–7/Malebranche 1997: 112.

41. La Forge 1974: 240/La Forge 1997: 146.

42. La Forge 1974: 240/La Forge 1997: 146–7.

43. La Forge 1974: 241–2/La Forge 1997: 148.

44. La Forge 1974: 241/La Forge 1997: 147. Schmaltz (2017: 194–8) finds it significant that, as La Forge sets up the hypothetical situation, the world is totally devoid of motion, just an undifferentiated plenum of matter. With everything at complete rest, God is required to get things moving; otherwise, even if God gave to one body the motive force to move itself, it could not move unless all other bodies move as well—such is physics in a plenum. As La Forge says, "that is why when God decided to move matter in various ways he had to apply the force that he chose to put into matter to many of its parts at the same time, so that they could give up their places to each other at the same instant, without which no motion could have been produce" (La Forge 1974: 241/La Forge 1997: 147). So if everything is at rest, God is required to set things in motion at the beginning; this, Schmaltz claims, is the "special" case in which no other creature can move things from the places in which they were created (at rest). But, Schmaltz suggests, once motion has been initiated, why could not bodies then continue to serve as efficient causes with a "determining force" to effect changes in motion? "God alone can initiate motion," he says, but "it does not seem to follow that God alone can put a moving body in the places where it exists successively." And yet, the idea that bodies can put other bodies in their places through their own causal efficacy does not seem to be La Forge's position. While I disagree with Schmaltz's claim that "there is no clear argument in La Forge from divine conservation" to body–body occasionalism, and that La Forge attributes "determining force" to bodies, even Schmaltz concedes, in the end, that "La Forge's account of the bodily determination of motion verges on occasionalism."

45. Sangiacomo (2014b) does not agree, and insists that the "continuous creation" argument needs to work together with the "no transfer of modes" argument. The latter, he insists, is complemented by the continuous creation argument. If I am reading him correctly, his position is that, for La Forge, the "no transfer" argument is the general argument that bodies do not cause motion in other bodies, and that it must be an immaterial mind that does so; and the "continuous creation" argument is the particular argument that it is God who does the requisite work. Platt (2020: 244–52) likewise does not see the "divine concursus argument" to be an argument for occasionalism.

46. See Pessin 2000, Garber 2001, Lee 2018, Schmaltz 2018, and Anfray 2019. As Garber notes (2001: 302), there is no reason to believe that Descartes saw occasionalist consequences for body–body relations as following from his doctrine of divine conservation as continual recreation, though Garber allows that there may be other considerations that rule out real causal efficacy in bodies.

47. *Theodicy*, §384, Leibniz 1960–61: VI.343.

48. See, for example, *De natura ipsa*, §15.

NOTES 307

49. For Aquinas, see *Summa theologia* I, Question 104, art. 1. For Suarez, see *Disputationes metaphysicae*, Disputation 21, section 1. Platt (2020: 252), too, notes that the argument is consistent with concurrentism.

50. This is Schmaltz's reading of Descartes (2008).

51. As Leibniz reads the Cartesians, they regard their occasionalism to follow directly from their account of divine conservation. "The Cartesians," he notes, "say, not wrongly [*non male*], that God creates all things continuously. For them, therefore, moving a body is nothing but reproducing it in successively different places" (Letter to De Volder, 1699, Leibniz 1960–61: II.193).

52. La Forge 1974: 242/La Forge 1997: 148.

53. La Forge 1974: 241/La Forge 1997: 147.

54. La Forge 1974: 242–3/La Forge 1997: 148–9.

55. Descartes to More, August 1649, AT V.403–5/CSMK 381–2; quoted at La Forge 1974: 243/La Forge 1997: 149.

56. *Principia philosophiae* II.43, where Descartes shows that "what it is that constitutes the power of any given body to act on, or resist the action of, another body . . . consists simply in the fact that everything tends, so far as it can, to persist in the same state" (AT VIII-A.66/CSM I.243).

57. On the complexities of force in Descartes, see Garber 1992: 280–99.

58. *Principia philosophiae* II.45, AT VIII-A.67/CSM I.244.

59. For other "deflationist" accounts of force in Descartes, see Garber 1992: 293–9, and Sophie Roux 2019.

60. *De la recherche de la vérité* VI.2.3, Malebranche 1972–84: II.309–11/Malebranche 1980: 446–50.

Chapter 9

1. Elisabeth to Descartes, 6 May 1643, AT III.661/S 62.

2. Descartes to Elisabeth, 21 May 1643, AT III.664–7/CSMK 217–9.

3. AT VII.341/CSM II.237.

4. AT IX-A.213/CSM II.275.

5. Of course, it is a completely different question as to whether Descartes, whether he realizes it or not, *does* have a heterogeneity problem, especially given his commitment to certain causal principles. There is long tradition of literature on this; for a helpful discussion, see Rozemond 1999.

6. *Metaphysica vera* I.8, Geulincx 1891–93: II.153/Geulincx 1999: 40.

7. *Corporis et animae in homine conjunctio*, IX.12, Clauberg 1968: I.215.

8. See *Meditationes* VI, AT VII.87–9/CSM II.60–61.

9. *Corporis et animae in homine conjunctio*, IX, XIV, and XVI, Clauberg 1968: I/215–6, 219–21.

10. *Corporis et animae in homine conjunctio*, XVI.10, Clauberg 1968: I.221.

308 NOTES

11. *Principia philosophiae/Principes de philosophie* IV.198, AT VIII-A.323/CSM I.285; the bracketed words are from the French translation.

12. AT VIII-B.358–9/CSM I.304.

13. See, for example, Thomas Aquinas, *Summa theologiae*, I, Question 13, Article 5.

14. La Forge 1974: 213/La Forge 1997: 124.

15. La Forge 1974: 216/La Forge 1997: 127.

16. La Forge 1974: 220/La Forge 1997: 130.

17. La Forge 1974: 244/La Forge 1997: 150.

18. La Forge 1974: 179/La Forge 1997: 95. In this passage La Forge is discussing the mind as the cause of ideas we have voluntarily, but it nonetheless indicates La Forge's view of the mind as a causally active substance.

19. La Forge 1974: 176/La Forge 1997: 92.

20. La Forge 1974: 245/La Forge 1997: 150.

21. La Forge 1974: 176/La Forge 1997: 93.

22. La Forge 1974: 177/La Forge 1997: 93.

23. On exemplary causation, see Platt 2020: 229–33.

24. Arnauld 1775: XLI.133. Arnauld seems later to have changed his mind and opted for an occasionalist account of the generation of ideas; see Nadler 1995.

25. AT XI.143, 176/G 119, 149.

26. I argue that for Descartes occasional causation is not a species of efficient causation in Nadler 1994; Schmaltz (2008: 157–62) argues that it is a species of efficient causation. See also Platt, though he does admit that it is ambiguous (2020: 230).

27. The fact that the laborers might still do the work without the promise of payment makes it problematic to see this particular factor, in abstraction from other relevant conditions, as a matter of true *sine qua non* conditionality. Perhaps we should think of a *sine qua non* condition in this context as increasing to a very high degree the probability of the outcome; likewise, in the body>mind case, God, absolutely speaking, could cause the sensory ideas in the absence of the bodily motions but, through his ordination of the laws of nature, is not at all likely to do so.

28. La Forge 1974: 93/La Forge 1997: 23.

29. La Forge 1974:145, 152, 244.

30. La Forge 1974: 163/La Forge 1997: 81.

31. La Forge 1974: 223/La Forge 1997: 132.

32. La Forge 1974: 227/La Forge 1997: 136. At this point, in Chapter 15 of the *Traité*, La Forge has not yet fully determined whether the will is, in fact, the efficient cause of motions in the body, but he is here at least entertaining it in the sense that he finds nothing that rules it out.

33. La Forge 1974: 213/La Forge 1997: 124. Most scholars are in agreement that La Forge grants to the human soul a truly efficacious power to move the body. Thus, Specht (1966: 140–41) says that "La Forge has not reached occasionalism in the full sense. The mind not only can move the body, but also it can think, and La Forge does not extend his causal critique to this. Divine intervention arrives only in the movements of the extended substance." See also Bardout 2002b, Platt 2020 (consistent with his concurrentist reading), Sangiacomo 2014b, Schmaltz 2017 (198), and Favaretti

NOTES 309

Camposampiero 2018. Bouillier claims that "the first of the Cartesians to remove from the human soul the power to direct motion, like the power to produce it, was not Delaforge but Géraud de Cordemoy" (Bouillier 1868: I.513–4). For a contrary view, see Sandrine Roux 2018 and, if I read her correctly, Antoine-Mahut 2021; as will become clear, I am in agreement with Roux and Antoine-Mahut.

34. La Forge 1974: 236/La Forge 1997: 143. The poet in question is Lucretius, *De rerum natura* I.304.

35. *Traité de l'homme*, AT XI.131–2/G 107.

36. To Elisabeth, 21 May 1643, AT III.665, 667/CSMK 218–9.

37. For Arnauld, 29 July 1648, AT V.222/CSMK 358.

38. To More, August 1649, AT V.403–4/CSMK 381.

39. To Elisabeth, 21 May 1643, AT III.667–8/CSMK 219; Appendix to Fifth Replies, AT VII.213/CSM II.275–6. See also Sixth Replies, AT VII.441–2/CSM II.297–8. For a discussion of this topic in Descartes and Malebranche, see Kolesnik-Antoine 2009.

40. Leibniz claims (incorrectly) that Descartes knew this all along, and thus adopted the "change of direction" account; see *Theodicy*, §§60–61. Garber (1983) has argued that the conservation of motion principle is intended to apply only to inanimate bodies, not the human body.

41. *Le Discernement du corps et de l'âme*, Cordemoy 1968: 140–41/Cordemoy 2015: 98.

42. La Forge 1974: 245–6/La Forge 1997: 151.

43. This and subsequent quotes from Clerselier's letter are from Descartes 1667: 640–43/ Clerselier 2021: 521–5.

44. Is this Clerselier's own view, or just a position that he, and others (like Leibniz), attribute to Descartes? Siegrid Agostini rightly cautions us to bear in mind the context of this discussion between Clerselier and La Forge (Agostini 2009: II.3.c)

45. La Forge 1974: 122/La Forge 1997: 47.

46. La Forge 1974: 246/La Forge 1997: 151.

47. Sandrine Roux (2018) provides an illuminating and relevant analysis of the *défaut de connaissance* principle in La Forge and others within the framework of contemporary theory of action by Arthur Danto and others. She refers in particular to the distinction between "basic actions"—those which are accomplished directly, simply by willing them, without having to will some other action as a means—and "non-basic actions," which require one also to will some other action as a means to effecting the desired action-outcome.

48. La Forge 1974: 240/La Forge 1997: 147.

49. Platt (2020), for example, reads it this way.

50. Sangiacomo (2014b) has argued against seeing the divine conservation argument as undermining the efficacy of the mind to move the body. He sees the "no transfer of modes" argument as the primary case against bodies moving each other, with the divine conservation principle functioning only as a supplement to show that, since bodies cannot move other bodies, God must be moving them. But since the mind moving the body would not require any transfer of motion (because minds do not have motion), this line of argument does not apply.

51. La Forge 1974: 242/La Forge 1997: 148. The italicized emphases are mine.

310 NOTES

52. La Forge 1974: 236/La Forge 1997: 143.
53. Sandrine Roux (2022) provides a different reading of the claim that "God does not do everything," whereby the mind makes a genuine causal contribution as a true efficient cause of its own volitions to occasion God to move the body. My own reading, however, is that God does not do everything because the *sine qua non* conditions—whether minds or bodies—are still relevant to the causal explanation. Notice that in the passage La Forge is referring to the counterfactual contribution of both minds *and* bodies, not just minds.
54. La Forge 1974: 245/La Forge 1997: 150.
55. *Le Discernement du corps et de l'âme*, Cordemoy 1968: 151/Cordemoy 2015: 107; 1968: 142/2015: 99.
56. Descartes to More, August 1649, AT V.403–5/CSMK 381–2; quoted at La Forge 1974: 243/La Forge 1997: 149.
57. La Forge 1974: 325/La Forge 1997: 214.
58. I am thus now in agreement with Sandrine Roux (2022) on the limited extent of La Forge's occasionalism, contrary to my earlier interpretation of La Forge on the power of the will to move the body (Nadler 1993b).

Chapter 10

1. To Elisabeth, 6 October 1645, AT IV.315/CSMK 272.
2. AT VIII-A.20/CSM I.206. This, at least, is his position in the *Principia philosophiae*. In his correspondence with Elisabeth, he seems more optimistic about reconciling human freedom with divine providence, when he says that "the independence that we experience and feel within ourselves, and which is sufficient to render our actions praiseworthy or blameable, is not incompatible with a dependence of another nature, according to which all things are subject to God" (3 November 1645, AT IV.333/CSMK 277).
3. *Metaphysica vera*, I.V, IX, Geulincx 1891–93: II.150, 154.
4. Cordemoy 1968: 253–4.
5. *Traitez de métaphysique*, Cordemoy 1968: 285–6/Cordemoy 2015: 152–3.
6. See *De la recherche de la vérité* I.1.ii, Malebranche 1972–84: I.46/Malebranche 1980: 4; IV.1; Malebranche 1972–84: II.12–3/Malebranche 1980: 267.
7. *De la recherche de la vérité* I.1.ii, Malebranche 1972–84: I.48/Malebranche 1980: 5 (paragraph added to third edition). See also *Traité de la nature et de la grace*, III.1. The complexities and problems of Malebranche's account of the will and its freedom are well discussed in the literature; see, for example, Robinet 1965: 367–474, and Dreyfus 1958.
8. Cordemoy never really addresses the issue.
9. *De la recherche de la vérité*, Éclaircissement I, Malebranche 1972–84: III.21/Malebranche 1980: 549.
10. See, for example, Chappell 1994: 184.

NOTES 311

11. The discussion of voluntary ideas or thoughts in the *Traité de l'esprit de l'homme* from which these passages are taken is in Chapter 10, La Forge 1974: 176–82/La Forge 1997: 92–6.

12. La Forge 1974: 148/La Forge 1997: 69.

13. La Forge actually makes this analogy; see La Forge 1974: 178–9/La Forge 1997: 94.

14. La Forge 1974: 182/La Forge 1997: 97.

15. De Villemandy 1686: 21. I am indebted to Sandrine Roux for bringing De Villemandy's treatise to my attention.

16. *Meditationes* IV, AT VII.57/CSM II.40.

17. La Forge 1974: 186/La Forge 1997: 100–101.

18. Some important recent contributions include Alanen 2002, Naaman-Zauderer 2010, Lennon 2013 and 2015, and Ragland 2016.

19. *Meditationes* IV, AT VII.57/CSM II.40.

20. *Meditationes* IV, AT VII.57–8/CSM II.40.

21. Descartes's account of materially false ideas is introduced in the Third Meditation.

22. *Meditationes* IV, AT VII.58–9/CSM II.41.

23. La Forge 1974: 182–3/La Forge 1997: 97–8.

24. I am indebted here to Lennon's discussion (2015: 70).

25. The most careful account of this letter is in Lennon 2013, who questions the piece's status as a letter (rather than a memorandum for future reference) and the traditional identification of the intended recipient as Mesland (by AT, for example).

26. Starting, for example, with Gilson 1913 and Alquié 1950. A more sophisticated and "moderate" kind of libertarianism is defended by Ragland 2016, although it is not clear to me that what Ragland is attributing to Descartes is not some version of compatibilism. Lennon (2013 and 2015)—correctly, in my view—argues against any kind of libertarian reading of Descartes.

27. To Mesland, 2 May 1644, AT IV.115–6/CSMK 233–4. Mesland's own view would be consistent with the Jesuit position.

28. To Mesland, 9 February 1645, AT IV.173/CSMK 245, italicized emphasis added.

29. It does seem strange, however, that if the highest grade of freedom consists in being determined by reasons to assent to a clear and distinct idea, then we can demonstrate our freedom by resisting that determination and suspending judgment (even if that suspension of judgment is determined by reasons).

30. Lennon (2013 and 2015), I believe, gets all this right.

31. Another possible reading of what is "morally" vs. "absolutely" possible here is that the former refers to the (im)possibility of withholding assent in the presence of the clear and distinct idea, and that latter refers to the two-way power that the faculty of the will has and maintains by its nature, independent of any present circumstances that may be determining it one way or the other.

32. La Forge 1974: 184–8/La Forge 1997: 99–102.

33. La Forge 1974: 146/La Forge 1997: 68.

34. La Forge 1974: 188/La Forge 1997: 102.

35. La Forge 1974: 191/La Forge 1997: 105.

36. Here La Forge seems to be following the more optimistic letter to Elisabeth (3 November 1645)—in which Descartes insists on the compatibility between the

312 NOTES

independence of the will that we experience within ourselves and "a dependence of another nature" upon God—rather than the appeal to faith of the *Principia*.

37. La Forge 1974: 192–3/La Forge 1997: 106–7.

38. I suspect that any attempt to account for God's foreknowledge of my willing when God is the cause of that willing would generate an infinite regress.

39. La Forge 1974: 71/La Forge 1997: 3.

40. La Forge 1974: 199/La Forge 1997: 113.

41. Nadler 1998.

42. Pessin (2000: 424) constructs this argument well on Malebranche's behalf: "Since God sustains not only larger bodies but also their constituent bodies, whose motion is responsible for the larger bodies' features, God's act of sustaining *all* bodies is effectively identical to His causing *all* bodily features."

43. Malebranche 1972–84: XI.160/Malebranche 1993: 147, italicized emphasis added.

44. Loeb (1981: 207) makes the same case for Malebranche. "Parity [with the case of the motion of body] suggests that at a particular time a created spirit either has no volition or some volition, and if some volition then it must have a determinate content or object, and hence that God cannot will that a created spirit exist at a particular time without willing that it has a specified determinate content or object. So God should be the sole cause of the volitions of minds as much as of the velocities of bodies."

45. See Schmaltz 2017: 195–6. Pessin (2000) and Platt (2020: 238–52) also take issue with my earlier reading and keep the divine conservation argument from undermining the soul's activity.

Conclusion

1. His skull, along with perhaps other parts, was apparently left behind in Sweden. On this, see Shorto 2009.

2. Baillet 1691: II.439.

3. Baillet 1691: II.439–41; McLaughlin 1979: 565–6.

4. Prost 1907a: 105.

5. Clair 1976 and La Forge 1974: 17–68.

6. Baillet 1691: II.399.

7. According to Antoine-Mahut (2021: 175), La Forge's importance in this regard is the way in which he reveals how "le cartésianisme se spécifie comme une psychologie empiriste."

8. *Principia philosophiae*, I.32.

9. La Forge 1974: 322–3/La Forge 1999: 212.

10. La Forge 1974: 186/La Forge 1997: 100–101; La Forge 1974: 78/La Forge 1997: 7; all italicized emphases are added.

11. La Forge 1974: 106/La Forge 1997: 34.

12. Sandrine Roux 2018: 121. Clarke (1989: 106), too, refers to La Forge's "reinterpretation" of Descartes.

13. Cook (2016) argues that even if bodies cannot cause an increase or decrease in motion, occasionalism does not follow; their properties as extended substances may still causally determine the properties of other bodies, including the direction of motion.

14. Thus I cannot agree with Clair's comment that "les Remarques de Louis De La Forge sur le Traité de l'homme de Descartes ont passé assez imperçues" (1974: 65).

15. *Journal des sçavans*, 3 May 1666, 214–6, accessible online at: https://gallica.bnf.fr/ark:/12148/bpt6k581215/f218.item

16. Quoted in Clair 1976: 65–6; see also McLaughlin 1979: 115–6.

17. Henkel 2022: 44n80.

18. André 1886: 12.

19. Gousset 1716: 44.

20. Malebranche 1972–1984: XX.237, #139.

21. *Entretiens sur la métaphysique et sur la religion*, VII.10–11, Malebranche 1972–1984: 160–3/Malebranche 1997: 115–7.

22. *De ipsa natura*, §10, Leibniz 1960–61: IV.509.

23. Robinet 1955: 360.

24. Henkel 2022: 125.

25. Desgabets 1983–85: 152.

26. Desgabets 1983–85: 156. My thanks to Tad Schmaltz for directing me toward this essay by Desgabets.

Bibliography

I. Works of La Forge

La Forge, Louis de. 1664. "Remarques." In *L'Homme de René Descartes et Un traitté de la formation du foetus du mesme autheur, avec les Remarques de Louys de la Forge*. Paris: Charles Angot.

La Forge, Louis de. 1666. *Traitté de l'esprit de l'homme, de ses facultez et fonctions, et de son union avec le corps*. Paris: Michel Bobin and Nicolas Le Gras.

La Forge, Louis de. 1974. *Oeuvres philosophiques*. Edited by Pierre Clair. Paris: Presses Universitaires de France.

La Forge, Louis de. 1997. *Treatise on the Human Mind*. Translated by Desmond Clarke. The Hague: Martinus Nijhoff.

La Forge, Louis de. 1999. *L'Homme de René Descartes et Un traité de la formation du foetus du mesme autheur, avec les remarques de Louys de la Forge*. Paris: Fayard.

II. Other Historical Sources

André, Yves. 1886. *La Vie du R. P. Malebranche, prêtre de l'Oratoire*. Paris: Poussielgue.

Arnauld, Antoine. 1775. *Oeuvres de Messire Antoine Arnauld*. 43 vols. Brussels: Sigismond d'Arnay.

Babin, François. 1679. *Journal ou relation fidele de tout ce qui s'est passé dans l'université d'Angers au sujet de la philosophie de Descartes en l'execution des ordres du Roy pendant les années 1675, 1676, 1677, et 1678*. Angers: n.p.

Baillet, Adrien. 1691. *La Vie de Monsieur Descartes*. 2 vols. Paris: Daniel Horthemels.

Bartholin, Thomas. 1651. *Anatomia reformata*. Leiden: Fransciscus Hackius.

Bayle, Pierre. 1737. *Oeuvres diverses de Monsieur Pierre Bayle*. 3 vols. The Hague: Compagnie des Libraires.

Buffet, Marguerite. 1668. *Nouvelles observations sur la langue française . . . avec les Éloges des illustres savantes tant anciennes que modernes*. Paris: J. Cusson.

Burgersdijk, Franco. 1634. *Institutionum logicorum libri duo*. Leiden: Abraham Comenius.

Burmann, Pieter. 1724. *Sylloges epistolarum a viris illustribus scriptarum, tomus V*. Leiden: Samuel Luchtmans.

Clauberg, Johannes. 1675. *Physica, quibus rerum corporearum vis & natura, mentis ad corpus relatae proprietates, denique corporis ac mentis arcta & admirabilis in homine conjunctio explicantur*. Amsterdam: Daniel Elzevir.

Clauberg, Johannes. 1968. *Opera omnia philosophica*. 2 vols. Hildesheim: Olms. (Reprint of the 1691 edition published in Amsterdam by Blaeu.)

Clerselier, Claude. 2021. *Les Lettres de Monsieur Claude Clerselier, 1644–1681*. Edited by Siegrid Agostini. Turnhout, Belgium: Brepols.

Collegium Conimbricense. 1602. *In octo libros physicorum Aristotelis*. Coimbra.

316 BIBLIOGRAPHY

Cordemoy, Géraud de. 1666. *Le Discernement du corps et de l'âme en six discours pour servir à l'éclaircissement de la physique*. Paris: Florentin Lambert.

Cordemoy, Gérauld de. 1968. *Oeuvres philosophiques*. Edited by Pierre Clair and François Girbal. Paris: Presses Universitaires de France.

Cordemoy, Géraud de. 2015. *Six Discourses on the Distinction between the Body and the Soul*. Translated by Steven Nadler. Oxford: Oxford University Press.

Descartes, René. 1659. *Lettres de Mr. Descartes: Tome II*. Edited by Claude Clerselier. Paris: Charles Angot.

Descartes, René. 1662. *Renatus Des Cartes De homine figuris et latinatate donatus a Florentio Schuyl*. Translated by Florent Schuyl. Leiden: Franciscus Moyardus.

Descartes, René. 1664. *L'Homme de René Descartes et Un traitté de la formation du foetus du mesme autheur, avec les Remarques de Louys de la Forge*. Edited by Claude Clerselier. Paris: Charles Angot.

Descartes, René. 1667. *Lettres de Mr. Descartes: Tome III*. Edited by Claude Clerselier. Paris: Charles Angot.

Descartes, René. 1964–76. *Oeuvres de Descartes*. 12 vols. Edited by Charles Adam and Paul Tannery. Paris: J. Vrin/CNRS. (Abbreviated in the notes as 'AT').

Descartes, René. 1984. *The Philosophical Writings of Descartes*, vols. 1 and 2. Edited and translated by John Cottingham, Robert Stoothoff, and Dugald Murdoch. Cambridge: Cambridge University Press. (Abbreviated in the notes as 'CSM.')

Descartes, René. 1991. *The Philosophical Writings of Descartes*, vol. 3: *The Correspondence*. Edited and translated by John Cottingham, Robert Stoothoff, Dugald Murdoch, and Anthony Kenny. Cambridge: Cambridge University Press. (Abbreviated in the notes as 'CSMK.')

Descartes, René. 1998. *The World and Other Writings*. Translated by Stephen Gaukroger Cambridge: Cambridge University Press. (Abbreviated in the notes as 'G.')

Descartes, René. 2018. *L'Homme*. Edited by Delphine Antoine-Mahut. Paris: Flammarion.

Descartes, René, and Elisabeth of Bohemia. 2007. *The Correspondence between Princess Elisabeth of Bohemia and René Descartes*. Edited and translated by Lisa Shapiro. Chicago: University of Chicago Press. (Abbreviated in the notes as 'S')

Desgabets, Robert. 1671. *Considerations sur l'état présent de la controverse touchant le Très Saint-Sacrament de l'autel*. Holland: À la Sphere.

Desgabets, Robert. 1983–85. *Oeuvres philosophiques inédites*. 7 vols. Edited by J. Beaude and Geneviève Rodis-Lewis. Paris: Du Puis.

De Villemandy, Pierre. 1686. *Traité de l'efficace des causes secondes, contre quelques philosophes modernes*. Leiden: Claude Jordan.

Fontenelle, Bernard le Bovier de. 1825. *Oeuvres de Fontenelle*. 7 vols. Paris: Salmon Libraire.

Geulincx, Arnold. 1891–93. *A. Geulincx Antverpiensis Opera philosophica*. 3 vols. Edited by J. P. N. Land. The Hague: Martinus Nijhoff.

Geulincx, Arnold. 2006. *Ethics*. With notes by Samuel Beckett. Edited by Han van Ruler and Anthony Uhlmann. Translated by Martin Wilson. Leiden and Boston: Brill.

Geulincx, Arnold. 1999. *Metaphysics*. Translated by Martin Wilson. Wisbech, Cambridgeshire: Christofell Press.

Gousset, Jacques. 1716. *Causarum primae et secundum realis operatio rationibus confirmatur et ab objectionibus defenditur*. Leuwarden: François Halma.

Heereboord, Adriaan. 1665. *Meletemata philosophica*. Amsterdam: Johannes Ravenstein.

BIBLIOGRAPHY 317

Huet, Pierre-Daniel. 1693. *Nouveau memoires pour servir à l'histoire du cartésianisme*. Utrecht: Guillaume van de Water.

Huet, Pierre-Daniel. 1810. *Memoirs of the Life of Peter Daniel Huet, Bishop of Avranches*. 2 vols. Edited by John Aikin. London: Longman.

Huet, Pierre-Daniel. 2003. *Against Cartesian Philosophy*. Translated by Thomas M. Lennon. Amherst, NY: Humanity Books.

Huygens, Christiaan. 1889. *Oeuvres complètes*, vol. 2: *Correspondence 1657–1659*. Edited by D. Bierens de Haan. The Hague: Martinus Nijhoff.

Le Gallois, Pierre. 1672. *Conversations de l'Académie de Monsieur l'Abbé Bourdelot*. Paris: Thomas Moette.

Leibniz, Gottfried Wilhelm. 1960–61. *Die philosophischen Schriften*. 6 vols. Edited by C. I. Gerhardt. Hildesheim: Georg Olms Verlag.

Madeira Arrais, Duarte. 1650. *Novae philosophiae et medicinae de qualitatibus occultis, pars prima*. Lisbon: Emmanuelis Gomez de Carvalho.

Malebranche, Nicolas. 1972–84. *Oeuvres complètes*. 20 vols. Edited by André Robinet Paris: J. Vrin.

Malebranche, Nicolas. 1980. *The Search after Truth*. Translated by Thomas M. Lennon and Paul J. Olscamp. Columbus: Ohio State University Press.

Malebranche, Nicolas. 1993. *Treatise on Ethics*. Translated by Craig Walton. Dordrecht: Kluwer.

Malebranche, Nicolas. 1997. *Dialogues on Metaphysics and on Religion*. Translated by David Scott. Edited by Nicholas Jolley. Cambridge: Cambridge University Press.

Régis, Pierre Sylvain. 1690. *Système de philosophie, contenant la logique, la metaphysique, la physique et la morale*. 3 vols. Paris: Thierry.

Rohault, Jacques. 1671. *Traité de physique*. Paris: Charles Savreux.

Rohault, Jacques. 1690. *Oeuvres posthumes de M. Rohault*. 2 vols. The Hague: Henry van Bulderen.

Spinoza, Benedictus. 1925. *Spinoza Opera*. 4 vols. Edited by Carl Gebhardt. Heidelberg: Carl Winters Verlag.

Steno, Nicolaus. 1669. *Discours de Monsieur Stenon sur L'Anatomie du cerveau*. Paris: Robert de Ninville.

Steno, Nicolaus. 2009. *Discours sur l'anatomie du cerveau*. Edited by Raphaële Andrault. Paris: Classiques Garnier.

III. STUDIES

Ablondi, Fred. 2005. *Gerauld de Cordemoy. Atomist, Occasionalist, Cartesian*. Milwaukee, WI: Marquette University Press.

Adam, Antoine. 1997. *Histoire de la littérature française du XVIIe siècle*. 2 vols. Paris: A. Michel.

Agostini, Siegrid. 2009. *Claude Clerselier: Editore e traduttore di René Descartes*. PhD Thesis, Università del Salento.

Alanen, Lilli. 2002. "Descartes on the Will and the Power to Do Otherwise." In *Emotions and Choice, from Boethius to Descartes*, 279–98. Edited by Henrik Lagerlund and Mikko Yrjonsuri. Dordrecht: Kluwer.

Alquié, Ferdinand. 1950. *La Découverte métaphysique de l'homme chez Descartes* Paris: Presses Universitaires de France.

318 BIBLIOGRAPHY

Andrault, Raphaële. 2009. "Introduction." In Niels Stensen/Nicolas Sténon, *Discours sur l'anatomie du cerveau*, 7–72. Edited by Raphaële Andrault. Paris: Classiques Garnier.

Andrault, Raphaële. 2016. "Anatomy, Mechanism and Anthropology: Nicolas Steno's Reading of *L'Homme*." In *Descartes' Treatise on Man and Its Reception*, 175–92. Edited by Delphine Antoine-Mahut and Stephen Gaukroger. Cham, Switzerland: Springer.

Anfray, Jean-Pascal. 2019. "Continuous Creation, Occasionalism, and Persistence: Leibniz on Bayle." In *Physics and Metaphysics in Descartes and in His Reception*, 213–42. Edited by Delphine Antoine-Mahut and Sophie Roux. London: Routledge.

Antoine-Mahut, Delphine. 2016. "The Story of *L'Homme*." In *Descartes' Treatise on Man and Its Reception*, 1–29. Edited by Delphine Antoine-Mahut and Stephen Gaukroger. Cham, Switzerland: Springer.

Antoine-Mahut, Delphine. 2017. "Reintroducing Descartes in the History of Materialism: The Effects of the Descartes/Hobbes Debate on the First Reception of Cartesianism." In *Descartes and Cartesianism: Essays in Honour of Desmond Clarke*, 125–48. Edited by Stephen Gaukroger and Catherine Wilson. Oxford: Oxford University Press.

Antoine-Mahut, Delphine. 2018. "Présentation." In Descartes 2018: 9–64.

Antoine-Mahut, Delphine. 2021. *L'Autorité d'un canon philosophique: Le Cas de Descartes*. Paris: J. Vrin.

Antoine-Mahut, Delphine, and Stephen Gaukroger (eds.). 2016. *Descartes' Treatise on Man and Its Reception*. Cham, Switzerland: Springer.

Armogathe, Jean-Robert. 1977. *Theologia Cartesiana: L'Explication physique de l'Eucharistie chez Descartes et Dom Desgabets*. The Hague: Martinus Nijhoff.

Armogathe, Jean-Robert, and Vincent Carraud. 2003. "The First Condemnation of Descartes's *Oeuvres*: Some Unpublished Documents from the Vatican Archives." *Oxford Studies in Early Modern Philosophy* 1: 67–110.

Ariew, Roger. 2007. "Descartes and Pascal." *Perspectives on Science* 15: 397–409.

Baigrie, Brian. 1996. "Descartes's Scientific Illustrations and 'la grande mécanique de la nature.'" In *Picturing Knowledge: Historical and Philosophical Problems Concerning the Use of Art in Science*, 86–134. Edited by Brian Baigrie. Toronto: University of Toronto Press.

Balz, Albert G. A. 1951. *Cartesian Studies*. New York: Columbia University Press.

Bardout, Jean-Christophe. 2002a. "Clauberg." *In A Companion to Early Modern Philosophy*, 129–39. Edited by Steven Nadler. Boston: Blackwell.

Bardout, Jean-Christophe. 2002b. "Occasionalism: La Forge, Cordemoy, Geulincx." In *A Companion to Early Modern Philosophy*, 140–51. Edited by Steven Nadler. Boston: Blackwell.

Battail, Jean-François. 1973. *L'Avocat philosophe Géraud de Cordemoy*. The Hague: Martinus Nijhoff.

Beyssade, Jean-Marie. 1979. *La Philosophie première de Descartes*. Paris: Flammarion.

Bitbol-Hespériès, Annie. 1990. *Le Principe de vie chez Descartes*. Paris: J. Vrin.

Bitbol-Hespériès, Annie. 1996. "Introduction." In René Descartes, *Le Monde, L'Homme*, iii–liii. Edited by Annie Bitbol-Hespériès and Jean-Pierre Verdet. Paris: Editions du Seuil.

Bitbol-Hespériès, Annie. 2016. "The Primacy of *L'Homme*." In *Descartes' Treatise on Man and Its Reception*, 33–47. Edited by Delphine Antoine-Mahut and Stephen Gaukroger. Cham, Switzerland: Springer.

BIBLIOGRAPHY 319

Black, Andrew. 1997. "Malebranche's Theodicy." *Journal of the History of Philosophy* 35: 27–44.

Bos, Erik-Jan. 2017. "Descartes and Regius on the Pineal Gland and Animal Spirits, and a Letter of Regius on the True Seat of the Soul." In *Descartes and Cartesianism: Essays in Honour of Desmond Clarke*, 95–111. Edited by Stephen Gaukroger and Catherine Wilson. Oxford: Oxford University Press.

Bos, Erik-Jan, Theo Verbeek, and Jeroen van de Ven. 2003. "Introduction." In *The Correspondence of René Descartes, 1643*, ix–xl. Utrecht: Zeno Institute.

Bouillier, Francisque. 1868. *Histoire de la philosophie cartésienne*. 2 vols. Paris: Delagrave.

Broughton, Janet. 1986. "Adequate Causes and Natural Change in Descartes' Philosophy." In *Human Nature and Natural Knowledge*, 107–27. Edited by Alan Donagan, Anthony Perovich Jr., and Michael V. Wedin. Dordrecht: Reidel.

Brown, Harcourt. 1934. *Scientific Organizations in Seventeenth-Century France*. Baltimore: Williams and Wilkins.

Carraud, Vincent. 2002. *Causa sive ratio: La raison de la cause, de Suarez à Leibniz*. Paris: Presses Universitaires de France.

Carriero, John. 2009. *Between Two Worlds: A Reading of Descartes's Meditations*. Princeton: Princeton University Press.

Chalmers, David. 1995. "Facing Up to the Problem of Consciousness." *Journal of Consciousness Studies* 2: 200–219.

Chappell, Vere. 1994. "Descartes' Compatibilism." In *Reason, Will and Sensation: Studies in Descartes' Metaphysics*, 177–90. Edited by John Cottingham. Oxford: Clarendon Press.

Chassagne, Albert. 1938. *Louis de La Forge, médecin et philosophe angevin*. Angers: A. Siraudeau.

Clair, Pierre. 1974. "Biographie." In La Forge 1974: 17–68.

Clair, Pierre. 1976. "Louis de la Forge et les origines de l'occasionalisme." *Recherches sur le XVIIième siècle* 1: 63–72.

Clair, Pierre. 1978. *Jacques Rohault (1618–1672): Bio-bibliographie avec l'édition critique des Entretiens sur la philosophie*. Paris: Editions du Centre Nationale de la Recherche Scientifique.

Clair, Pierre. 1990. "De Gueudreville, interlocuteur de Rohault." *Recherches sur le XVIIième siècle* 4: 47–52.

Clarke, Desmond. 1989. *Occult Powers and Hypotheses: Cartesian Natural Philosophy under Louis XIV*. Oxford: Clarendon Press.

Clarke, Desmond. 2000. "Causal Powers and Occasionalism from Descartes to Malebranche." In *Descartes's Natural Philosophy*, 131–48. Edited by Stephen Gaukroger, John Schuster, and John Sutton. London and New York: Routledge.

Clarke, Desmond. 2003. *Descartes's Theory of Mind*. Oxford: Oxford University Press.

Clarke, Desmond. 2014. "Louis de La Forge." In *The Stanford Encyclopedia of Philosophy* (Spring 2014 Edition). Edited by Edward N. Zalta. URL = <http://plato.stanford.edu/archives/spr2014/entries/la-forge/>.

Clarke, Desmond. 2016. *French Philosophy, 1572–1675*. Oxford: Oxford University Press.

Collacciani, Domenico. 2016. "The Reception of *L'Homme* among the Leuven Physicians: The Condemnation of 1662 and the Origins of Occasionalism." In *Descartes' Treatise on Man and Its Reception*, 103–26. Edited by Delphine Antoine-Mahut and Stephen Gaukroger. Cham, Switzerland: Springer.

Cook, Monte. 2016. "Cartesianism and Body-Body Occasionalism." *Studia de philosophia moderna* 2: 31–45.

320 BIBLIOGRAPHY

Cottingham, John. 1985. "Cartesian Trialism." *Mind* 94: 218–30.

Cousin, Victor. 1841. "De la persécution du cartésianisme en France," *Fragments philosophiques*. In *Oeuvres de Victor Cousin*, 3 vols., 2:181–91. Brussels: Société Belge de Librairie.

De Lattre, Alain. 1967. *L'Occasionalisme d'Arnold Geulincx*. Paris: Editions de Minuit.

Della Rocca, Michael. 1999. "'If a Body Meet a Body': Descartes on Body–Body Causation." In *New Essays on the Rationalists*, 48–81. Edited by Rocco J. Gennaro and Charles Huenemann. New York and Oxford: Oxford University Press.

De Vleeschauwer, H. J. 1978. "Les Sources de la pensée d'Arnold Geulincx (1624–1669)." *Kant Studien* 69: 378–402.

Dilucia, Niall. 2022. "Robert Desgabets' Eucharistic Thought and the Theological Revision of Cartesianism." *Intellectual History Review* 32: 669–90.

Dreyfus, Ginette. 1958. *La Volonté selon Malebranche*. Paris: J. Vrin.

Drieux, Philippe. 2016. "Machine and Communication of Corporeal Dispositions in Descartes and La Forge: The Mysterious 'Article 83' of *L'Homme* and La Forge's Comments." In *Descartes' Treatise on Man and Its Reception*, 127–38. Edited by Delphine Antoine-Mahut and Stephen Gaukroger. Cham, Switzerland: Springer.

Drieux, Philippe. 2019. "Louis de La Forge on Mind, Causality and Union." In *The Oxford Handbook of Descartes and Cartesianism*, 319–31. Edited by Steven Nadler, Tad Schmaltz, and Delphine Antoine-Mahut. Oxford: Oxford University Press.

Easton, Patricia. 2005. "Desgabets's Indefectibility Thesis: A Step Too Far?" In *Receptions of Descartes: Cartesianism and Anti-Cartesianism in Early Modern Europe*, 27–41. Edited by Tad Schmaltz. London and New York: Routledge.

Fakhry, Majid. 1958. *Islamic Occasionalism and Its Critique by Averroës and Aquinas*. London: Allen & Unwin.

Farrell, Alan P. 1970. *The Jesuit Ratio Studiorum of 1599*. Washington, DC: Conference of Major Superiors of Jesuits.

Favaretti Camposampiero, Matteo. 2018. "The Direction of Motion: Occasionalism and Causal Closure from Descartes to Leibniz." In *Occasionalism: From Metaphysics to Science*, 195–219. Edited by Matteo Favaretti Camposampiero, Mariangela Priarolo, and Emanuela Scribano. Turnhout, Belgium: Brepols.

Faye, Emmanuel (ed.). 2000. *Cartésiens et augustiniens au XVIIe siècle*. Corpus: Revue de philosophie 37.

Freddoso, Alfred. 1991. "God's General Concurrence with Secondary Causes: Why Conservation Is Not Enough." *Philosophical Perspectives* 5: 553–85.

Freddoso, Alfred. 2002. "Introduction." In Francisco Suarez, S.J., *On Creation, Conservation and Concurrence: Metaphysical Disputations 20–22*, xi–cxxiii. Translated by A. J. Freddoso. South Bend, IN: St. Augustine's Press.

Gabbey, Alan. 1971. "Force and Inertia in Seventeenth-Century Dynamics." *Studies in the History and Philosophy of Science* 2: 1–67.

Garber, Daniel. 1983. "Mind, Body and the Laws of Nature in Descartes and Leibniz." *Midwest Studies in Philosophy* 8: 105–33.

Garber, Daniel. 1992. *Descartes' Metaphysical Physics*. Chicago: University of Chicago Press.

Garber, Daniel. 1993. "Descartes and Occasionalism." In *Causation in Early Modern Philosophy: Cartesianism, Occasionalism, and Preestablished Harmony*, 9–26. Edited by Steven Nadler. University Park: Pennsylvania State University Press.

Garber, Daniel. 2000. "The Clauberg Connection: Descartes, Spinoza, and the 'Elegant Analogy.'" In *Descartes: Reception and Disenchantment*, 13–23. Edited by Yaron Senderowicz and Yves Wahl. Tel Aviv: University Publishing Projects.

BIBLIOGRAPHY 321

Garber, Daniel. 2001. "How God Causes Motion: Descartes, Divine Sustenance, and Occasionalism." In Daniel Garber, *Descartes Embodied: Reading Cartesian Philosophy through Cartesian Science*, 189–202. Cambridge: Cambridge University Press.

Garber, Daniel. 2002. "Defending Aristotle/Defending Society in Early 17th-Century Paris." In *Wissensideale und Wissenskulturen in der freuhen Neuzeit/Ideas and Cultures of Knowledge in Early Modern Europe*, 135–60. Edited by Wolfgang Detel and Claus Zittel. Berlin: Akademie Verlag.

Gilson, Etienne. 1913. *La Liberté chez Descartes et la théologie*. Paris: Alcan.

Gilson, Etienne. 1976. *René Descartes: Discours de la méthode, texte et commentaire*, 5th edition. Paris: J. Vrin.

Glauser, R. 2011. "Conscience et connaissance de la pensée chez Descartes." In *Descartes et ses critiques*, 13–32. Edited by Sébastien Charles and Syliane Malinowski-Charles. Laval, Quebec: Presses de l'Université de Laval.

Gootjes, Albert. 2013. "'A Smattering of the New Philosophy': Étienne Gaussen (ca. 1638–1675) and the Cartesian Question at Saumur." In *Church and School in Early Modern Protestantism*, 583–96. Edited by Jordan J. Ballor, David S. Sytsma, and Jason Zuidema. Leiden and Boston: Brill.

Gouhier, Henri. 1926. *La Vocation de Malebranche*. Paris: J. Vrin.

Gouhier, Henri. 1948. *La Philosophie de Malebranche et son expérience religieuse*. Paris: J. Vrin.

Gouhier, Henri. 1978a. *Cartésianisme et augustinisme au XVIIe siècle*. Paris: J. Vrin.

Gouhier, Henri. 1978b. *La Pensée métaphysique de Descartes*. 4th ed. Paris: J. Vrin.

Grigoropolou, Vasiliki. 2018. "Steno's Critique of Descartes and Louis de La Forge's Response." In *Steno and the Philosophers*, 113–37. Edited by Raphaële Andrault and Mogens Laerke. Leiden: Brill.

Gueroult, Martial. 1953. *Descartes selon l'ordre des raisons*. 2 vols. Paris: Aubier.

Hamid, Nabeel. 2022. "Substance, Causation and the Mind-Body Problem in Johann Clauberg." *Oxford Studies in Early Modern Philosophy* 11: 31–66.

Harth, Erica. 1992. *Cartesian Women: Versions and Subversions of Rational Discourse in the Old Regime*. Ithaca: Cornell University Press.

Hatfield, Gary. 1979. "Force (God) in Descartes' Physics." *Studies in History and Philosophy of Science Part A* 10: 113–40.

Hattab, Helen. 2001. "The Problem of Secondary Causation in Descartes: A Reply to Des Chene." *Perspectives on Science* 8: 93–118.

Hattab, Helen. 2007. "Concurrence or Divergence? Reconciling Descartes' Physics with His Metaphysics." *Journal of the History of Philosophy* 45: 49–78.

Henkel, Christian. 2022. *Grounding the World: The Dissemination of Occasionalism in Early Modern Germany*. PhD Dissertation, University of Groningen.

Hoffman, Paul. 1986. "The Unity of Descartes's Man." *Philosophical Review* 95: 339–70.

Isolle, Jacques. 1971. "Un Disciple de Descartes: Louis de La Forge." *XVIIième Siècle* 92: 98–131.

Janiak, Andrew. 2008. *Newton as Philosopher*. Cambridge and New York: Cambridge University Press.

Kolesnik (Antoine-Mahut), Delphine. 2006. "Les Occasionalismes en France à l'âge classique: Le 'Cas' arnaldien." *Revue de Métaphysique et de Morale* 49: 41–54.

Kolesnik-Antoine (Antoine-Mahut), Delphine. 2009. *L'Homme cartésien: La Force qu'a l'ame de mouvoir le corps: Descartes, Malebranche*. Rennes: Presses Universitaires de Rennes.

322 BIBLIOGRAPHY

Kolesnik-Antoine (Antoine-Mahut), Delphine. 2012. "Les Voies du corps: Schuyl, Clerselier, et La Forge lecteurs de *L'Homme* de Descartes." *Consecuto Temporum* 2: 118–28.

Kolesnik-Antoine (Antoine-Mahut), Delphine. MS. "Reason and Experiment in Regius and La Forge."

Kulstad, Mark. 1993. "Causation and Preestablished Harmony in the Early Development of Leibniz's Philosophy." In *Causation in Early Modern Philosophy*, 93–118. Edited by Steven Nadler. University Park: Pennsylvania State University Press.

Lähteenmäki, Vili. 2007. "Orders of Consciousness and Forms of Reflexivity in Descartes." In *Consciousness: From Perception to Reflection in the History of Philosophy*, 177–201. Edited by Sara Heinämaa, Vili Lähteenmäki, and Pauliina Remes. Dordrecht: Springer.

Lee, Sukjae. 2008. "Necessary Connections and Continuous Creation: Malebranche's Two Arguments for Occasionalism." *Journal of the History of Philosophy* 46: 539–65.

Lee, Sukjae. 2018. "Conservation as Continuous Creation: Just Like Creation but Not Necessarily Recreation." In *Occasionalism: From Metaphysics to Science*, 61–83. Edited by Matteo Favaretti Camposampiero, Mariangela Priarolo, and Emanuela Scribano. Turnhout, Belgium: Brepols.

Lennon, Thomas M. 1974. "Occasionalism and the Cartesian Metaphysic of Motion." *Canadian Journal of Philosophy*, Supplementary Vol. 1, Part 1: 29–40.

Lennon, Thomas M. 2013. "Descartes' Supposed Libertarianism: Letter to Mesland or Memorandum Concerning Petau?" *Journal of the History of Philosophy* 51: 223–48.

Lennon, Thomas M. 2015. "No, Descartes Is *Not* a Libertarian." *Oxford Studies in Early Modern Philosophy* 7: 47–82.

Lennon, Thomas M., and Patricia Ann Easton. 1992. *The Cartesian Empiricism of François Bayle*. New York and London: Garland Publishing.

Loeb, Louis. 1981. *From Descartes to Hume: Continental Metaphysics and the Development of Modern Philosophy*. Ithaca, NY: Cornell University Press.

Lucarini, Giulia. 2007. "La Corporis et animae in homine conjunctio plenius descripta di Johannes Clauberg." MS: Istituto di Filosofia Arturo Massolo, Università di Urbino.

Maimonides. 1963. *Guide of the Perplexed*. 2 vols. Translated by Shlomo Pines. Chicago: University of Chicago Press.

Manning, Gideon. 2012. "When the Mind Became Un-Natural: De la Forge and Psychology in the Cartesian Aftermath." In *Psychology and Other Disciplines: A Case of Cross-Disciplinary Interaction (1250–1750)*, 131–53. Edited by Paul J. J. M. Bakker, Sander W. de Boer, and Cees Leijenhorst. Leiden: Brill.

Matthews, Gareth B. 1992. *Thought's Ego in Augustine and Descartes*. Ithaca, NY: Cornell University Press.

Matton, Sylvain. 2005. "Un temoignage oublié sur le manuscrit du *Traité de l'homme* de Descartes." *Bulletin Cartésien* 36: 7–8.

McCrae, Robert. 1976. *Leibniz: Perception, Apperception, and Thought*. Toronto: University of Toronto Press.

McGuire, J. E. 1972. "Boyle's Conception of Nature." *Journal of the History of Ideas* 33: 523–42.

McLaughlin, Trevor. 1979. "Censorship and Defenders of the Cartesian Faith in Mid-Seventeenth Century France." *Journal of the History of Ideas* 40: 563–81.

Meschini, Franco Aurelio. 2011. "Filologia e scienza: Note per un'edizione critica de *L'Homme* di Descartes." In *Le Opere dei filosofi e degli scienziati: Filosofia e scienza tra testo, libro e biblioteche*, 165–204. Edited by Franco Aurelio Meschini. Florence: Olschki.

BIBLIOGRAPHY 323

Menn, Stephen. 1998. *Descartes and Augustine*. Cambridge: Cambridge University Press.

Moreau, Denis. 1999. *Deux Cartésiens: La Polémique Arnauld Malebranche*. Paris: J. Vrin.

Mouy, Paul. 1934. *Le Développement de la physique cartésienne, 1646–1712*. Paris: J. Vrin.

Naaman-Zauderer, Noa. 2010. *Descartes' Deontological Turn: Reason, Will and Virtue in the Later Writings*. Cambridge: Cambridge University Press.

Nadler, Steven. 1993a. "Occasionalism and General Will in Malebranche." *Journal of the History of Philosophy* 31: 31–47.

Nadler, Steven. 1993b. "The Occasionalism of Louis de la Forge." In *Causation in Early Modern Philosophy: Cartesianism, Occasionalism, and Preestablished Harmony*, 57–74. Edited by Steven Nadler. University Park: Pennsylvania State University Press.

Nadler, Steven. 1994. "Descartes and Occasional Causation." *British Journal for the History of Philosophy* 2: 35–54.

Nadler, Steven. 1995. "Occasionalism and the Question of Arnauld's Cartesianism." In *Descartes and His Contemporaries: Meditations, Objections and Replies*, 129–44. Edited by Roger Ariew and Marjorie Grene. Chicago: University of Chicago Press.

Nadler, Steven. 1996. "'No Necessary Connection': The Medieval Roots of the Occasionalist Roots of Hume." *The Monist* 79: 448–66.

Nadler, Steven. 1998. "Continuous Creation and the Activity of the Soul: Louis de La Forge and the Development of Occasionalism." *Journal of the History of Philosophy* 36: 215–31.

Nadler, Steven. 2005. "Cordemoy and Occasionalism." *Journal of the History of Philosophy* 43: 37–54.

Nadler, Steven. 2011. *Occasionalism: Causation among the Cartesians*. Oxford: Oxford University Press.

Nadler, Steven. 2019. "Spinoza and the 'Stupid Cartesians.'" In *The Oxford Handbook of Descartes and Cartesianism*, 659–77. Edited by Steven Nadler, Tad Schmaltz, and Delphine Antoine-Mahut. Oxford: Oxford University Press.

Ott, Walter. 2008. "Régis's Scholastic Mechanism." *Studies in the History and Philosophy of Science* 39: 2–14.

Ott, Walter. 2009. *Causation and Laws of Nature in Early Modern Philosophy*. Oxford: Oxford University Press.

Pellegrin, Marie-Frédérique. 2019. "Cartesianism and Feminism." In *The Oxford Handbook of Descartes and Cartesianism*, 565–79. Edited by Steven Nadler, Tad Schmaltz, and Delphine Antoine-Mahut. Oxford: Oxford University Press.

Perler, Dominik, and Ulrich Rudolph. 2000. *Occasionalismus: Theorien der Kausalität im arabisch-islamischen und im europäischen Denken*. Göttingen: Vandenhoeck & Ruprecht.

Pessin, Andrew. 2000. "Does Continuous Creation Entail Occasionalism? Malebranche (and Descartes)." *Canadian Journal of Philosophy* 30: 413–40.

Platt, Andrew R. 2020. *One True Cause: Causal Powers, Divine Concurrence and the Seventeenth-Century Revival of Occasionalism*. Oxford: Oxford University Press.

Prost, Joseph. 1904. "Le Cartésianisme à Saumur." *Revue de l'Anjou* 49: 201–15.

Prost, Joseph. 1907a. *Essai sur l'atomisme et l'occasionalisme dans la philosophie cartésienne*. Paris: Henri Paulin.

Prost, Joseph. 1907b. *La Philosophie à l'académie protestante de Saumur (1606–1685)*. Paris: Henri Paulin.

Pyle, Andrew. 2003. *Malebranche*. New York and London: Routledge.

Radner, Daisie. 1993. "Occasionalism." In *The Routledge History of Philosophy*, vol. 4: *The Renaissance and Seventeenth-Century Rationalism*, 349–83. Edited by G. H. R. Parkinson. London: Routledge.

324   BIBLIOGRAPHY

Ragland, C. P. 2016. *The Will to Reason: Theodicy and Freedom in Descartes.* Oxford: Oxford University Press.

Robinet, André. 1955. *Malebranche et Leibniz: Relations personnelles.* Paris: J. Vrin.

Robinet, André. 1965. *Système et existence dans l'oeuvre de Malebranche.* Paris: J. Vrin.

Roux, Sandrine. 2018. *L'Empreinte cartésienne: L'Interaction psychophysique, débats classiques et contemporains.* Paris: Classiques Garnier.

Roux, Sandrine. 2022. "La Forge's Partial Occasionalism: Why God Does Not Do Everything." *Oxford Studies in Early Modern Philosophy* 11: 67–96.

Roux, Sophie. 2013. "Pour une conception polémique du cartésianisme: Ignace-Gaston Pardies et Antoine Dilly dans la querelle de l'âme des bêtes." In *Qu'est-ce qu'être cartésien?*, 315–37. Edited by Delphine Antoine-Mahut. Lyon: ENS Éditions.

Roux, Sophie. 2014. "Was There a Cartesian Experimentalism in 1660s France?" In *Cartesian Empiricisms*, 47–88. Edited by Mihnea Dobre and Tammy Nyden. Boston: Springer.

Roux, Sophie. 2019. "A Deflationist Solution to the Problem of Force in Descartes." In *Physics and Metaphysics in Descartes and in His Reception*, 140–58. Edited by Delphine Antoine-Mahut and Sophie Roux. London: Routledge.

Roux, Sophie. 2021. "Une enquête sur Jacques du Roure." *Bulletin Cartésien* 50: 20–30.

Rozemond, Marleen. 1998. *Descartes's Dualism.* Cambridge, MA: Harvard University Press.

Rozemond, Marleen. 1999. "Descartes on Mind-Body Interaction: What's the Problem?" *Journal of the History of Philosophy* 37: 435–67.

Sangiacomo, Andrea. 2014a. "Defect of Knowledge and Practice of Virtue in Geulincx's Occasionalism." *Studia Leibnitiana* 46: 46–63.

Sangiacomo, Andrea. 2014b. "Louis de La Forge and the 'Non-Transfer Argument' for Occasionalism." *British Journal for the History of Philosophy* 22: 1–21.

Sangiacomo, Andrea. 2018. "Neither with Occasionalism Nor with Concurrentism: The Case of Pierre-Sylvain Régis." In *Occasionalism: From Metaphysics to Science*, 85–106. Edited by Matteo Favaretti Camposampiero, Mariangela Priarolo, and Emanuela Scribano. Turnhout, Belgium: Brepols.

Schmaltz, Tad. 2002. *Radical Cartesianism: The French Reception of Descartes.* Cambridge: Cambridge University Press.

Schmaltz, Tad (ed.). 2005. *Receptions of Descartes: Cartesianism and Anti-Cartesianism in Early Modern Europe.* Oxford and New York: Routledge.

Schmaltz, Tad. 2008. *Descartes on Causation.* Oxford: Oxford University Press.

Schmaltz, Tad. 2017. *Early Modern Cartesianisms: Dutch and French Constructions.* Oxford: Oxford University Press.

Schmaltz, Tad. 2018. "Continuous Creation and Cartesian Occasionalism in Physics." In *Occasionalism: From Metaphysics to Science*, 41–60. Edited by Matteo Favaretti Camposampiero, Mariangela Priarolo, and Emanuela Scribano. Turnhout, Belgium: Brepols.

Schmaltz, Tad. 2020a. "Cartesian Causation and Cognition: Louis de La Forge and Géraud de Cordemoy." In *Causation and Cognition in Early Modern Philosophy*, 61–82. Edited by Dominik Perler and Sebastian Bender. New York and London: Routledge.

Schmaltz 2020b. "*Mundus est Fabula*: Descartes's *Le Monde*." *Alvearium* 13: 35–48.

Schmaltz, Tad. Forthcoming. "The Pineal Gland in Cartesianism." In *The Cartesian Brain: Philosophical and Scientific Perspectives.* Edited by Denis Kambouchner, Damien Lacroux, Tad M. Schmaltz, and Ruidan She. New York: Routledge.

BIBLIOGRAPHY 325

Scribano, Emanuela. 2011. "'Quod Nescis Quomodo Fiat, Id Non Facis': Occasionalism against Descartes?" *Rinascimento* 51: 63–86.

Scribano, Emanuela. 2016a. "La Forge on Memory: From the *Treatise on Man* to the *Treatise on the Human Mind.*" In *Descartes' Treatise on Man and Its Reception*, 139–54. Edited by Delphine Antoine-Mahut and Stephen Gaukroger. Boston: Springer.

Scribano, Emanuela. 2016b. "The Return of Campanella: La Forge versus Cureau de la Chambre." In *Early Modern Philosophers and the Renaissance Legacy*, 169–84. Edited by Cecilia Muratori and Gianni Paganini. Boston: Springer.

Seyfarth, H. 1887. *Louis de la Forge und seine Stellung im Occasionalismus.* Gotha: Emil Behrend.

Specht, Rainer. 1966. *Commercium mentis et corporis: Über Kausalvorstellungen im Cartesianismus.* Stuttgart-Bad Cannstatt: Friedrich Fromman Verlag.

Specht, Rainer. 1972. "Über 'occasio' und verwandte Begriffe im Cartesianismus I." *Archiv für Begriffsgeschichte* 16: 198–226.

Stein, Ludwig. 1888. "Zur Genesis des Occasionalismus." *Archiv für Geschichte der Philosophie* 1: 53–61.

Thijssen-Schoute, Caroline Louise. 1989. *Nederlands Cartesianisme.* Utrecht: HES Uitgvers BV. [Originally published in 1954]

Van Otegem, Matthijs. 2002. *A Bibliography of the Works of Descartes, 1637–1704.* Utrecht: Zeno Institute.

Verbeek, Theo. 1988. *La Querelle d'Utrecht: Descartes et Martin Schook.* Textes établis, traduits et annotés. Paris: Impressions Nouvelles.

Verbeek, Theo. 1992. *Descartes and the Dutch: Early Reactions to Cartesian Philosophy, 1637–1650.* Carbondale: Southern Illinois University Press.

Watson, Richard A. 1966. *The Downfall of Cartesianism.* The Hague: Martinus Nijhoff.

Watson, Richard A. 1982. "Cartesianism Compounded: Louis de La Forge." *Studia Cartesiana* 2: 165–71.

Watson, Richard A. 1987. "The Cartesianism Theology of Louis de La Forge (1632–1666)." In Richard A. Watson, *The Breakdown of Cartesian Metaphysics*, 171–7. Atlantic Highlands, NJ: Humanities Press.

Weir, W. 1981. "Der Okkasionalismus des Johannes Clauberg und sein Verhältnis zu Descartes, Geulincx, Malebranche." *Studia Cartesiana* 2: 43–62.

Wilkin, Rebecca. 2003. "Figuring the Dead Descartes: Claude Clerselier's *Homme de René Descartes* (1664)." *Representations* 83: 38–66.

Wilson, Margaret. 1978. *Descartes.* London: Routledge and Kegan Paul.

Zittel, Claus. 2011. "Conflicting Pictures: Illustrating Descartes' *Traité de l'homme.*" In *Silent Messengers: The Circulation of Material Objects of Knowledge in the Early Modern Low Countries*, 217–60. Edited by Sven Dupré and Christoph Lüthy. Münster: LIT Verlag.

Index

For the benefit of digital users, indexed terms that span two pages (e.g., 52–53) may, on occasion, appear on only one of those pages.

al-Ashari, Abu Hasan, 162–63, 205–6
André, Yves, 259–60
animal spirits, 47–48, 63–64, 73, 77–78,
  137–38, 143, 224–25
Antoine-Mahut, Delphine, 253. *See also*
  Kolesnik-Antoine, Delphine
Ariew, Roger, 36–37
Aristotle, 8–9, 10–11, 13, 95–97
Aristotelianism, 1–2, 26, 28–31, 33,
  36–37, 45–46, 95–98, 203–4,
  225–26
Arnauld, Antoine, 12, 27–28, 31, 40–41,
  98–99, 104–6, 114–15, 116, 117,
  154, 155–56, 158–59, 222
Arnauld, Henri, 12
Aselli, Gaspar, 84–85
Augustine (Saint), 12, 40–41, 98–100, 106,
  107, 212, 224

Baillet, Adriaen, 15, 25–26, 253–54
Bartolin, Caspar (the Elder), 77
Bartolin, Thomas, 77, 80, 83–85, 141
Battail, Jean-François, 253
Bauhin, Caspar, 67–68
Bayle, François, 34, 39
Bayle, Pierre, 19, 143–44
Berkeley, George, 35
Bitbol-Hespériès, Annie, 67–68
Bouillier, Francisque, 3, 20
Boulliau, Ismail, 21–22
Boyle, Robert, 162
Buffet, Marguerite, 19
Burgersdijk, Franco, 10, 176, 223
Burman, Frans, 102–3

Cartesianism
  doctrines of, 33–42
  in France, 18–24, 27, 252–53
  in The Netherlands, 24–27

as the new philosophy, 2–3
  in Saumur, 12–13
causation, 177–78
  efficient, 168–69, 223–25
  equivocal vs. univocal, 217–18, 225
  exemplary, 221
  occasional, 167–69, 223–24
  procatarctic, 168–69, 174, 176, 216, 223
  See also concurrentism;
    conservationism; occasionalism
Chanut, Pierre, 52
Chapelain, Jean, 14–15, 92
Chouet, Jean-Robert, 12–13
Clair, Pierre, 253
Clauberg, Johannes, 4, 10, 25–26, 33,
  42, 43, 133–34, 168–69, 173–77,
  179–80, 184–85, 188–89, 192–93,
  215–17, 226, 258–59, 260, 262
Clerselier, Claude, 4, 6, 16, 17, 20–21, 22,
  23–24, 25, 33, 41–43, 44–45, 51–69,
  70–72, 89, 91–92, 227–29, 252, 259
Colvius, Andreas, 98–99
concurrentism, 163–65
consciousness, 101–7
conservationism, 163, 164–65, 251
continuous creation. *See* God: and
  conservation
Corbinelli, Jean, 258
Cordemoy, Géraud de, 4, 5, 18, 19, 20–21,
  23–24, 33, 37–39, 41–42, 43, 143,
  165, 180–93, 199–201, 213, 226,
  234, 236, 237–38, 239, 241, 248,
  253, 257–58, 259, 262
Cousin, Victor, 3

Da Fonseca, Pedro, 8
De Bruyn, Johannes, 25
De Champvallon, François de Harlay
  (Archbishop of Paris), 1

328 INDEX

De Fontenay, Claude, 18–19
De Launay, Gilles, 18–19
De Montmor, Henri Louis Habert, 14, 18, 20–22, 43, 180
Denis, Jean-Baptiste, 19
De Pontcourlay, Marie-Madeleine de Vignerot (Madame de Bonnevaux), 18, 19
De Rabutin-Chantal, Marie (Marquise de Sévigné), 258
De Raey, Johannes, 25, 33
De Roberval, Gilles, 21–22
Descartes, Catherine, 19
Descartes, René
   funeral of, 252–53
   works by
      Discours de la méthode, 107–8, 124
      La Description du corps humain, 89, 94
      La Dioptrique, 166–67
      Le Monde, 45, 49–50, 72, 171, 257–58
      Les Passions de l'âme, 45, 90, 93–94, 127, 136–37, 138–39, 154–55
      Meditationes de prima philosophia, 45, 90, 93–94, 118–19, 136–37, 171–72, 205–6, 236
      Notae in programma quoddam, 147, 171–72, 216–17, 219–20, 222
      Principia philosophiae, 45, 82, 90, 94, 107–8, 123, 169–70, 171, 210, 216–17, 254, 257–58
      Traité de l'Homme, 44–69, 70–90, 98, 136–37, 145–46, 154–55, 166–67, 222–23, 257–58, 262
De Scudéry, Madeleine, 19
De Sévigné, Françoise-Marguerite (Madame de Grignan), 258
Desgabets, Dom Robert, 2, 4, 5–6, 20–21, 22, 24, 25, 32, 33, 39–42, 122–23, 149–50, 152, 253, 262
De Toledo, Francisco, 8
De Villemandy, Pierre, 198, 241–42, 258, 260
De Vivonne, Catherine (Marquise de Rambouillet), 19
Dorlix, Pierre, 166–67
Du Roure, Jacques, 4, 23–24, 25, 33, 42–43
Dun Scotus, Johannes, 30
Durandus de Saint Pourçain, 163

Easton, Patricia, 33–34
Elisabeth, Princess of Bohemia, 52, 125, 151, 171–72, 214–15, 225–26, 236
Elzevir, Daniel, 51, 119, 257–58
eternal truths, 40
Eucharist, 1–2, 15, 24, 27–32
Eustacius a Sancto Paulo, 29–30

Fontenelle, Bernard le Bovier de, 169
force, 208–9, 211–12, 218–19, 232–33
freedom, 236–39, 241–48

Galileo Galilei, 50
Gassendi, Pierre, 19, 20–21, 35, 39, 109–10, 111, 112, 149, 154, 215, 225–26
Gausson, Etienne, 13
Geulincx, Arnold, 4, 10, 25, 33, 165, 177–80, 192–93, 215, 229, 237–38, 257–58
Gibieuf, Guillaume, 113–14
God
   and conservation, 205–8, 230–31, 248–51, 260–61
   as cause, 135–36, 175, 247–48 (*see also* concurrentism; conservationism; occasionalism)
   existence of, 118
   providence of, 236–37
Gouhier, Henri, 3, 253
Gousset, Jacques, 16, 17, 81, 194–99, 222, 228–29, 249–50, 258, 259–60
Guisony, Pierre, 53

Harvey, William, 75, 81, 83–84
Heereboord, Adriaen, 10, 25, 26, 33, 96, 176, 177, 223
Heidanus, Abraham, 25
heliocentrism, 49–50
Henkel, Christian, 259, 261–62
Hobbes, Thomas, 35, 109–10, 111, 112
Huet, Pierre-Daniel, 20–21, 143–44
Hume, David, 182
Huygens, Christiaan, 19, 21–22
Huygens, Constantijn, 157

ideas
   clear and distinct, 36, 146–47
   innate, 147–50

INDEX 329

nature of, 79, 145–50, 245–47
sensory, 146–47, 219–20, 221–24
imagination, 153

Kolesnik-Antoine, Delphine, 3. *See also* Antoine-Mahut, Delphine

La Flèche (Collège Henri IV), 7–9
La Forge, Louis de
commentary on Descartes's *Traité de l'homme*, 16, 70–90, 141, 254–55, 257–58, 259–60
education, 7–9
family, 7
illustrations for Descartes's *Traité de l'homme*, 53–69, 194
introduction to Cartesian philosophy, 13–16
as medical doctor, 9–10
Lallement, Pierre (Chancellor, University of Paris), 252
Lamy, Bernard, 12, 39, 262
Le Bossu, René, 33
Leibniz, Gottfried Wilhelm, 35–36, 117, 129, 162, 166, 171, 176, 201, 207–8, 261–62
Lennon, Thomas M., 3, 33–34
Locke, John, 35, 117

Madame de Bonnevaux. *See* De Pontcourlay, Marie-Madeleine de Vignerot
Madame de Geudreville. *See* Thiersault, Marie
Madame de Grignan. *See* De Sévigné, Françoise-Marguerite
Madame de Rambouillet. *See* De Vivonne, Catherine
Madame de Sévigné. *See* De Rabutin-Chantal, Marie
Maimonides, 162–63
Malebranche, Nicolas, 4, 5, 16, 39, 40–41, 99, 104–5, 106–7, 143–44, 165, 169, 170, 172–73, 180, 192, 205–6, 207, 212–13, 231, 237–39, 241, 248, 250, 253, 257, 259–61, 262
Martin, André (Ambrosius Victor), 12
matter, 35–36, 37–39
memory, 86–88, 154–61

Mersenne, Marin, 23, 31, 118
Mesland, Denis, 7–16
Michon, Pierre (Abbé Bourdelot), 18
mind
always thinking, 113–16, 123
causal activity of, 186–93, 195–97, 224–35, 236–51
interaction with body, 137–38, 175–77, 183–85, 197, 214–35, 256–57
nature of, 36, 90, 100–17
union with body, 123–43, 173–74, 256
See also soul
mind-body dualism, 35, 107–17, 118–21, 149
Molière (Jean-Baptiste Poquelin), 97
More, Henry, 170–71, 182, 210, 213
Mouy, Paul, 3

Newtonianism, 2–3, 35–36
Nicole, Pierre, 222
Noël, Etienne, 7–8

occasionalism, 3–4, 40–41, 162–93, 194–213, 218–35, 236–51, 255–57. *See also* causation

Paris, 14
academies and salons in, 18–24
Pascal, Blaise, 7–8
Pecquot, Jean, 84–85
Philippi, Guillaume, 25–26
pineal gland, 48, 79–80, 85–86, 136–46, 154–55, 224–25
Plato, 8
Platt, Andrew, 253
Plempius, Vopiscus Fortunatus, 26–27, 76–77, 82–83
Poisson, Nicolas, 262
Pollot, Alphonse, 54
Port-Royal Logic, 222
Prost, Joseph, 4, 253, 258

Régis, Pierre-Sylvain, 22, 25, 39, 40–43, 106–7, 117, 144, 150, 152–53, 253, 262
Regius, Henricus (Hendrik de Roy), 25, 33, 51–52, 129–30, 143, 149–50, 216–17

330 INDEX

Reneri, Henri, 25
Revius, Jacob, 26–27
Rohault, Jacques, 4, 18, 20–21, 22–23, 25, 33, 41–43, 253, 262
Roux, Sandrine, 253, 256
Roux, Sophie, 34
Rozemond, Marleen, 109

Sangiacomo, Andrea, 253
Saumur, 7, 9–13
   religious establishments in, 10–13
Schmaltz, Tad, 3, 39, 42, 253
Schuyl, Florent, 25, 54–55, 59–61, 66–68
Scribano, Emanuela, 253
sensations. *See* ideas: sensory
Seyfarth, Heinrich, 4, 253, 258
Sorbonne, 1–2
soul, 90
   immortality of, 118–23, 144–45, 151–54, 156–57
   See also mind
Specht, Ranier, 253
Spinoza, Bento de, 10, 27, 33, 35, 41–42
Steno, Nicolaus (Niels Stenson), 10, 141–42, 143–44

Suarez, Francisco, 29–30, 164, 208
substance, 34–35

Thévenot, Melchisédich, 19
Thiersault, Marie (Madame de Geudreville), 18
Thijssen-Schout, C. Louise, 3
Thomas Aquinas, 8, 29–30, 163–64, 166–67, 208

Van Gutschoven, Gerard, 25–26, 53–69, 79
Van Hogeland, Cornelis, 25
Vesalius, Andrea, 83
Villiers, Christophe, 139
Voetius, Gisbertus, 26–27, 129–30

Wallaeus, Johannes, 83
will, 36, 151, 179–80, 190–92, 237–39, 240–48, 249–50
Wilson, Margaret, 125–28, 131, 149
Wittgenstein, Ludwig, 42
Wolff, Christian, 261–62

Zittel, Claus, 57